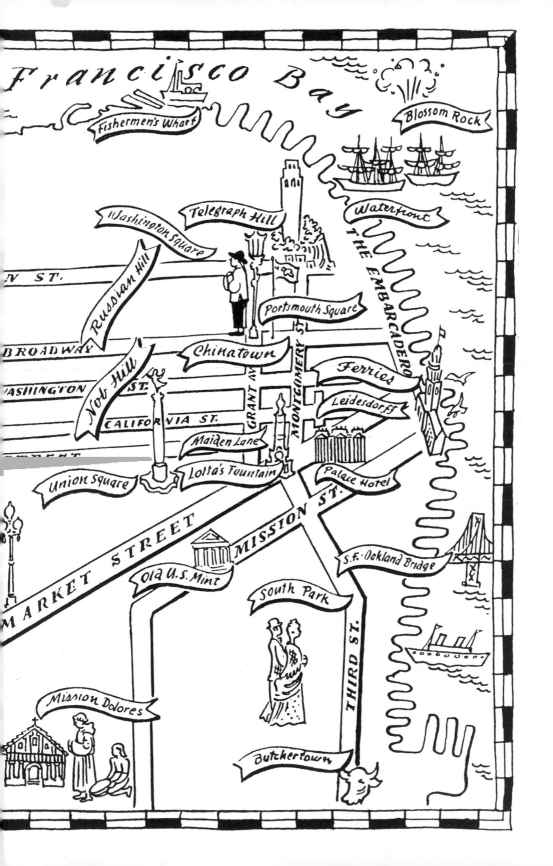

This Is San Francisco

A Classic Portrait of the City

ROBERT O'BRIEN

Foreword by Adair Lara

CHRONICLE BOOKS
SAN FRANCISCO

FOR MARY,
MOLLY, BRENDA, DEVON,
and REGAN

FIRST CHRONICLE BOOKS EDITION 1994.

Library of Congress Cataloging-in-Publication Data available.

Printed in the United States of America.

ISBN 0-8118-0578-6

Distributed in Canada by Raincoast Books, 112 East Third Ave.,
Vancouver, B.C. V5T 1C8

10 9 8 7 6 5 4 3 2 1

Chronicle Books
275 Fifth Street
San Francisco, CA 94103

FOREWORD

IN 1980 MY family and I moved to Petaluma for what would be a three-year stay. When I arranged the babies in their rusted twin stroller in the afternoons and wandered down to the river, the cobblestones that caught at the stroller's wheels and the mossy green pilings where steamboats once tied up would start to work on my sluggish sense of the past. I rather grandly decided that my brief residency and my postcollege literary pretensions equipped me to dash off a little history of the town.

For this I had to read a lot of local history. You will not be surprised to learn that it isn't all that interesting. Open some books of local lore, and you will learn where the First National Gold Bank stood and who the presidents were, and how often the name of the bank changed, until you want to blow your brains out right there and then in your living room, rather than risk being told anything further about the First National Gold Bank.

When I wrote my book, I was so determined to stay away from such dry stuff as facts and dates that the first fifteen pages I banged out on my portable Royal brought Petaluma from its rancho days halfway through the Civil War, when Petaluma loyalists set out to attack rebel Santa Rosa. Another fifteen would have launched it into the space age.

I had to slow down, and this meant I had to find the stories. I stopped polishing my dry little sticks of sentences and started over, spending days at the historical libraries and secondhand bookstores.

Everywhere I went I came across this out-of-print book called *This Is San Francisco*. Half the history writers I knew were shamelessly cribbing from it, never dreaming it would be reprinted. They'd pay the price marked in pencil on the flyleaf and hurry home with it, because the author, Robert O'Brien, didn't care where the banks stood and who the presidents were. He had put in his time bent over ponderous piles of original newspapers and blowing dust off old records, and then he just included every rollicking good story he could find.

Instead of the bank histories, we get the tale of a "crimp" named Calico Jim who shanghaied six policemen, one after the other, as they arrived at his boarding house to arrest him.

"After disposing of the sixth," O'Brien relates, "Calico Jim called it a day and left town. The legend goes that, when the cops got back from their cruises, they drew lots to see which one would take care of Calico Jim. The chosen one tracked him to Callao, Peru, and there, in the street, riddled the crimp with six shots, one for each of his victims."

Instead of History with a capital H, we get the saga of Dr. Henry Daniel Cogswell: "Any claim to romance in the doctor's life begins and ends with the statement he was a Forty-niner," says O'Brien. Cogswell first peddled goods in the mining country, then set up a dentist's chair in a tent on lower Washington Street. He made so much money at this and in real estate that in 1887 he founded Cogswell College, which is now the Ritz-Carlton Hotel. Before that he was able to take Mrs. Cogswell to Europe: "It was undoubtedly during the trip," says O'Brien dryly, "that he got the idea of perpetuating his memory by scattering statues all over America." Cogswell's commissioned statue of Ben Franklin stands in Washington Square.

O'Brien unfolds his anecdotes and history not according to subject or period, but in the way anybody should get to know a city: street by street. He begins at the Embarcadero and works his way west to the Great Highway. Along the way, we hear about all of it, the feuds, duels, the public hangings, the millionaires and matrons, the "hawk-nosed barkeeps," and the vigilantes. We hear about poet George Sterling, who swallowed poison in his Bohemian Club room, and gentle madman Emperor Norton, who was paid homage to wherever he went. We hear about old Laurel Hill cemetery, Sydneytown, Little Chile, the Broadway Jail, and the vanished Poodle Dog restaurant, near Clay and Dupont, where husbands dined with their wives on the first floor and their mistresses on the third.

For far too long this lively street map has languished on the dusty shelves of secondhand bookstores, the secret of history buffs and the legions of us who have been called "the writers of little histories." This new edition should put this book back where it belongs, in shop windows and on night tables.

Adair Lara is a native San Franciscan and the author of History of Petaluma, A California River Town. *Like Robert O'Brien in the 1940s and early 1950s, Lara writes a column for the* San Francisco Chronicle.

PREFACE

As I SHALL indicate elsewhere, the writing of *Riptides*, the column from which much of the material for this book was taken, was originally a project such as might have been assigned to any working (and lucky) San Francisco newspaperman.

An Easterner by birth, upbringing and education, I had come to San Francisco in 1939 and had been, as so many Easterners are, promptly bowled over by its romance and loveliness. By the time 1946 and *Riptides* came along, I thought I knew the city pretty well, and living in it had bred not only an increasing affection for it, but a pride in being able, if only in a *parvenu* sort of way, to associate myself, my work and my home with it.

But when, by force of my assignment, I was obliged to dig deeper into its past than cursory reading and study had taken me, I discovered that I did not know San Francisco well at all. True, I could not get lost upon her streets; I could (and did) display a smug familiarity with certain exotic, out-of-the-way places for the benefit of visiting friends from the East; I recognized and loved the smells and sights and moods of her at dawn and at noon and at midnight, in April and in October. But to *understand* the city, really to *know* her as you know your best friend or your wife or the house you lived in as a child—this understanding, I found, I did not have and would not possess until I knew how

and why she began; why she developed as she did; how she met the
challenges that sooner or later confront all cities; where she succeeded
and where she failed; how, from the beginning, her people played and
worked and lived; what made them laugh and what made them cry;
and, above all, what quality of sky, air or sea, sand, hills, fog or spirit
made them devoted to San Francisco with a fervor that became as innate
a characteristic of the San Franciscan as the grain of his muscles or the
fiber of his heart.

  Fumblingly and humbly, I began to learn. Here, in this book, is much
of what I have learned.

  It is by no means a complete history of San Francisco; it is rather an
informal biography, and some will quarrel with the judgment exercised
in presenting certain things at the expense of omitting others. Dominating personalities (such as the Big Four), notable pioneers (such as
Sam Brannan, William T. Coleman, Selim Woodworth and a dozen
others), exciting and important events (such as the Earthquake and Fire
of 1906, the general strike) have either been ignored entirely by the text
or presented with slightly more than passing reference. One reason for
this is that they have all received fuller and more able treatment than
I was able to give them. Another reason is that I thought it time that
someone paid a little less attention to the old stand-by personalities and
calamities and guidebook attractions, and a little more to certain quite
neglected aspects of the city and its past—Tar Flat and South Park,
South of the Slot and Bernal Heights and Cow Hollow, the Meiggs, the
Picketts, the Blythes, the Bancrofts and all the other districts and men
that most San Franciscans never get around to telling you about, but
that contributed so much toward shaping San Francisco into the wonderful and intensely human city that she is.

  My notes accumulated for a period of two years. When it came time
to organize them, they comprised many seemingly disconnected facts
and impressions, separated not only by chronology but also by their
special environments within the city. The clearest way to dissolve the
latter difficulty seemed to be to associate them all with the San Francisco
streets with which they were most closely identified and, by this arrangement, link environment with environment, just as the streets did and do.
And by tracing the evolution of each street from the muddy trail of the

Gold Rush to the distinctive thoroughfare of today, the stubborn obstacle of chronology was, in a measure at least, overcome.

There are (it is no secret) streets in San Francisco other than those presented here; my choice was determined mainly by the material at hand. The development of others would undoubtedly be an interesting and exciting addition to this or any book about San Francisco—Powell Street, for example, or Kearny, or McAllister, or Fillmore, or Macondray Lane. I wish time and space had permitted me to write about them, too; some day, perhaps, they will. . . .

Here, then, is the portrait of an American city. The subject is in no way liable for the deficiencies, in talent or perception, of the artist. In the spirit of love and respect, he has done the best he could do, hoping that through the lines and brush strokes there glows a suggestion of the warm and abiding magic of San Francisco.

ROBERT O'BRIEN

THE PREFACE, ONCE MORE

How and why and when I went to San Francisco; how it was a place where I felt at home and thought I would never leave; how I became a *Chronicle* columnist; how and why this book was compiled for the first time— just about all you need to know about these things is in the original preface.

But now, forty-five years later, to help explain the astonishing reappear-ance of the book in this attractive new edition, it seems appropriate to add several details.

First, I want very much to thank Chronicle Books and Senior Editor William LeBlond for giving *This Is San Francisco* another life. As for Adair Lara's warm, responsive introduction, it is everything I could have asked for and more, and verification that it was all worthwhile. For cheer-ful and indispensable help in making it happen, I am deeply indebted to Evie Steele of San Francisco for bringing us together.

It all proves one more time that San Francisco has always been the City of the Second Chance—a place to start over again, a city of happy miracles, where all good things are possible, no matter how steep the odds against them, how loaded the dice.

And after leafing through the first edition again, I want to thank my old friend, the late Antonio Sotomayor, more than ever for the spirit, humor, and lift he added to the text with his illustrations. Every time I'm in San Francisco I ride the Powell Street cable car to the top of Nob Hill to make sure his glowing murals of pioneer times are still there in the nave of Grace Cathedral.

Afterward, more often than not, I cross the street and linger a while on a Huntington Park bench, not to live nostalgically in the past, but to treasure it. There, on certain afternoons, ghosts of the Big Four and the Comstock Silver Kings mingle in the air with the clang of bells from passing California Street cable cars. There, on certain afternoons, perhaps in October with the dry leaves swirling along the sidewalks, San Francisco's rich and storied past drifts back to life in a kind of autumn reverie.

How neatly and clearly the epochs fall in line! Sharp climactic scenes, high points in the history of the West, bring each one to a dramatic close, then trigger the ones to follow:

The pastoral years of the Spanish, Mexican, and Franciscan eras end abruptly with the raucous whoop and holler of the gold strike at Sutter's Mill in 1848. Two brief decades later Mother Lode mines are petering out; the Gold Rush is all but over. With the driving of the Golden Spike and the completion of the cross-country telegraph, gone, just about forever, are the pioneer wagon trains. Silent now are the pounding hooves of the Pony Express.

Swiftly, the curtain rises on the Comstock Silver madness of the 1870s and the champagne days of the Gay Nineties, and San Francisco enters the twentieth century as the glamorous and world-acclaimed "Paris of the Pacific." Six years later—suddenly, in the stillness of an April dawn—earthquake! The proud city comes tumbling down. Water lines fracture. Fires break out. By nightfall that bonny city lies in ruins across its smoking hills.

Magically, an even more beautiful metropolis rises from the ashes of the old. In less than a decade jubilant San Franciscans, with their Panama-Pacific International Exposition, are celebrating the opening of the Panama Canal. After World War I, in what seems no time at all, growth, progress, and advancing technology are recreating not only the Golden West, but the nation and the world as well.

Late one autumn afternoon in 1940, with the Jazz Age and the worst of the Depression behind them, a loving and gallant throng of San

Franciscans gathers in the vast outdoor theater of the Treasure Island World's Fair for its closing ceremony. Sensing, perhaps, that it's their goodbye to still another San Francisco, many are in tears. Voices rising together in brave and touching sadness, they sing with Susannah Foster the fair's last song, "The Last Rose of Summer."

In the world beyond the bay, Europe is at war. A little more than a year later America, too, is at war. For the next three-and-a-half years, men and women in uniform shipping in, shipping out, coming back on leave, en route to the South Pacific, the North Atlantic and just about everywhere else, flood by the tens of thousands through San Francisco.

When the Pacific war ends on VJ-Day, 1945, still another epoch begins for the City by the Bay. The one we're in now. The one whose future we fashion each passing day.

At that time, on that note, the book *This Is San Francisco* ended. It went, gratifyingly, into five editions. Then, as later San Francisco books came along from fellow *Chronicle* columnists Herb Caen and Stan Delaplane and others, it gradually disappeared from the bookstores.

Libraries took to listing it as "o.p."–out-of-print. I began hearing of people who were amazed to learn that I was still alive. "What! After writing all those columns about the Gold Rush? I thought he died years ago." As long as I'm here to deny it, I'll be the last to complain.

I wrote "Riptides" for four more years after the book was published and another book, *California Called Them,* about some Gold Rush ghost towns I loved on the Mother Lode. My last column, "The Fork in the Trail," appeared in the *Chronicle* of December 19, 1952.

Four years after that, my wife, Mary, and I and our young family moved east to follow the meanderings of a writing career. As things worked out, I spent many busy and productive years writing books and magazine articles in a Connecticut town on Long Island Sound, forty miles from where I grew up.

But we couldn't stay away from the Pacific, and in this so-called time of "retirement" we live in Hawaii, where the sight of Honolulu takes our breath away every time we see it from a plane, or as we burst out of the Pali tunnel driving in from the Windward Side of Oahu. Stretched out down there in the sunshine along the white surfline and beaches, it's a city so radiant with promise, so fair, so much like San Francisco seen from across the Bay as you tool down out of the Waldo tunnel toward the Golden Gate Bridge, our hearts turn over at the peace and the grace and the feeling of coming back home.

So, in a world where people are cutting down tropical rain forests at the rate of 17 million hectares a year; where the over-fishing of the Atlantic has slashed the annual catch of Nimibian fisheries from two million tons to 100,000 tons in the last ten years; and 14,000 Canadian lakes have died slow deaths from acidification, mostly industrial—in this kind of world what does it matter? Mission bells and wagon trains, the Gold Rush and Lotta Crabtree, Emperor Norton and Luisa Tettrazini, Cow Hollow and Percy Montgomery and the Treasure Island Fair—what do they all matter?

For just a moment or two, or maybe even an hour, let's stop and think . . . if we, the living, fail to remember and respect San Francisco's past, fail to convey something of its glory to our children and grandchildren, then it all really *doesn't* matter, does it? The history books will all be there, gathering dust in the libraries. Who—then—will stand up and say that, deep down, San Francisco is an affair not of books, but of the heart?

Part of the abiding magic of San Francisco is that in spite of the bridges and jetlines, traffic jams and crowded sidewalks and dehumanizing skyscrapers—in spite of it all, most of us still feel that somehow that exciting, go-for-broke past all happened just yesterday. In a little park on Nob Hill, in a tucked-away restaurant off Montgomery Street or in North Beach—in a thousand different places, we hear it, smell it, reach out, perhaps, to touch it.

Time moves on. The past stands still. We'll be gone, but it will abide. A source of strength and courage. A light in the window.

On summer evenings the fog rolls in from the sea and smothers the coastal hills. Tides come in, and go out, and come in again. At high noon on bright, clear spring days, from high on windy San Francisco hills, we can look west to the shining sea. We can remember the mountains we crossed to get there. We can still hear bugles, out there—somewhere.

ROBERT O'BRIEN

ACKNOWLEDGMENT

THE MATERIAL for a book like this comes from a variety of sources; one could not say how many newspaper stories, reference books, manuscripts, pamphlets, letters, personal reminiscences.

Like anyone who has written of San Francisco's past, I owe an unpayable debt to the living and the dead who, out of love of San Francisco, were inspired to write and speak of the city as they truthfully knew it: the anonymous reporters writing for the old papers; the scholarly men and women whose months and years of patient research and composition produced the primary source books; all the pioneers and old-timers who passed along, in diaries and by word of mouth, the things they saw and knew and heard; their sons and grandsons, daughters and granddaughters who today keep alive the old spirit, the old legends, the old names and days. I want to thank them all—and would, if it were possible—for inspiration and encouragement, and the help they have so frequently and generously given, or offered.

If Edward Morphy, for instance, were alive, I should be quite incapable of expressing my obligation for the classic reporting he did in a series of historical sketches of San Francisco, a series which now lies largely forgotten in scrapbooks and in the *Chronicle* files of thirty years ago.

For all their assistance, I should consider similarly inadequate any mere expression of thanks to Harold J. Boyd, Percy Montgomery, Mrs. Gertrude Atherton, Frank Carroll Giffen and Billy Hatman, King of Cow Hollow, who adored their city and who now have gone where San Franciscans go when they die. They never told me where it is, but I know they believed it a place so fair that it is beyond the reach of mortal mind to imagine.

And, in the realm of the living, I can in no way give just recompense for the kind interest of hundreds of column readers who have written me to tell me what they know and feel about San Francisco, who have tolerantly borne with and corrected errors I have made and who have contributed much information that could have been gained from no source other than their own minds and memories.

George T. Cameron and Paul C. Smith, publisher and editor, respectively, of the *San Francisco Chronicle,* are entitled to an unlimited claim upon my gratitude for allowing me full permission to use, in any way it pleased me to use, material which originally appeared in *Riptides,* the column which for the last three years I have been writing for the *Chronicle.* This privilege also applied to the material in *San Francisco,* the column I wrote for the *Chronicle* for the three years prior to the inauguration of *Riptides.* If there were any more gratitude at my command, it would belong to Mr. Smith, who, for reasons he has never confided to me, assigned me the happy task of writing *Riptides* and basing it on the background, historical and legendary, of San Francisco and California.

Other staff members of the *Chronicle,* in the course of this daily work, have been most helpful in the editing of *Riptides,* and in supplying the suggestions, the material and the guidance that I could get nowhere but in the city room of a San Francisco newspaper. Among them, I must particularly mention Larry Fanning, Joseph Henry Jackson, John Bruce, Ben Macomber and Mrs. Marjorie D. Brown and her assistants in the *Chronicle* library.

Personnel of other institutions have been most patiently cooperative: City Librarian Laurence J. Clarke, Head Reference Librarian Miss Dolores Cadell and her staff, and Mr. Harry Sullivan, clerk of the newspaper files, all of the San Francisco Public Library; Mrs. Edna Martin

Parratt, managing director of the California Historical Society, and her assistants; directors of the Society of California Pioneers, who courteously placed that organization's abundant and valuable resources at my disposal, and Veronica J. Sexton, executive librarian of the California Academy of Sciences, who often has passed my way a story that I should not otherwise have known about or recognized.

Of the scores of friends, acquaintances and correspondents who have contributed to this book, I must mention especially Philip and Paul Bancroft, Edward F. O'Day, Harry Brook of the San Francisco City Engineer's Office, City Historian Guy C. Miller of Palo Alto, Drs. Don José Aubertine and Loren Taber, Joe Huff of the South of Market Boys, Fred W. Zimmerman and Billy Carr of the Native Sons of the Golden West, Jim Garbarino, and Charlie Smith of Sierra City. Still others to whom I am indebted are Louis Hicks, for furnishing certain material on the life of William A. Leidesdorff; George Mardikian, to whom every San Franciscan owes something, just because he is George Mardikian; and Mrs. Rainee Priest, for her willing and excellent assistance in research.

C. Gibson Scheaffer, the Whittlesey House editor who worked with me on the manuscript, assisted me with most understanding and constructive direction. Nothing else but this could have made so pleasant a task out of the customary drudgery of cutting and revision.

No less sincere thanks are due the University of California Press for permission to quote from Palóu's *Historical Memoirs of New California,* edited by Herbert E. Bolton, and from the Publications of the Academy of Pacific Coast History; Houghton Mifflin Company for permission to use material from *The Fantastic City,* by Amelia Ransome Neville; Alfred A. Knopf, Inc., for permission to use material from Professor Jerry Thomas's *The Bon Vivant's Companion,* edited with an introduction by Herbert Asbury. The author wishes to express his indebtedness also to Charles Scribner's Sons for permission to quote from *The Wrecker,* by Lloyd Osbourne and Robert Louis Stevenson, and from Stevenson's *Christmas Sermon;* to James H. Barry Company for permission to quote from *The Great Diamond Hoax,* by Asbury Harpending; to Bobbs-Merrill Company for special permission to quote from C. B. Glasscock's *Lucky Baldwin* (copyright 1933); to Philip Bancroft for permission to quote from *Retrospection,* by his father, Hubert Howe Bancroft; to The

Trade Pressroom for permission to quote from *Forgotten Pioneers,* by Thomas F. Prendergast.

Of the earlier, basic books about San Francisco and the Bay Region, I should add that, more times than one, I found indispensable not only Bancroft's *History of California,* but also his *California Pastoral, California Inter Pocula* and *Popular Tribunals. The Annals of San Francisco* and Bayard Taylor's *Eldorado* are also fundamental source books. For background on the exciting period of the Seventies, B. E. Lloyd's *Lights and Shades in San Francisco* is vivid and factual.

In conclusion, two things: In drawing upon the resources of all these people and these books, and many more I am not able to mention, I have tried hard to be accurate, and I hope the book is as accurate as I think it is. If it is not, the responsibility is totally my own.

Finally, I want to acknowledge the work and friendship of the illustrator, Antonio Sotomayor. I have told him that I would not censure a buyer for tearing the drawings out of the book, framing them, and throwing the text away. I did not quite mean that, but I will say, with all the sincerity that my jest did not possess, that their delightful freshness and originality make them a most welcome complement to what I have tried to say about San Francisco.

ROBERT O'BRIEN

CONTENTS

THE WATERFRONT   1

OLD TOWN 25

THE HILLS 113

MAIN STEM 211

SOUTH OF THE SLOT 255

THE SEA 319

INDEX 339

The Waterfront

1. EMBARCADERO

THE MAGIC CITY · THE FIRST SHIP ON SAN FRANCISCO BAY · GUNS OF MANIFEST DESTINY · THE WRECK OF THE "BROTHER JONATHAN" · THE BLASTING OF BLOSSOM ROCK · SHANGHAI KELLY'S BIRTHDAY PARTY · THE WRECK OF THE "RIO" · THE FERRY BUILDING · THE COMING-HOME OF THE THIRD FLEET

THE EMBARCADERO is the street where the city and the hills meet the sea.

It starts in freight yards, in warehouses and factories down by the Southern Pacific depot, runs north for a block or two, then begins its bend to the northwest and then to the west, passing far below the great arc and thrust of the Bay Bridge, ducking underground as it meets Market Street and the Ferry Building, emerging and bending again with the outward curve of the waterfront and plunging on westward until it comes abruptly to a stop at the dark, drying crab nets, the fishing boats and Italian sea-food emporiums of Fisherman's Wharf.

It is bounded on one side by the long, state-owned pier sheds jutting like fingers into the Bay, and always by the water lapping the gray timbers of the piers; on the other side it is lined by storage houses, industrial

3

plants and boxcars on the spurs of the Belt Railroad, by grimy water-front hotels, barrel houses and beer parlors, Navy tailors, secondhand clothing stores and longshoremen's quick-lunch counters.

In back of the Embarcadero and looming above it, the city's hills touch the sky, and they and all that space of sky are what lifts your heart when you see San Francisco, not only for the first time, but always. The hills and the sky cast their spell over the dullest of men, stirring him to poetry, inspiring him to liken the city to a beautiful and bewitching woman—an enchantress—with the face and body of a goddess, and a soul that could be as tender as that blue sky and as wistful as the fog that steals gently in from the sea.

But on the Embarcadero, where the piers are, there is no doubt about it: there, San Francisco is a weary drab, and looking at that street you can call her by many other names—Buenos Aires, Liverpool, Naples, Singapore, Sydney or Brooklyn. She's a waterfront, any waterfront, in any country.

That is in the daytime. At night, late at night, it's different. The magic about it then is that you can walk along the Embarcadero and know you're in no place in the world but San Francisco. The ships are there, with their sharp, steel prows touching the street and their lights blooming high above you in the dark, the way they are in Rio. There is the smell of salt water, and it smells the same as the East River or the Thames. Somewhere you hear a juke box playing the *Beer Barrel Polka,* and you could hear that on the waterfront of Hoboken, any night in the week. But you know you're not in any of those places.

The drabness the Embarcadero shares with any other waterfront is gone, and something tells you the Golden Gate is off there in the darkness. A bell rings low on the water, and you know that out there the tides are running swift and strong past Yerba Buena Island and the Island of the Angels, and past no other islands in the world. The twinkling lights on the inland hills give it away, and the damp of the tule fogs from the northern Bay tells you it's true: the light sweeping over Alcatraz can be no other light, and Telegraph Hill no other hill.

You're in San Francisco, and where you're standing was water a hundred years ago. San Franciscans made their waterfront out of sand they had to shovel out of the way before they could lay down her streets, and out of rock blasted from her hills. Start at a certain place on the water-front and you can walk inland six blocks before you come to where the water washed the shore a century ago, when they called the town Yerba Buena for an herb growing there. As you walk those six blocks, the buildings you pass are built over the rotten hulks of Gold Rush sailing ships left to founder by the Forty-niners. They're built on piles, tall trees from the redwood country pounded into the floor of the sea.

A few things have gone into that waterfront, and at night, without the bustle and the longshoremen and the traffic and the clatter of the steam winches, they come to you.

You see the lights of the bridges, and they seem to say that a bridge is not only a highway so cars and trucks and commuters can go from one shore to the other; a bridge, they say, is also a strong, lovely thing, linking lives with lives, people with people. It is a symbol of confidence, trust and hope.

Pick out by the street light the names on the pier sheds. "Java," they say, and "Singapore" and "Hong Kong" and "Pago Pago." Repeat them and look to the dark west and know that all America is at your back. You're at the end of the continent, and the water you hear whispering under the wharf has whitened the sands of Tahiti and tossed the ice floes in the Bering Sea. The spices you smell came from Cathay.

So stand there, with the cool night wind on your cheeks, with the sea and the lonely music the sea gulls make. Stand still in the night and listen. You are very close to San Francisco's heart. Maybe you will hear it beating, or maybe what you will hear will be only the restless stirring of the sea; but one is like the other. . . .

In the beginning, there was a little Spanish ship with sails like white wings.

Fate, that had passed by other, prouder ships—the Manila treasure galleons, Cabrillo's *San Salvador,* Drake's *Golden Hinde,* Cermeñon's *San Agustin*—reached out and touched the *San Cárlos,* and it was she who did what the others failed to do. It was she who became the first ship in history to sail through the Golden Gate and cast anchor in the fabulous lost port of the *Conquistadores.*

Seafaring men, hawk-eyed, bold and the greatest sailors of the Western World, had been trying to find it for centuries, but it remained for the leather-jacketed pathfinders of the ailing Gaspar de Portolá, onetime officer of the Catalan Dragoons and leader of a tiny overland expedition from the south, to scale the low Montara mountains and take their place as the first known white men to gaze upon the vast and shimmering waters of San Francisco Bay. The month was November; the year, 1769.

Six years later, the *San Cárlos* tacked laboriously up the California coast. Her young commander, Don Juan Manuel de Ayala, Lieutenant of Frigate of the Royal Spanish Navy, was under orders to explore the great Bay Portolá's men had seen. There were annoying, disconcerting things on Ayala's mind. The winds were stubbornly against him and his vessel. Before leaving San Blas, he had been struck in the foot by the accidental discharge of a pistol, and now, as his ship beat northward, Ayala lay confined to his bed with a festering wound. There had been a fire aboard ship.

It is recorded in the log of the *San Cárlos* that June 22, 1775, the day of the fire, whales were sighted and noted as the first sign of land. On the next day, the sailors saw seals, the second sign of land. On June 24, they spied a flock of ducks, positive and final proof that land was near. Later that day, a cry came from the lookout, and low to the southeast was Point Año Nuevo. Ayala brought the *San Cárlos* about and sent her pitching through the choppy seas toward the white beaches of Monterey. There his men would mend the sails, repair the damage of the stormy passage and take on ballast and water.

It was July 27 when a launch towed the *San Cárlos* to sea and into the sweep of a southwest wind. Her sails filled out, bellying before the breeze. Her spars creaked. She heeled over, and her prow pointed to the Golden Gate and her rendezvous with history.

But the wind changed, and again she fought against it in long, heartbreaking tacks. For eight days she inched her way northward. With the dawn of the ninth day, August 5, she was in sight of the end. Ayala saw the landfalls, Point San Pedro and the brown hills of the Coast Range to the east, the island cliffs of the Farallon Islands to the northwest, Point Reyes to the north. He turned the *San Cárlos* to the rising sun.

At four-thirty that afternoon, six miles outside the Gate, soundings were taken and the bottom was found at sixteen fathoms. At five o'clock, the *San Cárlos* was in fifteen fathoms, moving slowly toward the outer bay and heaving in the long swells that rolled to the heads. Ayala, limping along the deck on his wounded foot, wondered what to do. The sun was going down, and soon it would be dark. The pilot boat he had sent ahead to guide him through the channel had failed to return. The tide was ebbing swiftly, and although the *San Cárlos* was under full sail, he could see, by looking shoreward, that she was barely moving. Should he wait for his pilot's return, for a new day's light and a flowing tide? Could he wait, with the end so near?

Ayala made his decision, and the *San Cárlos* breasted the stream in the gathering dusk. At eight-thirty o'clock, her sixty-fathom line and its twenty-pound lead failed to touch bottom. She was past Point Bonita now, and past Mile Rock, and moving foot by foot along the southern shore of the harbor mouth. Then, just inside, the wind suddenly ceased. The *San Cárlos* lost headway, swung in the current and began to slide to the sea. Ayala shouted a command. An anchor splashed overboard. It dropped twenty-two fathoms—and held. The little ship was safe, the long voyage ended.

From the shore and through the darkness to her weary sailors, there drifted the sweet smell of yerba buena. . . .

So they were the first, and that was two months after the Battle of Bunker Hill.

The next year, while three thousand miles away the Liberty Bell was ringing, the Spaniards were building their adobe presidio huts on the rolling mesa above Fort Point, and their mission church beside the willowed bank of a little lake a few miles south and east. The United States was born in 1776, and so was San Francisco.

Years passed, and the great Bay slept. Now and then a ship would come from the south with supplies for the presidio garrison or the mission fathers. It would take on hides from the mission ranch, or tallow, or perhaps nothing at all, and then would sail away, and homesick soldiers would watch her stand out to sea and begin the long reach to the southwest.

Then the Russians, hungry for California meat and grain, sent their ships down from the Alaskan outposts. They anchored in the cove of Yerba Buena, rowing ashore to drive their bargains and to break the hearts of the soft-eyed *señoritas*. And there lay moored the English sloop *Raccoon* in 1816, and when her men heard the news of Waterloo, her guns cracked triumphantly, the echoes rolling sharply back across the Bay from the high dunes and the cypress-covered hills.

The trading ships came more often, and now they were Yankee ships, flying the Yankee flag, and their skippers were tough and their crews swaggered across the dusty plaza, booting out of their way the pigs that rooted there in the sandy ground. One day, some Yankee ships sailed into the Bay, and they were neither traders nor Sag Harbor whalers; they were men-of-war, the substance of manifest destiny, and the name of one was *Portsmouth*. It was to give its name to the plaza, when the plaza became a square.

It was 1846, and America was on the march from sea to shining sea. Musket fire rattled along the Rio Grande. Covered wagons rocked westward across the Kansas plains. A handful of trappers in coonskin caps captured Sonoma, and the reluctant Sloat captured Monterey, although "captured" is a pretty glamorous way of putting it; no lives were lost and no shots fired, and when it was over the natives went back to dozing in the sun, and finally slept once more. Getting his orders from Sloat, Captain Montgomery of the *Portsmouth* fired a twenty-one-gun salute, rowed ashore with his Marines, raised the Stars and Stripes over the little plaza, and Yerba Buena was a piece of America.

Thus, to El Dorado, came the pathfinders and the conquerors.

Three years later, five hundred ships came bearing gold-seekers, and rode at anchor hard by the little cove. So myriad were the masts, they say, they resembled a forest of leafless trees; beneath the masts, the deserted ships swung silently with the tides. They had weathered the gales of Cape Horn, had carried treasure hunters to the western shore. And now, abandoned by their gold-hungry crews, they belonged to the rats.

For the Forty-niners who came by white top, the journey was an ordeal in the sun, and it was an ordeal in the swamps for those who crossed the

Isthmus. For those who came by sea, it was a six- or eight-month trial by monotony, where a fish, a bird, the raising of an island on the horizon electrified the bored and sea-weary Argonauts.

Stand on the Embarcadero, and you stand where their ships came in and dropped their iron hooks. You stand where their land of promise ran to the sea; you stand on the shore of their golden mirage and dream. You stand where the Gold Rush began.

Above you, a few years later, the tall masts of the clipper ships reached for the same stars, and off there, toward Telegraph Hill, rose the groggy laughter of the whores, the thieves, the pimps, the cutthroats and dim-brained criminals of the Barbary Coast.

By then, there were rickety wharves at the ends of the streets, which ran hundreds of feet into the Bay and which were jammed from dawn to sundown with wagons and drays, swarthy seamen speaking a Babel's Tower of tongues, merchants and crafty-lipped bartenders, miners in their red shirts, with the red mud of the Yuba, the American, the Sacramento and the Feather rivers still caked on their knee boots. Pile drivers hammered the long timbers, chuffing steam paddies dumped their sand on the shores between the wharves and the beached hulls, and the top-heavy Irish men-of-war dropped their cargoes of rocks to the mud of the harbor floor. Slowly, foot by foot, the little cove was disappearing; the waterfront was moving eastward and into the harbor.

Sea and ships were the town's life then, and when the signal tower on Telegraph Hill announced an approaching vessel, tradesmen closed their shops, roulette wheels in the gambling halls ceased their spinning, drinks lay half-finished on the bars and the town rushed to the waterfront to greet her. That happened, too, when the ships sailed away.

In *Annals of San Francisco,* by Frank Soulé, Dr. John H. Gihon and James Nisbet, there was a description of Steamer Day and the departure of the steamer *Brother Jonathan*. In the Fifties, the *Jonathan* was on the Nicaraguan run and her passengers were bound east via the Isthmus. The narrative was richly detailed, telling of the passengers about to start the long journey home and of the well-wishing friends and relatives who thronged to the Jackson Street wharf to see them off. It told of the last-minute champagne cups, of the roar of escaping steam, the shouts of the mates, the casting off of the lines, the cries of those leaving and those left behind, the exuberant scaling of hats by passengers and spectators alike, then the crashing of the paddles, the cheers, the good-bys and the slow disappearance of the ship behind the shoulder of Telegraph Hill. It was the *Brother Jonathan,* when she struck the rocks of the desolate northwest coast, that gave San Francisco her first major marine disaster. Down with her went one hundred eighty men, women and children. Among them was James Nisbet, who had written so glowingly of a happier day for the *Jonathan.*

She stood through the Gate July 28, 1865, on a routine run to Portland and Victoria for the California Steam Navigation Company. Her commanding officer was Captain S. J. De Wolf. On board were one hundred forty-five passengers and a crew of fifty-four. In addition to Nisbet, then an editor of the *San Francisco Daily Evening Bulletin,* the passenger list included Brigadier General George Wright, en route to take command of the Army's Department of Columbia, and A. G. Henry, close friend of Abraham Lincoln, former United States Surveyor General and newly appointed Governor of the Territory of Washington. (Treasure hunters still insist the *Jonathan* carried from $300,000 to $1,000,000 in government gold and United States Treasury notes. Official records fail to support this belief.)

Late in the afternoon of July 30, a small boat containing eleven men, five women and three children, all numb with terror and exhaustion, reached the rugged coast of Del Norte County, near Crescent City and the Oregon border. They were the only survivors of the *Jonathan's* last voyage.

When the news reached San Francisco, the entire city mourned the victims of the disaster. Flags hung at half-staff. Bells tolled. Buildings were draped in black crepe. And little by little, as the sea cast body after body on the lonely north coast, San Franciscans learned the story:

It was noon, and there was a northwest wind of gale force. Mountainous seas were breaking over the *Jonathan.* De Wolf ordered her put about; he was going to take her back to Crescent City and safety. At one-fifty o'clock, eight miles southwest of Point St. George and some ten miles from her haven, the *Jonathan* struck a submerged rock. The shock sent the passengers pitching to the deck. De Wolf tried vainly to back her off. For five minutes, she wallowed helplessly. There was another deep thump. A section of her keel floated to the surface. Her foremast tore loose, dropped, punched a hole through her bottom and crashed to rest with its foreyard across the promenade deck. Three lifeboats were lowered. One, filled with women, capsized. Another, filled with men, capsized. The third somehow stayed right side up, and started for shore.

Forty-five minutes after she hit, the *Jonathan* sank in twenty-five fathoms. Nothing was ever recovered except the bits of wreckage washed up by the sea. The sea also gave up some half a hundred of her dead, and Nisbet was one of them.

In one of his pockets, they found four sheets of paper covered with calm and deliberate handwriting, in pencil and still quite legible when he was taken from the water. They were headed: "At Sea, On Board the *Brother Jonathan,* July 30." There followed his will, coolly written in the last minutes of his life on the cracking deck, and a note to the Hopkins family of San Francisco, with whom he had lived and by whom he was fondly known as "Grandpa."

"A thousand affectionate adieus," the letter said. "You spoke of my sailing on Friday—hangman's day—and the unlucky *Jonathan.* Well, here I am with death before me. My love to you all—to Caspar, to Dita, to Mellie and little Myra—kiss her for me. Never forget

Grandpa."

In one of the Embarcadero beer halls, or perhaps in a Howard Street sherry tavern, you might still find a grizzled old-timer who would sneer at the cosmic blasts of the atomic bomb. He would take another pull at his beer, or another gulp of his sherry, and snort, "Son, they were nothing. By God, you should've been there when they blew up Blossom Rock."

He would be thinking fondly back to that day when San Franciscans opened the Seventies with a bang—a bang that lifted the top off the great submarine shelf midway between Alcatraz and Yerba Buena Island.

Captain Frederick Beechey of the British Navy discovered the rock in 1826 by the simple method of ramming it with his ship, the sloop *Blossom.* Forty years later, Major R. S. Williamson of the Army Corps of Engineers was ordered to do something about it, for it presented a constant threat to ships bound from San Francisco to Mare Island up the Bay, or to the Sacramento River and the San Joaquin River channels. The Major had a survey made, and it showed that at low tide the top of the rock was five feet under water. It was sandstone, about one hundred ninety feet long and one hundred feet wide.

Deciding it should be removed to a depth of twenty-four feet at low tide (it has since been lowered to forty-two), the engineers called for bids. The successful bidder was Colonel A. W. von Schmidt, a civil engineer already noted in San Francisco for skill and ingenuity. The Colonel's price was $75,000.

Getting down to work in October, 1869, von Schmidt anchored a coffer-dam ten feet square to the top of the rock and began sinking a shaft. When the shaft was about thirty feet below low water, his workmen struck out into lateral galleries and eventually hollowed out a great chamber. Over this submarine room, the top crust of the rock formed a roof about fifteen feet thick. The plan was to pack the chamber with forty-three thousand pounds of powder, touch it off by an electric current and blow the roof to bits. The fragments would drop to the chamber floor and then be swept by tides into deep water.

On Friday, April 22, 1870, the Colonel issued a bulletin. The following day, it said, San Francisco would witness the greatest explosion in her history. Glaziers gleefully rubbed their hands, expecting every window in town to shatter. Scientists suggested that timers be stationed along the road between San Francisco and San José, fifty miles to the south, to clock the progress of the anticipated "earth wave" the blast would cause. Yachtsmen organized boating parties to cruise around and pick up the dead fish that were to float to the surface of the Bay.

The explosion was scheduled for one-thirty in the afternoon, but by ten that morning spectators were scaling the steep sides of Telegraph Hill. "By one o'clock," wrote the *Chronicle* reporter assigned to Telegraph Hill, "there was hardly standing room over all the northern face of the slope." With these spectators, plus the sight-seers packed on North Point and Meiggs' Wharf and those in steamers and some two hundred smaller craft, the crowd was estimated at between fifty and sixty thousand.

As the time for the blast drew near, the Telegraph Hill group began to get restive. Rowdies amused themselves by pegging oyster shells at stove-pipe hats and parasols that blocked their vision. Other ruffians tapped a couple of barrels of beer. When the barrels were empty, they rolled them down the hillside, clearing a way through the crowds, said the reporter, "like a charge of cavalry."

At one-twenty-eight, there was a puff of white smoke and a boom from Alcatraz. It was the warning gun. But one-thirty came, and nothing happened. Von Schmidt, in a small boat a discreet eight hundred feet from the rock, sent men over in another boat to find out what was the matter. They readjusted a displaced wire and rowed back to von Schmidt.

At two-five, the Colonel gave his battery crank a sharp twist, and there was a muffled thud. A column of water two hundred feet in diameter and jet black in color shot high into the air, lifting skyward on its crest timbers and fragments of rock. As they dropped, another wave boiled seventy feet upward and then rolled away in great, circular swells.

A spontaneous cheer broke from the crowd. Steamers tooted their whistles. People fired guns, and for several minutes the Bay echoed with an appreciative din. But the Telegraph Hill crowd went away grumbling; they had been too far away to hear the thud, there had been no earth tremors, not a pane of glass was broken and there were no dead fish.

In an editorial the next day, the *Chronicle* granted the blast had been instrumental in removing a marine hazard, but, as a spectacle, it rated the explosion a failure. An Alcatraz cannon, it said, could make a lot more noise than von Schmidt's forty-three thousand pounds of powder. Most San Franciscans, who would have felt hoodwinked at anything short of utter vaporization of the Bay, agreed.

Although the sledge that drove the Golden Spike had knocked the props out from under San Francisco's shipping trade with the East Coast (tonnage of ships entering the port dropped 41 per cent between 1867 and 1870, the year after the transcontinental railroad was completed), she was still the greatest harbor on the West Coast, and the flags of every maritime nation in the world fluttered from the mizzen trucks of the ships that came through the Gate.

The men who sailed most of these ships reached San Francisco after a long time at sea, two years, maybe three. They were sick of the sea, sick of the bad, inadequate food, sick of the cursing martinets that ran the hellships. So they wanted to forget all that in a gaudy pageant of wine, women and song. As a matter of fact, if they got enough wine and enough women, why, the hell with the song.

Naïvely, they all believed they could get drunk the quickest; stay drunk the longest; and enjoy the most glamorous whores, at the lowest prices, on the Barbary Coast—a row of brothels, gin mills and honky-tonks along six or eight blocks of Pacific and Kearny Streets and Broadway. The longer they were at sea, the more delightful their imaginations pictured the shabby bars and the fat and frowsy harlots that waited for them at the voyage's end. As they neared port, they happily told each other that all the world was divided into three parts—the sea, the ship and the Barbary Coast.

Thanks to a brutal side of San Francisco waterfront life in those days, many of them were unconscious during their stay on the Coast. Minutes after they reached shore, many of them were hit on the head either with a Mickey Finn or a heavy club. And when they were kicked awake the next day, they were miles at sea again, bound for Singapore, or perhaps a three-year whaling cruise. When this happened, they knew they had been shanghaied.

Not long after the turn of the century, this practice waned before the growing power of the seamen's unions and corrective legislation, but in the earlier days it was frequently the only way the rough, hard-driving masters of the trading ships could get together a crew.

The mechanics was simple. The moment a ship appeared in the Bay, it was immediately swarmed upon by runners representing sailors' boardinghouses on shore. By promising the crew unlimited supplies of free liquor, plus harems of desirable and willing drinking companions, the runners lured the sailors to these boardinghouses. Once there, the first drink served them was a tumblerful of equal parts of brandy, whisky and gin, with a dash of opium. A couple of these, and the sailor just did not care. To make sure he didn't, the boardinghouse proprietor worked him over with a billy. Then he dropped the sailor through a trap door, flung him into a boat and rowed him to a ship that needed a crew.

The profit for the proprietor, or crimp, was the $20 or $30 he charged the ship's master for supplying a sailor, and whatever he managed to steal from the victim. Frequently, the captain also handed the crimp an advance on two months of the sailor's pay, which was entered on the ship's records

15

as reimbursement for getting the sailor a job. These gains the crimp split, on a percentage basis, with his runner.

The boardinghouses grouped themselves in a row of witches' nests along lower Pacific Street. Policemen walking this beat carried knives in their breast pockets, because knives were faster to draw than pistols. The story was told (by the late Edward Morphy, San Francisco newspaperman and annalist) that Sergeant Tom Longford of Harbor Station entered a secondhand store in this block one night to investigate a suspicious noise. As he stepped into the dark interior, a man sprang from the blackness. With one motion, Longford drew his knife and swung it blindly in a long, powerful, random sweep. The room was suddenly silent. Striking a match, Longford looked down. There, at his feet, lay his victim, neatly decapitated.

Perhaps in retaliation for this, a crimp named Calico Jim years later shanghaied six policemen, one after the other, as they arrived at his boardinghouse to arrest him. After disposing of the sixth, Calico Jim called it a day and left town. The legend goes that, when the cops got back from their cruises, they drew lots to see which one would take care of Calico Jim. The chosen one tracked him to Callao, Peru, and there, in the street, riddled the crimp with six shots, one for each of his victims.

On Davis Street, around the corner from Pacific, was the boardinghouse of the notorious female crimp, Miss Piggott, who, in her day, sent many a sailor off to a hellship passage with a tap of her bung starter. Another lady crimp, Mother Bronson, had a tavern on Steuart Street. She was a strapping wench who was capable, when aroused, of lifting a customer from the floor to the top of the bar with one kick.

It was the crimp Shanghai Kelly, however, who engineered the classic in the dismal annals of shanghaiing. One dull day in the Sixties, Kelly heard of three crewless ships in the Bay—crewless because their masters were so tough no sober sailor would touch their registries with a fifty-foot jib boom. The canny Kelly chartered a tugboat and announced that it was his birthday and he was sponsoring a junket around the Bay for all his friends. Drooling over his promise that liquor on the house would flow like water, a hundred friends piled on the tug and started on the cruise. Three hours later, doped whisky had knocked out everybody but Kelly and his toadies.

Kelly then ordered the tug around and headed for the three ships. Stopping alongside each one, he passed over the bulwarks a full crew, stiffer than planks, but solid hands—every one of them—when they regained consciousness. The next day, the ships and Kelly's birthday-party guests were far at sea.

After a stroke like that, no one, as long as men were shanghaied, ever questioned Kelly's right to the title "King of Crimps."

The sea has her secrets and murmurs of them as she ripples darkly past the Embarcadero piers. They become part of the waterfront legend and of the tales told by old salts over their beer. Like the ghostship that comes riding through the Gate on the sea fogs. Like the dipping sea gulls they believe to be the souls of dead mariners. Like the decaying hulk of the *Rio,* where and how many fathoms deep in the swiftly flowing waters of the Golden Gate?

It happened that on the morning of Washington's Birthday, 1901, M. J. Fitzgerald, a reporter for the San Francisco Marine Exchange, stood on Meiggs' Wharf, at its end, where it met the Embarcadero sea wall. He was peering into the thick gray mist that had closed down over the Bay. "Damned bad weather," he muttered. "Shouldn't wonder if she decided to stay outside till it lifts."

Five minutes more went by, and suddenly Fitzgerald heard a sound, a sound like the rhythmic thudding of oars, muffled by the fog. A moment later, a dark shape loomed in the mist, swung in toward the sea wall. Fitzgerald recognized it in an instant as a lifeboat. In it huddled a dozen men, half-clad and shivering. Some were bleeding from cuts on their heads and arms. One look at the lifeboat's bow told Fitzgerald that the ship he had been waiting for had come in. Across it were the words, *City of Rio de Janeiro.*

In a matter of minutes, San Francisco confronted the greatest marine disaster in harbor history. All day, newspaper and Marine Exchange switchboards were jammed with anxious queries. Lifeboats, Italian fishing boats and scores of other craft plied the Gate in a grisly search for floating bodies or pieces of wreckage. Thousands of the curious stood on the bluffs above the Gate's south shore, watching the seekers and staring at the swift, inscrutable tides. But the tides yielded nothing but the dead—the dead and a few broken timbers, a few sacks of mail. Of the two hundred eleven on board the *Rio,* all but eighty perished.

The facts were these:

Because of mechanical difficulties, the *Rio,* proudest steamer of the Pacific Mail Line and a former Spanish-American War transport, arrived off the headlands two days behind schedule. Approaches to the Bay were blanketed in tule fog, and she dropped her hook four miles west of the Cliff House at noon, Thursday, February 21.

At five o'clock that afternoon, she was boarded by Captain Fred Jordan, a Bay pilot known as "Lucky" Jordan. He had never had a bad break in all his professional career, and now he was about to pay for it.

Later that evening, the skies cleared slightly, and the *Rio* steamed to a position off Point Lobos. Again the fog closed in. Jordan decided to wait it out. Captain William Ward, thirty-eight-year-old master of the *Rio,* turned in for the night, leaving orders to be awakened if the weather cleared again. At four o'clock the next morning, it began to look as though the fog were lifting. Jordan, on the *Rio's* bridge, saw stars through rifts in the mist. He saw the bright lights on the headlands. He sent for Captain Ward.

Later, survivors said Rounsevelle Wildman, United States Consul General at Hong Kong and the most important person on the passenger list, was in a hurry to catch a train from Oakland that afternoon so that he could reach Washington in time for President McKinley's inaugural ball. It was also said that Captain Ward himself, engaged to marry a San Francisco girl, was impatient to see his fiancée after the long voyage from the Orient.

At any rate, the clearing skies seemed to Jordan to justify an immediate approach to port. Captain Ward concurred. "Take her in," he ordered, and against a swirling, six-knot ebb tide, the *Rio* headed for the Golden Gate. Cautiously, at half speed, she steamed past Point Lobos, past Land's End. At five o'clock, she hit a dense fog bank. Safely through it, Pilot Jordan took his bearings on Point Bonita. To starboard, the dim shape of Mile Rock slipped past and to the stern.

Another fog bank, more dense than the first, rose before the *Rio.* She slipped closer and closer to the fog-shrouded coast.

She struck the Fort Point ledge at five-twenty-five o'clock. With a long-drawn grinding, her stern heaved out of the water. She trembled, and listed sharply. Her lights blinked out. Spars crashed to the deck. Cries of alarm, running footsteps and the desperate shrieking of her whistle echoed through the ghostly fog. At five-thirty-five, with fourteen feet of water in her holds, she slid gently off the ledge and went down by the bow.

A few managed to get away in lifeboats. Rescue vessels picked up the others. Wildman and his wife and son were among the one hundred thirty-one passengers and members of the Chinese crew who drowned. Captain Ward was last seen entering his cabin. He had said if anything ever happened to a command of his, he would blow his brains out and go down with her. Survivors did not believe he had time for the pistol.

For years, waterfront legend had it that the *Rio* carried with her to the bottom a fabulous amount of gold, and the legend still lives along the Embarcadero. Surviving officers and Pacific Mail officials, however, testified her cargo comprised only $300,000 in opium and $400,000 in silk.

A number of attempts have been made to locate the wreck of the *Rio,* but all have failed. Mariners believe she has settled into one of the great submarine cavities where Gate tides have washed the channel floor to a depth of four hundred feet. They say the sea will never surrender the *Rio* until it runs dry. Then they smile and add, "And when that time comes, what will it matter?"

If the Embarcadero has a soul, it's something shaped like the Ferry Building. The world over, the Ferry Building stands for San Francisco the way the Campanile stands for Venice, the Eiffel Tower for Paris, or the Empire State Building for New York. Its lofty tower is a sight that will bring a lump to your throat if you're a San Franciscan and seeing it for the first time from the deck of the train ferry that's bringing you back home. And, if you're going away, it's a part of that last look that you'll never forget.

To examine it, you might think it had always been there and the Spaniards had found it when they arrived, but that would be to be deceived by its drabness, its curious stillness and the air it has of waiting for something to happen.

At the time, the papers were pretty busy with Admiral Dewey's capture of Subig Bay, and so all there was in the *Chronicle* of July 14, 1898, were four paragraphs leading off the Ocean and Waterfront column.

"The new union ferry depot," they began, "was opened yesterday to the Southern Pacific Company, and the Harbor Commissioners were interested observers and expressed themselves as delighted with the satisfactory manner in which everything worked. . . ."

Thus, quietly and several years before its completion, the Ferry Building started its life of service to the city and the waterfront. In the years that followed, it became the hub of the Bay Area's transportation system, and commuters and travelers trod its marbled and mosaic floors at the rate of fifty million a year—a volume of traffic exceeded by no other terminal in the world except London's historic Charing Cross Station. That was before the bridges sent the commuter ferries sailing into history.

When that happened and the Ferry Building halls grew deserted and lonely, newspapers carried sentimental stories saying the Ferry Building was not dead, it was only sleeping. Most San Franciscans still like to believe that.

The reason is, there are things about the Ferry Building that a San Franciscan carries in his heart. They are the memories of the good times, the happy comradeship, the inspiring and exhilarating moments that came with the ferryboat rides back and forth across the Bay. They are the remembered glimpse of lighted clock dials in the tower at night, and the tenderness of the slanting afternoon light on the tower as you stand at Lotta's Fountain, say, and look eastward down the gentle slope of Market Street. The Ferry Building means the tears of all the farewells that were ever spoken there, and the embraces of all those who ever greeted each other there. These, and fifty years of hurrying footsteps.

They say the tower is modeled after the famous Giralda, the Moorish bell tower of the Cathedral of Seville in Spain. And that is true, but a San Franciscan will tell you there isn't another tower in the world like the Ferry Building tower, and you've got to be a San Franciscan to know what he's saying.

Then you'll know he's talking about all the times the building has lived through: the time of the laughing, cheering soldiers of the First California Battalion, off to do or die and remember the *Maine* in the faraway jungles of the Philippines; the proud ships of the Great White Fleet as they lay in the stream, on their way to show the world what Teddy Roosevelt meant by a big stick; the freighters and the troopships of the First World War; the Matson liners and the gay farewell parties at the piers before they left for Waikiki; the Japanese liners and the American President ships, backing into the channel with bands playing and confetti bursting in flurries from their decks; the white ferryboats to Sausalito and Oakland, and the Sacramento River boats; the ferries to Treasure Island during the Exposition, and the blue, halcyon skies of those days, and the hot sunshine; then the war days when the Ferry Building siren gave no time signals, so if you heard it you'd know it was an air raid warning; the days when the ships suddenly disappeared from their places in the harbor, and you didn't know where they went, and you didn't ask; the battle wagons, and the coming home of the shell-ripped cruiser *San Francisco* who got hers in the Savo Islands when the battle was Guadalcanal; the white hospital ships, and the submarines slinking down the Bay to Hunter's Point; the P-38's whistling overhead; the convoys moving out in the nighttime; the stillness of the siren on V-E Day, because the war was still going on in the west, and then the happy sound it made, rising and falling, rising and falling, when that was over and, later, when Admiral Halsey brought the Third Fleet back to the Gate. . . .

That was the end of the war for the Ferry Building and the Embarcadero, and the place to be was above the waterfront on Telegraph Hill. The Golden Gate Bridge was hidden in the morning mists that day, and the fog closed in like a gray wall over the gray water just beyond Fisherman's Wharf. The crowd came early and stood on the steps that lead to the base of Coit Tower. Four and five deep, they stood on the walk and concrete steps that circle the crest of the hill and strained their eyes into the mist.

The old-timer standing in a group of old-timers was disappointed. He surveyed the drab freighters at the piers and in the stream and snorted contemptuously. "They oughta dress their ships. Every ship in the harbor oughta be dressed. I remember when Fighting Bob Evans came in with the Great White Fleet, there wasn't a ship in the Bay that didn't have her flags up and flyin'." One of his companions nodded. "That's right . . . that's right." Beyond them and in the distance, the mists rolled over Russian Hill, brushing the tops of the tall buildings on that hill and Nob Hill, and graying out the Top o' the Mark.

There was a long delay, and the curious, filtered, flat light fell unkindly on the city and the faces of the people standing and waiting, the way San Franciscans have always stood and waited on Telegraph Hill to see important things happening in their harbor. They peered through field glasses, or fumbled in paper bags for sandwiches they had brought with them against just such a delay. Women stood on the hoods of parked automobiles with shoes off, holding the shoes in their hands.

Two blimps, gray like the sky, suddenly poked their blunt noses through the fog and hovered close to the water. A thin, dark submarine emerged from the mist and knifed slowly up the stream, inshore and close to the Embarcadero.

It was ten minutes to one when the first whistles came from the ships at the North Beach piers. Soon the people on Telegraph Hill saw what the men on the ships down there had seen before them—the low hull of a destroyer escort. Inch by inch (so slowly did it seem to travel), it slid into view from behind the corner of an apartment house between the hill and the Bay.

And, one by one, the destroyers moved up past the waterfront. The welcoming horns and whistles blew, and against their bass the yelp of a ship's siren rose and fell. There was a fireboat off Fisherman's Wharf, and suddenly water feathered from her nozzles in four white plumes. Like the grim ghosts of ships came the others—the cruiser *Vicksburg,* her blinker lights flashing shoreward; the battleship *Alabama;* the battleship *Wisconsin;* the battleship *Colorado;* the battleship *South Dakota,* with her victory pennant trailing like a serpent across her stern.

Dark and menacing, their guns angled slightly toward the sky, they stole silently up the Bay. Behind each of them followed a school of tiny, eager landing craft, and behind the landing craft were the white, spreading wakes.

All at once there was that glad burst of the Ferry Building siren, sending its weird and triumphant anthem across the Bay. In the waterfront factories and warehouses, workmen tied the whistles down and let them blow.

On the hill, the crowd began to break up, and there was the sound of many automobiles starting at once. The school children formed their lines and marched back to their school on Union Street, and hill dwellers, who had watched from their windows and roof tops, put away their field glasses and returned to the open fires you knew about because there was in the air, and had been all morning, the smell of smoke from the coal they use in their fireplaces up there on the hill.

Soon the people had all gone, and the hill again belonged to the gloomy sky and the still, dripping trees.

Down below the hill and around the base of the hill was the Embarcadero, black and slick in the fog. Ships coming home were an old story to that street. That's what it was there for, that was its life.

It lay there, waiting for them.

Old Town

2. MONTGOMERY STREET

"GOLD FROM THE AMERICAN RIVER!" · THE CORPSE IN THE WELL · THE
STRANGE DELIGHT OF DOCTOR JONES · THE GREAT FIRES · VIGILANTES OF
'51 · "HALLECK'S FOLLY" · THE ASSASSINATION OF JAMES KING OF WIL-
LIAM · VIGILANTES OF '56 · "PISCO JOHN" AND HIS POTENT PUNCH · THE
TODDY TIME-TABLE · ON THE FIELD OF HONOR: GILBERT VS. DENVER. GWIN
VS. MC CORKLE. HUNT VS. HUBERT. FERGUSON VS. JOHNSTON. TERRY VS.
BRODERICK · THE AMBROSIAL PATH · THE LOST MINE OF PEGLEG SMITH ·
SOLDIERS OF THE LORD · THE LEGACY OF P. MONTGOMERY

WHEN YOU'RE on a noisy, narrow, downtown street where the tallest
buildings and the biggest banks go soaring into space, where a hoyden
wind snatches your hat or lifts your skirt above your knees, where Market
Street goes by at one end and Telegraph Hill cuts off the sky at the other,
and the sun sets at two in the afternoon—when you're on that street,
you're on Montgomery Street.

A little more than a hundred years ago, it was an imaginary line named in questionable tribute to the Navy captain who wrested the pueblo from the dreamy, almond-eyed natives. And it was the place where the sea came to in those days. At high tide, the sea even surged beyond the imaginary line and formed a tiny lagoon at the base of the Broadway cliffs. It was across the neck of this lagoon, in 1844, that a flimsy planking was laid to accommodate pedestrians who wanted to walk from the tent-and-shanty settlement to Clark's Point, a quarter of a mile away.

That was San Francisco's first bridge, and its completion was the biggest thing that had happened since the panther carried off the Indian boy from Jacob Leese's backyard on Dupont Street. Proudly, the white settlers (all twenty-five or thirty of them) inspected the structure, jumped up and down on it to test its strength, and vowed that Yerba Buena was certainly the most up-and-coming community west of Chicago.

Four years later, when it was no longer Yerba Buena, but San Francisco, and the pine-board shacks and adobe huts numbered two hundred and the people eight hundred, the Mormon firebrand, Sam Brannan, ran stumbling through the muddy potholes of Montgomery Street, holding aloft a quinine bottle from whose contents the sun struck a gilded light. "Gold!" he cried, waving his hat. "Gold from the American River!"

For months, San Franciscans had been hearing reports about the gold at Sutter's Mill, a hundred fifty miles to the north and east—there had even been a couple of paragraphs in the local papers about it—but they were from Missouri. "When we see it, we'll believe it," they said, and went back to the Portsmouth House billiard tables.

So now they saw it.

"I looked on for a moment," one of them wrote. "A frenzy seized my soul; unbidden, my legs performed some entirely new movements of the polka steps—I took several; houses were too small for me to stay in; I was soon in the street in search of necessary outfits; piles of gold rose up before me at every step. Castles of marble, dazzling the eye with their rich appliances; thousands of slaves bowing to my beck and call; myriads of fair virgins contending with each other for my love: these were among the fancies of my fevered imagination. The Rothschilds, Girards and Astors appeared to me but poor people; in short, I had a very violent attack of the gold fever. . . ."

He was no isolated case, for, in a matter of hours, the whole town had it bad. Barbers, butchers, millers, bartenders, shoe clerks—three-fourths of the male population, in fact—took one look at Brannan's bottle, dropped whatever they had been doing and nailed up their shop doors and windows. Then they kissed the wife good-by, chucked the kids under the chin, hung out a sign that said, "Gone to the diggings," and were off in a cloud of dust.

The town was never the same after that.

When they came back, most of their wives were still where they left them; the bare, tawny hills were still there, and the sand dunes and the dwarfed and twisted oaks; the streets were still so muddy you could sink up to your neck and above it in the tide-flat slime if you didn't watch your step, and not much time had passed.

But it wasn't a small town any more. There were all those Gold Rush ships in the cove and Bay, and by the end of '49 there were thirty thousand people; and houses, shacks, sheds and stores were going up at the rate of one every hour, slapped together from packing boxes, sailcloth, sections of abandoned ships—anything you could drive a nail into and that would shed water.

A year or so before, at A. J. Ellis's boardinghouse and grogshop on Montgomery Street, just across the lagoon bridge, some of the boys complained about the taste of the whisky Ellis was serving. "All right," growled Ellis, "drink water then. The well's in the backyard."

"God damn it, we will," vowed the boys. They trooped to the well, let down the bucket and pulled up a dead sailor.

Something like that had handed the town laughs for months, but, now, Ellis was gone, the bridge was replaced by a levee and industrious citizens were filling in the lagoon. If you'd tried to tell them the story of the dead sailor, you'd have been talking to yourself after the first sentence. They were too busy. There was money in reclaimed land.

The town was spreading the way ink spreads on blotting paper. West beyond Mason Street and up the sides of Russian Hill, and south beyond California Street, and even Market Street. Lots that two years before you could have picked up in trade for a goat or a keg of whisky were selling for $10,000 and up. Eggs were a dollar apiece; stores with a twenty-foot frontage rented for $3500 a month; and a gambling house paid $15,000-a-month rent for a drafty room in a Portsmouth Square hotel.

It was a boom town now. Anyone who could saw wood could earn $12 to $15 for a few hours' work. Hack drivers called it a bad day if they didn't make at least $20, and even waterfront loafers sneered at anything less than $5 or $10 for an odd job. Once, a tough sea captain climbed from a ship's boat to Long Wharf, set his bags down and tossed a half dollar to a seedy-looking bystander. "Here," he said gruffly, "take these bags to the Parker House." The roughneck eyed him coolly, spat over the side of the wharf, tossed two half dollars to the planking and snarled, "Take 'em yourself."

This gold fever probably achieved its most picturesque stage in the person of a Doctor Jones, whose idea of a good time was to spread a sheet on the floor, scatter gold dust on it and walk through the dust in his bare feet. Then he would take his clothes off and roll in it. When he got bored with this, he would scoop it up in his hands and pour it on his head. Eventually, he wound up back East in a place where they kept people like that.

Montgomery Street, whose merchants not long ago had advertised their location as "Montgomery Street on the Beach," was a noisy lane of brokerage houses, saloons and auction shops. Their proprietors could, at low tide, walk out the back door and on to the barges that held their merchandise in storage.

Those places set the tone of the street, but there were other people and establishments, too. The Sydney Ducks, for instance, off the Australian convict ships, who lived at the Telegraph Hill end of the street, swigging cheap green ale at The Magpie or The Bird in Hand, sleeping with Chilean harlots in the two-bit cribs and sandbagging after-dark pedestrians for what they could steal from their victims' pockets.

All that went on a couple of blocks away from the offices of such upright citizens as J. S. Hager, later a United States Senator; James King of William, whose assassination would, in a few years, send the Vigilantes reaching for their muskets; Kentucky-born A. P. Crittenden, who would get shot through the heart on the afterdeck of a Bay ferryboat; and a mild, prosperous commission merchant named Joshua Abraham Norton, who would one day dress himself in a soldier suit and call himself an emperor. The first brick building was on Montgomery Street, and the

Tontine gambling house, and a Mexican saloon. Rowe's Olympic Circus (featuring Ethiopian Serenaders) was down toward California Street, where massive towers now scrape the sky; and there, too, were Lütgen's Hotel, Kloppenburg's Grocery and Al Wilkie's lemonade factory.

They were all flimsily built, and so when the fires came they went flaring up like orange crates. There were six fires, the first roaring through the block between Portsmouth Square and Montgomery Street on the day before Christmas, 1849. When volunteer firemen got through fighting it with water-soaked blankets and bucket brigades, fifty jerry-built structures lay in ruins. So fast was the block rebuilt, you could have circled it a month later and sworn it had been standing like that all the time.

The second fire came the next May and raged for seven hours across three blocks, bounded east and west by Montgomery Street and Dupont Street, on the slope of the Clay Street hill. This time it was a top-flight fire: buildings destroyed, three hundred; damage, $4,000,000 plus. But within ten days, more than half the burned area was rebuilt. They were going strong on the other half when, five weeks later, a third fire leveled another $3,000,000 in property between Kearny Street and the Bay. The fourth struck in September (this is still 1850) and destroyed several more blocks between Dupont and Montgomery, this time farther north and closer to Telegraph Hill.

The biggest one of all came May 3-4, 1851. Starting in a paint and upholstery shop off Portsmouth Square, it got away fast and hard. You get the best picture from H. H. Bancroft, the California historian:

"Aided by a strong northwest breeze, it leaped across Kearny Street upon the oft-ravaged blocks, the flames chasing one another, first southeastward, then, with a shifting wind, turning north and east. The spaces under the planking of the streets and sidewalks acted as funnels, which, sucking in the flames, carried them to sections seemingly secure, there to startle the unsuspecting occupants with a sudden outbreak all along the surface. Rising aloft, the whirling volumes seized upon either side, shriveling the frame houses, and crumbling with their intense heat the stout walls of supposed fireproof structures, crushing all within and without. The iron shutters, ere falling to melt in the furnace, expanded within the heat, cutting off escape, and roasting alive some of the inmates. Six men who had occupied the building of Taafe and McCahill, at the corner of

Sacramento and Montgomery, were lost; twelve others, fire fighters in Naglee's building, narrowly escaped; three were crushed by one falling wall; and how many more were killed and injured no one can say. The fire companies worked well, but their tiny streams of water were transformed into powerless vapor. More effectual than water was the pulling down and blowing up of buildings. . . . Voluntary destruction went hand in hand with the inner devastation, the boom of explosion mingling with the cracking of timbers, the crash of tumbling walls, and the dull detonation from falling roofs. A momentary darkening, then a gush of scintillating sparks, followed by fiery columns, which still rose, while the canopy of smoke sent their reflection for a hundred miles around, even to Monterey. It is related that the brilliant illumination in the moonless night attracted flocks of brant from the marshes, which, soaring to and fro above the flames, glistened like specks of burnished gold. . . ."

Ten hours of this, and the city lay in ashes. Glum San Franciscans, counting their losses once more, figured they had been burned out of two thousand buildings and about $12,000,000 worth of property.

The next month, there was still another. There hadn't been time to put up anything that wasn't temporary, but even so, some $2,500,000 in homes and business establishments went up in smoke at the base of Telegraph Hill.

While rival communities smugly observed that San Francisco was, and always would be, a firetrap because it was so windy, and preachers mounted beer barrels in Montgomery Street to cry that God was getting even with the city for its debauchery and licentious ways, tough and determined men began building all over again.

They began something else, too. Several of the fires had undoubtedly been set. There had been a lot of looting. Corrupt courts and a graft-infested police force were no help whatever. So certain public-spirited citizens organized their own street patrols. On June 9, 1851, they formed a Committee of Vigilance, named Sam Brannan their leader, and grimly prepared for action. They didn't have long to wait.

Within forty-eight hours, they had seized, tried, convicted and hanged a Sydney Duck known as John Jenkins, or The Miscreant. He had been careless enough to get caught stealing a safe from the Long Wharf shipping office of George W. Virgin (who later, by the way, for a local-boy-makes-good touch, went to Siam and became Admiral of the Royal Siamese Navy).

The next month, while ships in the harbor roared salutes, the Vigilantes hanged James Stuart, another Sydney cutthroat, from the end of the Market Street wharf. Before they got through, they lynched two more and deported half a hundred other characters who were low, but not low enough to rate a necktie party.

By September, when the Committee called it a day, The Magpie, The Tam o' Shanter, The Bird in Hand and the other Sydneytown rookeries were quieter than a redwood grove at midnight, and on the verge of becoming respectable. Vigilance had slipped their best customers a Mickey Finn.

On Montgomery Street, a few blocks from the home office of the world's richest bank, A. P. Giannini's Bank of America, there stands a certain building with a wealth of its own, a wealth of pioneer associations and memories. It may not be there much longer, for it has recently passed from the hands of staid and conservative owners to those of forward-looking businessmen, who, it is said, would like to tear it down and erect a garage in its place.

On the day that happens, San Francisco will wake up and discover it has lost one of its most historic buildings. Indignant citizens will cry, "Why didn't somebody do something?" Gray-bearded sons of pioneers will tear their hair, and politicians will nod sadly, not over the loss of the building, but because they missed a chance for publicity by failing to campaign for its preservation. In the end, everyone will settle for a bronze plaque on the garage cornerstone, marking the site of the once famous Montgomery Block. Sometimes, San Francisco is like that.

While it stands, it is No. 628, a weary-looking four-story building covering the southeast corner of Montgomery and Washington Streets. For years, San Franciscans have regarded it as a sort of aviary for the strange, nocturnal birds of the city's artistic element, and that is a fairly accurate appraisal. A Montgomery Block residence is the equivalent of a membership card in the poor man's Bohemian Club.

Once in a while, it makes the papers. For example: a blue-nosed cop on duty at the Hall of Justice County Jail on Kearny Street a block away will complain to his superiors that he can't get the prisoners away from the windows, not even to eat, because they're all hanging on the bars watching artists' models sun themselves in the nude on the Montgomery Block roof. His shocked superiors put a stop to the sun bathing, and the story (with pictures) usually rates a breezy treatment in the local dailies.

But publicity is an old story to the Montgomery Block, for, even before it was built, it was making news.

Beginning about a year after the Vigilantes cleaned up the town, San Francisco entered the post-Gold Rush letdown. The fires had been discouraging, and it was obvious the mines weren't going to make every man a millionaire. Purchasing power took a dive, leaving merchants stranded with whole cargoes of surplus commodities. The bottom fell out of the real estate market. Grafting politicians robbed the city treasury with one hand, and with the other signed ordinances boosting the tax rate. Civic morale was wearing thin.

In 1852, Henry W. Halleck met with a group of citizens to talk the situation over. Halleck had come West in 1847 with the Third United States Artillery to inspect the fortifications of the Pacific Coast, had stayed to help draft the state constitution, and now was anxious to do something to get San Francisco back on its feet. (Halleck was later the man President Lincoln appointed as General-in-Chief of All Union Armies.)

For a while he listened as the others gloomily discussed the state of affairs and wondered what they could do to restore people's confidence in the future of the city. Then he advanced what he thought was the answer: a building, a big building, an expensive building. As a matter of fact, he said, he had already planned such a building with G. P. Cummings, an architect whom he had brought with him to the meeting. After he had given them time to consider his proposal, Halleck turned to Cummings. "In your opinion, Mr. Cummings, how much would this building cost?"

The architect replied, "Three million dollars."

The civic leaders threw up their hands. "Halleck," they said, "you're a fool," and walked out.

Halleck went ahead without them, borrowing money wherever he could—from eastern financiers, from foreign banks, from the railroads—and late that year he put hundreds of Chinese coolies to work excavating for the foundation. Day after day they toiled on that street corner of the young metropolis, scooping up the tide-flat mud in baskets.

When their work was finished, redwood logs, floated across the Bay from Contra Costa County, were fashioned into a huge mat and placed in position on the floor of the excavation. Crosswise over them was laid another layer of redwoods, and, above that, a layer of twelve- by twelve-inch ship's planking. Sidewalk superintendents, watching the progress of construction, shook skeptical heads; the building would either sink out of sight into the mud, or else a good high tide and a strong blow would send it right out through the Gate. They called it "Halleck's Folly." Some wag offered a derisive alternative, "The Floating Fortress."

But it kept on growing bigger. Into it went cement from England, glass from Belgium, France and Germany, iron fittings, beams, doors and balconies brought around the Horn from Philadelphia, and 1,747,800 bricks. When Halleck was through, he had the largest building on the Pacific Coast, the first earthquake-proof building in San Francisco and (it is said) the first commercial structure in the world to have inside rooms opening on an inner courtyard.

It had taken fourteen months to build, and, two days before Christmas, 1853, "Halleck's Folly," or, more formally, the "Washington Block," was opened to the public. It wasn't long before both names were forgotten; San Franciscans, by everyday usage, automatically changed one of them to the "Montgomery Block." As for that business about Halleck and his folly, they figured the less said about it the better.

Perhaps the building did strengthen the public confidence in the city's future, but its success, and Halleck's triumph, had no effect whatever on the knavery of the City Hall politicians; three years later, they were still bribing and plundering. Finally, James King of William, a newspaperman, decided the city had had enough. He was waging against them the best fight he could, almost singlehandedly, when they struck back—with a bullet.

King had been a Montgomery Street financier who had lost out in the post-Gold Rush depression, had gone into the newspaper business, and now, as editor of the *Daily Evening Bulletin,* was turning the town upside down with his incendiary editorials and attacks against corrupt politicians. (His curious name developed from the fact that in his early life in Georgetown, D. C., there had been several James Kings in the community. His father's name had been William, so the boy added the "of William" to distinguish himself from the others.)

At three o'clock on the afternoon of May 14, 1856, King's *Bulletin* appeared on the streets carrying a bitter onslaught against James P. Casey, a member of the Board of Supervisors. Among other uncomplimentary details, King mentioned Casey's record as a onetime inmate of New York's Sing Sing prison.

An hour later, Casey burst into King's office on Montgomery Street. He was very excited. He blustered that he resented King's reference to his past. King coldly told him to get out. "Never show your face here again!" he commanded. And Casey went.

It was a little after five when King left his office for dinner. He walked north in front of the Montgomery Block. He reached the Washington Street corner of the block and paused for a moment in front of the Bank Exchange saloon. Then he stepped from the curbing and started diagonally across the intersection toward the Pacific Express offices. He was halfway across when Casey stepped from behind a wagon, pointed a Navy revolver at King's breast and fired. King staggered back. "Oh, God, I'm shot!" he said, and lurched on toward the corner. Casey ran a few steps up Washington Street to Portsmouth Square and the sanctuary of the police station.

Minutes after the attempted assassination, angry mobs milled in the streets around the Square and demanded that Casey be hanged from a lamppost. Fearing for Casey's safety, Sheriff David Scannell and a flying wedge of deputies rushed him into a carriage and drove him at breakneck speed to the County Jail on Broadway, several blocks away. The crowd ran after them, yelling, "Kill him! Lynch Casey!"

Above their cries rose the slow, grim tolling of the Monumental firehouse bell. It had been the tocsin of the Vigilantes in 1851, and it still was. . . .

The next day, the Committee of Thirteen of the Vigilance Committee began the enrollment of members. By noon, there were fifteen hundred. Within several days, there were eight thousand.

Now, on Sacramento Street, a couple of blocks toward the waterfront from Montgomery, there is a four-story brick building occupied by the Underwriters' Salvage Company. In those days, a two-story granite structure stood on that spot. The Vigilantes took it over, sandbagged it, mounted fieldpieces in the windows, placed armed sentinels in the street in front of it and on the roof, and called it Fort Gunnybags.

At noon on the Sunday after King was shot, twenty-six hundred of them, with bayoneted muskets on their shoulders, marched through the streets to the County Jail and arranged themselves in perfect order in front of the tiny building. Several of them dragged forth a cannon, loaded it with powder and ball and trained it on the jail door. A lovely, luminous Sunday it was, and the thousands of men, women and children who silently looked on from the nearby slopes of Telegraph Hill and Russian Hill could clearly see every move the Vigilantes made.

As the linstock of their cannon sputtered there in the street, the leaders stepped forward, mounted the jail steps and delivered their ultimatum to Sheriff Scannell. Some elements in the city, proclaiming themselves for "Law and Order," had protested against the Vigilance Committee, but in the face of its swift and determined organization, there was nothing authorities could do. And with only thirty deputies he could rely on, there was nothing Scannell could do. He called the cowering and trembling Casey out of the jail and turned him over. He also surrendered Charles Cora, a gambler who had been awaiting trial for the murder of United States Marshal William H. Richardson.

While the Vigilantes were trying Cora and Casey in the big committee room in Fort Gunnybags, James King of William died in Room 207 of the Montgomery Block. That was on Tuesday.

On Thursday, six thousand mourners followed King to a martyr's grave in Lone Mountain Cemetery. Grim-faced men, standing on the wrought-iron balconies of the Montgomery Block, watched the slow cortege move westward up the Clay Street hill and disappear over its crest. Even as they watched, they heard the plangent tolling of the Monumental bell, telling them that down the street and around the corner at Fort Gunnybags the

plank gallows of the Vigilantes were exacting a life for a life—Cora's for
Richardson, Casey's for King. Later, as they gathered at the Bank Exchange to talk things over, they learned from spectators that Cora, the
gambling man, had gone out quietly and stoically, the way a gambler
would; Casey, the tough ex-convict, died screaming for his mother.

(The murderers are still lying in sun-swept corners of the tiny Mission
Dolores cemetery on Dolores Street. A six-foot stone marks Cora's grave,
and over Casey's stands a massive, brownstone marker erected "with
respect and esteem" by fellow members of his volunteer fire company,
Crescent Engine Company No. 11. Across the bottom of the monument's
marble plaque are Casey's last words, "May God forgive my persecutors.")

In the next three months, the Vigilantes hanged two others, deported
twenty-five and convinced some eight hundred small-time thieves, pick-
pockets, ballot-box stuffers and would-be yeggs of all types that there was
no future for them in San Francisco. Most of these quietly departed for
the more healthful altitudes of the Sierra; the rest just went back where
they came from.

In August, the Vigilantes staged a big parade, and then disbanded.

"Crime," says Bancroft, "never again reached dangerous proportions in
the city." Politicians, in a sudden frenzy of reform, cut municipal ex-
penditures from more than $2,500,000 in 1855 to $856,000 in 1856, and to
$354,000 in 1857. Real estate values advanced. Business got better. In a
little while, the kids in the street stopped pretending they were Vigilantes,
and went back to making believe they were trail riders and Indians.

On the corner of the Montgomery Block where an Italian travel agency
is now, there is a small bronze plaque, placed there by *E Clampsus Vitus,*
an old-time miners' organization revived a few years ago by history-
conscious Californians. Lettering on the plaque reads, "Here in the Bank
Exchange 1853-1918 Duncan Nicol invented and served Pisco Punch.
Benefactor Humani Generis. Dedicated by *E Clampsus Vitus* 29 January
1938."

There is no doubt that Nicol influenced California drinking—in two
ways. He arrived in San Francisco from Glasgow in the early Seventies,

and somehow scraped together enough money to take over the Bank Exchange. Although he was not a gold seeker in the literal sense of the word, he struck his own personal bonanza when (the legend says) a dying stranger he had befriended imparted to him the secret formula of a rare punch that went down as lightly as lemonade and came back with the kick of a roped steer. Its basic ingredient was a brandy made of a Peruvian bark.

From the moment he passed the first Pisco Punch over his bar, Nicol was made. Seafaring men, who nicknamed him "Pisco John," scattered his fame across the seven seas. Visitors to the Bank Exchange returned to their homes in New York, London and Berlin and restlessly pined for another sip of the potent ambrosia they had tasted in the old gaslit bar on Montgomery Street. To one impressed reporter of the day, the invention of the Pisco Punch did more to advance civilization than the driving of the Golden Spike. "Step," he wrote, "into the foyer of the Hotel Cecil in London and inquire in a loud voice the location of 'Pisco John's' and from a dozen throats will come the reply: 'Southeast corner of Montgomery and Washington Streets, San Francisco, America!'"

Convinced he was indeed an Isaac Newton of the soul, Nicol decided to spread his contribution to mankind around, and that is where his second point of influence emerged. There was no reason, he thought, why the fair sex should be denied the delights of Pisco Punch. So he opened a special ladies' entrance on the Washington Street side of the saloon and arranged a few booths and tables off in a corner where a girl could drink in unmolested peace. This is said to have been the city's first cocktail lounge.

And although it was an era when most ladies would rather lose their bustles on Market Street than be seen at a bar, they didn't seem to feel that way about Pisco John's. Their eyes glowed with excitement (and anticipation) as they gave their orders to the waiter. They got a *femme fatale* look and feeling about them. One or two may even have had the nerve to light up a cigaret.

Nicol never revealed all the ingredients of his drink. He even guarded it from his bartenders, mixing it in the cellar and sending it upstairs on a dumb-waiter. When Prohibition closed down the Bank Exchange, it got around that the base of the Pisco Punch was Peruvian brandy. But what was the something added? What made it so terrific? Only Nicol knew.

Reporters badgered him for the answer. What difference did it make now? they demanded. But Nicol stood his ground. "Even Mr. Volstead," he replied firmly, "can't take the secret from me." When he died in San Francisco in 1926 at the age of seventy-two, with him to his grave went the mysterious recipe of Pisco Punch.

To many a mountain man and miner, the very thought of Pisco Punch, or anything like it, was undoubtedly as revolting as the thought of milk. They wanted their whisky straight, in quantities bordering on the oceanic and in pointed containers so they couldn't put it down until they had finished it.

These boys were monumental drinkers, and there were several reasons for it: they were a long way from home and their family ties; they were a lonely lot and craved the easy camaraderie of the tavern; and there was just nothing else to do for relaxation from their highly competitive search for gold.

"All nature here," wrote Bancroft, "was filled to overflowing with that intoxicating power which carries men onward in their wild career to happy success or soul-crushing destruction. Here so often they might with the Cyclops sing, 'Ha! Ha! I am full of wine, Heavy with the joy divine.' Thousands every day were as drunk as birds of paradise—so drunk that ants might eat their legs off."

The story goes that a traveler arrived at the Rich Bar diggings on the Feather River at three o'clock in the morning and was politely astonished to find that all hell was breaking loose in the Bluebird saloon. "Isn't it a trifle late for that sort of thing?" he asked the grizzled hotel proprietor.

"Hell, no," swore the innkeeper proudly. "In Rich Bar, three o'clock in the morning is just the shank of the evening. They won't quiet down for another two days."

Some of the back-country hamlets became the base of operations for a perpetual spree on the part of hunters, *vaqueros,* vagabonds and wrecks in various stages of disintegration. To tourists and other travelers who happened into their pet saloons, they passed out gilt-edged cards headed "Toddy Time-Table." This timetable outlined their daily drinking schedule as follows:

6 A.M.—Eye-Opener	4 P.M.—Social Drink
7 A.M.—Appetizer	5 P.M.—Invigorator
8 A.M.—Digester	6 P.M.—Solid Straight
9 A.M.—Big Reposer	7 P.M.—Chit-Chat
10 A.M.—Refresher	8 P.M.—Fancy Smile
11 A.M.—Stimulant	9 P.M.—Entre Act
12 M. —Ante-lunch	10 P.M.—Sparkler
1 P.M.—Settler	11 P.M.—Rouser
2 P.M.—A la Smyth	12 P.M.—Night Cap
3 P.M.—Cobbler	Good Night

In those days, it took only a few brandy smashes, a few sulky sangarees, an odd look, the wrong word at the wrong time, and the innocent by-standers would have to dive for the tables or the back bar while a couple of the boys blazed away at each other in the middle of the barroom floor. Prudent bartenders along Montgomery Street even provided for this emergency by sandbagging their bars, or armoring them with sheet iron.

Shooting on sight was a favorite outdoor sport, and more than one trigger-happy Forty-niner stood over a dying victim, smoking sixgun in hand, and said for what it was worth, "Sorry, pard, my mistake. I thought you was somebody else."

But this sort of thing was for the rabble, a little crude for the professional classes and the men of honor; in the best tradition of the Continent and the Old South, they favored the more cavalier procedure—the formal challenge, the acceptance, seconds, surgeons in attendance, an audience, and Navy revolvers at dawn. So established was the duel that, once called out, public opinion almost forced a man to see it through. Wrote one observer of the times, "The man in California who refused to fight when challenged was considered outside the pale of genteel society."

It became an occupational hazard with San Francisco newspapermen; they were constantly finding themselves involved in duels as a result of their rabid editorials. One editor, resigned to the perils of his profession, hung this sign over his desk: "Subscriptions received from 9 to 4. Challenges from 11 to 12 only."

It was a San Francisco newspaperman, as a matter of fact, who launched the state's most sensational affair of honor of the early Fifties. He was quick-tempered Edward Gilbert, thirty-three-year-old editor-in-chief of the *Daily Alta California* and one of California's first two Congressmen.

The exchange started when Gilbert, in the columns of the *Alta California,* accused Governor Bigler of making political hay out of the question of relief for emigrant wagon trains. Gilbert's sarcastic remarks were resented by General James W. Denver, a personal friend of the Governor. (Later, Denver also became a California Congressman, served as Governor of the Territory of Kansas and was the man for whom Denver, Colorado, was named.)

In the traditional manner, Denver published a card giving Gilbert the lie direct. Gilbert then challenged Denver to a duel, and Denver accepted. Under the code, Denver had the right to name the weapons. Being an expert shot with the rifle, the General discreetly chose the rifle. They met at dawn, August 2, 1852, at Oak Grove, some forty miles from Sacramento. It was the first time they had ever seen each other.

At the first fire, Denver deliberately missed. Gilbert also missed. Rejecting efforts of the seconds to call the whole thing off, the editor again took up his position.

Denver threw off his coat. "Now I must defend myself," he said. "I'm not going to stand here all day to be shot at." A moment later, he sent a bullet through Gilbert's heart. As his second bent over him, Gilbert smiled, and died.

San Franciscans, who had liked and respected Gilbert, draped their buildings in mourning. Civic bodies passed dolorous resolutions in his honor. Newspapers carrying his obituary appeared on the streets edged with black lines. And the practice of dueling grew more popular and more public.

Sometimes the contestants announced the time and place of their duels in the papers and invited everyone they knew to come along and bring a friend. When they were held in town (usually in the pastures near the Mission), half the population locked its doors, trooped to the field of honor and jeered blatantly if the conflict failed to end with a fatality. When the duels took place across the Bay, at Benicia or in Contra Costa County, hundreds of citizens piled on ferryboats and steamed to the scene.

Most of the time, a duel was a pretty grim thing, but once in a while the crowd went away laughing. In the next year, William M. Gwin (he became a United States Senator) and J. W. McCorkle quarreled over a horse race, and met with rifles at thirty paces near the Santa Clara County line. Conditions: wheel and start firing. After three ineffectual shots, one of which felled a donkey half a mile away, the antagonists saw that someone might get hurt if they kept that up; they decided they weren't mad at each other after all, and adjourned to the nearest bar for a round of bourbon for everybody.

Montgomery Street, which in those days was crowding Portsmouth Square for first place as the town's diversion spot, came in for more than its share of arguments that were settled with pistols.

One May night in 1854—in the street's latest attraction, Catherine Sinclair's gilt-and-red-velvet Metropolitan Theater—George T. Hunt, a lawyer, put his feet on a chair just as Numa Hubert, a hot-blooded Southerner from New Orleans, was about to sit on it. In a matter of seconds, friends were holding them apart. The next day, Hunt received Hubert's challenge. He accepted it, and four days later, they confronted each other near San Francisco's Pioneer race track with dueling pistols at ten paces. On the third exchange of fire, Hunt fell with a mortal wound in the abdomen.

"Hubert! Hubert!" cried the dying man. "I forgive you, Hubert, and God forgives you."

For the rest of his life, these words rang in Hubert's ears, and the man he had killed haunted him day and night. Ten years later, he confessed to a friend, "The phantom of Hunt never leaves me." And leave him it never did, until his own death in Chicago, in 1872.

But even unhappy endings like this were no deterrent to dueling. "During the year 1854," wrote Bancroft, "there appeared to be a mania for duels. Editors fought. Lawyers, judges, shoulder-strikers, doctors, loafers fought. The Legislature of this year was called the fighting legislature, and if a week or two passed without the notice of a hostile meeting in the public journals, men looked at each other as if something were wrong."

Montgomery Street's most dramatic contribution to the annals of dueling got its start four years later in the Bank Exchange. One of the principals was George Pendleton Johnston, Kentucky gentleman, clerk of the United States Circuit Court in San Francisco and an ardent sponsor of antidueling legislation. The other was State Senator William I. Ferguson, known up and down the state as a brilliant orator, a wit and a high-wide-and-handsome drinker who, when drunk, liked to be called "Yip-see-Doodle." Twenty-five years after his death, the *San Francisco Morning Call* remembered the titanic benders of "Yip-see-Doodle" with these words: "In his convivial hours—or days—he was hilarious to a point quite inconsistent with the dignity of the senatorial character, even drunken senatorial dignity. . . ."

Anyway, on an August evening in 1858, over a brandy smash at the Bank Exchange, Ferguson told an off-color story involving a girl friend of Johnston. Eyes blazing with anger, Johnston challenged Ferguson on the spot. At five o'clock a few afternoons later, they stood ten paces apart in a secluded glen on the eastern shore of Angel Island in San Francisco Bay. Looking on were their seconds, three physicians and scores of spectators who had rowed or sailed over to the island to watch the encounter. The weapons were pistols.

The first fire took no effect. They shortened the distance and fired again. Again both missed, and this happened a third time. Seconds then attempted to talk them out of going on, but Johnston insisted on an apology, and Ferguson refused to give it. So they lined up once more, six paces apart, and fired their fourth shots. Johnston's wrist was grazed. Ferguson fell back into his seconds' arms, wounded in the right thigh.

Going over to the prostrate Ferguson, Johnston grasped his hand and said, "Uncle Ferg, I'm sorry for you."

"That's all right," Ferguson whispered.

He died three weeks later while surgeons were amputating his wounded leg.

Johnston was tried in a Marin County court for violating the antidueling legislation he himself had sponsored. But the courts of those days didn't convict duelists—it just wasn't done—and he was freed on the contention that Ferguson had died, not as a result of the duel, but because he refused to submit to an operation until it was too late to save his life.

From then on, Johnston, like Hubert, lived with a ghost. He tried to appease the ghost with alcohol, and even though it didn't do any good, he kept on trying until it finally killed him, twenty-six years after that afternoon on Angel Island.

This business of dueling reached its climax in what Major Ben C. Truman, international authority on the subject, called "the fourth most noted fatal duel in the United States." The contestants were United States Senator David C. Broderick and David S. Terry, Chief Justice of the State Supreme Court.

Every California school child knows the story: Broderick, the former stonecutter, saloonkeeper and New York fireman who came to the Coast in 1849 and became the lonely and powerful leader of the anti-Lecompton wing of the Democratic party. Terry, the tall, broad-shouldered Kentuckian and Southern fire-eater who also arrived with the Argonauts, defied the Vigilantes as a whip of the opposition "Law and Order" group and rose to prominence in the pro-slavery element of the Democratic party. The remarks Terry made about Broderick in a speech in Sacramento. Broderick's bitter words when he read Terry's speech at the breakfast table in San Francisco's International Hotel. The inevitable exchange of notes. And then, on the chilly morning of Tuesday, September 13, 1859, in the thin sunlight, in a ravine near Lake Merced—the duel.

Now, at the southerly shore of Lake Merced (a twenty-minute drive from the San Francisco City Hall), a road branches from Lake Merced Boulevard, winds two-tenths of a mile around the shoulder of a little hill and comes to an end in a wide parking circle. From there, a path takes you to the small valley selected by the Native Sons of the Golden West as the site of the Broderick-Terry duel. Whether this is the true site is debatable, but there is the marker where Terry is supposed to have stood, and, ten paces to the south, hidden beneath the drooping branches of young evergreens, is the stone marking the spot where Broderick is supposed to have stood. You smell the evergreens there, and the dry grass, and hear the smack of driven golf balls from a country club tee across the vale.

If the Native Sons are right, there Broderick stood and pulled the delicate trigger of the dueling pistol too soon and sent his bullet into the ground three paces short of the mark. And there he fell a moment later, a bullet through his chest, and lay with his pale face to the sky.

"The shot is not mortal," said Terry with disappointment. "I have struck two inches to the right."

Gently, tenderly, they placed Broderick on a mattress in the bed of a spring wagon and drove him back to San Francisco.

Four days after that, he lay in state in the Union Hotel on Portsmouth Square. The entire city was in mourning. Thousands filed past his bier to pay their last respects, and one old man said what most of them were thinking when he touched Broderick's cold forehead and murmured, "God bless you. California has this day lost her noblest son."

The next afternoon, thirty thousand—nearly the total adult population of San Francisco—jammed Portsmouth Square and the nearby streets to hear the funeral oration of the silver-tongued Colonel Edward D. Baker. Then, to the tolling of the fire bells in the engine houses and at the head of a mile-long procession of mourners, Broderick was borne to his grave in Lone Mountain Cemetery.

Dueling in California was never fashionable after that. There were later fatalities on the field of honor, but not many, and none worth writing about. They added only a futile postscript to a bloody and fantastic passage in California history.

The street wasn't all like that. It was just that it was Main Street in those days and a lot of life was lived on it and drinking and dueling were a side of that life. There were other sides.

Montgomery Streeters could get excited over patchwork quilts, stiletto embroidery and a life-size painting of the royal family of Hawaii on horseback, and did get excited over them at the first Mechanics' Institute Fair in 1857. They could toss their hats in the air, dance a jig on the plank sidewalks and throw an all-out parade over the month-old news (brought by Panama steamer) that the Atlantic cable had been laid. And when one of the town's leading judges solemnly proclaimed it the greatest news the globe had heard since Columbus discovered America, they believed him with all their hearts.

San Franciscans stood in Montgomery Street, stared soberly at the newspaper blackboards and wondered if it was war when they read the chalked words (relayed from St. Joe by pony express) saying Fort Sumter had fallen. They stood there and wept as they read, in the de Young brothers' *Daily Dramatic Chronicle,* the story of Lincoln's assassination.

And every afternoon around four, they promenaded along Montgomery Street to meet their friends, to gossip, to window-shop at the smart jewelry

stores and the dress shops—the women in their rich Parisian gowns, their velvet cloaks and Paisley shawls, daintily lifting their flounces clear of the splinter-edged boards of the makeshift sidewalks; the spade-bearded men in their cream-colored trousers, their fancy vests crossed by heavy gold watch chains, their frock coats and broad-brimmed sombreros.

There, along that "Ambrosial Path," almost every day of the week, you ran into the people that made San Francisco's world go round: tall, imposing William T. Coleman, who had been president of the Vigilantes; the blue-blooded elite of the fashionable South Park and Rincon Hill society crowds—the Hall McAllisters, the William Blandings (of the South Carolina Blandings), the Louis McLeans (of the Baltimore McLeans), playboys like Billy Botts (son of the Governor of Virginia) and Charley "The Baron" Fairfax, the Sweringen girls, Sue and Bell.

Or you might see the sultry Lola Montez, swinging along the street in her black-velvet bolero jacket and sweeping silk skirt, her large, gray eyes veiled behind the black lace that fell from the brim of her broad hat. There would be miners down off the Comstock in their rough beards, their red shirts and battered hats, gamblers from Portsmouth Square in high, polished boots and stovepipes and ruffled shirt fronts that glittered with diamonds. You would meet the characters—the street preachers; Emperor Norton moving regally in the direction of the Donohoe-Kelly Bank to cash his worthless drafts on the royal treasury; The Guttersnipe on the prowl for a discarded crust or the butt of a half-smoked cigar.

You would hear the chatter of the crowd, the rhythmic pounding of the pile drivers down along the waterfront, the rumbling of hoofs on the street planking, the nasal cries of the auctioneers on Long Wharf a block or two away, the jangling of barrel organs. And if the afternoon was hot enough and sunny enough to drive a desert rat to drink, and suddenly you heard a Chickasaw war whoop razoring the other sounds to shreds, you knew that Pegleg Smith was in town and on the rampage again. . . .

To Montgomery Street, Pegleg Smith brought alkali dust, the touch of drifted sands and a mystery that has never been solved, the mystery that has become the fantastic legend of the Lost Pegleg Mine.

A couple of years ago, the *San Francisco News* carried a story out of San Bernardino headed, "Old-time Shootin' Iron May Be Clue to Fabulous Mine." The story said that while passing through a desert arroyo a man kicked over a rock and there, cached beneath it, was an 1849-model cap-and-ball Colt revolver with the name Smith scratched on its frame. A prospector in the party "believed the gun might be another link in the mysterious disappearance of Smith, whose quest for gold in the Colorado desert seventy-five years ago led him and many other gold seekers to death."

Although the story said the finding of the revolver would revive efforts to discover the Lost Pegleg Mine, the quest, actually, has never ceased. Positive that they and they alone have the secret, weather-beaten and desert-wise prospectors have been combing the Southern California badlands for more than a hundred years in search of the "burned, black gold" of Pegleg Smith. Some try to find it by piecing together scraps of gossip and the muddled descriptions of its location that have come down, by word of mouth, since stagecoach days. These, added to a hunch, a jealously guarded theory, a trust in their own luck, keep them looking. Some have even blindfolded their burros and set them loose on the desert in the belief that a mystic sense would lead the animals to the lost mine. Many of them have died looking for it, and desert mice have built nests in their sun-blanched skulls.

To go back to the beginning, the original Pegleg Smith, mountain man, Indian fighter, souse and tale spinner, was born in 1801 in Kentucky. His name was Thomas L. Smith (no relation to Pathfinder Jedediah Smith), and he was one of twelve children. After two years of diligent study in a country school, he succeeded in mastering the first three letters of the alphabet. When, at the end of another two years, he had progressed no farther than the letter *k,* he walked out of the classroom in disgust, and never went back.

He hung around the house for a couple of years and then, at the age of sixteen, resolutely rebelled against the beatings he took from his father. "I didn't keer about the old woman wallopin' me," he said, "but the old man had no right to treat me so blame bad."

From there on, he led a bizarre life. He was a bouncer in the river saloons of St. Louis and Natchez. He hunted and trapped with Choctaw and Chickasaw Indians, taking an indefinite number of their squaws as wives and boasting, after accompanying them on forays against other tribes, that he never killed an Indian without relieving him of his scalp.

Smith was twenty-six and on a trapping expedition out of Santa Fé when an Indian shot him in the leg and shattered his ankle. Smith severed the muscles himself with a butcher knife, and one of his companions completed the amputation with a pocket saw. Miraculously, the wound stopped bleeding the next day. After a few months of recuperation in a Utah Indian village, Smith was up and around again, hobbling on a stout oak stump he had whittled during his days of convalescence. He became known to Indians as Wa-ka-to-co, or "the man with one foot." White men called him Pegleg.

Two years later, while seeking water in the desert ranges somewhere between Yuma and Los Angeles, he came upon three buttes. The summit of one of them was covered with curious black stones. He struck one against another rock, and the blackness scaled off. "The exposed surface," he said later, "showed a yellow color like copper. I put a number of small pieces in my pocket, because I thought I might be able to use them for lead (bullets). . . . When I got to Los Angeles, I found out my yellow stuff was solid gold."

He went back to look for the three buttes, but they were never there, where he thought they were, and he never found them. Nor has anyone else found them, and lived to tell of it.

Pegleg was an old man and that was far behind him when he landed in San Francisco to stay. Still peppery and plenty tough in a barroom brawl, he would gleefully unship his wooden leg at the drop of a bar glass and have at the boys, cracking skulls left and right. When really in his cups, he would stand at the corner of Clay and Montgomery and curdle the blood of passers-by with his war whoops.

He spent the last months of his life in the San Francisco City and County Hospital, where he was kept alive by a crony who smuggled him a bottle of rye whisky a day. He died there in October, 1866, at the age of sixty-five. With his death, the chances against finding that nugget-littered butte in the Colorado desert advanced to a million to one.

After that, the legend began to get confused. Another Pegleg Smith (the one referred to in the *San Francisco News*) happened along who seemed to have struck a bonanza on or near the Colorado desert. One scorching July day in the early Seventies, he started for his secret mine with three burros and a thirty-day supply of food. He never came back. A few years later, an Army deserter tottered into San Bernardino, delirious from heat and thirst and dragging a bag of gold. In a lucid moment, he told of finding the bag in the desert wastes beside a peg-legged skeleton. Then he died.

There was still a third Pegleg Smith, no prospector, but a Colorado desert holdup man who was ultimately taken out of circulation by the Arizona Rangers. Then, close to the end of the century, a Canadian stumbled upon a desert mine near the foothills of the Superstition Mountains. He visited it every spring, returning with enough gold to support himself handsomely in San Diego for the rest of the year. He died mumbling unintelligible directions to the mine. His name was Henri Brandt, but he walked with a rolling limp that, in time, identified him as a man with a pegleg. And as memories grew blurred and fuzzy, Brandt became Pegleg Smith.

To further baffle desert rats still searching for the Lost Pegleg Mine, a Los Angeles wag takes a periodical trip into the Colorado desert and plants artificially weathered wooden legs along the wasteland trails.

Then there are the squaws who come in off the desert with handkerchiefs bulging with nuggets. Gold-hungry prospectors have promised them carloads of dime-store jewelry and have even married them in order to find out where the nuggets came from, but always, at the last moment, fear and superstition frighten the squaws into tight-lipped silence.

Some prospectors swear a colored ranch hand named Jim Green found the Lost Pegleg Mine. Jim, they say, had a secret bonanza on the Colorado desert whose location was revealed to him by a dying French-Canadian miner. One day, Jim left the tiny desert town of Banner and was never seen again. The most he ever disclosed about his mine was that once, when he went there to get some nuggets, he found it guarded by a human skeleton eight feet long.

Incredible as all this is, the fact remains that the desert sun is bleaching the bones of men who have followed the quest for the fabulous butte covered with black gold. Undoubtedly, other seekers will die the same slow death. And to their last dry and choking gasp, they will believe that out there, somewhere in those shifting sands, lies a gold mine of untold richness, waiting to be discovered. Perhaps they are myth believers and dreamers, but it could be true. Maybe it is there, somewhere.

Things became so tame along Montgomery Street, and everyone became so honest, they say a well-heeled miner left a hefty poke of gold dust on top of a hitching post while he went into the Bank Exchange for a few quick ones with a friend. When he came out, he found a silver dollar resting on his poke. Beneath it was the scribbled note, "To help out." Up the line a block or two and around the corner, however, sin had dug itself in for a last-ditch stand.

Just south of that corner, there is now a bronze tablet set low, at sidewalk level, in the façade of a two-story brick building. The building is No. 809 Montgomery Street, and if you should stand in front of it and throw a stone at random, you might hit anything from a Chinese broom factory to a South Seas night club. The words on the plaque read: "On this site the work of the Salvation Army on the Pacific Coast was started by Major Alfred Wells, July 22, 1883." Major Wells was a brave fellow.

Street preaching in early San Francisco was a harrowing and thankless job. Upright, devout citizens, and there were many of them, attended regular services at the city's churches (thirty-seven in 1852, and nearly one hundred by 1880). The others were prone to regard a sermon as something to be heckled and, if possible, to be broken up with brickbats. So a street preacher ran a good chance of getting personally roughed-up by hoodlums. If that didn't happen, his meeting could be interrupted by any number of coincidental events, including dog fights, "Stop, thief!" chases through the streets, or cries of "Fire!"

The first recorded instance of street preaching is noted in the good Rev. William Taylor's book *Seven Years' Street Preaching in San Francisco, California; Embracing Incidents, Triumphant Death Scenes, Etc.* One night in December, 1849 (he wrote), he mounted a carpenter's workbench on Portsmouth Square in front of a packed gambling house "where many a jolly circle drank to each other's health the deadly draught." He commenced singing a hymn in a high key.

"The novelty of the thing," he recalled, "had a moving effect. The people crowded out of the gambling house and gathered together from every direction. . . ."

He then proceeded to lecture them for an hour on the text. "For what is a man profited, if he shall gain the whole world, and lose his own soul?" Oddly enough, there was no violence, which you can attribute to mass astonishment and curiosity rather than good manners or interest in the soul. At any rate, that was the beginning.

Later, street preaching fell to such noted divines as Old Orthodox, Hallelujah Cox and Crisis Hopkins, who, after haranguing the sinners for an hour or two, would descend from their brandy-keg pulpits and head for the Bank Exchange for a well-earned round of drinks.

By the time Major Wells mounted a beer barrel on Montgomery Street, he was within earshot of one of the hottest spots on earth—the Barbary Coast. Around the corner on Pacific Street a few steps away were the crimping joints; they didn't have much business now, but they were still there. Closer at hand were such sensational dives as Johnny McNear's Whale and Maggie Kelly's pothouse, the Cowboys' Rest. From these places and a dozen others like them, a great caterwauling arose by day and by night.

One of the star boarders at The Whale, for instance, was Tip Thornton, whose specialty was slicing off the noses or ears of people he did not like. In The Whale alone, he is said to have lopped off at least twenty noses. Maggie's snuggery, too, was the scene of many a historic fray. When searchers probed the ruins after the 1906 disaster, they found, within arm's reach of the bartender's station, an arsenal of fifty pistols and enough knives, daggers, blackjacks and brass knuckles to stock six police headquarters' showcases.

In spite of this competition, Major Wells, that night in 1883, was able to note proudly that he had won five converts to the Army's cause at his first night street meeting. Not long after that, reinforcements arrived from the East, and for them, Sherman, Clay and Company, the music store, collected twelve instruments—at the time the most complete assortment of band instruments on the Coast—and equipped the West's first Salvation Army band.

More and more of the Army Lassies circulated through the bars with their tambourines, ever alert for a stray soul to save, or the opportunity to slip a tract into a drunkard's pocket. Gradually, with the help of police protection, abuse from rowdies ceased. Rarely were the Salvationists forced to cover, as in the old days, by a barrage of beer bottles; hecklers no longer knocked their caps off, or kicked in their drums.

Cowboy Mag, Tip Thornton, Chicken Devine, Shanghai Kelly and the rest of the Barbary Coast broads, dips, thieves and cutthroats probably spun like pinwheels in their graves, but that's the way it got to be.

It was a day in June, 1946, and late afternoon. The tall office buildings had just closed for the day and the bankers, the brokers, the clerks, the accountants and the stenographers were descending to the street level in crowded elevators and pouring into Montgomery Street and hurrying for the trains that would take them to their suburban homes down the Peninsula, or the trains that would take them across the Bay Bridge, or the streetcars that would lurch and clatter out to the avenues on the other side of Twin Peaks. Four lanes of automobiles moved slowly south to Market Street on the one-way thoroughfare. They blew their horns; the feet shuffled on the pavement; a California Street cable car, loaded to the outside steps with people going home, frantically sounded its strident bell, cut across the traffic lines and began its slow climb up Nob Hill.

I turned into the Collins and Wheeland Grill on the corner of California and Montgomery. It had been standing there since the Sixties. If you didn't know that by the sign on the front window, you could have told it by the long, narrow interior, the tile wainscot behind the lunch counter and the dark wood paneling above it, the line of tables from front to back, and the massive old bar that also extended lengthwise down one side of the room. Waiters were setting the tables for the dinner-hour rush.

I exchanged a few words with the manager about a story, and then, as I was about to leave, I saw Percy Montgomery sitting alone at a table at the back of the restaurant. He saw me at the same time and motioned me over.

He was in his late sixties or early seventies, and had been travel editor of the *Chronicle* when I went to work there in 1939. But when the war came, what paper had any use for a travel editor? He had got a job as a

receptionist at a Montgomery Street bank, but then he had lost it, and now I didn't know what he was doing for a living.

He still looked the same. Massive head, bald but tanned, with a fringe of white hair over the ears and around in back. The pince-nez over the tired gray eyes, fastened to his coat lapel with a black silk ribbon. The immaculate white shirt, wing collar and a dark-blue tie. A dark coat over his short, portly figure. Gold cuff links.

Two old-fashioneds sat on the table just beyond his knife and fork.

"Will you join me in a cocktail?" he asked graciously.

I declined it, and he looked offended. "You will not accept a gentleman's offer to join him in a drink?"

"No, thanks, Percy. I'm not drinking."

"Ah, that is another matter," he said in his precise way. "In California we respect a gentleman's attitude toward drink. If you wish to refuse on moral or physical grounds, that is your pleasure. I will shoot any son of a bitch who says you are not entitled to it."

He held up his old-fashioned and looked me seriously and squarely in the eye. "I toast your health," he said, and drank. He put the glass down and daintily wiped his lips. Then he began to talk.

"I have not seen you in a long time. Our paths have diverged. Nevertheless, I know the work you have been doing. As one interested in the ways of San Francisco, you may like to know that every day at five o'clock, I come through that door, walk down this room and hang my hat on that hat rack. I sit down at this table. Every day at five o'clock, John, my waiter, places two Scotch old-fashioneds on this table. They are here when I sit down. I do not order dinner; John knows what I like, and brings it to me. I have done this daily, month in and month out, year in and year out, for forty-two years."

He said it slowly and significantly, as if he wanted to be very sure I got it right.

"I know this street, and I tell you," he continued, "that this was once a street of men. Big men. Real men. The street of the Comstock kings—Jim Flood, Jim Fair, J. W. Mackay, W. S. O'Brien, William Ralston, Senator Sharon—every one of them rich enough to pave the street with silver from here to Telegraph Hill. This street knew them, knew the tread of their footsteps.

"There was a day when, if you refused a drink from a gentleman on Montgomery Street, you would not have had time to explain that you were not drinking. You would have been shot while your mind was phrasing your explanation. Honor, the code of gentlemen, did not wait for explanations.

"This was a street of talented men. I have sat in Coppa's restaurant before the Fire, when it was in the Montgomery Block, and watched George Sterling, Jack London, Gelett Burgess, Will and Wallace Irwin, Maynard Dixon, Frank Norris. Men of talent. And before them, the street knew Ambrose Bierce, Bret Harte and Mark Twain. It has known the Booths, Lola Montez and Lotta Crabtree, the California Diamond. Rudyard Kipling has walked on this street, and Robert Louis Stevenson and a young French naval officer named Pierre Loti.

"This was also a street of brave men. This morning, in his office on the second floor of the Montgomery Block, I talked with Oliver Perry Stidger, the son of pioneers, in whose very office Sun Yat Sen and Wong Sam Ark, leader of the mighty Chinese clan of Wong and past supreme grand master of the world-wide Order of Chinese Masons, plotted the overthrow of the Manchu dynasty and the foundation of the Chinese Republic. On that April day in 1906, when God took this city and shook it down into powder and set it afire, Oliver Perry Stidger told an officer of a demolition squad, come to blow up the building to stop the spread of the flames, that he dare not lay a hand on that building. From his desk drawer he drew a pistol and swore that he would shoot the first man that tried to lay a dynamite charge in the Montgomery Block.

" 'Give the building thirty minutes,' Stidger demanded. The officer told his men to wait. The wind shifted. The fire went the other way. Because one brave man stood his ground, the Montgomery Block was saved, and the next day it stood out like a beacon of courage and inspiration amid the smoking rubble of San Francisco. Block after block and mile after mile of buildings lay in ruins. But the Montgomery Block was still there, telling the heartsick people, telling all the world that San Francisco could come back, had to come back—"

The old man's eyes were flashing. His pince-nez trembled. His features were set and stern and his hands were clenched at the edge of the table.

"God damn it!" his expression said, "can't you see how important that was?"

Then he relaxed. His eyes turned sad and wistful. His hands smoothed the napkin in his lap. He reached for his second old-fashioned, sipped it and put it down.

"And so she did. . . . San Francisco did come back, stronger, more lovely than ever," he said gently.

If there were only time, his words seemed to say, if there were only time, how much I could tell you of this wonderful city, how much about her that is brave and beautiful, how much about the old times we used to have, and the old days . . . but there is not the time and there never will be the place, and I am not sure you would understand; all this was long ago, years ago, before you were born, when things were different. . . .

"I tell you all this," he said, "because perhaps some day you will write a story about those people and those days. If I can, I will give it to you. I am getting along in years. I will not be here much longer, and I have nothing else to leave behind me."

He finished his cocktail, and exactly at that moment John arrived with his dinner. Percy neatly tucked the end of his napkin into his shirt front and selected his soup spoon.

"You will pardon me," he said politely, and began to eat.

When I went outside, Montgomery Street was quiet. Beneath the tall buildings the shadows were deep, and the bars had already lighted their neon signs. Nearly all the automobiles were gone. Around on California Street and high on the side of Nob Hill, up by Chinatown, the bell of Old St. Mary's dropped seven slow, wise notes into the evening stillness. I turned to the right and walked toward Market Street.

Percy didn't give me that story, because I never saw him again. A month later, it said in the paper that he was dead.

3. LEIDESDORFF STREET

THE DARK SECRET OF WILLIAM LEIDESDORFF · THE HEARSE WITH THE
WHITE PLUMES · LEIDESDORFF'S LIFE AND DEATH AT YERBA BUENA · PAU-
PER ALLEY · EARLY EVENING

THE STORY is like a Hollywood period piece of the antebellum South.
New Orleans in the 1830's, with its white, pillared mansions and gleaming porticos, its shuttered windows and the smell of honeysuckle. A passionate, dark-haired youth. A lovely and delicate blonde girl, and, in the
years afterward, whenever he saw the wild blue lupine on the California
hills in the springtime, he would remember her eyes.

The youth was William Alexander Leidesdorff, son of a wandering
Dane and a West Indian native girl. An English planter had taken a
fatherly interest in him from his infancy. The planter had educated the
lad, and then, prudently cautioning him against disclosing the exotic
strain of his blood, had sent him to New Orleans to work in the office
of his (the planter's) brother, a wealthy cotton merchant.

59

Softly plucking his guitar and singing romantic ballads in his low, rich voice, young Leidesdorff made the heart of more than one New Orleans society belle beat faster. But he kept his fancy free, until the day he saw the girl with the golden hair and the lupine blue eyes. Her name was Hortense, and she was the daughter of a family that proudly traced its forefathers to the aristocracy of Louis XIV's France.

The planter died and the cotton merchant died, leaving their estates to Leidesdorff. So, financially, at least, he was in a position to ask the hand of Hortense in marriage. But what of the strange and forbidden alliance which had begotten him? According to the uncompromising standards of New Orleans society, his mother's blood coursed through his veins with a ruthless taint, and to reveal it meant to sentence himself to instant exile. Yet, Leidesdorff was a young man of honor; Hortense, he felt, must know.

At first, he didn't have the courage. He confessed his love for her and proposed to her, and, with happy heart, she accepted him. Her father gave his approval, pleased that his daughter had selected such a popular and promising young man for a husband. Leidesdorff presented Hortense a handsome diamond engagement ring.

But the secret tormented him day and night. Torn by this conflict between love and honor, he couldn't sleep, and walked the streets of New Orleans until dawn; he grew pale and weary with the struggle. At last, one evening, just before their wedding, on his knees and begging her forgiveness, he told her.

Weeping bitterly, Hortense answered that her father would never consent to the match, and she could not disobey him. They must never see each other again. Nevertheless, in spite of his mother's blood, in spite of everything, she said, she would love him until she died.

The next day, Leidesdorff received a package containing every gift he had given her, and the diamond engagement ring. With it was a note from Hortense's father, severing all relations between his family and Leidesdorff.

Leidesdorff sold everything he had, bought the one-hundred-six-ton schooner *Julia Ann* and stocked her with merchandise for a trading voyage to the Pacific; he was leaving New Orleans and never coming back. A day before his departure, as he walked along Canal Street, he saw a funeral procession. White plumes waved from the hearse, indicating the death of one young in years. To avoid the cortege, Leidesdorff stepped into a store. He watched it go by and saw, sitting in the first carriage, Hortense's father, mother and little sister.

Leidesdorff went pale. "My God," he whispered, "whose funeral is that?"

"A young society girl's," replied the storekeeper. "Poor thing, she almost married a mulatto. She died yesterday—from the shock, they say. Very pretty she was, too. She used to come in here once in a while with her mother. . . . Her name was Hortense something-or-other. . . ."

That night, the priest who had administered the last rites to the dying girl brought Leidesdorff a tiny gold crucifix. It had been hers, and the priest said she sent it to tell him that she had loved him to the end.

A few years later, in 1841, after many a lonely reach across the Pacific, the *Julia Ann* dropped anchor in Yerba Buena cove. Time and faraway ports had softened his memories, and her master was through with roving. He was home at last, and it was his home until he died of brain fever in May, 1848, at the age of thirty-eight.

During those seven years, Leidesdorff threw himself wholeheartedly into the commercial, political and social life of the outpost community. He built its first hotel, the verandaed, one-and-a-half-story City Hotel on the plaza. Down on the cove beach, below the line of what later became Montgomery Street, he put up a large warehouse. In his cottage on the outskirts of the village—a step from where the Russ Building now reaches thirty-one stories to the sky—he sipped mellow Mission wine with the Mexican provincial administrators and Army officers, and proudly conducted them to the cottage's backyard to show them Yerba Buena's only flower garden.

In 1845, he was appointed American vice-consul, and, the next year, he openly aided Frémont and the Bear Flag rebels in their seizure of northern California. Under American military rule of the territory, he became a member of the town council, and town treasurer. In 1847, he was one of a committee of three which supervised the building of the territory's first public school. (It opened on the plaza in the April of the next year with Thomas Douglas, a Yale man, as schoolmaster.)

A man of consuming energy, and still, perhaps, trying to drive from his head the haunting words of Hortense's good-by, Leidesdorff sought other, even frivolous, outlets. He bought a spirited horse from Lansford W. Hastings, a professional guide, and, late in '47, staged California's first formal horse race on a meadow flat near Mission Dolores. Not long after that, he imported from Alaska a cranky, thirty-seven-foot launch originally built as a pleasure craft for Russian officers stationed at Sitka. Driven by side paddle wheels and powered by a small steam engine, the *Sitka,* as Leidesdorff christened her, was the first steamer to ply the coastal waters of California.

Six months later, Leidesdorff was dead.

If he had lived, he would have witnessed the happening of strange and unpredictable things within the next brief years.

The Gold Rush started, and in a matter of months they had pushed back the waterline to a point even with his warehouse. They ran a street along the beach there, and named it Leidesdorff Street. On it they built the two-story Pacific Mail steamship office, and, to make a sidewalk from Montgomery Street a block away, boom-struck merchants recklessly sank one-hundred-pound cases of first-class Virginia tobacco (worth seventy-five cents a pound) into the tide-flat mud. To accommodate the Gold Rush fleet, they began building Long Wharf, and by October, 1850, it extended nearly half a mile into the Bay from its shore end on Leidesdorff Street. Auction houses and commission offices mushroomed overnight on the street, and hotel, taverns and boardinghouses—R. B. Woodward's famous What Cheer House; the Kremlin; Mrs. Moon's Cottage; the Kennebec House; and Squiro's, celebrated from the Mother Lode to Los Angeles for its volcanic punches.

But as the city grew, the waterfront left Leidesdorff Street farther and farther inland, and most of those places moved to more promising localities. It was thirty years after Leidesdorff's death that a number of grain and mining brokers opened their bucket shops on that block of the street which lies between Pine and California Streets. Until the 1906 disaster brought them down, this block was known throughout the West as "Pauper Alley," and a lot of long chances, greedy hopes and desperate dreams flourished and died there in the breasts of the shabby down-and-outers and "mudhens"—beggars, tramps, peddlers, ragpickers, servant girls, scrub women, streetwalkers—who shuffled to the alley to gamble their pennies on the exchanges.

Now, Leidesdorff Street is a crooked, four-block lane connecting the A. Paladini fish market on Clay Street with the San Francisco Chamber of Commerce on Pine. Three of the blocks afford drab and unpretentious sanctuary to commercial binderies and print shops. The fourth, still called "Pauper Alley" by nostalgic old-timers, is a windy, financial district canyon where the sun shines only an hour or two a day during the summer noons. It's a quiet place, deep down and close to the earth between the towering cliffs of the high office buildings, and what sounds there are are the sounds of the Pine Street traffic, the grinding of the cables in the California Street slots and the clicking heels of the financial district stenographers who, coatless, shivering and leaning into the wind, hasten along the alley for their afternoon cup of coffee at Eddy's Sandwich Shop. The shoe-shine man in the tiny San Francisco Wall Street Shoe Shine Parlor bends to his cloth and brush. Here it is evening at three o'clock in the afternoon, when to the north, beyond the roofs of the produce district, you can see sunlight gleaming on the white houses of Telegraph Hill.

And Leidesdorff, lover of the lost Hortense, man of honor and pioneer, to whose tainted blood San Francisco never gave a second thought, sleeps beneath the stone floor of the Mission Dolores, three miles southwest and an eternity away.

4. GRANT AVENUE

THE IMPRESSIONS OF CAPTAIN MORRELL • THE FIRST DWELLING • THE
STREET OF THREE NAMES • HONEST HARRY AND HIS COLOSSAL FRAUD •
MEIGGS' WHARF. THE COBWEB PALACE • CHINATOWN MOODS • LITTLE
PETE AND THE SEE YUPS • FIRECRACKERS AND VIOLETS • THREE WORLDS

ON ONE side of the continent in 1825, New York was a thriving metropolis of nearly one hundred seventy thousand; the Union had twenty-
four states, and they were in the first year of the administration of John
Quincy Adams. On the other side of the continent, Captain Benjamin
Morrell, master of the American ship *Tartar,* visited the Mexican wilderness outpost on San Francisco Bay and promptly became one of California's first real estate promoters.

"The Bay," he wrote, "presents a broad sheet of water of sufficient extent
to float all the British Navy without crowding; the circling grassy shores,

indented with convenient coves, and the whole surrounded by a verdant, blooming country, pleasingly diversified with cultured fields and waving forests; meadows clothed with the richest verdure in the gift of bounteous May, etc. Man, enlightened, civilized man, alone is wanting to complete the picture and give a soul, a divinity to the whole. . . ."

There were men around—Mexicans and Indians—but apparently the Captain did not consider them enlightened or civilized; as far as he was concerned, they didn't count. Yerba Buena had a while to wait before divinity and a soul would come along in the form of its first, Anglo-Saxon settler and resident.

His name was William Anthony Richardson. He was a native of Kent and a former mate of the English whaler *Orion.*

It isn't clear whether he was kicked off the *Orion,* whether he jumped her, or whether he left by agreement with her master. At any rate, she had entered the Bay in 1822 for supplies, and when she sailed away, there was Richardson, on the beach.

He did not settle down at once, but decided that while in California he would do as the Californians did. First of all, he obtained permission from Mexican officials to stay there and teach navigation and carpentry to the natives. The next year, at Mission Dolores, he was baptized a Catholic. He changed his middle name to Antonio. In 1825, the year Captain Morrell stopped off at Yerba Buena, Richardson married Maria Antonia Martinez, daughter of the commanding officer of the San Francisco Presidio. He was then twenty-nine years old.

Richardson made both ends meet by piloting visiting mariners around the Bay, supervising Indian crews of ship caulkers, dabbling a bit in livestock and (some say) a little smuggling on the side in partnership with his father-in-law.

During all this time, he had been living either at the Presidio or the Mission. For some reason, in 1829, the year before he became a naturalized Mexican citizen, he moved to San Gabriel, in Southern California. Six years later, however, he returned to the Bay to stay. In casting about for a place to live, he selected a likely spot on a sandy hill overlooking Yerba Buena cove, hacked a clearing out of the chaparral and pitched a tent.

That tent was San Francisco's first civil dwelling.

If you stand on Grant Avenue, where it crosses Clay Street, you're in the heart of the biggest Chinese community in the world outside of China, and forty steps from where Richardson put up that crude canvas shelter.

It was nothing but a windy slope, loosely held together by chaparral, red-barked manzanita and scrub oak. Later, after Richardson had replaced the tent with his adobe Casa Grande, and Jacob Leese, the Ohio trader, had erected his wooden house nearby, and a few other buildings appeared on the same frontage line, the planners ran a street along there, on the hillside. They called it Calle de la Fundacion.

But after 1846, and the Stars and Stripes were flying over the plaza, that name seemed no longer appropriate; the name of the street was changed to Dupont, in honor of the American admiral. (With characteristic insouciance, they got his name wrong, making and keeping it "Dupont," instead of the way he spelled it, "Du Pont.") Much later, when Dupont Street became synonymous with whoring and hitting the opium pipes, merchants around the Market Street end had three or four blocks of it changed to Grant Avenue, to commemorate the deeds and nobility of the Union general. When the rest of the street, with its harlot warrens, its slums and opium dives, was wiped out in the 1906 disaster, the city decided to give it a clean break from its shady past and renamed it Grant Avenue all the way from Market Street to the North Beach waterfront.

Nevertheless, some of the old Chinese living in the narrow alleys off the avenue still call it Dupont Street. That's what it was when they arrived there, and, to them, that's what it still is.

Dupont Street got off to a modest but respectable start. Two blocks up the hill from the confusion of Montgomery Street and the waterfront, and one block up the hill from the disorder of the Portsmouth Square gambling halls, it seemed to many a nice quiet place. In 1849, T. Dwight Hunt, founder of the First Congregational Church in San Francisco, was supervising the construction of a chapel at Dupont and California Streets.

Nearby, Rev. Albert Williams was conducting Presbyterian services in a tent. For a while, Sam Brannan published the town's first newspaper, the *California Star,* on Dupont Street. There were several hotels—the Globe, the Albion, the Excellent, the American and, at Clay Street, on the former site of Jacob Leese's house, three cottages, superimposed one on top of the other, collectively formed the first Hotel St. Francis. At Jackson Street rose the three-story armory of the California Guard, the city's first military company.

But as it wandered north across the Presidio Trail, across Pacific Street and Broadway, Dupont Street lost itself among the shanties, the dairies and market gardens and abattoirs of the flatland that ran past Telegraph Hill to the Bay and were called, then as now, North Beach.

In those days, North Beach was the happy and prosperous little realm of Harry Meiggs, a New York lumber merchant who had gone west with the Forty-niners. Turning a deaf ear to the call of the Sierra diggings, Harry determined to stay with what he knew. Down by the North Beach waterfront, he found a brook fed by two springs, and beside the brook he erected a sawmill. He supplied the mill with lumber cut in the forests across the Bay and up the Mendocino coast, and, as an unloading point for the lumber, he built a pier not far from where Fisherman's Wharf stands today.

A back-slapping, easygoing, well-dressed extrovert, Harry Meiggs represented the nineteenth-century version of Rotary Club president, Y.M.C.A. secretary, Boy Scoutmaster and all-round civic spark plug rolled up in one sleek package. In addition to that, impressionable San Franciscans opined, he was honest as the day was long. "Well, there goes 'Honest Harry,'" they would say, as they watched him stride purposefully along Montgomery Street to an appointment with his banker. But that was in 1850. Four years later, if they could have got their hands on him, Honest Harry would have dangled from the flagpole in Portsmouth Square.

During those four years, no grass grew beneath the well-shod feet of Honest Harry. By bringing around the Horn with him a cargo of lumber and selling it at twenty times its cost, he had made himself $50,000 almost before he stepped off the boat. Before one year had passed, he had five hundred men cutting wood for his sawmill, and he was worth $500,000. In another year, he was reputed to be the richest man on the Coast, and could well afford a public display of his passion for music by building the Bush Street Music Hall and sponsoring the appearances of itinerant singers and musicians.

Side by side with this delight in music went a singular faith in the future of North Beach; he was its first and greatest booster. Its possibilities as a real estate development, he believed, were unlimited, for where else could the growing city expand? Using his influence as a member of the Board of Aldermen, he engineered the extension and grading of streets in the North Beach area. Feverishly, he bought all the land he could lay his hands on, and when his own money ran out, he borrowed huge sums with which to buy more land. When he vaguely mentioned security, the bankers told him not to be foolish; his word was as good as gold. Money in the bank, that's what his word was. Honest Harry smiled, slapped them on the back and vowed they had said a mouthful.

The whole trouble was, North Beach didn't develop. On the contrary, the city was expanding south toward Market Street instead of north to North Beach. Furthermore, as we have seen, 1854 was about the time real estate values began to tumble. Honest Harry, owing by now some $1,000,000 and with interest on his loans piling up at the rate of $30,000 a month, lost some of the starch from that famous smile; he was getting worried. So were his creditors.

There were at City Hall some blank city warrants, or municipal promissory notes, already signed by the mayor, to be filled in as to date and amount when the occasion arose. Somehow, perhaps with the help of his brother, John G. Meiggs, who had been elected city comptroller in September, 1854, Honest Harry obtained them, made them payable to himself in large amounts and converted them into cash. He forged personal notes in his favor, and cashed them in, too. To raise another $75,000, he overissued $300,000 worth of stock in his lumber company.

About the first of October, Honest Harry took a good look at his position. To put it mildly, he was in a jam. He had just about exhausted his stopgap measures. North Beach real estate values were still plunging dizzily. He had forgeries, bad checks, unkeepable promises to pay all over the city. After his gloomy inventory, Honest Harry heaved a long sigh and got in touch with his old friend, Captain Jacob Cousins, skipper of the bark *American*.

Within a couple of days, a two-year supply of provisions, including $2000 worth of delicacies and vintage wines, had been placed in storage on the ship. Four small cannon were mounted on her decks. When asked by waterfront idlers what was going on, Captain Cousins replied that a couple of wealthy gamblers had chartered the bark for a pleasure cruise to Australia.

It was midnight of October 3 when everything was ready and Captain Cousins knocked on the front door of the Meiggs mansion at Montgomery Street and Broadway. On a table were two bags of gold, each containing $5000. Honest Harry pushed one over to Cousins. "Captain," he said, "this is hell, but I can't help it. There's nothing else to do. We've got to leave tonight."

Taking the newly elected city comptroller with him, he got in a carriage, drove to Mission Point, and transferred to a small boat which carried him out to the *American*. Minutes later, in the pre-dawn darkness, the bark was under way.

"Where do you want to go?" asked the Captain.

"Anywhere you please," replied Honest Harry.

After two anxious days spent rolling off the heads in a dead calm and foggy weather, a north wind filled her sails and the *American* dropped below the western horizon, bound for Tahiti.

The morning after he boarded her, and even as she lay becalmed just outside the Gate, San Francisco learned of Honest Harry's crash and flight when a brokerage firm, to which he had written a farewell note confessing he owed it $200,000, attached his North Beach property. Within hours, dazed citizens discovered he had left them holding a bagful of forgeries, spurious notes and worthless stock. Although first, frantic reports placing his debts at $2,000,000 and the cash he took with him at $500,000 were later scaled down to $750,000 and $250,000 respectively, it was clear that Honest Harry had promoted one of the epic swindles of history.

The town took it hard as it faced the fact that Honest Harry, the most popular man in California, was a rogue. "Then," says Bancroft, "a thousand fingers pointed that way, bony, bloodless fingers, and plump, fat fingers, digits horny with hard labor, belonging to washerwomen and working men, and the diamond digits of merchants, bankers, and frail, fair ones. Few escaped the fangs of Harry, for he was clever, he was popular and, above all, he was honest. . . . Now the community cursed him. Congregating upon street corners, men told their losses and swore if they could catch him they would hang him."

But while all this was going on, Honest Harry was sailing over the bounding main to the isles of the South Seas. After tarrying pleasantly at Tahiti, he ordered Captain Cousins to put about and head for Chile. The legend is that there Honest Harry went through his cash to the last dishonest dollar and was forced to pawn his watch to pay the rent.

For a long time, San Francisco did its best to forget it ever heard of Harry Meiggs. But, some ten or fifteen years later, travelers returning from South America brought back romantic tales about a man named Meiggs who was known up and down the west coast of that continent as "the financial wizard of the Andes." Finally, someone who had known him in his San Francisco days came back and said it was true: Honest Harry was in the chips again.

Forsaking lumber, he had become a successful railroad contractor in Chile. After thirteen years there, he moved on (in 1868) to Peru, where they called him "Don Enrique Meiggs, the Messiah of the Railways." With characteristic dash and imagination, he completed some 700 miles of railroads in Peru, including 87 miles of the spectacular Callao-La Oroya road, which clings to the almost vertical cliffs of the Rimac gorge, the Mollendo-Arequipa railroad, and its 225-mile, South Trans-Andean Railway extension to Puno, which crosses the Andean summit at Crucero Alto at an altitude of more than fourteen thousand feet. The accomplishments of his engineers on these and other mountain lines are still among the wonders of·the railroad world. Meiggs is said once to have boasted to the Peruvian cabinet, "Anywhere the llama goes, there I can take a train."

By the early Seventies, Honest Harry's personal fortune was estimated at $100,000,000, and not only Chile, but all Peru, hailed him as a genius. With a fraction of his wealth he made some attempt to redeem the bad debts he left behind him in San Francisco. Some say he paid them off to the last penny; other authorities, however, say he cannily bought up his notes for sums far less than their face value. There is no way of telling which report is right.

Like most Americans, Californians pull for the underdog, and they like a winner; Honest Harry had turned out to be both. So when they heard that the one thing he wanted most in life was to visit California, the state lawmakers in 1874 forgot the state constitution for a moment and passed a bill exonerating Harry, washing his San Francisco record off the slate and saying, in effect, that all was forgiven. And when Governor Newton Booth refused to sign the measure, they passed it over his veto. But the Governor's disapproval deprived the gesture of the unanimity he longed for; because of this, and increasing complications in his business affairs, Honest Harry never returned.

On his death there in 1877, Peru mourned him as the nation's hero. San Franciscans, whom a quarter of a century had mellowed into good and genial losers, called him their "splendid outcast." After all, they argued, if Honest Harry had been a swindler, he had been one of the biggest and best the world had ever seen. What more could a San Franciscan ask?

North Beach never did live up to Harry Meiggs' expectations, but it got to have an air about it. Before the drives to the Cliff House or through Golden Gate Park became fashionable, before Woodward's Gardens became the place to have an outing, North Beach was where San Francisco rolled up its shirt sleeves and opened its parasols and enjoyed its Sunday afternoons.

For instance, it was the thing to do to go to Meiggs' old lumber wharf, which ran from the North Beach shoreline some sixteen hundred feet into the Bay. You rented a bathhouse and went in swimming there, or you promenaded along the wharf with your girl friend on your arm, or you stood at the end of it and watched the catboats leaning to the leeward reach across the harbor. On the way back in from the end of the wharf, you stopped at Cockney White's museum and lost a quarter to the educated pig that played seven-up. Where the wharf met the shore, you stopped at Abe Warner's Cobweb Palace for a free dish of his wonderful crab chowder.

Warner, a native New Yorker who had been a Fulton Market butcher in his day and always wore a butcher's top hat, loved spiders and never killed one, and as you sipped your chowder you marveled at the festoons of cobwebs that hung from the gloomy rafters, the light fixtures and the cages in which he kept the monkeys, bears and kangaroos of his menagerie. You bought a bag of peanuts from Zachariah Colby, the crippled sailor who hung around Warner's, and fed them to the monkeys. You prodded Warner's parrot into squawking its famous line, "I'll have a rum and gum. What'll you have?"

Yes, Sunday was the day at North Beach. The breweries there were quiet—Schwarz's, the Bavaria, the Empire, the Lafayette, the Old Stock, the St. Louis—and no smoke issued from the chimneys of Senator Jack Fay's soap factory. The Pacific oil refinery of Josiah Stanford (Leland's brother) was still, and so was John Everding's starch works.

If you were a blade with a hang-over from what you'd done on Saturday night, you stood in line on Sunday morning at Driscoll's Salt Water Tub Bathing Emporium a block or two from Abe Warner's and waited for your turn for a dip in the steaming sea water and a rubdown by Bathhouse Jack. Or maybe you'd gone to North Beach not to cure a hang-over, but to get one, and if that was the case you started with the great crabs (cracking their shells with mallets on the redwood block) and the cool lager at Charlie Schwartz's, or the tall tankards of steam beer at the place run by the man who wore wooden shoes, or the famous cocktails of Paddy Gleason, who stirred them with his right forefinger, the only finger he had on that hand. ("It saves the trouble of keepin' me eye on the spoons," he once explained, and took his place among the gossoons and bully boys as a rare one and a card.)

But if you were one that brought your girl with you, you left the Cobweb Palace and crossed the street to Riley's shooting gallery and showed her how good a shot you were with an air rifle. After that, you strolled to Mason's lot, where Jimmy Kenovan, who could dance a jig for twenty-four hours without stopping, had his greased pole with the five-dollar gold piece on top of it and a ham a little lower down and a silver dollar between the ham and the ground. You laughed for a while at the people trying to shinny up the slick pole after the prizes, and then wandered over to Heydenaber's Atlantic Hall for the dance, or whatever entertainment they happened to have that night. Later, if there was a moon, you went back out to the end of the wharf and held your girl's hand and maybe stole a kiss or two.

The biggest things that happened in North Beach in those days were like the time in George Doherty's barn at Jones and Francisco Streets when Joe Kane, the pride of the Beach, knocked the hell out of Jim Aitken, the champ of Tar Flat. Interest in the fight ran so high that North Beach mothers stationed their children on corners near the barn with orders to run for home with the results when the battle was over. The boys from the Beach swaggered around town for months after that. Or like the time the whole city turned out to watch Henry Hoyt and Dan Leahy row their Whitehall boats in a race out to Yerba Buena Island and back.

That was in 1880, and by then the other resorts were taking the trade from Meiggs' Wharf. The Alcatraz and the Sausalito ferries weren't using it any more. The sea wall of the new waterfront was cutting it off from the Bay, and ragged vagabonds like "The King of the Dumps" and "Spoony the Dumper" were foraging beneath it at low tides for junk or odds and ends that struck their fancy in the rubbish now tossed there by the inhabitants of the waterfront shanties.

Abe Warner, still wearing his top hat, stuck it out at the Cobweb Palace until 1897 and then, at the age of eighty, retired. There were too many other places for people to go, and besides, those who could afford a high time didn't get a kick any more out of a stroll on a wharf, free crab chowder, air-rifle shooting galleries, cobwebs or talking parrots, and steam beer wasn't good enough for them any more. When they went out stepping now, it was at Harbor View or the Cliff House or the Poodle Dog, and they ordered champagne. The old North Beach, which had given San Francisco the best years of its life, was finished.

Something else to end an era happened in 1897. "Little Pete," one of the chieftains of the Sam Yup Tong, organizer of the racketeering "protective" society Gi Sin Seer, and Chinatown vice king, was murdered in a Chinese barbershop on Washington Street, a few steps off Portsmouth Square. The highbinders went on killing after that for a while, but never with the same old zest, and now the tongs have a peace association that settles their arguments without resorting to hatchets.

When 1850 began, there were seven hundred eighty-nine Chinese men in California, and two Chinese women. At the end of that year, the men numbered four thousand eighteen, the women seven. By the end of 1851, there were twelve thousand men, and the same seven women.

A quarter of a century later, there were about one hundred thousand Chinese in California, and B. E. Lloyd, in his *Lights and Shades in San Francisco,* said that between forty-five and fifty thousand lived in San Francisco. Of these, two thousand were women, and of the two thousand women, nineteen hundred were whores. With the exception of a handful scattered through other districts of the city, every Chinese lived in eight square blocks—that's about six thousand to a block—straddling Dupont from Sacramento to Pacific.

"A family of five or six persons," wrote Lloyd in 1876, "will occupy a single room, eight by ten feet in dimensions, wherein all will live, cook, eat, sleep and perhaps carry on a small manufacturing business. . . . In the lodging houses, they huddle together and overlay each other, like a herd of swine that seeks shelter in a strawpile on a cold winter night. . . .

"A space in a wall of no greater dimensions than a large dry-goods box furnishes ample room for a cigar stand; and a cobbler will mend your shoes in an area window, or on an unused doorstep. . . . Even the oxygen in the air is totally exhausted by repeated inhalings. . . .

"In Chinatown, there is not a basement, cellar area, dormitory, porch, loft, garret, or covered court, but teems with . . . Chinese inhabitants, night and day. The sidewalks are monopolized by them, with their little tables of fruits, nuts and cigars; the cobbler, tinner, chairmender, and jack-of-all-trades, claim, by squatter right, a seat upon a box or doorsill where to ply their trades; the alleys, lanes and byways give forth dense clouds of smoke from the open fires, where cooking is performed, and the house tops are white with drying garments, fluttering from the network of clotheslines. . . ."

The Chinese represented a way of life and a problem that San Francisco couldn't take lightly. Sand-lot agitators bellowed in protest against cheap Chinese labor. The W.C.T.U., or whatever its equivalent was, shrilled against the Chinese "slave girls," some of whom were far too desirable to be tolerated on the loose by suspicious and waspish wives. Hoodlums cornered a Chinese whenever they could and strung him up by his queue from a lamppost. Reporters out to make a hit with their city editor wrote lurid stories on their adventures in Chinatown opium dens, or their idea

of hilariously funny yarns on Chinese funerals. On Sunday, ministers thundered from the pulpit against Chinese fan-tan parlors, and on Monday the cop on the beat knocked on the doors of these same fan-tan parlors and collected his "protection" fee.

There were many complex elements involved in the Chinese situation, and if you're interested in going further into it, Charles Caldwell Dobie's *San Francisco's Chinatown* is as complete a study as any; for a sensational treatment of Chinese vice and the plight of the Chinese whore, try Herbert Asbury's *The Barbary Coast*. In the main, the Chinese were a problem because there were so many of them; because they would work for lower wages than white laborers; because they infuriated Americans by preferring their own way of life to the American way of life; because, as an underprivileged, an illiterate and a not-too-bright nationality group, they were shamefully exploited by unscrupulous whites.

Little by little, they began to get civilized treatment. The Six Companies became a strong and intelligent influence toward giving the Chinese some idea of civic consciousness, and did its best to improve Chinatown's living conditions and health standards. The Protestant and Catholic churches buckled down to their mission work. In 1887, the San Francisco Board of Education decided to make an honest document of the Declaration of Independence, and permitted Chinese children to attend a public school.

Although they brought with them this situation and these problems, the Chinese added things to San Francisco, things almost as far away and as exotic as the clanging of a temple gong in the purple hills of K'un Lun: joss sticks burning, paper lanterns glowing on the high balconies in the night, the teeming streets, a gust of weird and alien music from clashing cymbals, flute, moon fiddle and butterfly harp, peddlers balancing their baskets on their bending shoulder poles, the sing-song chanting of the crib girls behind their lattice windows, an open doorway and the reek of tobacco smoke from clay pipes and the rattle of dominoes drifting through it, the smell of sandalwood, the patter of slippered feet down dark and sinister alleys, lilies like carved ivory in a tenement doorway, an old woman wailing a Cantonese lament, moonfaced children flying dragon kites in the streets, the click of abacus beads in an herb shop, a bolt of royal-blue silk in a store window, and a jade tree. . . .

In this Chinatown arrived the ten-year-old, shifty-eyed boy who was destined to be for fifteen years its most feared and hated citizen, and its ruler. He was Fong Ching, from the Kow Gong district of Canton.

Fong Ching got a job in a Chintown shoe shop at $10 a month, and on this he supported himself, two uncles and a cousin. He was a bright youngster and did his job well; before long his pay was raised to $18 a month. He regularly attended the Sunday school of the Methodist mission, applying himself so well to the study of English that within a few years he was the official interpreter for the Chinatown association to which he belonged, the Sam Yup Company. However, sometime during his adolescent years, Fong Ching decided there were easier ways to make money than slaving in someone else's shoe store. And before he reached twenty-one, he had become a full-fledged racketeer and gangster, in the strict latter-day Chicago sense of the words. He was now known as Little Pete.

Not content with being the recognized head of the Sam Yups, he started the Gi Sin Seer, whose membership list was soon a Who's Who of Chinatown's leading hatchet men, highbinders (later, in the white underworld, they were called "trigger men"), thugs and criminals. "Through this organization," reported the *San Francisco Chronicle*, "he levied tribute on the vices as well as on the industry of his countrymen. No Chinese lottery, no gang of opium smugglers, hardly any business, in fact, could be carried on in Chinatown without paying tax or tribute to Little Pete."

Another association, the See Yup Company, numerically far bigger than the Sam Yups and said to represent four-fifths of Chinatown, rebelled against the graft-riddled autocracy of Little Pete. Its members launched a boycott of all stores operated by Sam Yups. The dispute moved into violence as, back in China, in an effort to stop the tong war, authorities arrested relatives of See Yups, threw them in jail and confiscated their property. A few See Yups were found dead in the gutters of Chinatown alleys, shot in the back. Nearby, where they had been dropped by the killers, police would always recover the guns, and that was all.

When one of his highbinders was tried for the slaying of a See Yup, Little Pete nonchalantly attempted to bribe a police witness to perjure himself on the stand. Indicted and convicted, Little Pete was sentenced to five years for bribery. He served eighteen months in Folsom and San Quentin state prisons, and was then released on parole. Back in Chinatown, he blandly returned to his rackets.

Little Pete, a small, nervous man who, when he spoke, seemed to twitch the words out of his mouth, was an Oriental dandy. It is said he spent two hours a day brushing and oiling his queue, and owned forty suits and thousands of dollars' worth of rings and stickpins. He constantly carried a cane with a curiously carved head of jade. (Little Pete willed this cane to his lawyer, who, in turn, willed it to a friend. Its jade head, set into a ring, now adorns the hand of the friend's wife, a Nob Hill society matron.)

He could well afford ease and luxury, for, by Chinatown standards, he was a wealthy man. In his earlier days, he had borrowed $100 at interest of five per cent a month and had started his own shoe factory in a Washington Street tenement building. One of the few legitimate enterprises he ever indulged in, the business prospered. To conceal from customers the fact that his shoes were produced by Chinese labor, he called it the F. C. Peters Company, and employed a white traveling salesman to whom he paid the handsome salary of $250 a month. In fixed horse races at the Bay District and Ingleside tracks, he won $100,000 before the fraud was discovered and his dishonest jockeys barred from the saddle. This money he invested in the lucrative, artificial fish-pond industry in China.

That was in 1896, and Little Pete was thirty-two and getting overconfident. When he learned the See Yups had placed a price of $2000 on his head, he smiled and hired a white bodyguard named Ed Murray. "I'm not afraid of them," he boasted. "They don't dare kill me."

On Saturday, January 23, 1897, a week before the Chinese New Year, they got Little Pete as he sat in a barber's chair at 819 Washington Street. He had sent Murray down to the corner for evening papers with the late race results. Two of the barbers were back in the kitchen getting hot water. A third barber stood in front of another patron, his back to the door and blocking his customer's view. Two Chinese in blue cotton suits and black hats ran up the two steps into the barbershop and began shooting.

The barber and his customer bolted for the kitchen. The gunmen fired five shots, backed out the door, ran around the corner into an alley, dropped their forty-five and a sawed-off shotgun in the gutter and vanished into a tenement house. Little Pete lay on the barbershop floor with two bullets through his head and one in his side. He was very still, and near his shattered head the dark, liquid mirror of his blood reflected the gaslights.

That night, there was an almost festive air in Chinatown. Happy See Yups stood on street corners, one paper said, "talking and laughing like schoolboys on a holiday." They decorated their windows with red paper and hung extra lanterns on their fire-escape balconies. Up on Stockton Street, the Luey Sings, relatives of one of Little Pete's victims, gleefully shot off fusillades of ceremonial firecrackers.

Three days later, in the workshop of Little Pete's shoe factory, where he lay during the period of mourning, relatives garbed in white Chinese mourning robes closed the satin-lined lid of the metal casket on what the *Chronicle* described as "the powder-marked face of the shrewd and potent Chinese who bribed jockeys and jurors, sold women and shoes, made and spent money corruptly, purchased murder, and died by the bullet." Reverently, the pallbearers carried the casket down the dark stairway to the street and the hearse. The six shining black horses that were to draw the hearse pawed impatiently, striking pale sparks from the Washington Street cobblestones. They slid the casket on to the carriage, placed beside it an enlarged, flower-framed photograph of the gangster and a pillow of white flowers with "Good-by" lettered on it in violets. The driver cracked his whip, and the strange procession moved up the side of Nob Hill toward the Fook Yam Tong burial ground in the sand hills by the Golden Gate.

Preceding the hearse were an American band playing a Beethoven funeral march and a Chinese band, with its fiddles, flutes and crashing cymbals, playing at the same time an exotic dirge. Behind the hearse walked Little Pete's widow, dressed in jute sackcloth edged with white piping. She was wailing, and staggered so in her grief that relatives supported her between them; other relatives in blue half mourning carried her four now-fatherless children. And still others scattered handfuls of imitation paper money into the air to purchase the good will of the spirits. Behind them followed a long slow file of more than a hundred carriages. It is said that thirty thousand Chinese watched the cortege go by from the sidewalks and balconies and house tops. So inscrutable were their faces, one could not tell Little Pete's friends from his enemies, and among them somewhere were the faces of the two who shot him down. Which two they were, white men never learned.

There was yet a final touch of violence to be added to the crime-ridden career of Little Pete. At the cemetery, a mob of three thousand whites, most of them women, surged about the hearse, laughing and yelling and all but trampling the grief-stricken widow as, on her knees, she wept before the catafalque. They fought over scraps of ribbons and papers and stole them for souvenirs. When the procession departed, leaving behind ceremonial roasts of lamb and pork for the spirit of Little Pete, they fell upon the meat and ate it, and when that was gone they flung the bones to the gravestones, and left.

Now, the worlds of Grant Avenue are three.

At one end of the street, where a sand hill used to be, the Market Street cars clatter past; there, too, Grant Avenue meets O'Farrell and the end of the line for the cable cars of the O'Farrell Street rope. The avenue is level for a few blocks; then it rises, skirting the flank of Nob Hill and the flank of Telegraph Hill a mile or so to the north, and then it dips sharply to the Embarcadero and Pier 39, where the ships of the Blue Star line strain at their hawsers with the tides. Within these limits, between Market Street and the Bay, lie the three worlds.

There is the world of smart shops and flower stands on the corners and well-groomed women, and that is downtown and close to Market Street. Grant Avenue is broader there, and when people write to you or tell you how beautiful the women of San Francisco are when they walk, how elegant their carriage, how fashionable their clothes, they are thinking of the women they saw on Grant Avenue, just off Market.

It's a world of mansions in St. Francis Wood and Pacific Heights, of gowns by I. Magnin, orchids by Podesta and Baldocchi and diamonds by Shreve; a world of *filet de sole Marguery* and strawberries Romanoff at the Palace for lunch, and dry Martinis tonight on Nob Hill; a world of cool blue-tiled swimming pools down the Peninsula over the week end and golf at the Burlingame Country Club, and a Pan-American Clipper flight to the Islands when the summer fogs start rolling in from the sea.

It is a world, too, of psychiatrists' bills and divorces, of children who live half the year with one parent and half the year with the other, and of pampered lap dogs sitting in the front seat beside the chauffeur; a

world that has expensive mistresses in its penthouse apartments, and sleek-haired, expensive gigolos in Sierra mountain lodges.

For the most part, this is a world that began a hundred years ago with a sweating, red-shirted miner digging for Mother Lode gold, or a saloon-keeper making his pile on redeye and forty-rod, or a cursing, driving, two-fisted sea captain making his with cargoes and wooden hellships. Today, the names of their great-granddaughters are in the bluebook, and, clean-limbed, they stride down Grant Avenue with the grace of thoroughbreds. . . .

Between that world and the next is Bush Street. You start where Bush crosses Grant Avenue, and you leave behind the flower stands and the smart dress shops and the discreet bars, and you're in Chinatown. There is always, it seems, the smell of sandalwood. Wind bells tinkle on the lampposts. You climb the short hill, past the Chinese art goods stores, past California Street, past Old St. Mary's. You stroll on, across Sacramento Street, across Clay, and you come to a pillar that divides the front doors of the Dick-Young Apartments and the Tin Shen Tong Company, Herbs. Above your head and fixed to that pillar is a small plaque. "The Birthplace of a Great City," it reads. "Here June 25, 1835, William A. Richardson, founder of Yerba Buena (later San Francisco), erected its first habitation, a tent dwelling, replacing it in October, 1835, by the first wooden house, and on this ground, in 1836, he erected the large adobe building known as 'Casa Grande.'"

As you read the plaque, old Chinese shuffle by, talking in tight bursts of Cantonese, and Chinese housewives shop for groceries in the markets. When the noon siren drifts from the Ferry Building, Chinese school children—the girls in sweaters, skirts, bobby sox and saddle shoes and the boys in sweaters and jeans—swing along the avenue on their way home to lunch. They chatter in Chinese and show their even white teeth in laughter and sometimes sing a hit-parade song.

Above their heads are the corrugated iron awnings of the shops, and above the awnings rise the balconied façades that hide the city's worst slums, where sometimes eight Chinese live in a cell-like room and sixty families in one three-story tenement building. Here, Grant Avenue is only three lanes wide, and cab drivers with impatient fares honk their horns behind dawdling trucks. Black-eyed street gamins shout as they play in the streets, and from the open doors of a Chinese bar flow the strains of Bing Crosby's *Mexicali Rose.*

The farther you go, the more incredible and bizarre is the incongruity of the world of Chinatown. Store windows confront you with Buddhas and back-scratchers, vases of sheerest porcelain and tawdry nude statuettes, teakwood chests and brass candle snuffers, mandarin robes stiff with gold brocade, and dime-store tops, jade goddesses and table radios in model galleons, and ash trays made in Japan, elephant bells and cinnabar boxes and plastic teacups. Side by side on liquor shelves stand Ng Ka Py and Golden Tassel Kentucky Corn, Gop Gai and Haig and Haig pinch, Mui Kwai Lu and Mariachi tequila.

On the sidewalk in front of a market is an open case of steel-gray squid with staring golden eyes, and beside it are a Chinese crone and a bloodyaproned butcher, haggling over the price of dried fish bellies. In the windows of the Chinese delicatessens, grocery stores and herb shops are bottles containing preserved chickens or preserved snakes or dried sea horses. There are platters of crooked ginger root, green mongo beans, candied melon rinds and lichee nuts. There are dark, brown, leathery-looking deer testicles strapped with Scotch tape to the backs of ceramic Bambis; aging Chinese buy them at the rate of $150 a pound and with them (or deer antlers, with the velvet still on them) make a brew they drink to restore their "vitality." There are cellophane-wrapped boxes of green and shredded sharks' fins for sharks' fin soup, imported from Hong Kong's Sai Woo Lane. And live rabbits and quacking ducks and squawking chickens, all in wire pens and doomed to the quick knife and the slaughter.

At night, Chinese characters in neon blaze blue, green, purple and pink over the Grant Avenue sidewalks, beckoning the tourists to the bazaars, the bars, the night clubs and the walk-up sky rooms. Some of these places eagerly amuse their white customers by playing recordings of Chinese music, and you hear it coming from an open window somewhere above you, the striking of wood on wood, the pentatonic music of fiddle and reed, and a girl singing in a minor key. Old Chinese in black suits, black hats and tieless white shirts stand gossiping on the street corners, or read the bulletins pasted to the windows of Chinese newspaper offices, or sit drinking tea in the basement restaurants, or sit in their association rooms playing cards. Tourists window-shop for souvenirs for the folks back home. Sailors, who know they can't be blamed for trying, whistle at pretty Chinese girls.

A block down the hill to the east is the old plaza, and three blocks west is the top of Nob Hill, and here, in between, are fifty thousand Chinese in an alien land. In the apartments, in the hotels, in the tenement flats, in the alley cubicles, most of them are sleeping, and by the time the bell of Old St. Mary's strikes two, the store windows will be dark, the bars will be closed, the tourists will be gone, and their world will be a world of shadows and stillness and a night sky and the faraway stars. . . .

The third world begins at Broadway, and this is a world of Neapolitans and Tuscans, Romans and Venetians and assorted *paisani* from the toe to the knee of the Italian boot. Cross Broadway, and you leave behind the kingdom of *chow mein* and *jow won ton* and jasmine tea, and enter the realm of *ravioli*. The vowels you hear now are soft and liquid, and the music is something from *La Tosca*.

In fact, a step from the corner of Grant Avenue and Broadway is a café called "La Tosca." Scenes from the opera are painted on the walls; Caruso sings from the juke box, and you drink a *cappuccino,* gray, like the robe

of a capuchin monk, and made of chocolate that is laced with brandy or rum, and heated by steam forced through coffee.

This is a world of round *brovolette* cheeses hanging in store windows, and garlic sausage, and *capretti* at Easter time. Of the lovely smell of baking bread coming from ovens beneath the sidewalk, of picturesque and brightly colored family washings on clotheslines strung high over narrow alleys, of flowers in window boxes and canaries singing. Of Tony's Shaving Parlor, and the Panama Canal Tagliarini and Noodle Factory and the Roma Macaroni Factory. Of steep lanes on the side of Telegraph Hill, and fat Italian housewives leaning on their window sills and laughing in the sunshine, and wiry Italian boys playing ball in the street.

West from here to the Marina and to Fisherman's Wharf lies the rest of North Beach, the gilded bubble of Honest Harry Meiggs. Not far from where his lumber pier struck out into the Bay, the fleet of the crab fishermen nudges the docks of the lagoon. Sienna nets dry in the sun. Steam rises from the sidewalk vats where the crabs are boiled, barkers browbeat diners into overrated restaurants and tourists buy tiny, live turtles with names painted on their backs. Vacant lots lie across the line of Honest Harry's once famous wharf, they, and a couple of Italian restaurants, some tenements, the Belt Line railroad tracks, the Embarcadero.

Three-quarters of a century ago, perhaps, the people who lived on Grant Avenue above the Bay were wakened in the morning by a bugler on Alcatraz, blowing reveille for the boys of an Army detachment stationed there. Old-timers who were children then say they hear him yet in their dreams, and, waking, remember the days when they saw windjammers from their windows. You see them sitting in the sun and sipping their red wine, and you think of many amazing ways in which their world has changed, and only a few things that are the same. Like their sun and the taste of their wine. Like the laughter of children and the flight of gulls. Like the tides that ebb and flow in the Bay below them, the way they did when Grant Avenue was Dupont Street, the way they did when there wasn't any street at all.

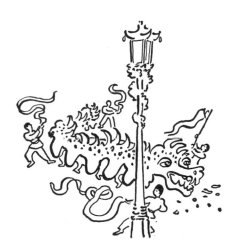

5. MAIDEN LANE

AN ALLEY OFF UNION SQUARE · THE HAPPY FAMILY OF IODOFORM KATE ·
AN ARTIST'S MASTERPIECE · THE RAPE OF "ELAINE" · WHEELER THE
STRANGLER · RECHRISTENING · APRIL DAFFODILS

IT'S A short street and a narrow one, with Kearny Street and Fred Solari's
bar and grill at one end, and Stockton Street and Union Square at the
other. Natives sometimes refer to the block nearer Union Square as "the
upper block," and to the other one as "the lower block."

There is a Maiden Lane in London, and another in New York. Both
are centuries older than this one, but it happens that a San Franciscan
gets a wonderful feeling when he passes the window of John Wooster's
optical shop, where the little flags of the radiometers spin in the sun, and
rounds the corner of the Maiden Lane that meets Union Square. It is the
feeling that now, in this quiet place, he can slow his stride, he can drift
for a while, he has time to look at the puppies and the goldfish in the pet

86

store window, and admire the flowers in a florist's shop. For him, a walk down that upper block is a five-minute vacation, a time to forget what's on his mind, to window-shop, to pass the time of day with the green boxwood, the privet and the comprosma that grow in sidewalk boxes.

Many years ago, when there was a murder a week on Kearny Street's Battle Row and Spanish Kitty was the toast of the Barbary Coast, Maiden

Lane was Morton Street and two blocks of depravity ruled by a lady known as Iodoform Kate. Compared to the cribs she operated, the worst dive in Pacific Street was as chaste as a Southern Pacific waiting room. Harlots, naked from the waist up, sat in the crib windows and for a few pennies permitted passers-by to fondle their breasts. The rest they had to sell they sold for not much more, and Asbury says a hard-working girl on Morton Street entertained from eighty to a hundred customers a night. Respectable women caught slumming on Morton Street were upbraided from the crib windows for giving away the only thing an honest whore could market, and were driven from the alley by choruses of catcalls and jeers. Except for these infrequent intrusions, the residents of Morton Street were one big industrious family, obscene but happy, with a chicken in every pot, and a red light over every door.

Paradoxically, the street's best story has nothing to do with the bawdy tarts of Iodoform Kate. Its heroine, indirectly, at least, is Tennyson's Elaine, the Lily Maid of Astolat.

In 1875, a San Francisco boy named Toby E. Rosenthal was acquiring an international reputation as a painter. He was not a native of the city, but his father had brought him there as a child, and he had grown to adolescence on the slope of Telegraph Hill. The father now had a tailor-shop crowded between a fruit stand and a laundry on Stockton Street, and the young man was over on the Continent. His paintings were anecdotal in subject, and photographic in treatment; he was a sort of Victorian Norman Rockwell.

On the strength of canvases with titles like *Love's Last Offering, Spring's Joys and Sorrow* and *The Exile's Return,* European critics were calling Rosenthal a genius, when Tiburcio Parrott, a wealthy San Francisco merchant, commissioned him to do a painting based on the lines from *Idylls of the King,*

> *And the dead steered by the dumb*
> *Went upward with the flood.*

It was to be a five-by-three oil painting illustrating the scene where the corpse of Elaine, dead of unrequited love for Lancelot, is ferried on a funeral barge to Camelot by her father's deaf-mute servant.

For some reason, the finished work did not please Parrott, and Rosenthal sold it for $3500 to another San Franciscan who dropped into his Munich studio one day, a Mrs. R. M. Johnson. Rosenthal proclaimed it his masterpiece, and back in San Francisco his home-town papers proudly played *Elaine* for all it was worth.

They carried feature stories on the artist's father, telling how, sitting cross-legged on his bench, he had stitched far into the night for years to earn the money to send his boy to the Royal Academy of Munich. They reported breathlessly that Crown Prince Frederick William of Germany had fallen in love with *Elaine* and had offered Rosenthal $25,000 for the painting, but alas! he had already sold it to Mrs. Johnson. They told how Rosenthal had obtained the corpse of a young girl and propped it in position in his studio, and made the first sketches for *Elaine* from the dead model.

When they announced that Mrs. Johnson was going to exhibit *Elaine* in San Francisco, it gave the city its biggest thrill since Laura D. Fair had been acquitted of the murder of A. P. Crittenden three years before. Elaine clubs were organized overnight. As fast as they could get them from the printer's, music stores sold hundreds of copies of *The Elaine Waltzes,* hastily composed in honor of the great art event. Booksellers frantically sent east for caseloads of *Idylls of the King,* as the demand for the poem which had inspired the masterpiece boomed it to top place on the best-seller list.

At the galleries of Snow & May, on the corner of Kearny and Morton Streets, the painting was unveiled March 30, 1875, a Tuesday. More than five thousand men, women and children, silent with awe and admiration, filed past *Elaine* that day and Wednesday and Thursday. Many of them, following advice given in the newspapers, were armed with opera glasses in order to detect and appreciate the minute details. Some were so moved by Elaine's sad fate and the melancholy gloom of the picture, they burst into tears and were led away weeping.

It was on Friday that the entire city, from the waterfront to the sand dunes, from North Beach to the Mission, staggered under the news that *Elaine* had been stolen—cut from its frame by vandals during the night. Excited San Franciscans read the headlines in the papers: "Alas! Elaine," mourned the *Daily Alta California.* Echoed the *Chronicle,* "Farewell, Sweet Sister!" They rushed out to tell the neighbors. Tongues wagged in Montgomery Street taprooms, in Market Street beer cellars, over Nob Hill tea tables and the backyard fences of Telegraph Hill.

Those who could hastened to the Morton Street corner to verify the report with their own eyes, and jammed the gallery to the doors. "The occasion seemed like a funeral, and the endless procession like a mournful cortege following some friend to the grave," said the *Chronicle.* "All spoke in hushed tones, and some ladies actually shed tears while looking on the empty frame. . . . The hands of ancient ladies were raised in holy horror. . . ."

Mrs. Johnson, the owner, received the news with sad but dignified calm. Contradicting a widespread rumor, she said she would offer no reward for the return of the painting, on grounds it would encourage wholesale robbery of other valuable works of art. But, she flashed, ordinary punishment was too good for the man who stole *Elaine*.

"He should either be hanged, drawn and quartered, or broken on the wheel," she said. "But, since those antique methods of punishment cannot be revived, I would have him scourged at the whipping post, after the manner of the baser criminals in Delaware."

Meanwhile, as the *Chronicle* dramatically put it, "that astute and energetic terror to evildoers, Police Captain I. W. Lees, had begun, at the very instant the loss became known, to revolve all the circumstances in the secret recesses of his busy brain."

Luckily for the Captain, an anonymous tipster reported seeing four sinister-looking characters standing in Morton Street outside Snow & May's basement window late the night of the crime. One had a scar on his face. Something in Captain Lees' busy brain clicked. "Scar, eh?" he mused. "That must be my old friend, Cut-Face Donahue." And, banking on this slender clue, he hatched some plans.

He and his men struck between two o'clock and four o'clock Sunday morning. At a Third Street lodginghouse, he picked up John Curran, James E. Allen and Tommy Wallace. Another member of the gang, James O'Neill, was routed out of bed in a Dupont Street brothel. Cut-Face Donahue, alias William Cloonan, was arrested in a house on lower Mission Street. After he had worked them over for a while, Captain Lees knew where the picture was—under the bedclothes in the back room of a shanty on Langton Street, a South of Market alley. And that's where he found it, undamaged, wrapped in cotton cloth, sealed, and labeled, "Custom House Official Maps."

The news that *Elaine* had been recovered caused no less excitement than the report of its theft. The *Chronicle* put out a Sunday-morning extra and sold five thousand copies. Churchgoers forgot the morning services and dashed to police headquarters to gaze at the famed painting. Announced the *Daily Alta California,* "A broad smile spread over the face of the community and caused a very perceptible sensation of pleasurable surprise and gratification as the news was heralded through the streets that 'Elaine is found! Elaine is found!' The news spread like the flame amid prairie grass, and, gathering as it advanced, blazed into fiery excitement."

When the painting was tacked back into its gilded frame and again placed on exhibition (guarded, this time, by two burly patrolmen), beside it hung a large photograph of the bearded man of the hour, Police Captain Lees.

Two months later, Allen, who had cut the canvas from the frame; Curran, his assistant, and Cut-Face Donahue, the brains behind the crime, started long prison terms at San Quentin. They confessed they had stolen *Elaine* in hopes of claiming a large reward, and never quite understood what all the commotion was about. It was Allen who put their disgust into words. "Hell," he sneered, "there's a little picture in the stores of a young hood nippin' a cigar from an old stiff who's lookin' in a window, that you can get for two-fifty. I'd rather have that than *Elaine* any day."

Maybe you would agree with him, and maybe you wouldn't, but you can find out the next time you're in Urbana, Illinois. That's where *Elaine* is now, on the wall of the art gallery of the University of Illinois.

There were other stories that added a bit of local color to Morton Street, such as a few stranglings. Once, a man named George Wheeler, occupying rooms above Snow & May's with his wife and sister-in-law, sat down in a chair and asked the sister-in-law to sit on his lap. She yielded prettily, and Wheeler rewarded her by choking her to death on the spot. In the Eighties, a barefoot man garroted two Morton Street harlots in their cribs and left them lying on the floor.

But nothing ever happened again to create the sensation caused by the stealing of *Elaine,* and the street's carnival of obscenity played its last-night stand on April 17, 1906. The next day, its tawdry props, its ramshackle, rat-ridden scenery, went up in smoke.

After that, Morton Street began another life. Big department stores rose on Post and Geary Streets, which paralleled it on the north and south, and their trade entrances opened into the narrow alley. From morning until night, it was crowded with wagons, carts and horses, and rang with the shouts of teamsters.

In 1909, its name was changed to Union Square Avenue, but for years nothing else about it changed except that trucks took the place of horses

and wagons. Then a restaurant or two appeared on the street: Gobey's Steak House, Girard's French Restaurant and the famous German Coffee Shop. Fred Solari's opened at the Kearny Street end in 1921, the year they changed the name again, this time to Manila Avenue, to extend the spirit represented by the Dewey Spanish-American War monument in Union Square. In the next year, at the suggestion of a businessman who had a jewelry store where the alley met Kearny, city officials renamed it once more, and called it Maiden Lane, after the street which is the center of New York's jewelry and silverware trade.

The new name seemed to be a happy thing for the little street. In time, the back doors gave way to small, independent establishments: a shoe-repair shop, a florist's. Fashionable restaurants moved in. Two or three bars, catering to late shoppers and white-collar girls, took Maiden Lane addresses. And now you can buy a cocker spaniel puppy on one side of the street, and a piece of Orrefors glass on the other. You can step into a chic beauty salon, get a permanent, and then walk next door to the Pan-American Airways office and buy a Clipper seat to Bali.

A few Aprils ago, there was a surplus supply of daffodils in San Francisco. Maiden Lane merchants bought one hundred fifty thousand, decorated their block with them and invited the city to a party. The block was closed to traffic, and San Franciscans, who love flowers in the street anywhere, milled around by the thousands. Bands played. Hundreds of canaries twittered from cages hung above the sidewalks. Troubadours strolled through the crowd singing Spanish songs. Warm sunshine flooded the street, filling it with bright light and a haze of daffodil yellow.

After the war was over, the merchants did it again, and now it's called the Daffodil Festival, and it's an annual affair. There isn't anything colossal about it; Los Angeles has probably never heard of it. But Maiden Lane during the Daffodil Festival is where San Francisco smiles, and tells you it's spring.

6. BUSH STREET

THE STREET TODAY • SHIPS OF THE DESERT • CHRISTIAN RUSS, PIONEER • BUSH OF BUSH STREET • THE THEATER • THE HOUSE OF MYSTERY. MAMMIE PLEASANT'S SORCERY. SARAH HILL AND SENATOR SHARON. THE FORGERY. SARAH'S LOVE CHARMS. "YOU DIRTY SCRUB!" DAVID TERRY'S ASSAULT ON JUSTICE FIELD, AND ITS VIOLENT CLIMAX. THE HALLUCINATIONS OF TERESA BELL. THE GHOST OF MAMMIE • THE ORIGINAL POODLE DOG AND THE EARLY FRENCH RESTAURANT. A MILLION MEMORIES. THE DECLINE OF ELEGANCE • VIOLATED GRAVES

IF YOU have ever been on Bush Street, you won't remember it; you will get it mixed up with some street in Seattle or Chicago or that Armageddon of drabness and futility, Pawtucket, Rhode Island.

Bush Street misses out from start to finish. Where it starts, on lower Market Street, it is neither in nor out of the financial district. Where it crosses Grant Avenue, the elite shopping district ends, and Chinatown begins. A little farther out, it is halfway up the side of Nob Hill, not high

enough to be fashionable, not low enough to be included in the Tenderloin. Still farther out, it gets lost in a series of colorless residential streets
that look alike, sound alike and smell alike, and the smell is one of stale
cooking.

Even San Franciscans don't seem to give it a second thought. Most of
them don't know anyone who lives on Bush Street, because it's an apartment house street, a street whose most prominent feature is the front fire
escape. Its residents are undoubtedly good, hard-working, respectable,
lonely people, finding, somehow, recompense for their two-rooms-with-
bath-and-kitchenette existence, perhaps in a fox terrier, a canary, pulp
magazines, the movies or a table-model radio. Once in a while, one of
them cracks under the drabness and takes an overdose of sleeping pills,
or seals himself in the kitchenette and turns on the gas. But that doesn't
happen very often, no more than on any street like it in Pawtucket. When
it does, it may rate a paragraph in the local papers, and the city editor,
assigning the story to a rewrite man, will say, "Here, take a Bush Street
suicide from the police beat. It can't have class. Keep it short."

To anyone who doesn't live there, the city editor's judgment is right;
that's the way the street adds up—no class.

It had a sort of bizarre distinction once, a portion of it recent enough
to be remembered by nostalgic old-timers. There are, for example, some
of these around who still cackle over their port, exchange sly winks and
dig each other with their elbows at the mention of the old Poodle Dog,
when it was at Bush and Dupont. There may even be one or two old
enough to remember, as they totter along the street, the tread of
camels. . . .

Every once in a while, you see a wire-service story announcing that
someone in Texas or Arizona is going out to shoot a camel. Very probably, the story is a fake, but if, by some curious chance, it isn't, then the
home address of that camel could at one time have been the Bush Street
Music Hall. In 1860, fifteen Mongolian Bactrians (they have two humps;
a dromedary has one) lived there and gazed dolorously back at the San
Franciscans who came to gape at them. Like all camels in California in
those days, they were the unhappy victims of an experiment launched in

a we're-willing-to-try-anything-once frame of mind by the United States Army. With their ungainly frames and shaggy humps, they did for Bush Street what Pegleg Smith, a few years later, did for Montgomery; they brought to it the touch of vast and vacant skies, desert suns, and drifting dunes.

The experiment began in the 1850's, when an Army officer named Major Henry C. Wayne suggested to the War Department that it import some camels for transportation and supply purposes in California and the Southwest Territories. The War Department investigated the care, feeding and environmental necessities of the camel, and finally, with the backing of Secretary of War Jefferson Davis, got Congress to appropriate $30,000 to finance the project.

In all seriousness, Wayne and several other officers (including Captain George B. McClellan, later the distinguished Union general) were sent abroad to study the camel. After they had studied it, they bought some at prices ranging from $15 to $1000, and eventually shipped seventy-six dromedaries to Texas. The second and last boatload of them arrived there in February, 1857.

Their first serious test came in that same year, when the War Department commissioned E. F. Beale to break a wagon road from Fort Defiance, New Mexico, to Los Angeles, using camels. Disadvantages were quick to appear: camels didn't get along with horses, the men didn't like camels, and furthermore, how in hell did you tie a thousand pounds of supplies to a camel's hump so it wouldn't fall off?

In spite of all this, Beale, when he reached Los Angeles, was convinced the Army had something. Impressed by their speed, their endurance, their ability to thrive on desert shrubs, he reported to the War Department that the camels were "the salt of the party and the noblest brute alive. . . . I look forward to the day when every mail route across the continent will be conducted and worked together with this economical and noble brute."

Beale's enthusiasm turned out to be premature. It became evident that California was not a camel's idea of heaven. Some said it was because the California sands were formed of oblong, crystallized grains, instead of the round grains he was accustomed to in the old country. Others believed he didn't like the rocky, mountainous terrain he frequently had to cross. Still others thought he was just homesick and depressed. Several attempts to establish dromedary lines between California and Arizona ended in dismal fiascoes. Then the Civil War came along, and no one had the time to give them proper care and attention.

At last, in a weird safari, thirty-five of them were driven up the Coast to Benicia, at the northern end of San Francisco Bay, and sold at auction. Most of these camels eventually found their way to Nevada, where they were used to carry salt and other supplies to the silver mines.

Three years before this, Otto Esche, a San Francisco speculator, suffered an attack of camel fever and decided to import Bactrians from Mongolia and start a camel express between San Francisco and Salt Lake City. Seventeen died during the trans-Pacific voyage, but ultimately fifteen arrived safe, and more or less sound. While he wondered what to do with half the herd he had planned on, Esche pastured them on an oasis hard by the Mission Dolores.

Finally abandoning his camel express idea, he hired the Bush Street Music Hall, paraded the Bactrians through the streets and put them on exhibition. San Franciscans, many of whom had never seen a Bactrian, were enchanted by the beasts and supported the exhibition for several weeks before losing their interest in the solemn-eyed ships of the desert. At length, Esche sold them to a commission merchant who put them out to graze beyond the western limits of the city, near Washerwoman's Lagoon, and kept them nimble by exercising them under six-hundred-fifty-pound packs in the sand dunes near the Presidio.

In the next two years, Esche managed to get thirty more Bactrians to San Francisco alive; but none of his plans for them ever worked out. Of the total of forty-five that arrived alive, about half of them were sent to the Nevada mining country; the rest were bought by a Canadian visionary who thought they would come in handy in the mining regions of British Columbia.

On the whole, authorities on this experiment agree that the camel did not get a fair trial. He was overloaded, overfed and overwatered. The native drivers imported with them developed into problem drinkers and spent much of their time in jails. Ultimately, the camels employed in Nevada were turned loose to roam wild, thus sharing the fate of those discarded by the Army years before in Arizona. Once in a while, as the years passed, Southern Pacific passengers crossing the southwestern deserts would see a distant herd plodding slowly across the sands. And what was most probably the obituary to the whole curious episode appeared in the *Chronicle* of May 28, 1899:

"The last wild camel in America," said the report, "was killed and eaten by the Indians in Yuma a few days ago. . . . It seems sad that the noble beast should have such an inglorious end, and yet some sympathy must be given the poor Indians, for they must have been awful hungry to be able to masticate the tough, seventy-five-year-old camel. . . ."

The first person on record as living anywhere near the present line of Bush Street was J. C. Christian Russ, a well-to-do New York jeweler who closed his shop one night and went to see a torchlight procession in honor of General Jackson. The next day, he was no longer well-to-do. While he had been watching the parade, thieves had broken into his shop and cleaned it out. Disgusted with Manhattan, Russ and three of his sons enlisted in Colonel Jonathan D. Stevenson's New York Volunteers to fight the Mexicans. All of them, plus Mrs. Russ and several more children, arrived at Yerba Buena on the transport *Loo Choo* in March, 1847.

Too late to see any action, Russ dragged a ship's cabin to Montgomery Street, near Bush, and made himself at home. At that time, he was on the outskirts of town. In fact, he couldn't see the town from where he lived because it was on the other side of a sand hill. Nevertheless, he had a certain stolid faith in the future of the settlement. He opened a jewelry shop and later an assaying office, and bought real estate. The Russ Building skyscraper stands on it today.

There are conflicting stories about the naming of the street. One says it was named in honor of a pioneer doctor; another claims Jasper O'Farrell, who laid out the city the way it is today, named it after one of his assistant surveyors, John Bush, a former cabin boy who had deserted the New England whaler *Margaret* when she put into the Bay in 1845. (Most ardent supporter of this claim was John Bush himself. He returned to San Francisco in the 1890's after an absence of thirty-odd years, set out to paint the town red and fell into the hands of a couple of Barbary Coast bawds who drank up most of the money he had on him and then rolled him for the rest. That, he complained at police headquarters when applying for a police escort back to his hotel, was a fine way to treat "Bush of Bush Street.")

As the city entered the post-Civil War period and Comstock gold and silver poured down from the Washoe, something glamorous happened to Bush Street: the Poodle Dog restaurant moved out of Chinatown to the southeast corner of Bush and Dupont, where, for the next half century, its private upstairs dining chambers and love nooks would lend a sort of Parisian air to the city's night life. A year later, and half a block away, W. C. Ralston, the financier, opened his California Theater.

"Find out the biggest theater in the world, and make this one ten feet bigger," he had instructed his architect.

So, with the California and two smaller theaters, the Bush Street and the Standard, all within less than two blocks, the street took the theatrical play from the Portsmouth Square area, and kept it there for a couple of decades. A lot of famous old stars—the pin-up boys and girls of their day—strode the hardwood boards of the California stage, though their names now mean nothing to anyone but octagenarians and students of the American drama. But it was the big time, and San Francisco, which had always prided itself (and still does) on being a great theater town, could pat itself on the back and boast that it took a back seat to no theater capital in the world. Take your pick—Booth? Sothern? Davenport?

Scott-Siddons? Modjeska? Boucicault?—they had all played the California.

In the middle Seventies Ralston died, a couple of new theaters went up on Market Street and Mission Street, and the California slid into a decline, taking Bush Street with it. Perhaps as the result of an emerging Irish influence, the pendulum of public taste swung away from the serious drama to a combination of the rowdy and sentimental which found its best expression in vaudeville and minstrel shows, and with a gaudy repertoire of these the Bush Street and the Standard kept plugging along.

It was at the Standard that Billy Emerson laid the town flat with his rendition of *The Big Sunflower* and *Mary Kelly's Beau;* and Phil Beckhardt sang *Only a Pansy Blossom* and woke up the next morning to find himself the shopgirl's dream man. Dick José, who became a local immortal because he could sing *Silver Threads Among the Gold* in a way that tore the heart out of sentimental San Franciscans, made his debut there, bringing down the house with his bell-like tenor as he crooned *It's a Flower from My Angel Mother's Grave.*

But by the late Eighties, the minstrel show (even Hoyt and Dockstadter's Minstrels, which had succeeded the Billy Emerson and Charley Reed shows at the Standard) was on the way out, and the old theater crowd no longer hung around and tossed silver dollars in front of Steiner's saloon, next door to the Bush Street Theater. No longer did the big white horses at the Bush Street firehouse, just beyond the California Theater, feel the light, affectionate touch of the pretty actresses stopping by to pat their velvet noses and feed them carrots and sugar lumps.

On that street, an era had come and gone, leaving behind it nothing more substantial than the filaments of memories. As it receded into the past, it became invested, perhaps, with a glamor and a happiness it never had. Nevertheless, San Franciscans, believing it in retrospect to have been a happy, glamorous era, made it so. When they thought of it, they remembered the good things—the good times, the carefree nights, a play, a famous name, a personality, a sentimental ballad, blazing footlights, the crash of applause, the fall of a curtain. The frontier was a state of mind, a youth, an earliness, a recklessness, the time of an open heart, and all of that was passing.

As the theaters darkened and grew silent, there were left to Bush Street a house of mystery, a house of joy and a house of the dead. So far beyond recalling is the old town, not even the dead are there now.

On a Bush Street corner (the cross street is Octavia), stand a small hospital and six eucalyptus trees. The corner was once the site of a gloomy, three-story, Victorian Gothic mansion with a mansard roof, an inner courtyard and rooms of many-mirrored walls. Fire destroyed the house in the 1920's, but it left the row of eucalyptus trees thad had screened the old dwelling from the stares of curious passers-by.

If you had been on the sidewalk beneath their rustling branches at half past ten on the night of October 16, 1892, you would have heard a man cry desperately, "Where am I?" You would have heard the sound of running footsteps. Then, a moment later, utter silence as the house of mystery gathered to itself its first, unhappy ghost.

That would have been the ghost of Thomas Bell, pioneer, multimillionaire, and master of the mansion with the mansard roof.

For at that time, and with that cry, Bell pitched to his death from the second-floor landing of a circular stone staircase at the rear of the mansion. Some said that he was ill, and stumbled, and fell. Others whispered that he had been pushed—by the voodoo priestess known as Mammie Pleasant.

This gaunt Negress, one of the most picturesque and sinister of all San Franciscans, was born Mary E. Williams on August 19, 1814, in Philadelphia. Her father's background is confused, one contemporary account describing him as a Kanaka and another as a Cherokee Indian. But they agree that her mother was a Louisiana Negress at whose knee Mammie could have learned the black, swampland magic that she was said to practice with so compelling an art in San Francisco.

When she was six, she was placed with a family named Hussey in Nantucket. Eventually, she moved to Boston, where she married James W. Smith, a rich Cuban and an ardent Abolitionist. Before he died in 1844, he made her promise to devote some of his $45,000 estate to promoting the Abolitionist cause.

(Years later, Mammie returned to San Francisco from a trip East and confided to her friends that she had at last carried out Smith's deathbed wish. She had, she said, met John Brown at a rendezvous in Canada and had given him $30,000 with which to finance his raid on Harpers Ferry. When Brown was captured, this note was found in his possession: "The ax is laid at the foot of the tree. When the first blow is struck, there will be more money to help. [signed] W. E. P." Mammie said the note was hers; she always, she said, made an *M* like a *W*, and the initials stood for her real name, Mary E. Pleasant.)

After Smith's death, Mammie married one of his overseers, John J. Pleasant, and in 1849 they sailed around the Horn to California. Pleasant, the husband, vanishes from the record at this point, and you hear no more of him. As for Mammie, her reputation as a cook seems to have preceded her to San Francisco, for on her arrival wealthy merchants and mine operators bid as high as $500 a month for her services. But she turned these offers down and started her famous boardinghouse at Dupont and Washington Streets. For years, it was the leading establishment of its kind in the city; on its register were the names of Sharon, Newton Booth, Broderick, Terry and others who later rose to positions of importance in the state.

It would appear that Mammie ran another business on the side, that her efforts to make her boarders feel at home were not limited to Louisiana shrimp, Southern fried chicken and corn-meal pones, but included other "dishes," such as blonde ones. This, undoubtedly, was the source of the "mysterious influence" that she seemed to wield over the local mighty later, when, at her approach, more than a few Senators, judges and opulent Nob Hill citizens would hear a rattling in their skeleton closets.

After twenty-five years of running her boardinghouse and allied enterprises, Mammie moved in with the Bells, and it was then that she began to take on the sinister and enigmatic aspect that clung to her for the rest of her life, and even after that was over. She clearly had Bell, her onetime boarder and now a wealthy vice-president of the Bank of California, in the palm of her hand. It was no secret, for example, that he had the gloomy mansion at Bush and Octavia built according to Mammie's own specifications, and it was registered in her name. She went shopping alone in the Bell family carriage. She managed the household, spending as much as $3000 a month. Somehow, no one knew how or why, she dominated Bell, and Bell's wife, Teresa. Those with imaginations, recalling the mother from the Louisiana bayous, said Mammie was a dark sorceress and had cast over them a voodoo spell. Those without imaginations said Teresa had been one of the added attractions at Mammie's boardinghouse; consequently, Mammie knew too much about both Bell and Teresa, and neither of them dared to rebel against the authority she had assumed.

Mammie at this time is described as a bizarre figure, riding through the streets shopping-bent in the Bell carriage. Although her skin was ebony black, her features were as stern and chiseled as a patrician's. She sat bolt upright in the carriage with a bright scarlet blanket around her shoulders and a vividly colored sunbonnet tied on her head. (According to the Bush Street legend, Mammie's scarlet blanket was found beside Bell's body after he had plunged to his death from the spiral staircase of the house of mystery.)

But even before Bell's strange accident and the things that happened later to Teresa, it appeared that an ill and blasting wind blew upon those who yielded to the magic of the gaunt witch of Bush Street. In her cauldron bubbled insanity and sudden death.

In 1880, United States Senator William Sharon of Nevada, a former California real estate operator who had made $10,000,000 on the Comstock Lode, met a girl in San Francisco named Sarah Althea Hill. He was in his late fifties, she was in her twenties. In a businesslike arrangement, she became his mistress for an "allowance" of $500 a month.

A couple of years later, Sarah's charms palled on the Senator, and he ordered her out of her apartment in San Francisco's Grand Hotel, which he owned. Sarah didn't like it; she refused to budge. But, while she looked on in dismay, workmen under instructions from Sharon entered the apartment, calmly rolled up all the carpets, removed all the doors and walked off with them. Sarah went to live with a girl friend.

Not long after that, Sarah had Sharon arrested on a charge of adultery. She had, she claimed, a written marriage contract signed by him (under California law, it would have been as binding as a legal ceremony); he had had an affair with another woman, and now she wanted a divorce and half the $10,000,000. Sharon countered with a United States Circuit Court suit declaring he had never entered a marriage contract with Sarah.

If she had a copy of any such contract, he said, it was a forgery. He wanted the court to make his contentions official and a matter of record.

Thus, in 1883, began a series of state and federal trials that lasted until Sharon's death two years later and was carried on by his executors until 1889, when Sarah's claim was once and for all dismissed as a counterfeit.

Through all these years, Mammie Pleasant hovered at Sarah's side like a combination Svengali and an ambitious mother, advising her, consoling her, goading her on, paying the lawyers who pleaded Sarah's perjured cause. How much Mammie spent on the case, she would never tell. Guesses range from $5000 to $100,000.

In one of the opinions handed down against Sarah, United States District Judge Matthew P. Deady had this to say about Mammie:

"Mammie Pleasant has taken charge of this case from the beginning, and, to use her own phrase, is making the defendant's 'fight,' whom she supports, and to whom she was forced to admit, after much evasion, she had advanced more than $5000, and how much more she would not tell. In my judgment, this case, and the forgeries and perjuries committed in its support, have their origin largely in the brain of this scheming, trafficking, crafty old woman. . . ."

During the course of the trials, it developed that Sarah and Mammie had decided to go to court only after witchcraft had failed to soften Sharon's attitude toward his discarded mistress.

Soon after she was ejected from the Grand Hotel, Sarah went to a newly dug grave in a San Francisco cemetery and there deposited a package containing several articles of Sharon's underwear. Conditions of the charm were that if they remained there, beneath a coffin, until they rotted, Sharon would either marry her or die. The magic spell was broken, however, when health department officials, tipped off by a cemetery employee who had seen Sarah place the package in the grave, opened it a few days later and retrieved the Sharon underwear.

Also, Sarah wore one of Sharon's socks tied around her left leg, and slept in one of his shirts; it was not clear what either of these charms was supposed to accomplish. And another time, she tried to get Ki, Sharon's Chinese servant, to admit her to Sharon's Palace Hotel rooms. All she wanted to do, she told Ki, was to sprinkle some black powder around his chair, some white powder in his liquor bottles and between his bed sheets. She gave Ki $5, and promised him $1000 besides, and $40 a month for life if the charm worked.

Ki told her he would think it over. Then, a few days later, fearing she wanted to poison Sharon's whisky, the wary Chinese told his master about Sarah's proposition, and from then on refused to let Sarah near the apartment.

So nothing worked, and it all developed into a pattern of intrigue that must have delighted the black soothsayer and led her to observe with satisfaction the quickening bubbles in her cauldron.

Sarah married one of the lawyers whom Mammie had hired, David S. Terry, the former Chief Justice of the California Supreme Court, the hot-blooded fire-eater, the slayer of Broderick. In one of their last courtroom scenes, as Justice Stephen J. Field of the United States Supreme Court was reading his adverse opinion, Sarah stood up in the courtroom and accused him of having been bribed by Sharon's executors. Justice Field ordered her removed.

As the court marshal advanced to her side, Sarah struck him in the face. "You dirty scrub!" she sneered. "You dare not remove me from this courtroom."

Terry, who had been sitting next to Sarah, leaped to his feet. "No God-damned man shall touch my wife," he said grimly. He was clutching his bowie knife when deputy marshals bore down on him and threw him to the courtroom floor. Then, while they fought, scratched, kicked, bit and cursed their captors, Sarah and her husband were dragged from the room.

Justice Field remarked with classic restraint, "As I was saying when interrupted—" and resumed the reading of his decision.

For this celebrated display of contempt Terry received six months and Sarah thirty days in jail. They came out swearing vengeance against Justice Field. "The earth is not big enough to hide him from me," Terry declared. "The first time I see the son of a bitch, I will horsewhip him."

Later that year, en route from Los Angeles to San Francisco, Field's train stopped at Lathrop, California. Field and David Neagle, his body-guard, sat down in the station restaurant for breakfast. A few moments after that, Sarah and Terry, who had boarded the train at Fresno, entered the restaurant. Sarah got up and went out again to return to her train seat for her revolver. While she was gone, Terry left his place, rushed at the Justice and struck him two blows on the head from behind.

As Terry set himself for yet another blow, Neagle drew his revolver and stepped between them. Terry reached for his bowie knife. Without hesitation, Neagle fired twice and Terry fell to the floor with two bullets in his heart. He died instantly.

Sarah never recovered from this final shock. Three more years went by, and, at the end of them, she was a mental wreck and in the last home she ever knew—the insane asylum at Stockton. The person who had her committed was her old friend and counselor, Mammie Pleasant.

So 1892 was a big year in Mammie's life, Sarah mad and Bell dead from a mysterious fall. She still had Teresa left, and now, more grim and gaunt than ever, Mammie drew the meshes of her web closer about the wealthy widow. But her magic was losing its potency; her hold on Teresa was slipping. At last, in 1899, Teresa broke completely away from her and ordered her out of the mirrored rooms, out from under the haunted mansard roof. And Mammie, now a bony crone of eighty-six, went. A few years later, a Mrs. L. M. Sherwood of San Francisco found her living in poverty on Webster Street, in the city's Negro quarter. She took Mammie into the Sherwood home and nursed her until her death on January 11, 1904. Mammie was buried in the Sherwood family plot at Napa, some fifty miles north of San Francisco.

Teresa lived on until 1922. In a most weird will, she denied parenthood of the four living children everyone had assumed to be hers and Bell's, and ordered her $1,000,000 estate divided among charities and her first cousins, if she had any. If she didn't have any, their share was to go to the state. She left the children $5 each.

The children contested the will, maintaining their mother had been insane. At the end of a sensational trial, a jury agreed, breaking the will after considering these and other eccentricities attributed to Mrs. Bell: she carried a nine-inch dagger; she believed she could write poetry equal, if not superior in literary quality, to William Shakespeare's; she heard voices in the wind; she claimed she could fly through the air and had made several aerial trips to New York and back.

No sooner was this case settled than a crippled music teacher named Viola Bell Smith announced she was Teresa's daughter by a former marriage. After more lengthy litigation, her claim was upheld, and, four years after Teresa's death, the estate was distributed among charity and the surviving children.

Meanwhile, superstitious San Franciscans said the dark mansion at Bush and Octavia had received into its shadows another ghost—the desolate shade of Mammie Pleasant. Until the day the flames destroyed the house, they said you could hear it up under the eaves, sometimes giggling, but most of the time whimpering and moaning softly, like the wind in the six eucalyptus trees.

It wasn't long ago that an advertising firm took over a solid-looking, five-story brick building at 415-425 Bush Street, on the corner of Claude Lane and just across the street from the telephone company offices. You can go from Claude Lane, through a side entrance of the building and down a flight of marble steps, stained and worn by the footsteps of many years. You cross a mosaic landing, descend a few more steps and find yourself on the threshold of a large, square room with radiators high on the walls and a lofty ceiling supported by massive pillars. This room, now the pressroom of the *Wall Street Journal,* was once the main dining room of Bergez-Frank's old Poodle Dog restaurant.

Perhaps it's symbolic of something that omelet soufflés and guinea hen *sous glace,* the popping of champagne corks and the rich scent of Havana cigars have given way to stock market quotations, the grind of a press and the smell of printer's ink; at any rate, the fate of the Poodle Dog is a typical example of what has happened to the old French restaurants for which San Francisco was once so famous.

For the perspective, you have to go back to an indefinite day in the early Fifties, when a family, said to be New Orleans French, opened the first Poodle Dog near Clay and Dupont Streets. (Exactly how it got its name is not known. There are three legends: its real name was Poulet d'Or, which miners mangled into Poodle Dog; it was named in honor of the mistress' pet lap dog; while the founders were trying to think of a name, a stray poodle kept appearing at the place and begging for food, and they adopted it as a mascot and named the restaurant after it for good luck.)

The Poodle Dog—and other establishments like it—satisfied the Gold

Rush demand for good food at a time when nearly everyone had to eat out because there were no women around to supply home cooking. The arrival of more women had little effect on this practice, because, for a few years anyway, most of the women who arrived were hardly the home-cooking type.

There were no cultural heritages in San Francisco, no Back Bay traditions, no snobbery, no phony class distinctions. The Harvard man dug ditches shoulder to shoulder with the Bowery bartender. The Yale man was the hireling of a Philadelphia bootblack who had made a fortune hawking newspapers on Long Wharf. Socially, it was a free-for-all, and sooner or later society was bound to develop along lines established by the amount of cash with which you emerged from the scramble. There wasn't the time or the foundation for any other kind of social structure; the old Spanish and Mexican families had become weakened and exhausted by decades of colonial existence, and, anyway, California wasn't Spanish or Mexican now. It was American, and proud of it.

So San Franciscans were a race of self-made men. And if they wanted to sit down and relax over a good meal, they were going to have it; and it would not only be good, it would be nothing but the best.

On this basis then, the Poodle Dog prospered, and so did the others, like the Maison Dorée and Marchand's. It remained in its first location, next to the original Hotel St. Francis, until 1868, when, lured southward by the expansion of the city, it moved to Bush Street. Here, it took on a sophistication it didn't have before. Instead of the raw miner, its patron was the stiff-collared banker, the frock-coated judge, the spade-bearded lawyer—the Argonaut with a little more culture and grayer hair, but neither of these to the extent where he didn't have a twinkle in his eye, a sprightliness in his step and a fondness for sipping champagne from a lady's slipper behind the discreet curtains of an upstairs dining room.

Writing of the Poodle Dog in the Seventies, Lloyd put it somewhat mildly when he said, "If a registry were kept of all the after-dark patrons, giving also their companions, the publicity of it would be a startling disclosure to the social world."

It was in the Nineties, however, that the Poodle Dog reached its greatest popularity as a rendezvous and a restaurant. In that gilded era, when *bons vivants* and men about town wanted to dine, the Poodle Dog was their destination. In its first-floor dining room husbands could and did eat in public propriety with their wives; in its well-appointed and cozy third-floor nooks, they could and did dine with their mistresses in an atmosphere suggestive of naughty but tender abandon.

Edward Morphy, the late newspaperman and historian, described the Poodle Dog of the Champagne Days as "the shrine of a million happy memories," and rhapsodized, "That was where Bohemia gathered and quaffed the wine when it was red and kissed the lips of comrades fair. . . . Poets, painters, journalists, physicians, politicians and luminaries of the law, all foretime gathered there and bandied wit and pleasantries. . . . One can picture it in dreams across a shadowy spirit cloud of frogs' legs, omelet soufflés and *escargots bordelais,* with scalloped edges of *pompanon au gratin* and *pâté de foie gras aux truffes de Perigord.* . . ."

But the disaster of 1906 put an unhappy end to all that. After a few years in a temporary location west of the downtown district, the Poodle Dog came back to Bush Street, to the corner of Claude Lane. With it then became identified some of the best-known names in the recent French restaurant history of the city: Jean B. Pon, Calixte Lalanne, Jean Bergez, Louis Coutard and Camille Mailhebeau.

Looking back to those times, you can see why the restaurants which did so much to establish San Francisco as a gourmet's paradise were fading from the scene: the old-school French chefs were dying off; also, a certain ease, a certain elegance, a certain richness, was disappearing from the city's way of life, for the disaster had sobered the city, and aged it and thrust upon it the responsibility of reconstruction. French cooking was no longer an important thing, and a secret rendezvous with a chorus girl no longer alluring.

This is the way, for example, it went with the Poodle Dog. Bergez, who with Coutard and Mailhebeau reopened the Bush Street Poodle Dog, died in 1917. Mailhebeau struck out for himself; he opened Camille's on Pine Street in 1923, but died a year later. After this instability and unrest, along came Prohibition and dealt the Poodle Dog (and all the other old-time restaurants like it) the finishing blow. The old rendezvous, the shrine of a million happy memories, closed its doors forever the night of April 15, 1922.

"I am in despair," said Jean Pon that night. "I am going back to France."

Here and there are things the Poodle Dog left behind. J. C. Lalanne, son of Calixte and proprietor of Post Street's Ritz restaurant, has some of the glassware and a few of the old menus. A piece of the bar adds a bit of glamor to the rumpus room of a wealthy San Franciscan who lives in suburban Hillsborough. Still other traces were inherited by the advertising firm when it took over the building at Bush Street and Claude Lane, but these swiftly disappeared.

The fifth-floor ballroom was partitioned into artists' studios. Private dining rooms on the fourth floor were knocked apart to make way for modern printing and photographic plants. Downstairs in the basement was an entrance to a secret passageway that led to convenient hotel rooms next door, where a man and his girl friend could finish what they started over their *café diable*. Now there is no entrance, but just a blank section of newly laid brick, in the shape of an arched and narrow doorway.

Out where Bush Street ends in shabby, two-story frame houses that have caught the overflow of the colored and the Japanese from the Fillmore district—out there, north of Lone Mountain, is a neat and modern housing development bearing the name Laurel Village. It was put there at great cost to the builders, but, more than that, it exacted a most dear price from the city in pride and tradition.

For it was there, beneath the fifty-odd acres of the housing project, that San Francisco buried her pioneers and many of her Native Sons and Daughters. In 1854, Colonel E. D. Baker spoke at the dedication ceremonies of Laurel Hill Cemetery, and he said, "The truth peals like thunder in our ears—thou shalt live forever!" He meant that there, beneath the pines and the oaks and the bending willows, the memory of the sleeping dead would be forever green.

But some eighty years later, faced with a housing shortage, San Franciscans voted Laurel Hill Cemetery out of existence, and workmen began the evacuation of forty-seven thousand graves. The remains of ten thousand were buried elsewhere by their descendants; those of the rest were taken to Cypress Lawn, a few miles south of San Francisco, to await another resting place. Mausoleums were left with their doors gaping open, and many headstones were carted to Ocean Beach and dumped in the sand to reinforce the sea wall.

Just before the bulldozers went to work filling in the yawning pits and grading the hills, you could walk through that city of the dead and see, for example, a small, Gothic, brownstone structure looking like a chapel and with the name "Luning" carved on the front. The door was gone and the vaults untenanted. Above one of them, in good faith, had been lettered, "To my hearing, thou shalt give joy and gladness, and the bones that have been humbled shall rejoice."

Across a weed-grown avenue was the proud stone of William Squire Clark, October 3, 1807-November 16, 1889. It was Clark who, with a makeshift pile driver, sank the piles for the first wharf in Yerba Buena cove. Over a rise and around a bend was a modest shaft five feet in height, standing over an open grave. On its side was carved, "Andrew Smith Hallidie, London, England, March 16, 1836. San Francisco, Cal., April 24, 1900. Inventor of Cable Railway System. Builder of First Cable Railway. A Loyal Citizen."

Not far away was a tall pillar "Erected to the memory of our Chief by the officers and members of the San Francisco Fire Department, December, 1895." It marked what was once the grave of David Scannell, who had stormed the heights of Chapultepec in the Mexican War. He was the first sheriff of San Francisco. Later, he became the city's most revered and picturesque fire chief, and when he died in service March 30, 1893, the department's bells all over the city dolorously tapped seventy-three times, once for every year of his life.

Beneath an air raid siren on Senator's Hill were the remains of Laurel Hill's most imposing monument, the great column that stood above the grave of David S. Broderick. Some of the blocks that formed the monument had been piled to one side, but others had been tipped into nearby graves and left there. All trace of other historic dead—the Floods, the Fairs, the Sharons, the Ralstons, the Lathams, the Donahues—had disappeared.

Scattered across the slopes, half-buried and covered with matted vines, were less pretentious stones, and bits of stone. On one of these was the sentimental epitaph for a child,

This lovely bud, so young and fair,
Cut off by early doom,
Just came to show how sweet a flower
In Paradise would bloom.

You couldn't tell whose grave it had marked, for there was only the carved fragment, lying beside the road.

The Hills

7. BROADWAY

A STREET HAS A LIFE · THE FIRST WHARF · A MACABRE PICNIC · THE
BROADWAY JAIL · THE MAGNETIC MURDERESS · "ADIOS, SEÑORES!" · ALECK
GOLDENSON, WHO MURDERED MAMIE KELLY · "YOICKS!" · THE HOUSE
OF DEMONS · POP DEMAREST, HERMIT OF RUSSIAN HILL · GEORGE STERLING,
PRINCE OF PARADOX. "O SINGER FLED AFAR. . . ."

You CAN say that a street has a life, like a man.

A certain street, for example, ages with dignity, and when it does its life is one of good content; its face has peace upon it, like the face of a man who has grown not only in years but in wisdom, humor and gentleness.

A street can age into frayed but brave respectability, leading a modest and temperate life and presenting to the world a face that is lined and careworn, but nevertheless one that says it has done its best; if it did not quite fulfill its expectations or live up to its possibilities, well, that is life.

115

A street can also fail, and know a fall from ease and grace of living. Howard Street and Second Street, south of Market, are such streets, and, when this happens, the result, as in a man, is sometimes pathetic to see.

But there are, in San Francisco, streets that defy generalities like these, and one of them is Broadway. It has more than one life, and more than one face; and the faces are those of peons and pimps, millionaires and matrons, chefs and chippies—faces that take you from Manila to Mazatlan, from Mazatlan to Boston's Beacon Hill, from Beacon Hill to the Bronx.

Where it lies in the shadow of Telegraph Hill, where it stands between the world of Chinatown and the world of North Beach, it is a five-block nocturne by Reginald Marsh; of chili joints and spaghetti joints and neon lights, hamburger parlors and poolrooms, a walk-up heaven for homosexuals in one block and a strip-tease show in the next.

That is the life there, and the faces are those of hawk-nosed barkeeps, fat Italian mammas, Filipino boys with Hollywood haircuts, hay-headed vipers high as the sky and twice as wide, flabby burlesque queens with the blank eyes of marionettes, lisping youths adjusting peroxided locks with delicate, ringed fingers, paunchy stockbrokers stuffing themselves with two-inch steaks and plenty of red wine, a lonely Mexican slumped over a bar and riding back to Guadalajara on a glass of tequila and a juke-box lament.

Beyond and to the west, there is the hill called Russian, and beyond the hill and still farther west, close to the cypress-covered mesas of the Presidio, Broadway lives another life—life in a twenty-room mansion, life at a picture window overlooking the Golden Gate, life beneath the shade trees and on the clipped green lawns. Here, the faces you see are the faces of Swiss nursemaids in starched uniforms and children in clothes by Lanz, of men whose fathers were rich before them and whose grandfathers founded the city, of women whose grandmothers danced at the Apollo Hall cotillions, of sons educated by Yale and the Navy, of daughters educated by Miss Burke's finishing school and the Red Cross Motor Corps.

They used to say, and many still believe, that Nob Hill was and is the dwelling place of San Francisco society, but Nob Hill, in the socially elite sense, is as dated as the cable cars that, buglike, crawl upon its slopes.

Nob Hill, in that sense, long ago moved west—to Pacific Heights, and Broadway.

So Broadway, down by the waterfront, has its own east, and out by the Presidio its own west, and they seldom meet. When they do, they do not speak, or even nod. If they share anything, it is a pity for each other, that and the name of their street, and nothing more.

When Portsmouth Square was a cow pasture, Broadway was the north end of town. Spurs of Telegraph Hill blocked it in one or two places, and before they were removed, you had to go around them or scale them if you wanted to stay on what the map said was Broadway. About a mile from the waterfront, Broadway ran headlong into the sheer side of Russian Hill and stopped. To go farther west, through the wild mustard fields and the thistle to the dunes, you took the meandering Presidio Trail.

The reason it was the north end of town, and that they made a street there, was because of the rocky point where it met the Bay. This point was one extremity of the crescent beach of Yerba Buena cove. It was called Clark's Point after its owner, William Squire Clark, who went west from Maryland in '46 and whose white marble stone was one of the last to yield to the bulldozers of Laurel Hill.

The rocky shelves of the point played an important part in the ship-to-shore service of those early days; instead of running straight to the beach, where passengers would have to wade the last few yards to land, ships' boats went to Clark's Point, and there the passengers stepped to the rocks without getting their feet wet. Then they scrambled up Broadway and along the side of Telegraph Hill and down to the bridge spanning the neck of Laguna Saluda, crossed the bridge and there they were, on Montgomery Street and in the heart of town.

Clark, a man who was convinced that Yerba Buena had a future (he had served with Leidesdorff on the first school committee), decided to improve his natural landing, and in the early spring of 1848 obtained some pig iron ballast from a ship anchored at Sausalito across the Bay, and with ropes and pulleys rigged it into a crude, manually operated pile driver. With this contraption, he drove some redwood piles into the floor of the cove close to the point ledge. Then he laid down a few planks, and had the first wharf on the West Coast able to handle a seagoing vessel. Clark's first customer at the new wharf stood between the heads in September, 1848; she was the brig *Belfast,* out of New York with a cargo of lumber. The moment her gangplank slammed to the timbers of Clark's Wharf, and her crew began unloading her cargo directly from ship to pier, the cash value of Clark's reef as well as that of all the property in the vicinity boomed to figures nearly a hundred per cent higher than they had been the day before.

Three years later, when deserted Gold Rush ships rode at anchor by the hundreds in the cove and Bay, the end of the Broadway wharf was out over the water two hundred fifty feet from the ledge, and to the north and south of it eleven other piers jutted from the busy waterfront. Warehouses stood between the point and the base of Telegraph Hill, where, a few years before, the wooden markers of a pioneer cemetery had weathered in the sun and rain.

Offices of harbor and river pilots, commission merchants and shipping agents went up on the wharf, and it was where the people flocked by the thousand to see the Pacific Mail steamers chuff around the hill and come in for a landing, and where they stood and cheered or wept as the same ships hauled in their lines, tooted their whistles and backed into the stream on Steamer Day with passengers, homeward bound for the East, waving from their decks.

Enterprising capitalists built hotels where the wharf met the land and Broadway—the Illinois House, the Broadway House, the Broadway Hotel, Lovejoy's Hotel and the Lafayette Hotel. Corrugated-iron buildings nearby housed grocery stores, butcher shops, drugstores, auctioneering offices, coffeehouses, sailors' boardinghouses, taverns, a saddler, a hat merchant, a tinsmith. Up the street and a block or two from the waterfront was Couzen's slaughterhouse, and above the slaughterhouse and to the steep Telegraph Hill cliffs clung the tents and shanties of Sydneytown, where the Ducks lived. Another block or two and you came to the shacks of Little Chile, and the noisy Mexican fandango parlors which comprised a bawdy, raucous annex to the Barbary Coast on Pacific Street, one block to the south.

Across the way from the fandango parlors, between Kearny and Dupont

and about where you would go now for one of New Joe's North Beach
hamburgers, was the two-story brick building called the Broadway Jail.

In May, 1856, the *Sacramento Union* tartly observed that the Vigilantes
of San Francisco had good reason to take up where they left off in 1851; it
was time, it said, that somebody did *something*. "They have stood calmly
by," it declared, "and seen and heard of some fourteen hundred murders
in San Francisco in six years, and only three of the murderers hung, under
the law, and one of those was a friendless Mexican."

To the friendless Mexican, incidentally, went the unique distinction of
being the first person legally hanged in San Francisco. His first name was
José; his last name has come down variously as Forni, Formi and Forin.
One night he and another José—José Rodríguez—quarreled over a monte
game in Happy Valley, south of Market Street. In a few moments, there
was nothing happy about Happy Valley; angry cries, triple-decked ob-
scenities and the clash of knives rang from one end of the area to the
other. When they got through slashing each other, Rodríguez was dead
and Forni was figuring out a case of self-defense.

That, as far as Forni was concerned, was a waste of time. Determined
to set an example, the jury brushed aside his defense, declared him guilty
and sentenced him to be hanged at the end of Broadway, on Russian Hill.

Bang-bang went the hammers and up went the gallows, and when the
prisoner's last day arrived, more than half the population of the city
toiled to the hilltop to watch the hanging. "It was a glorious sight!" wrote
Bancroft. ". . . Russian Hill was thronged with a great concourse of
people. The Marion Rifles and the California Guard were out, flaunting
their gayest attire. The streets were lined with carriages; husbands
brought thither their wives, and mothers their children, to witness the
rare entertainment. Three or four clergymen with attendant interpreters
assisted at the exodus of this soul. . . ."

As the crowd looked on, the executioners bound Forni hand and foot,
slipped a black hood over his face and with a hatchet chopped the rope
that supported the platform beneath his feet, and the guest of honor at
this macabre picnic hung in mid-air.

Eighteen months later, ten thousand San Franciscans were diverted by another public hanging. Two more years went by, and then, early in 1856, the third execution mentioned by the *Union* took place. With this one, authorities stopped looking for suitable natural surroundings, and exacted the life of the guilty man in the relative privacy of the Broadway Jail yard. From then until the Nineties, when the task of execution was transferred to San Quentin state prison, this was where the gallows was erected whenever San Francisco justice called for a hanging.

It was there, perhaps, that Cora and Casey would have swung if the Vigilantes, that Sunday in May, 1856, had not marched into Broadway and up to the jail and demanded of Sheriff Scannell the surrender of the two murderers; and when Scannell yielded his prisoners and thus consigned them to the gibbet beams of Fort Gunnybags he cheated the Broadway gallows of a double feature that would have supplied a grim chapter to the annals of the street.

The same thing happened, but not in the same way, sixteen years later. The condemned in this instance was not a gambler like Cora, or an ex-convict like Casey, but the gentle assassin, and easily the most glamorous inmate the Broadway Jail ever had, Laura D. Fair.

For eight years, ever since she had met A. P. Crittenden in Virginia City when she was a boardinghouse keeper and he was a wealthy Comstock Lode lawyer, Laura had lived off his promises that he would divorce his wife and marry her. Finally, she wearied of promises and came to believe Crittenden had ruined her, and one November evening in 1870, as he sat with his wife on the upper deck of a Bay ferry, Laura stepped up to him and shot him through the heart. He lingered miraculously and then, a few days later, died.

After a sensational trial, Laura was convicted of murder. On June 3, 1871, the day Superior Court Judge Samuel Dwinelle passed sentence, Laura became the first woman ever condemned to death by the State of California; on July 28, a Friday (California's traditional execution day), she was to hang in the courtyard of the Broadway Jail.

A few weeks after she received her sentence, a *Daily Alta California* reporter who signed his story "Loftus" went out to Broadway to interview Laura in her cell, Cell No. 32. It was a cold foggy night. The jail, to Loftus, was "small and grim looking," and lighted as if by day with flaring gas jets. He ascended a circular stairway to the women's quarters on the second floor.

Laura's cell was ten by twelve feet, with whitewashed walls and a well-scrubbed floor. It contained a cot, a looking glass, a washstand, a rocking chair and two other chairs, and a painted bureau on which flickered two candles. As Loftus put it, Laura sat "demurely oscillating in the rocking chair."

For his readers, he sketched an attractive picture of the wan murderess, mentioning her personal magnetism, her tall, well-proportioned figure, her square shoulders, her sensuous lips, her light curly hair, her tapering fingers, her eyes, "blue and vivacious in expression."

"Happily," Loftus parenthetically informed his readers, "her optics made no impression on us, but perhaps this was not their fault. We have become so deeply embayed in the ice of cynicism that nothing, not even an 'angel from Heaven,' could thaw through the ice that surrounds the 'little beating thing' in the left-hand side of our *cuerpo*."

Maybe it wasn't her optics, but something about Laura raised his temperature a few degrees above freezing point. His paper had been loud in its applause of the death sentence, yet Loftus, looking back on the interview, permitted himself to wonder if hanging were the gentleman's answer. He concluded his story with these words:

"Although we are far from sentimentalists, are aware that she was impartially tried and as impartially convicted, although we know that her crime was flagrant and can admit of little extenuation; yet we question whether the purposes of justice would be imperiled were her sentence commuted to life imprisonment."

Jail attendants hadn't even started to build the gallows in the courtyard before Laura obtained a stay of execution. The next February, the State Supreme Court granted her a new trial, and the next September a jury went Loftus one better; it acquitted her and freed her. And the small, grim-looking, brick jail on Broadway settled back again to the standard, run-of-the-mill cutthroats and thugs that came its way.

They never did execute a woman at the Broadway Jail, and when the state finally had to do it, it involved nothing so crude as hemp and a crossbeam; it was done in what officials like to believe is a modern and humane manner, although you would be inclined to doubt that if you had seen it. The murderess was one Juanita Spinelli, grotesquely known as "The Duchess," a thin, gaunt woman whose dark hair was streaked with gray. She always felt that to kill with a gun was a little dull and unrefined; she preferred a hatpin, plunged neatly into the victim's ear.

When covering the story of "The Duchess'" execution, reporters made a point of saying she was the first woman legally executed in California. Another woman, they added, had been executed, but it wasn't legal, because she had been lynched. It happened far from Broadway, in 1851, the year the Broadway Jail was built. Oddly enough, her name was Juanita, too. . . .

Now, as you drive west on California Highway 49, you leave Sierra City and follow the course of the north fork of the Yuba River past Ladies' Canyon, dropping down the fir-covered slopes of the Sierra at the rate of a hundred feet a mile. After a while, you come to a sudden turn in the road, a turn toward the river, and there is Downieville, a picturesque and sleepy town of perhaps seven hundred, and the county seat of Sierra County. Two iron bridges link the town's main section on the north bank with Jersey Flat on the south bank and Durgan's Flat, also on the south bank, but some two hundred yards down the river.

Here the Yuba was good to the Forty-niners. It was November, 1849, and the mountain winter was setting in, they say, when a Major William Downie arrived at that river bend with thirteen men and started panning the river gravel. So rich it was, he decided to stay, and sent nine of his men down into the Sacramento Valley for winter food and supplies. The next spring, when Downie and the others who had remained were on the verge of starvation, one came back—Jim Crow, a Kanaka. And close on his heels was a gold-hungry horde of Argonauts; they had seen the gold dust Jim Crow had flashed in the Valley bars and stores, and they wanted some like it.

Before the end of April, the shanty boom town named Downieville sprawled across the flats, and its population was five thousand. And from there, other gold-seekers fanned out up and down the river, along Slate Creek and Canyon Creek, to Steamboat Bar, Port Wine, Whisky Diggings, Charcoal Flat, Poker Flat, Big Rich Bar and Little Rich Bar.

It was the year after this that Juanita got in trouble. The tale brings her down as a lovely, twenty-four-year-old Spanish-Indian with large and shining eyes, long raven hair and an olive skin. She was the mistress of a Mexican monte dealer, and lived with him.

To celebrate the Fourth of July, 1851, and to hear the Independence Day oration of John B. Weller, destined later to become Governor of California, the miners flocked to Downieville from the gulches, the river bars and flats. By sundown, the town was rocking with celebrating drunks, and one group of revelers staggered along the street kicking in doors and picking up free drinks at each house. In the course of this alcoholic pilgrimage, Big Joe Cannon kicked down the door of the Mexican monte dealer.

When he awoke the next day, it didn't seem so funny to Big Joe, and he went back to apologize to the gambler. As he stood in the doorway, still muddled from the night before, he saw Juanita in the cabin room. He said something to her, and, for all anyone knows now, it might have been a couple of four-letter words, or it might have been "Good morning."

At any rate, whether it was what he said, or simply the sight of him, Juanita's dark eyes lost their softness. She left the room. She returned with a long knife and with passionate strength drove it through Big Joe's breastbone and into his heart.

Cannon was carried to a split-board shanty nearby and laid on its puncheon floor and there, an hour later, he died. Howling for revenge, his friends seized Juanita, dragged her to the platform near the St. Charles Hotel where Weller had spoken the day before, and went through the motions of a trial. It was a travesty from the moment it started.

There were two bridges in those days too, and some say it was the bridge to Jersey Flat, and others say it was the bridge to Durgan's Flat. Still others say she wasn't hanged from a bridge at all, but from a gibbet erected on the riverbank. Wherever it was, Juanita went out like a princess.

As an angry, milling mob of two thousand miners looked on, Juanita, wearing the best and prettiest dress she had, shook hands with her few friends. She mounted the scaffolding. Pulling off the man's hat she had borrowed to wear while they were hustling her through the streets, she scaled it with flawless aim back to its owner. Then she seized the noose and adjusted it about her slender throat. She took one last look at the green mountains, the wide blue sky. *"Adios, señores!"* she cried.

A moment later, as the crowd cheered, the crude scales of frontier justice balanced once more, and were even.

Ninety years after that, the other Juanita, who never had the class of the Spanish-Indian girl with the raven hair, died strapped to a metal armchair in the little green gas chamber of San Quentin.

The last time a mob surged in Broadway in front of the jail and demanded a life was in 1886, two days after Aleck Goldenson, an eighteen-year-old art student, shot and killed Mamie Kelly.

They lived next door to each other, in the neighborhood of what is now San Francisco's Civic Center, and one day Mamie, pretty, brown-eyed and fourteen, was returning home from school. Goldenson intercepted her at a street corner. They talked for a few minutes. Suddenly he pulled out a .32 calibre revolver. "You can take that!" he said, and shot her in the head.

Mamie fell dying on an egg crate in front of a grocery store, and Goldenson ran to City Hall, then at Larkin and McAllister Streets, where he surrendered to police and babbled his story: Mamie had been madly infatuated with him, had badgered him and tormented him when he refused to respond to her affection, and finally had so stung him with insults that in a frenzied rage he shot her.

Forty-eight hours later, a crowd of four thousand jammed into Metropolitan Hall on Fifth Street, just off Market. There were twice that many, reports said, who couldn't get into the hall and were left standing in Fifth Street and on the steps of the nearby United States Mint. Inside, and before the meeting was called to order, the hall became a bedlam when someone marched up the center aisle waving an eight-foot pole from the end of which dangled a hangman's noose. "Hang him!" roared the crowd. "Lynch Goldenson!"

Vainly, calmer spirits, who had thought the purpose of the meeting was to raise funds for Mamie's bereaved family, called for sober consideration of the crime and a legitimate trial under the law. They were shouted down by the mob, which now seemed to crave not only Goldenson's life, but the lives of twenty-three other prisoners in Broadway Jail who had either been convicted of murder or were awaiting trial for murder.

Meanwhile, other speakers harangued the crowd outside. Someone suggested that on the way to the Broadway Jail they take time out to hang all the Chinese in Chinatown. Someone else thought it would be a good idea to find Goldenson's lawyer and string him up, too. A gang of hoodlums seriously plotted the demolition of the jail by means of dynamite bombs.

At length, some two or three thousand strong, the mob swarmed out Dupont Street and Kearny Street to Broadway, where it promptly came to grips with deputy sheriffs and police. Rocks and bricks rained upon the officers, who retaliated with flying-wedge rushes upon the crowd and a great flailing of billies.

All around the jail and on its roof stood tight-lipped deputies armed with Martini-Henry rifles, under orders from Sheriff Peter Hopkins to shoot to kill, if necessary. But after three or four hours of scattered street fighting the crowd grew discouraged. Its yelps subsided to a snarl, and finally to silence.

The next day, thousands attended Mamie Kelly's funeral at St. Joseph's Church. Her rosewood casket rode to its resting place in Calvary Cemetery in a white-plumed hearse drawn by two white horses.

It was not quite two years later that the state accomplished what the mob had on its mind that night in Metropolitan Hall, and there are many old-timers around who remember how the pounding of hammers echoed from the jail courtyard and up the side of Telegraph Hill when the carpenters nailed together Goldenson's gallows and its thirteen steps.

For his last moments, Goldenson wore a yellow satin tie and the suit he had on when he committed his crime. Tied to his left hand was a photograph of Mamie, taken in her confirmation dress. In his right he clutched an American flag. After kissing Mamie's picture and making a brief speech in which he said she was his "first and only love," he shook hands with the guards and officials on the gallows platform, placed the noose around his neck and died, witnesses admitted, "as game as any man who ever faced death on the scaffold."

He was the last murderer of any note who was hanged on Broadway, in the cobblestoned courtyard of the old jail, with Telegraph Hill looking

down from one side and Russian Hill from the other, and a soft, blue
San Francisco sky above. To some San Franciscans, the Broadway Jail
was never quite so glamorous after that, but most of them were glad. San
Francisco, they thought, had had her share of that sort of thing, and it
was good to get it over with at last.

So in those first years, you could walk through the Broadway dust past
the jail, and there you would be right across the street from the Barbary
Coast and the northern border of what everybody called "the Devil's
Acre," that hell-on-wheels collection of gin mills, brothels, gambling dens,
beer cellars and crimp joints.

But a block farther on, there was the Charlemagne Private College,
where, no doubt, children of some of the town's best and most decorous
families sat through their classes with the strains of Barbary Coast melo-
deons drifting through the open windows. Then you would come to
Henry Brader's soda factory, and then, a block beyond and where Broadway began the climb up Russian Hill, the city's first synagogue lifted its
strangely severe lines above the broad and sandy thoroughfare. That was
the temple of Congregation Emanu-El, built in 1854 at a cost of $20,000,
and its members were those Jewish Forty-niners who had held the first
religious meeting of their faith in Louis Franklin's tent in Jackson Street
on the Day of Atonement in 1849.

From the synagogue, the land sloped sharply and steeply upward, so
sharply and steeply that even today one block of Broadway is not paved
for traffic; nor is Vallejo Street where it ascends the hill a block north of
Broadway; and Lombard Street uses so many switchbacks to get up the
side of it that one block is believed by San Franciscans to be the crook-
edest stretch of street in the world.

The top of this hill then was grass, bleached in the summertime, and
rock and mustard and, the legend goes, the graves of the Russian sailors
who gave the hill its name.

On the hill's western rampart, in those early days, stood a white and
many-gabled Swiss chalet. There is a tall apartment house on its site

now, but then it was the outermost fringe of town, and the occupant of
the cottage was an expatriate Englishman named Colonel J. P. Manrow.

Manrow was a celebrated figure in the San Francisco of the Fifties and
served as an official of the Vigilance Committee of 1856. To a brawling,
roistering, two-gun community he contrived to bring a sort of old-school-
tie touch by riding to the hounds every morning in a black silk top hat,
scarlet hunting coat, white whipcord breeches, English riding boots and
jangling silver spurs. Fair weather or foul, he leaped upon his hunter,
rallied his hounds and any other dogs that happened to be around, and
lashed madly over the sand dunes pursuing rabbits and uttering hoarse
cries of "Yoicks!" and "Tallyho!"

One day, at a Vigilance Committee meeting several months after the
assassination of James King of William, Manrow casually mentioned that
strange things were happening in his house. Tables, he said, were tipping,
invisible hands were rapping and spooks were raising general hob with
his household. When two friends ridiculed these reports, Manrow invited
them to sit in on a little séance. These friends were William H. Rhodes,
an attorney who wrote Victorian science fiction on the side under the nom
de plume Caxton, and Almarin Brooks Paul, a mining engineer.

On the night of September 19, 1856, Rhodes and Paul sat down in the
library of Manrow's house with Manrow, Manrow's wife, her sister and
her sister's daughter, both of whom had recently arrived from Honolulu.
They sat in a circle holding hands. Suddenly, knocks were heard in all
parts of the room. The table rose a foot from the floor and swung about
in mid-air. Sofa cushions flew in all directions, books leaped from the
shelves, the doorbell rang violently, and all six present were simultaneously
struck on the head with invisible hands or kicked by invisible feet. A book
hurtled across the room and struck one of the ladies. Paul picked it up
and placed it on a table. It flew open. He closed it, and again it opened.
Upon examination, the open page was found to contain the only biblical
quotation in the volume, which was a collection of travel sketches. The
quotation: "Cannot ye discern the signs of the times?"

Using the rapped alphabet, they struck up a conversation with the
spirit, and at first it insisted it was the ghost of James King of William.
After some cross-questioning, however, it confessed it was not James King
of William's ghost, but the shade of Capitana, a Kanaka crone Mrs. Man-

row's sister had known years before in Hawaii. They asked Capitana to endorse her statement with a physical sign. Instantly, a bush outside the window shook violently, and they saw a form which materialized and then vanished before their eyes.

Then, while they stared in fright out of the window, another shape materialized out of the ground. Its countenance was so hideous and repulsive that everyone but Paul fled from the room in terror. As he watched, it advanced on the house and disappeared into the wall.

Pulling themselves together, they sat down again and asked to be visited by kinder and more peaceful spirits. As if they had been awaiting the summons, soft hands caressed and patted their cheeks. These hands then took substance, and as many as twelve were counted hovering about the head of a single person.

Rhodes and Paul returned the next night and the night after that, and the same things happened. Both insisted as long as they lived that there could have been no possible fakery.

For many more months, the spirits plagued the Manrows. They dashed flower pots against the walls, spilled water, rang the doorbell, turned off lamps. Once, in a playful mood, a spirit threw a hatchet at Manrow. Narrowly missing his head, it whizzed past him and buried its blade in the kitchen wall.

Gradually, however, the spirits withdrew and left the Manrows alone, but until the day in 1919 when it was torn down, the Swiss chalet on Russian Hill was known to San Franciscans as "The House of Demons."

One by one, pioneers built their homes on Russian Hill. It was hard to get to—Broadway at the hill's base dwindled to a goat trail that zigzagged up the slope—but the town was pushing out. Besides, Russian Hill had a view that was worth a little trouble to live with.

No one, it is true, paid much attention to the view until Captain David Jobson, a retired mariner, erected a forty-foot tower upon the hill's summit, in the middle of a lot he used for a cow pasture and potato patch. Then San Franciscans suddenly became Russian Hill-conscious, and on clear Sundays hundreds panted up its steep sides, handed the Captain a quarter and toiled on up to the wooden crow's-nest to gaze at a panorama they could have seen just as well, for nothing, from the foot of the tower.

That lasted for a few years, until the west winds weakened the tower and it was torn down before it collapsed of its own accord. By then, Manrow had neighbors on Russian Hill, occupying large and stately houses, four or five of them, on the Broadway side of the slope, some with stables and all with elaborate gardens. As long as they lived, the owners of these homes—the Atkinsons, the Ranletts, the Homers, the Turners—would remember how, to get down into town, they had to cut across the grassy hillside to Pacific Street a block away, then the only east-west street planked all the way to Van Ness Avenue. They would remember, too, the rhythmic and hollow clip-clop of a horse's hoofs that told them Al Evans, an editor of the *Daily Alta California,* had put his paper to bed and was riding his bay mare out Pacific Street toward home; or the sharp clatter of Frank Pixley's wagon and mule team (he was the *Argonaut* editor) as they too made their way homeward to Cow Hollow in the evening. Sometimes, it was the long rumble of cattle being driven out Pacific Street to the Black Point slaughterhouse, and then it would not only be the low thunder of hoofs on the planks, but the bawling of steers, the crack of the herders' whips and the yapping of their dogs.

A few more years passed, and there, on the hill, in their terraced gardens, in their homes paneled with imported English oak and toa wood from the South Seas, lived the Shafters, the Selden S. Wrights, the Edward L. Bosquis, the William P. Taafes, the James R. Boltons and their lovely daughters May and Frances and Lizzie, the Joseph L. Moodys, the John Dolbeers and the Numa Duperus.

The vacant spaces, the grassy lots, the bare and rocky crags left behind by the earth movers, disappeared beneath other homes and streets. Willis Polk, the architect, lived there and gave fashionably bohemian tea parties before his open fireplaces; Charles Rollo Peters had a studio on the hill; Helen Hunt Jackson, the poetess, gazed wistfully from a Russian Hill window and died there; the Cadenassos sang and played the piano and entertained in their house on Macondray Lane, and the hill got itself a reputation as a sort of artistic Olympus; but it had no single quality, really, and has none now.

With the city changing, at least two of the old mansions have, since the passing of their builders, served as elite and expensive brothels. Nothing raucous, but (the madames boasted) quiet, dignified and refined, well in the best old tradition of the hill. Others have become "guesthouses," as San Francisco calls its *pensions,* and next to them, or a block away, twelve-story apartment houses rear against the sky, towering above the cypress and the eucalyptus trees and the gardens that were planted long ago. And there are cottages with window boxes clinging to the cliffs, hanging high above the city.

One group of these cottages borders what is known to Russian Hill as the Compound, a pleasant tangle of grass, shrubs and wild flowers at the top of the Broadway steps, which ascend the hill from Taylor Street. These four or five cottages were originally built to house refugees from the 1906 disaster, but in the years since then they have afforded decrepit sanctuary to dozens of transient newspapermen and magazine people, arty old ladies and arty young men and bohemians living in respectable poverty.

The king of this picturesque roost until his death in 1939 was Pop Demarest, who in his obituaries stood revealed as "The Hermit of Russian Hill" and an aged and amiable libertine with eighty-seven years of un-inhibited living behind him. Reporters, paying an attention to him after he was dead that they never gave him while he was alive, learned that he had died of complications that developed after he fell down his front steps and broke a leg. They learned, also, a few of the traits and circum-stances that had for years endeared him to residents of the Compound.

For a long time, it was said, Pop lived in an abandoned cistern pipe under the Compound. In the last years of his life, he found the pipe a little cramped and moved into the basement room of one of the Com-pound cottages. When reporters examined this room a few days after his death, they found a witch's nightmare of a cave, dank, dark and fes-tooned with ancient cobwebs. Dried animal skins hung from the ceiling. Bones littered the floor. The cats that Pop had collected were everywhere, crouching in the dusty corners, slinking in and out the door, quarreling in the middle of the floor over old scraps of meat. Phonograph records (one reporter estimated there were twenty-nine thousand) were piled from floor to ceiling. Four antique phonographs with bell-shaped horns stood on orange crates and chairs. Littering many shelves was Pop's life-long accumulation of curios, which included bits of broken china, old

cups, clocks and hundreds of cheap and useless trinkets of the sort heaped upon trays in pawnshop windows—buttons, pins, spectacles, old lodge emblems.

Pop had built the cottages and owned the half acre of land they stood on, and is said to have refused $50,000 for it. He scorned money, never pressing his tenants if they fell behind in their rent, and he scorned baths. "Earth," he once said, "is one of the few honest things in this world. Because it clings to me, am I to banish it to the sewers?"

What he loved most in his life were: the great singer Patti, whom he adored from afar ever since the moment he first heard her voice; his phonograph records, which he sometimes played until dawn on his squeaky talking machines; and drinking. Every month, until they took him away to the hospital to die, Pop went on a prodigious bender. On these memorable occasions, he would sometimes caper stark naked through the Compound garden, throwing bottles about and scattering his cats with wild and piercing cries; and his tenants, who were tolerant people and loved him, would lock their doors and wait patiently for the bearded anchorite to sober up. This always took a day or two; then he would emerge from his gloomy den with his face the very portrait of meekness and humility. A few more days and that stage would pass, and then life in the Compound would fall back into its old, quiet routine.

By those who knew him, Pop Demarest was sincerely mourned, and San Franciscans who hadn't known him mourned him, too, when they read about his life and his death. The town is a live-and-let-live town. Just be yourself, have a good time and all the laughs you can get, and don't hurt anybody. That's all it asks, and that's the way Pop Demarest lived, and that's why it missed him when he was gone.

On Russian Hill, far above the garish life and neons of Broadway and the shadowy warehouses that stand where Clark made his wharf, far, also, above the mansions that seem to stare, heavy-lidded with boredom, at each other across Broadway on the city's western ridge—far above these and close to the sky and the stars is a piece of San Francisco that is apart and alone. Yet so tender are its trees and silence, it seems sometimes to be humming a wistful song whose words, if words there were, would tell of the long-ago hills and how lonely they were before the people came to live upon them.

It is a little park, and in it, with the trees and two paths, is a bench, a long bench made of varicolored tiles. A bronze tablet is set into the tiles, and its inscription starts, "To Remember George Sterling . . ."

The words must seem ironic to those who knew him, for, knowing him, how could they forget him? To them, he was a moody and lovable poet of genius, a true and loyal friend. To those who didn't know him, and read of his exploits in the newspapers, he was other things: an eccentric bard, a buffoon, a Pagliaccio of the Water Lilies, the Count of Poppa Coppa's Montgomery Block café.

But everyone, whether they knew him or not, was shocked when the morning papers of November 11, 1926, gave them the news that George Sterling had swallowed poison in his Bohemian Club room and was dead. It was, one writer said, as if Golden Gate Park had slipped into the sea.

Sterling rose to uncontested leadership of San Francisco's Bohemia from an Oakland real estate office. Born in Sag Harbor, Long Island, in 1869, he attended St. Charles College in Maryland, went west in 1890 and started to work for his uncle, F. C. Havens, an Oakland realtor and capitalist. It wasn't long before he commenced to chafe under the humdrum limits of his clerical existence. He looked for companions in another world and found them: Joaquin Miller and Ambrose Bierce, Jack London and Robinson Jeffers.

In 1905, two years after the publication of his first volume of poetry, *The Testimony of the Suns,* Sterling left Oakland and the real estate business and went down the coast to Carmel, where, bewitched by the white sand and surf, the twisted cypress and the metallic blue sky, he lived and wrote for six years. Then he returned to San Francisco and, except for brief periods spent in Carmel and New York, remained there for the rest of his life.

In his later years, Sterling moved in unpredictable ways across the San Francisco stage. He would cut an elfin caper, as when one midnight he stripped and plunged into a Golden Gate Park lake to pluck a water lily for a lady. Or he would be a brooding stalker, a man who one minute would be standing on a street corner talking to a friend and the next minute would turn, without saying good-by, and silently vanish into the fog.

To many, he was a sort of Prince Paradox. Poet though he was, and Dantesque in appearance, he was an excellent boxer and yachtsman. He labored over a sonnet for months, wedging his soul into its implacable form, and then with a jest gave the sonnet to a friend. He wrote poetry that was sheer music, but detested concerts of any kind. His sense of humor was generous and gay, but he flew into a rage at the very mention of dominoes, the Sutter Street car line, rhubarb pie or women who left face powder on his coat lapels, all of which he hated.

But toward the end, the fires in Sterling began to burn low. He fell ill, and was consumed with gnawing pains that he tried to appease with alcohol. He abandoned himself to depression and despair and saw the world as a never-ending pageant of dreariness and suffering. One night, in his room, he burned his photographs and letters. When they were ashes and the smoke curled upward no longer, he lay down on his bed and died.

It was a little less than two years later that a handful of his friends gathered on the wind-swept western reach of Russian Hill for the dedication of the bench. There were brief eulogies, the singing of two songs— *Song of Friendship,* whose words Sterling had written, and his favorite ballad, *The Soft Caress of Night*—and the ceremonies were over.

Now, that bare hillside is covered with cypress, sycamore and acacia. The bench is at the end of a broad, tree-lined walk, and Russian Hill mothers take their babies there to play. The bench has settled and the tiles have cracked deeply in one place, but old men sit upon it and sun themselves. Occasionally, lovers stroll down the path to a little clearing and stand very close to each other and look west, over the Marina house tops to the Golden Gate and the sea. An apartment building towers overhead. Only once in a while, from nearby streets, comes the sound of traffic.

8. WASHINGTON STREET

CANDELARIO MIRAMONTES' POTATO PATCH · THE PLAZA · THE REDWOOD
SCHOOLHOUSE. "HO FOR THE DIGGINGS!" MASSETT'S CONCERT · THE FIRST
PLAYS · THE JENNY LIND · GAMBLING HELLS · "HOME, OR THE MINES" ·
PROFESSOR JERRY THOMAS. BIRTH OF THE DRY MARTINI. THE INVENTION
OF THE BLUE BLAZER · THE RIALTO OF THE WEST · MENKEN RIDES A WHITE
HORSE · THE FIRST CABLE CAR · ROBERT LOUIS STEVENSON IN SAN FRAN-
CISCO · MIDAS AND THE SCIENTIST. GEORGE DAVIDSON. THE HAUNTED HOUSE
ON THE HEIGHTS. ELLINOR DAVIDSON'S BARGAIN · THE PHANTOM GALLEON

THERE WAS once, a few hundred feet inland from the shore of Yerba
Buena cove, an open space amid the chaparral and the scrub-oak trees.
The hills were all around, and it was a good, sheltered place, a place that
got the sun, and not too much fog. In 1833, the American trading bark
Volunteer dropped her anchor in the still cove, and one day her eleven-
year-old cabin boy, William Heath Davis, Jr., went ashore and in that
clearing saw a potato patch which was producing potatoes for the ragged

135

garrison at the Presidio of San Francisco. It was tended by a Mexican named Candelario Miramontes. Davis borrowed a horse from Miramontes and rode over the hills and sand dunes on a sight-seeing expedition to the dilapidated Presidio fort.

Years later, when he had become a prosperous San Francisco merchant, Davis was fond of strolling up Washington Street with a newcomer to the city, and recalling that experience of his youth. He related it carefully, so that it led to a question in the mind of his listener, and always the listener, sooner or later, asked it: "And where, Mr. Davis, was that potato patch?"

Davis would pause at the busy corner of Washington and Kearny Streets, where buildings rose on every side and carriages rolled past and pedestrians thronged the sidewalks. He would point across the intersection to Portsmouth Square, a tiny green island of grass and trees that was the center and the hub of the city's life. And he would say, "Right there."

Even today, a San Franciscan can get a proud and prejudiced thrill out of showing Portsmouth Square to a tourist and exclaiming, "Just think, that was once a potato patch!"

The thing is, the unbelievable incongruity to him is, that this piece of earth could ever have been so prosaic. Looking back, he sees it as a place where San Francisco history was made, day and night. He hears a fife playing *Yankee Doodle* and sees the Marines raising the American flag there, and he sees The Miscreant swinging there from the Customs House rafter, still in the moonlight and with a half-smoked cigar clamped between his rigid jaws. He sees the first public schoolhouse, and lights blazing in the Bella Union saloon, and hears the rattle of the roulette ball and tinny music coming from the El Dorado, the Verandah and Dennison's Exchange. He feels the hush and solemnity of the thirty thousand as they stood in the Square on that Sunday and heard the rolling flow of words with which Baker (like Marc Antony over Caesar, they said afterward) eulogized the slain Senator Broderick. He can hear the miners yelling themselves hoarse over Lotta Crabtree in Gilbert's Melodeon and the spider dance of Lola Montez. He sees Emperor Norton, the fairy-tale monarch, strolling regally beneath the trees in his tattered uniform. He sees the first cable car climbing the Clay Street hill beside the Square, and the pale, emaciated Robert Louis Stevenson resting beneath its shade trees. He thinks of fire bells clanging and flames dancing against the night sky and the rich bass voice of Curly Jack Carroll singing *The Fireman's Bride* for the volunteers as they battled the raging blaze—"Hark, don't you hear the Hall bell a-ringing? Hark, don't you hear the doomful sound? Hark, don't you hear the firemen a-running? As they cry, 'Pull on, brave boys, pull on!' " He thinks of the dramas of passion and lust that played themselves out on Portsmouth Square, all that excitement and movement and life, and he can't believe that a Mexican named Candelario Miramontes once grew potatoes there.

Portsmouth Square was then, and is now, half a city block, lying one block west of Montgomery Street and three blocks from Broadway. On two sides of it, Washington and Clay Streets passed it and scaled the hill to the west. On another side lay Kearny Street, one of the town's main and busiest thoroughfares. The fourth side was bounded by a lane called Brenham Place, which connected Washington and Clay.

Sixteen years after the lad Davis borrowed the horse and rode over the sand hills, another traveler landed on the shore of the cove and found a strident, bustling boom city of six thousand people. He was Bayard Taylor, an author.

On the August day that he arrived in San Francisco, the summer wind raised choking clouds of dust and blew them across the town. "On every side," he wrote in *Eldorado,* "stood buildings of all kinds, begun or half-finished, and the greater part of them mere canvas sheds, open in front, and covered with all kinds of signs, in all languages. Great quantities of goods were piled up in the open air for want of a place to store them. The streets were full of people, hurrying to and fro, and of as diverse and bizarre a character as the houses. . . ."

He tried to get a room at the Parker House, on the corner of Kearny and Washington, but it was filled. He crossed Portsmouth Square to the adobe City Hotel and there obtained an attic room whose ceiling was so low he bumped his head on the rafters the next morning when he sat up in bed.

At sunrise, he found the town wide awake and humming. At six-thirty, the hammering of breakfast gongs rose from every building and every street.

"By nine o'clock," Taylor wrote, "the town is in the full flow of business. The streets running down to the water, and Montgomery Street, which fronts the Bay, are crowded with people, all in hurried motion. . . . The eastern side of the plaza, in front of the Parker House and a canvas hell called the El Dorado, are the general rendezvous of business and amusement—combining 'change, park, club room and promenade all in one. . . . The very air is pregnant with the magnetism of bold spirited, unwearied action. . . .

"But see! the groups in the plaza suddenly scatter; the city surveyor jerks his pole out of the ground and leaps on a pile of boards; the venders of cakes and sweetmeats follow his example, and the place is cleared, just as a wild bull which has been racing down Kearny Street makes his appearance. Two *vaqueros,* shouting and swinging their lariats, follow at a hot gallop; the dust flies as they dash across the plaza. . . ."

Six weeks later, when he returned from a trip to Monterey, the jaw of the sophisticated New Yorker dropped even lower; during his absence, the city had grown and spread to more than twice its former size. Three-story buildings stood where tents had been before, and the houses now ranged to the hilltops, as far from the waterfront as the eye could see, and instead of six thousand people, there were fifteen thousand, every manjack of them on the make and out to find the end of the rainbow that arched through the California sky and touched the earth somewhere in the pine-covered foothills of the Sierra.

So the Square, the plaza, was the heart of town, where the Forty-niners met and did business, or relaxed together and parted, where Mexican cowboys roped runaway steers and where, if you put a two-bit piece in its mouth, Constable Charley Elleard's trained black pony would trot to the bootblack stand on the corner, drop the coin into the shoe-shine boy's hand and lift its hoof to the boot rest for a polishing.

As a setting for that faraway, magic-lantern life, the plaza changed almost from day to day. The early fires shifted the scenes and shuffled the landmarks. The constant pushing, the pressures of expanding trade, ex-

panding population, sent the settlement fanning out from the cove shores
to the hills and beyond, and, when it was possible, they carted the hills
away and dumped them in the Bay. So nothing much stayed the same
very long except the Square itself.

That first public schoolhouse, for example. The first class in the one-room,
redwood building on the corner of the Square comprised six pupils, and
it met for the first time, with Yaleman Douglas as its teacher, on April 3,
1848. The month after that, thirty-seven of the town's estimated sixty
school-age children were going to the school. Two months later, however,
the school board, Yaleman Douglas and perhaps some of the pupils
themselves were hotfooting it for the Mother Lode, not caring, literally,
whether school kept or not.

As a matter of fact, it didn't; but the schoolhouse went on serving the
settlement as a meetinghouse for all sorts of groups and organizations,
from Mormons to Odd Fellows. The next June, a ruddy-cheeked and roly-
poly Englishman named Stephen C. Massett presented a sort of grab-bag
program of entertainment in the building before an audience of about
one hundred fifty, including four women. Massett gave them monologues,
impersonations and renditions of such songs as *When the Moon on the
Lake Is Beaming* and *When a Child I Roamed*. As theatrical entertainment it was the first faltering start for the town that, a few years later,
would go mad over the silvery voice of Elisa Biscaccianti, the American
Thrush, and the somber Hamlet of Edwin Booth.

Other schools were built, and the plaza schoolhouse became a court-
house, then a police station, and then, in 1850, after a short, eventful life
of two years, it was labeled an eyesore and torn down.

On Washington Street, across from the Square and above the *Alta
California* printing shop, was a drafty, barnlike room called Washington
Hall. There, in January, 1850, a group of traveling players from Sacramento's Eagle Theater presented San Francisco's first legitimate stage
attraction, a double feature of *The Wife* and *Charles II*. A week later,
the troupe's treasurer lost all the profits in a monte game. Disgruntled
and broke, the company quit. Eighteen months after that, the *Alta California* plant and Washington Hall went up in smoke in the sixth great
fire.

On the Kearny Street side of the Square, dapper Tom Maguire, the former New York hack driver, opened over his Parker House saloon and gambling hall a theater he named the "Jenny Lind," not because Jenny Lind ever sang there or any place else in California, but just because he admired her. This theater opened in October, 1850. It burned to the ground in the fire of May 4, 1851. On June 13, Maguire opened the second Jenny Lind Theater in a new building on the same site. Nine days later, fire destroyed this theater. Undaunted, Maguire raised $160,000 and sank it in a third Jenny Lind, prudently building, this time, of stone. It opened October 4, 1851. Two years after that, deep in the red, Maguire sold it to the city for $200,000 for use as a City Hall.

That is what happened to three Portsmouth Square landmarks in the space of two or three years. The backdrops were constantly moving, constantly shifting, but always in front of them was this bizarre throng, this carnival crowd, in a Saturday-night mood every day and night of the week.

But the gaiety, the exuberance, sometimes, was a little forced. Many of those earliest San Franciscans were desperately homesick, lonely and unhappy. Because they couldn't go back home with their name on a gold mine, many of them regarded themselves as failures. They'd come to California with a banjo on their knee and hope in their heart; they were going to grab themselves a yard of that golden fleece, take the first boat back home, pay off the mortgage, sit back with their feet up on the front-porch railing and spend the rest of their life telling the neighborhood kids how they fought the Indians and the grizzly bears and struck it rich in Dead Man's Gulch, a thousand miles the other side of the Rockies. But it didn't turn out that way. Instead of golden fleece, all they had was the red wool shirt on their backs.

Native stability, or a sense of humor, or both, saved a lot of them, and they sensibly squared accounts with themselves, either packing up quietly, going back to Ohio or wherever they came from and chalking the whole thing up to experience, or staying in California and making a new and serious start in a field that had nothing to do with gold mines. As for the others who failed to find what they had come for, some decided they might as well be drunk as the way they were, and ordered another double whisky and escaped their problems that way. And there were some who figured all they needed was one, good, lucky break, and they'd go home with a bag of gold in spite of everything. These were the ones who were going to break the bank at the El Dorado.

Taylor says he could have left the City Hotel, crossed Portsmouth Square toward Washington Street and stepped into any one of seven gambling halls: the El Dorado at the corner of Washington and Kearny, Dennison's Exchange, the Parker House, the Verandah, the Aguila de Oro, the St. Charles and the Bella Union.

It was the El Dorado, where the sky was the limit, that always got the greatest play. Starting as a flimsy room made of canvas tacked over two-by-four scantlings, it ended, after the early fires, a handsome, four-story stone building gaily decorated with flags and streamers and with a flashy interior that led many a passer-by to wonder why he should go to his flea-ridden bunk and go to sleep when he could go in here?

Frescoes smiled from the ceiling, above the glittering chandeliers. Lush nudes, painted in poses of abandon, hung on the walls. A band played familiar tunes from a balcony across the far end of the room, its lively music rising above the hum of voices, the sound of ball on wheel, the solid chink of coins and the thud of pokes slapped down, the calls— "Make your bets, gentlemen"—of the croupiers and the bankers. Immense cut-glass mirrors gleamed behind the bar, and around the leather-covered gaming tables piled high with nuggets, gold dust and gold and silver coins, milled the picturesque crowd—seraped *vaqueros* and pigtailed Chinese and ponchoed Chilians, laborers and lawyers, merchants and top-hatted professional gamblers, miners and newsboys, deacons and buck-skinned mountain men.

You could play faro or monte, roulette or rondo or chuck-a-luck, and you could win a hundred thousand dollars or drop your last ounce. Some of them made it and went home heroes, but the favorite anecdote of the times pictures a young man, down from the Mother Lode and on his way home with $10,000 or $20,000 which he had dug from the earth with months of backbreaking work, and which he had saved and hoarded through many days and nights of clean living and saintly self-denial. He is going back to the Vermont village he came from and marry the sweet and innocent girl who is yearning for his return. While waiting for his boat to sail, he wanders past the El Dorado. He drifts inside, observes the feverish crowd with amused disdain. "What fools," he says to himself, "frittering away their money and their souls in this house of Satan."

After an hour or so of this, he gets bored; he decides to risk a dollar, just to pass the time and see what happens. To his pleasant surprise, he wins. He doubles his bet, and wins again. A little later, he has a stack of several hundred dollars in double eagles at his elbow. Now, he is begin-

ning to get a little feverish himself. He pictures himself laying $40,000 in Mary's lap instead of a paltry $20,000. He has a couple of White Tiger's Milks to steady his nerves. Then his luck changes. Now he is down several hundred dollars. He has another White Tiger's Milk. From his savings, he stakes just enough to break even; if he wins this time, he will quit. He loses.

A few hours later, you see the hero of the story disheveled and desperate. He has reached his last five hundred. Shattered is the vision of his happy homecoming, his smiling Mary (perhaps he can never marry her now, for he is unworthy of her wholesome goodness). Now he realizes he is but a foolish toy of Fate; but he still has his steamer ticket, and if his luck will change just this once, he will sail away from this accursed California, go back home, ask Mary's forgiveness on bended knee and maybe some day she will take him back. Eyes glowing in his pale, haggard face, he pushes his last bet across the table. "Home—or back to the mines," he says in sepulchral tones.

The wheel spins. The ball bounces playfully over the grooves. The crowd around the table bends forward, tense and intent. The young man bends forward, beads of sweat on his brow, hands clenched in the agony of suspense.

The wheel slows down. The ball finds its last groove and swings around and stops. The young man sinks back in his chair and closes his eyes. "The mines, by God," he sobs. He rises, pushes his way through the crowd and lurches through the swinging doors and out into the cheerless night.

Patrons who, from the bar, have witnessed the young man's downfall, watch him go and sadly shake their heads. "What a fool," they say, and order another drink.

There was another young man who, when he left the El Dorado, neither lurched nor staggered; he walked out calmly with the situation well in hand, launched on a happy and prosperous career. His name was Jerry Thomas, and when he died some forty years later tipplers the world over mourned the passing of the best bartender in American history.

Although less than twenty-five years old when he left the El Dorado bar, he already had one triumphant notch in his mixing spoon, representing his invention of the cataclysmic Blue Blazer. He moved on to the Planters' House in St. Louis, where he perfected the holiday wallop known as the Tom and Jerry. After a few years there, he became head bartender at William M. Tweed's Metropolitan Hotel in New York. Then he returned to San Francisco, to the Occidental Hotel bar.

With a few dashes of imagination, you can easily reach the conclusion that there, in the early Sixties, the "Professor" (an honorary title conferred upon him by his "patients") gave to the world the Martini cocktail.

The Martini, according to a footnote to Recipe No. 105 in Thomas' book, *The Bon Vivant's Companion,* was originally called the "Martinez." In those days, before the "Professor" developed it into a social, afternoon appetizer, the cocktail was a tonic, a morning eye opener. It is highly probable that one morning a shivering customer entered the Occidental Bar and said, " 'Professor,' I'm going on a cold trip to a town across the Bay. Give me something to keep me warm."

In an inventive mood, the "Professor" started out with gin and bitters, added a touch of maraschino to give a little color, and then, with the swift inspiration of genius, poured in some vermouth. "Where are you going?" he may have asked idly, as he filled the traveler's glass.

"Martinez."

"Very well, here is a new drink I invented for your trip. We will call it the Martinez."

As it grew in popularity, and became subject to analysis by connoisseurs, the maraschino was abandoned as superfluous, the name understandably was corrupted to "Martini" (after three or four, that final *z* would get very much in the way), and there you had that cool and amber package of dynamite which, even today, is still making so many friends and influencing so many people.

At any rate, the merry pilgrims who trod San Francisco's famed Bacchian Way in 1862 felt they had lost their best friend when Jerry Thomas packed up his $4000 set of solid silver bar implements and moved on to Virginia City, the Nevada boom town on top of the Comstock Lode. After a few years there, Thomas returned to New York and for the last twenty years of his life ran the world-famous Thomas' Exchange at No. 3 Barclay Street.

The story of how the "Professor" took his first, sure step toward immortality is one of the legends of the old El Dorado and is sympathetically told in Herbert Asbury's introduction to a modern edition of Thomas' book.

It seems that one day a rawboned miner strode in from the diggings and slapped his poke on the El Dorado mahogany. "Barkeep!" he roared. "Fix me up some hell-fire that'll shake me right down to my gizzard!"

Thomas pondered a moment, measured his man, and then said, "Come back in an hour." He retired to the back room to figure out what he was going to do. An hour later, with spectators crowded five deep around the bar, he took down two silver mugs. Into one he poured a tumblerful of Scotch and a tumblerful of boiling water. He lighted a match, set fire to the drink and tossed the blue-flaming liquid from one mug to the other. Then he emptied it into a glass, smothered the flames, stirred in some sugar, added a twist of lemon peel, set the glass in front of the miner and bowed. "Sir," he said solemnly, "the Blue Blazer!"

The miner raised the glass to his lips and drank. He put it down empty with a dazed look on his sunburned face. His teeth chattered. He trembled as if seized with ague. He sank with a sigh into the nearest chair. "He done it!" he said in an awed whisper. "Right down to my gizzard. Yes, sir, right down to my gizzard."

It was three whole days before the miner touched another drop.

They graded Portsmouth Square and put a fence around it in 1854, and its days as a cattle corral were over. But the added dignity in no way diminished the color and force of the life that moved through the Square, around it and along the three or four blocks of Washington Street that reached from the Square to the Bay.

Lights of the gambling halls still blazed all night long, and the music of their bands drifted over and beneath the swinging doors and into the street a block and a half from the First Baptist Church up between Dupont and Stockton Streets, and a half a block from the decorous and innocent Louis Quatorze interior of Peter Job's fancy-pastry-and-ice-cream parlor, where, of an evening, hoop-skirted ladies with Eugénie curls and their bearded, frock-coated escorts poised themselves on gilded chairs and fastidiously sampled the confections of "The Sherry of the Pacific."

Down Washington Street from the Square was the theater which had started out as Bryant's Minstrels and then became San Francisco Hall, and then, in 1856, Tom Maguire's Opera House. That was a few years after the tiny Biscaccianti, enthusiastically hailed as "the Columbus of the Musical Pacific," melted the town's heart with her clear soprano voice, and $50 gold slugs rained upon the American Theater stage in tribute to Kate Hayes, the blue-eyed Irish Linnet, and Lola Montez enthralled the boys (and netted herself $16,000 a week) with her sexy and suggestive spider dance.

As far as this investment was concerned, Maguire had nothing to worry about over his Opera House; San Francisco had established itself as a community that would toss the key to the city at the feet of an artist who captured its fancy. When it fell in love, it was head over heels; it gave its heart away, and a fig for what the world said or thought.

The dramatic critic of the *Daily Alta California* summed it up when, following a wildly acclaimed performance of Juliet by the hitherto unrecognized eastern actress, Matilda Heron, he wrote: ". . . If Miss Heron was neglected night after night by your New York audiences, if she was shoved away from the Broadway and pushed down to the Bowery or some worse stage, the San Franciscans boldly pronounce her to be among the very brightest geniuses of the age. Crowded houses follow in her train; California will lay a fortune at her feet, and wherever she may go, however she may be received in London or New York, she is always sure of a hearty welcome and a shower of bouquets from us."

And later, with the town backing him to the last man, this same critic further announced to anyone it concerned: "The stamp of a San Francisco audience, of however little weight it may be among the Cockneys or the Knickerbockers, is no such small matter after all, for when we pronounce a favorable verdict, we are able to back it up with a fortune and snap our fingers in the face of the world!"

Down where the street crossed Montgomery, there was not only the Bank Exchange, but the Occidental restaurant, where Dave Scannell and the other boys from the volunteer fire company Engine No. 1 sat four and five hours over their dinners of underdone canvasback duck; and M. L. Winn's popular Branch Extension, described in its advertisements as "A refectory of the highest order, furnished in most tasteful and elegant manner," and glamorized by the after-the-show patronage of actors and actresses from Maguire's, the Metropolitan on Montgomery Street and the American on Sansome.

A few doors toward the waterfront, the Clipper restaurant was packed to the doors day and night, serving "three for two"—any three dishes for two bits—and sending the orders from kitchen to tables on the flatcars of a miniature railroad. Across the street from the Clipper, at their Auction Lunch saloon, James C. Flood (a Staten Island boy) and William S. O'Brien poured slugs of redeye and forty-rod for the men down from the diggings, and shrewdly kept their ears open as they polished the glasses and swabbed the floor; gold was in the hills and in the drunken babbling of the men who came from the hills, and twenty years from then, playing a tip here, a wily hunch there, putting two and two together and plunging at the right time, the two saloonkeepers and their partners, James G. Fair and John W. Mackay, would be worth a cool $20,000,000 each in Comstock gold and silver.

In spite of all this, it was Maguire's that set the tone of the street and was the reason why the town called Washington Street "the Rialto of the West." The volunteer firemen, with their silver-plated fire engines and their gold-plated trumpets, were the apple of San Francisco's eye in those days, but even they took a back seat for a while when Edwin Booth was playing at the Opera House, or Charles Kean, the great English tragedian, or Edwin Forrest.

Maguire himself was a noted Washington Street character then, dressing with flash and jauntiness, calling himself "the Napoleon of the Impresarios" and risking large sums of money to satisfy his ambition, which was, he modestly admitted, to give San Franciscans the best the world had to offer in the way of theatrical entertainment.

Even by his own standards, Maguire achieved a splendid pinnacle in 1863 when he brought to Washington Street and the Opera House the most celebrated actress of her time, the dazzling Adah Isaacs Menken. As the star of *Mazeppa,* she had ridden to theatrical glory in daring flesh-colored tights and on the back of a white horse, which, during a climax of the play, galloped up a stage runway and out of sight with Adah lashed to its back.

To do justice to the appearance of "the Menken," Maguire assembled in a supporting cast "the finest corps dramatique ever having an organization in this city," and from Long Wharf to the Mission pasted up playbills hailing "the great sensation scene of the flight of the wild steed and his helpless rider up the rocky passes."

On that opening night in August, a packed house caught its breath at the sight of the "naked" Menken, and when her spectacular exit was over and she and her horse vanished high into the flies, the audience applauded with a roar of approval that rolled up Washington Street to Portsmouth Square and beyond it. Menken took the town by storm as it had never been taken before. "Every curve of her limbs," wrote Author

Charles Warren Stoddard ecstatically, "was as appealing as a line in a Persian love song. She was . . . a living and breathing poem that set the heart to music and throbbed rhythmically to a passion that was as splendid as it was pure." In less than three weeks, thirty thousand San Franciscans crowded into the Opera House to see *Mazeppa* and gape at the nearest thing to nudity that had ever appeared on the American stage. Over their toddies at the Bank Exchange after the performance, plug-hatted theatergoers fingered their flowing moustaches, winked at each other and opined that where riders were concerned, Boston could have Paul Revere; they'd take Menken.

No wilder triumph had ever hit Washington Street, and none like it ever came again. A few years later, the opening of Ralston's California Theater ended the street's run as "the Rialto of the West." By that time, San Francisco wasn't a boom town any more, and Portsmouth Square was no longer a village green. The city was still growing, and Washington Street was one of the things it left behind.

During his visit to San Francisco, Rudyard Kipling was impressed by the cable cars. These contraptions, he reported to the readers of his newspaper back in India, had leveled the city's famous hills. "They take no count of rise or fall. . . . They turn corners almost at right angles, cross other lines, and, for aught I know, may run up the sides of houses."

To this day, the cable cars inspire in the visitor to San Francisco a sort of bewildered wonder; and to many San Franciscans they are a beloved institution to be babied, nursed along and protected with maternal ferocity against a progressive element that says cable cars belong in the museum along with the Stanley steamer, horsecars and the Wright Brothers' flying machine. But books and poems have been written about them, artists have painted them, songs have been sung about them, love has bloomed on them; you can buy a hobby kit and put the pieces together and have a model cable car; florists' shops sell glazed pottery models, suitable for centerpieces, and miniature sterling silver cable cars for charm bracelets have been sold at the jewelry counter in the Palace Hotel lobby. And in spite of progress, in spite of the fact that many of the old cable lines have yielded to electric cars and gasoline busses, there are still some left, climbing the city's hills and coasting down the other side, lurching around curves and making with their bells the sweetest music a San Franciscan ever heard.

Portsmouth Square in the 1870's still had some history to live through, and it was on August 2, 1873, on Clay Street between Kearny and Jones, that the first cable car, slowly and gingerly, went up and down a hill. Although it was the result of great engineering skill and ingenuity on the part of Andrew S. Hallidie, and was to open up extensive living areas to the growing city's population, the five-block odyssey rated only a feeble play from the local newspapers.

The big news the next morning was a $1,500,000 fire which had destroyed twenty blocks in downtown Portland. Below this Page One story in the *Chronicle,* San Franciscans read a laconic few inches of type under the headline, "The Uphill Road—The First Car Run over the Clay Street Track Yesterday."

"Successful experiments (the story said) were made yesterday in running cars on the Clay Street railroad. At five o'clock in the morning, the first car was sent down the hill and back again by means of the wire rope. No difficulty was experienced in stopping at any point desired, and the success of the experiment fully realized the anticipation of the projectors. . . . Some days will elapse before regular travel will be conducted on the road."

Behind the story was a rainy night in 1869. Hallidie, a wire-rope manufacturer and an inventor, was standing in Jackson Street watching five horses trying to pull a crowded horsecar up the steep Jackson Street grade. One of the horses slipped and fell. The driver jammed on the brake. A chain snapped. The car slid backward down the hill, dragging the horses with it. At the level of an intersection, the driver managed to stop the car. After Hallidie helped extricate the horses from their tangled harness, he continued his walk, pondering. There must, he thought, be another way.

Four years later, his other way was ready. The innumerable technical difficulties had been tackled and met. Some $100,000 had been spent. Public indifference had been bitterly recognized and accepted. And now the trial was about to take place. Steam hissed from the boilers of the powerhouse at Clay and Leavenworth Streets. The tracks, the slot and the endless cable beneath the street reached down the hill, past Dupont Street, past Portsmouth Square to Kearny. Poised on the hill's summit was the dummy car, with the cable grip mounted on it, and behind the dummy, the tiny, top-heavy passenger trailer. The city was dark and quiet in the early morning fog.

At a signal from Hallidie, the wheels in the powerhouse began to turn and there rose for the first time the high, eerie song of the cables that you still hear whining from the California and the Powell Street slots. With the inventor at the controls and a few of his friends and backers nervously holding their hats and clutching the trailer seat, the first cable car moved over the crest of the hill. Gradually and smoothly, it descended the hill. Responding to Hallidie's testing, it stopped and started, stopped and started. At the end of the line at Kearny Street, it was swung around on a turntable. Then it climbed back up past Portsmouth Square, past Dupont, to the top of the hill. When they reached the starting point, Hallidie and the passengers stepped to the street and solemnly shook hands. The damned thing worked.

It is said the only nonparticipating eyewitness to the experiment was a Frenchman living in Clay Street. Wakened by the rattling of the cable, he stuck his head out the window, tossed a musty bouquet of flowers at the cable car, and went back to sleep.

That afternoon, to the accompaniment of considerable rowdiness, the cable car made its first public journey up and down the hill. Happy spectators, including a breezy element from the Barbary Coast a few blocks away, shoved the dummy onto the turntable so enthusiastically that a grip bolt broke and had to be repaired on the spot before the trip could begin. When the car got under way at last, nearly a hundred passengers jammed the dummy and trailer, built to hold twenty-five. Hanging from the roof, bawling themselves hoarse, they rode up the hill and back again. At Dupont Street, firecrackers popped in salute and grinning Chinese in ceremonial robes stood at the curbing watching them go by. One of them—no Confucius—summed up the cable car with a saying that has become a San Francisco classic: "No pushee, no pullee. Allee samee go like hellee."

Back at the Kearny Street turntable, on the corner of Portsmouth Square, beaming city officials congratulated Hallidie and agreed that it was indeed a great day for the Queen City of the Pacific. The cable car, they said, was an engineering miracle; it was here to stay.

Six years after that, a tall, lean, young foreigner, outlandishly dressed, wandered into Portsmouth Square and sank slowly to a bench. Anyone could see from the strange way his dark eyes glowed and from the almost luminous pallor of his sensitive face that he was ill. But he had come a long way to be there on Portsmouth Square, in San Francisco, and he looked about him with lively curiosity, absorbing the sights and sounds and smells of the Square, the feel of the still young and fabulous city.

On his arrival from Monterey, he had toiled up the Bush Street hill, looking for a home. A step beyond Stockton Street, he came to a curious house, the house of Mrs. Mary Carson. Originally, it had been a two-story cottage that had been brought around the Horn in sections. But some time during its existence its owners had decided to enlarge it, which they accomplished by jacking up the cottage and building a new ground floor beneath it. Across its front, on all three floors, extended balconies and green-shuttered windows. But what interested the stranger most was a sign in the front window. It read, "Furnished Rooms to Let." He knocked on the door, and, when Mrs. Carson answered, he said he would like to inspect a room.

Mrs. Carson hesitated. Two foreigners had just disappeared from her house, leaving behind an unpaid bill for several months' rent, and this caller was, without a doubt, also a foreigner. "He was such a strange-looking, shabby shack of a fellow," she said later. "He wore a little brown rough ulster, buttoned up tight under his chin, and Scotch brogues, the walking kind, laced up high, and his pants stuck in the tops, and a dicer hat."

So it was with no eager cordiality that Mrs. Carson led him upstairs to a large room, second floor front, threw open the door and said, "Here is all there is of it." But the stranger was satisfied with what he saw; he gave Mrs. Carson an advance payment on the rent, departed, and later that same day returned with two pieces of luggage and moved in. The signature she read in her registry by no means allayed Mrs. Carson's fears,

for she had never heard of it. Neatly and finely, it said, "Robert Louis
Stevenson."

Far from his native Scotland, desperately poor and suffering from lung
trouble, Stevenson lived at 608 Bush Street (now above the Stockton
Street tunnel and the address of a barbershop) until May, 1880, and there
spent what he once said were the unhappiest days of his life. It was in the
bare room at Mrs. Carson's that he finished *The Amateur Emigrant,* a
series of sketches based on his Atlantic crossing, and wrote a large part
of *Across the Plains,* a collection of travel pieces describing his journey
from New York to San Francisco.

It was from there, too, that he set out on his long streetcar rides about
the city, and his trips to the waterfront, where he would board a ferry
and ride back and forth across the Bay. On days when he was too weary
to ride, he would wander down to Portsmouth Square and watch the
people come and go.

In contrast to Kipling, who lived and dined elegantly at the Palace
during his visit to San Francisco, Stevenson ate a ten-cent breakfast of
coffee and rolls in a Sixth Street restaurant, just off Market Street. He
would have a meager lunch at Donadieu's, on Bush between Dupont and
Kearny, and then return to Sixth Street for his dinner. When this proved
too extravagant, and he was forced to limit his eating expenses to forty-
five cents a day, he eliminated the lunch at Donadieu's.

In the unhappy days of that winter, the lonely traveler sat in Portsmouth Square, brooding and dreaming in the warm February sun. He
saw the pigtailed Chinese in their blue linen suits and hats of woven
straw; the sailors in from the South Seas, where he one day was destined
to die; the bustling stock traders; the wretched derelicts of Pauper Alley;
the street venders and the street preachers, selling salted peanuts and
liniments and salvation; the beggars and the castaways, resting like him
and like him feeling the sunshine on their shoulders and their gaunt
faces; the Kearny Street promenaders, fashionably and expensively
dressed, the women daintily lifting their dust ruffles and flounces clear of
the dusty pavement or shutting their bright parasols as they crossed the
street to the corner by the cable car turntable to board a car bound up
the hill, or engage a hack at the stand on that corner of the Square.

As he sat there, watching the movement and the life with his dark, thoughtful eyes, Stevenson could not help but marvel at what he saw. "I wonder," he mused, "what enchantment of the *Arabian Nights* can have equaled this evocation of a roaring city in a few years of a man's life, from the marshes and the blowing sand."

West of Portsmouth Square, Washington Street climbed through Chinatown to Stockton Street, past the gardens and the hand-wrought iron fence of the mansion that stood on that corner (it was the home of Captain Martin R. Roberts, the shipping baron, and father of Actor Theodore Roberts); past the mansion, stables and green lawns of the millionaire J. B. Haggin; past the old Ebbets homestead (built by a pioneer whose mercantile firm, one year in the Fifties, had made $50,000 from the sale of top hats); past that, and up over the shoulder of Nob Hill. Then it descended to Van Ness Avenue and then, like Broadway, its parallel street three blocks away, it scaled the heights called Pacific.

There was in those days on the summit of the heights a little park called Lafayette Square. Children play there now; the nursemaids from the nearby and palatial homes of the rich wheel their baby carriages along its gravel paths, and oldsters sit on its benches swapping yarns and admiring the view; but in the early Seventies two men erected a small telescope there, and gazed at the stars.

This crude observatory brought together on that hilltop a strange pair— George Davidson, the cultured and learned president of the California Academy of Sciences, and bewhiskered James Lick, the crude, shrewd and illiterate realist, the crafty Midas, the Pennsylvania piano maker who had arrived in San Francisco in '47, amassed a $4,000,000 fortune in real estate and now lived in conditions bordering on squalor in a private room of his own Lick House, the best and most elegant hotel in town. (So eccentric was he, it is said, he once discharged a gardener for refusing to obey orders; he had given the gardener a rare shrub, and commanded him to plant it upside down.)

Peering through Davidson's telescope, Lick fell in love with the stars and their serene and mysterious fire, perhaps because even with all his power and money they were forever unobtainable and beyond his reach. But he resolved to do what he could to bring them to earth, and in 1879, three years after his death, with $700,000 he had set aside in his will for that purpose, workmen began construction of the great Lick Observatory on Mt. Hamilton.

Davidson, the man who revealed to Lick the majestic pageant of the stars and perhaps the only beauty that ever touched his lonely life, was in many respects the more remarkable of the two. There are authorities who say he was the most remarkable man who ever lived in California. His name is perpetuated in San Francisco by Mt. Davidson, upon whose summit (the highest point in the city) stands the massive, one-hundred-three-foot Easter cross.

A picture taken of the scientist in 1910, the year before his death, showed him as a white-haired, white-bearded man of strongly molded features and an intense and domineering air. By that time, he had received awards from some thirty-five distinguished scientific organizations of Europe and America. World-famous institutions of learning had granted him honorary degrees, and foreign rulers had showered him with decorations. His published books, scientific papers and reports numbered more than three hundred, and covered subjects ranging from the transit of the planet Venus to micrometers, from the sewers of London to the temperature of the waters of the Golden Gate, from the boomerangs of California Indians to the static oceanography of the coastal waters of Alaska.

Davidson was a self-made scientist. Born in Nottingham, England, he had been brought by his parents, at the age of seven, to Philadelphia. What education he had he received from his mother and the Philadelphia public schools. But the genius he possessed revealed itself early in his life; at seventeen, his grasp of astronomy earned for him a position as night observer and computer at the observatory of Philadelphia's Girard College. At twenty-five, he arrived on the Pacific Coast as head of a geographical and astronomical expedition sent out by the United States Coast Survey. The year was 1850, and from then on, except for the many months he spent traveling and at sea, his home was San Francisco.

In 1858, Davidson married Ellinor Fauntleroy, youngest daughter of Robert Henry Fauntleroy of Virginia and granddaughter of Robert Owen, the noted Scotch philanthropist and educator who had founded the Owenite community at New Harmony, Indiana. Early in their marriage, they had three children, Thomas, George and Ellinor.

You would think that these three children were indeed fortunate, that they had every advantage wealth, a distinguished father and an aristocratic mother could give them. And so they were; but George committed suicide in 1900 at the age of thirty; Thomas, the first-born, died in 1934 after a lonely and unhappy life, and only Ellinor lived to achieve a happiness. It came to her, mostly, in the last years of her life, in the years when, to the children at their games in Lafayette Square, she was known as the Lady of the Haunted House.

A few years ago—it was 1946—there stood on the heights half a block from the square a four-story, twenty-room, brown-shingled house, No. 2221 Washington Street. Built in the 1890's, it towered gloomily over the gleaming and modern duplex homes that surrounded it, and stood as a sullen rebuke to their clean white stucco, their bright flowers, their shining windows, their smooth, trim lines. In that house, Ellinor Davidson had lived alone in a world that had been dead for many years.

The house was empty in 1946; it had been more than a year since neighbors called police to investigate its strange quiet, and the police broke through the massive front door to find Ellinor dead in her bed, the victim of a heart ailment. Soon the children of the neighborhood would no longer whisper about the mystery of the house and the candlelight that glimmered from its dark windows in the nighttime when Ellinor was alive. No longer would they have a house to call "The Haunted House of Washington Street," for Ellinor had written in her will that if her heirs refused to live in the house, it was to be destroyed. And now, within a few weeks, the wreckers would be going to work.

She had lived alone there since Thomas' death. He had been an expert title searcher in a San Francisco law firm, and had been little company for her. Of his own accord, he went to work at four o'clock in the afternoon and stayed at the office until midnight. Then, every night, he would seal his personal valuables—his rings, his watch, his wallet—in a stamped, self-addressed envelope and put the envelope in an outside coat pocket, where, if accosted by a thief, he could easily reach it and perhaps drop it in a mailbox before turning to confront the bandit.

Thomas had a strongly mechanical turn of mind; he claimed the invention of the stop-and-go traffic signal, and his hobby was the dismantling of clocks and watches.

One night, he arrived home, left his hat on the hall table downstairs, went up to his room and died of a heart attack. Ten years later, when the police entered the house seeking Ellinor, his hat was still there, dusty and untouched, on the hall table.

Twelve months passed before the executors of Ellinor's $250,000 estate had organized and catalogued the thousands of souvenirs and relics, objects of art and books, the clothes and the furniture, the scientific instruments and heirlooms which had littered every room and every closet of the old house. Four moving vans had carted away to the University of California and the California Academy of Sciences the priceless collection of books, papers and maps that had belonged to her father.

But even so, even after all that had been taken away, to step into the chill and sunless rooms was to step into an era and a life that had been illuminated by the steady flare of gaslight. Standing in the gloomy downstairs hall and looking into the three large living rooms, you felt that the clocks in this house had stopped ticking a long time ago.

Gaslight chandeliers of ornate brass, with crepe-covered glass reflectors, hung from the moldering ceilings. On one wall hung a large, original William Keith landscape; on another, over a fireplace, the ponderous head and antlers of a moose. A fifth van load of books and papers was stacked in bookcases and on the floors. In one corner stood a lacquered chest which the Japanese government had presented Professor Davidson after he had been to Japan to observe the transit of Venus. A card attached to it said it was to be crated and shipped to the Metropolitan Museum in New York.

The furniture was simple and sturdy, and cane-bottomed chairs rested on rich Persian rugs. Here and there, on tables and window sills, were plain candlesticks, still holding the half-burnt candles that Ellinor had used to find her way around the house at night; she had never permitted the installation of electricity in her house. In one corner of the last large room was a tiny coal fireplace, and one of the two overstuffed chairs in the house. On another chair nearby was an old-fashioned battery radio, with a loop aerial and receivers on a headset.

In the high, dark butler's pantry on the same floor was the two-burner gas range on which Ellinor cooked her own meals. In the dining room, beside the cheap pottery cups and saucers she used, was stacked a complete set of Wedgewood china. Upstairs, in Professor Davidson's study, was the wooden bedstead he had slept on. Over the head was draped an American flag. Its field bore thirty-five stars. When executors broke into a closet in this room, they discovered five urns on a shelf; the urns contained the ashes of Ellinor's father, mother, two brothers and an aunt.

Two stuffed owls sat on the floor of the upstairs hall. Workmen, ripping open the door of a closet in this hall, fled in fright when they beheld a dozen human skulls on the closet floor—anthropological specimens brought back by the professor from one of his trips to the South Seas.

On the bureau in Ellinor's room was the tortoise-shell ear trumpet she used and her steel-rimmed spectacles. Stuck into the mirror frame was a photograph of her, taken at the 1940 Golden Gate International Exposition. It showed a tall, gaunt woman with dark hair and eyes, and there was nothing about it to tell that she was a lonely or a haunted woman. There was even the suggestion of a happy smile on her face.

But there was no doubt about it. As you walked through the damp and gloomy house and saw the things she had treasured—the notebooks with old theater programs pasted in them, the worn copy of Burke's Peerage of the year 1915, the newspaper clippings of three decades ago, her mother's trousseau, the letters from friends long since gone—you knew that Ellinor had made a bargain: she had traded the present for the past, the living for the dead. As she sat in the candlelight, there must have been faces in the shadows, faces she had loved. And so real and vivid did they seem, their presence warmed her heart, even as the dancing flames in the fireplace warmed her body. And in them lay her reality, and the secret of her strange content.

That house is gone now, and in its place stand two of the white modern homes against which it held out for so many years. Over the hills and three miles east on the waterfront, the theaters and bars of Washington Street are gone too, and where they were are the sheds and warehouses of the commission district, destination of the Diesel trucks that come pounding in from the valleys in the early morning with lettuce and grapefruit, oranges and artichokes, avocados and the deep-purple egg-plants, still warm from the rich valley earth and the hot valley sun.

Portsmouth Square is a drowsy place where old men sleep under the trees and Chinese bootblacks play on the bright grass and roving evangelists beseech you to consider your ways and repent before it is too late. The Hall of Justice rises somber and foreboding on the site of the old El Dorado and the Jenny Lind Theater, and the cable cars no longer climb Clay Street, past the Square.

There is a monument now beneath the trembling poplar trees of Portsmouth Square, erected to the memory of the lonely young author who sat there in the sun in his brogues and ulster and dicer hat, and watched the world go by. On a small granite shaft are inscribed the tender lines from his *Christmas Sermon,* "To be honest, to be kind—to earn a little, to spend a little less, to make upon the whole a family happier for his presence, to renounce when that shall be necessary and not be embittered, to keep a few friends, but these without capitulation—above all, on the same grim condition, to keep friends with himself—here is a task for all that a man has of fortitude and delicacy."

On top of the shaft is a little bronze galleon, pennants streaming out and sails swelling as if before a good and steady wind.

There is a legend about the ship, and one about the Square. It is said that on moonlight nights the little vessel slips her moorings and puts out to sea, manned by a phantom crew. And it is said that on these same nights, if you listen hard in the moonlight, you can hear the pounding of hoofs across an old plaza; you can hear a croupier calling, and the far-away strains of a gambling-hall tune.

9. CALIFORNIA STREET

THE WASHOE, AND RAILS REACHING EAST • "LOOK OUT FOR THE SOUND-
INGS!" • THE MOUNTAIN'S SECRET, AND THE WASHOE CURSE. THE GROSCH
BROTHERS. DEATH AT LAST CHANCE. OLD PANCAKE STATES HIS TERMS.
FORTUNE'S FOOLS • THE COMSTOCK MADNESS. "BEDLAM LET LOOSE" • DIA-
MONDS IN THE DESERT. ASBURY HARPENDING AND THE CONFEDERATE PLOT.
THE GREAT HOAX. "HONOR BRIGHT—?" • THE NABOBS OF NOB HILL •
NORTON I, FAIRY TALE MONARCH • OLD ST. MARY'S: CATHEDRAL OF PIO-
NEERS • PAST AND PRESENT

THINK OF a blazing sun in a hot, blue sky, and a barren mountain in the
region called the Washoe. Think of a handful of bearded, sweating, sun-
burnt men swinging their puny picks beneath that sun and that sky,
plunging them into the mountain's crumbling crust while the dry desert
wind sears their throats and stings their eyes.

Think, also, of two steel rails, reaching north and east from the willow-
shaded banks of the Sacramento, bending together, climbing together,
reaching to the foothills of that river valley, mounting through the Sierra
pines and bridging the Sierra canyons to Emigrant Gap, where the west-

159

ward plodding wagon trains left the summit twenty years before and lurched on their high wheels down to the Bear Valley flats; reaching onward, tie after tie, rail after rail (as the Chinese coolies dug the earth from their path and broke the granite for the rail beds and gasped from the pain of the thin, sharp, pine-scented air stabbing their lungs); twenty miles and twenty days more and through the Donner Pass, the twin rails snaking beneath the snowsheds and then down among the cottonwoods of the Truckee River Valley, and then across the sweet-smelling meadows, and ever toward the sunrise.

Think of all this when you think of California Street as it is today, because, before these things happened, and even while they were happening, it was just a street that began down near the waterfront, ran west and level to Montgomery Street, and then climbed a steep and grassy hill and lost itself in the chaparral, trailing off in the shifting dunes of the western city.

When Montgomery Street was the town's Fifth Avenue and Washington Street its Rialto, Forty-niners pitched their tents in the middle of California Street, up the hill from Leidesdorff's cottage. The Tehama House was also on the street, a shipping firm or two, and some boarding-houses—Mrs. Moon's, Mrs. Petit's, Mrs. Leland's—but in 1853, horses and carts fell through the holes in the planks of California Street and foundered in the mud beneath, and wags scrawled arrows pointing to the holes, and scrawled signs which read, "Office to let in the basement; William Diver, agent," and "Horse and dray lost below; look out for the soundings."

That was the year, with wood from China, they started building the church now called Old St. Mary's halfway up the California Street hill, on the corner of Dupont, and some of the parishioners grumbled because it was so far from town. And by that year time, chance and the lust for gold had drawn closer together from Dublin and County Tyrone, from Ohio, Connecticut and the Hudson River valley, the shrewd peddlers, the wily adventurers and the saloonkeepers who would one day rule this street from the vulgar and garish mansions they built upon its hilltop.

Where were they then? The suave and charming Billy Ralston was selling shipping space for a steamship agency in Panama. Charlie Crocker was driving bargains in hairnets and chemises from behind the counter of a

Sacramento dry-goods store, and learning the secret of his success: "Make a dollar buy a dollar and five cents' worth of material." Hopkins and Huntington hawked beans and bacon, shovels and nails, to Mother Lode miners. Mackay was handling a pick at Downieville and Fair was panning the Feather River sands for specks of gold dust, and Flood and O'Brien were pushing rum across the bar of their Auction Lunch saloon in Washington Street, sweeping the floor and swabbing the mahogany and passing the time of day over a game of euchre with the boys in the back room.

Two or three hundred miles east, on the other side of the Sierra divide, the bleak and rugged mountain rose to meet the Nevada sky, as it had for so many eons. Two men knew, or thought they knew, the secret that lay hidden beneath its peak and deep within its bowels. Emigrants, toiling westward across the Nevada wastelands, cursed it because it stood in their path, circled it and stumbled on to El Dorado, and in a few days it grew blurred and blue on a horizon they had left behind.

In a canyon cut deep into the southern face of the mountain, not far from where the swift Carson River veers to the southwest, Mormon emigrants discovered gold in 1850, and they named it Gold Canyon. But the dust was thin and pale, and nuggets the size of their fists (they believed) awaited them beyond the Sierra, and so they pushed on to California. A few years later, there was a tiny mining community at the mouth of Gold Canyon, and another one a few miles above it, a settlement of a dozen shanties and a few tents called Johntown. Out of these camps, in the winter and spring when there was water in the canyon bed, went miners to whom thin, pale dust was better than none at all, and with their toms and rockers they took $5 or $10 a day from the canyon gravel, enough to see them through an evening of faro or twenty-one, or the "grand ball" that rocked Dutch Nick's saloon in Johntown every Saturday night. Wherever they worked, they encountered a strange and aggravating blue substance, like sand or like tiny scales of sheet lead, that clogged their rockers and delayed the washing of the gravel. Cursing it, they clawed it out of the rockers and threw it aside and swore that if they had to put up with much more of it, they'd pull up stakes and head for the Hang-town diggings over on the Mother Lode.

Among them were two young brothers from Utica, New York, Edgar Allen and Hosea B. Grosch, who had come over the Sierra from Vol-cano, California, in 1852. Intelligent, well educated and schooled in min-eralogy, they grew curious about the blue substance. Secretly they tested it, grinding it, baking it, exposing it to acids. When they were through, they filled their trembling hands with the blue mineral and stared at it, bright-eyed and incredulous. Now they knew, and it was beyond belief: those hands held an ore that was nearly solid silver!

Looking back to what happened to them, and what later happened to the others, superstitious miners can say that at that moment there fell upon the young brothers the curse of Mt. Davidson, which hounded to their graves the men who first blundered upon its secret, just as the curse of the Mother Lode mocked and tormented its discoverer, James Marshall, until the day he died a pauper. For even before they began to mine the silver mountain they had found, Hosea and Edgar Allen Grosch were dead.

Hosea struck a pick into his foot, and died of blood poisoning. Three months later, Allen started across the Sierra to raise money with which to open the great vein. Caught in a swirling mountain blizzard, he stumbled and crawled over the desolate wastes for eleven days. Then, near collapse from hunger and exhaustion, he was found by a party of deer-hunting prospectors on the western slope of the divide, and was taken to the Placer County mining camp Last Chance. Both legs were frozen from his thighs to his toes. He refused to have them amputated, and died babbling crazy things about his brother, Gold Canyon, and a strange ore that was the color of the Nevada sky.

Like a devil, the mountain haunted the others, too; to the peddlers and adventurers and saloonkeepers, it yielded staggering riches, and treasure enough to pave California Street with silver and gold, but to the men like the Grosch brothers, the men who unlocked its fabulous magazines, it dealt poverty, madness and death.

There are no monuments to them in California Street, no stone to the memory of those who at last revealed that Big Bonanza which, in less than two decades, showered $300,000,000 on San Francisco and crowned her a queen among cities.

There is no plaque, for instance, saying it was on a clear and lovely day in June, 1859, that two men—Irishmen named Pete O'Riley and Pat Mc-Laughlin—drove their picks into the black dirt of Six Mile Canyon, a few miles northeast of Johntown. . . .

The black dirt contained gold, and plenty of it, and the prospectors shook with excitement as they swung their rockers and dumped the yellow stuff into a pile on the ground. There was the blue sand again, and now a blackish rock which hampered their work. They swore at it and tossed it out of their way. Above them blazed the sun, and all around them the western breeze stirred the sage, and beneath them as they worked, warm and deep within the mountain, lay the vein of Ophir that would give up $20,000,000 in silver, but not to them.

That evening, Old Pancake Comstock, another prospector, roamed the mountain side in search of his straying mustang. When he found it, he rode to O'Riley's and McLaughlin's little camp. He dismounted, got down on his knees and ran his fingers through their gleaming dust. "Boys," he said as he rose, "you've struck it." He looked at the diggings, at the spangled earth that lay about them. "There's just one thing," he added. "You're working on my land."

Coolly, he laid his terms on the line: O'Riley and McLaughlin had to move on unless they let him and his friend Manny Penrod in on the claim. Furthermore, Old Pancake went on, there was the matter of the sluice boxes and the spring whose water they were using to wash the dirt; he owned all of that, too, he and Jim Hart and Jim Fennimore, the grizzled, hard-drinking miner known the length and breadth of the Washoe as "Old Virginia."

Confronted by these complications, O'Riley and McLaughlin decided they might as well yield to Comstock. Within the next few days, there were some very swift deals. Legend has it that Comstock persuaded Old Virginia to sell his share in the claim for a blind horse, a pair of blankets and a bottle of whisky. J. D. Winters bought out Hart's interest for a horse and $20 cash. Winters, along with J. A. Osborne, agreed to furnish two arrastras, or mule-powered quartz grinders, and Osborne was admitted into the partnership.

So that made six men in the Ophir Company, staking out the first claim along the vein—O'Riley, McLaughlin, Comstock, Penrod, Winters and Osborne.

Before long, several things happened. The first was that Old Pancake's bragging and blustering about the strike led people to believe he had discovered the Ophir, and it began to be known as his mine and as the Comstock Lode. The second was the discovery of what the Grosch brothers had known six years before and died without revealing: the blue substance the Johntowners had damned and thrown away—and not only that but the black rock, too—was loaded with silver.

Within a matter of weeks, the mountain passes from California were choked with fortune hunters, Washoe-bound to make a million, and Virginia City was a wide-open, rip-roaring boom town. And the six men were off on their hay ride to oblivion.

Dazzled by cash offers for their shares in the mine and convinced the vein would dwindle to nothing in a matter of days or weeks, they began to sell out. Comstock sold for $11,000, and gloated over the hard bargain he had driven. McLaughlin sold for $3500, Osborne for $7000, Penrod for $3000. O'Riley, last of the six to leave the Ophir, got $40,000. Winters' price does not seem to have been recorded, but it's safe to say that, like the rest, he sold for a song. Bancroft, who later traced him, says he left the Lode and went to California, "where he was no better off than the others."

Osborne went east, and faded out of sight. Penrod died broke. McLaughlin, in 1875, twenty-six years after he and O'Riley made the great strike, was working as a cook in Southern California. As for O'Riley, he took his $40,000 and built a hotel in Virginia City. A few years later, he plunged heavily in mining stock, lost, and died insane. Old Pancake, whose name the Lode bears to this day, failed at merchandising in Carson City, and took to roaming the mountains, lured from gulch to gulch, from canyon to canyon, by the will-o'-the-wisp belief that he would once more strike it rich. But one day he got tired of looking and sat down beside the Bozeman trail in Montana and blew out his brains.

What happened to San Francisco in the years following the discovery of the Lode they sometimes call "the Comstock madness." As the subterranean drifts and crosscuts of the Ophir, the Yellow Jacket, the Kentuck, the Gould and Curry, the Con. Virginia, the Hale and Norcross, the Eclipse and some forty other mines yielded million after shining million, California Street and the rest of the town climbed on a stock market merry-go-round that whirled dizzily for the next twenty years.

It was a rough ride; but the lucky ones, the tough ones, the ones with a long reach, managed to grab a brass ring now and then, and when they did it was the life of Riley for them for the rest of their days—blooded horses and Nob Hill mansions, mistresses and Poodle Dog champagne, and enough left over to buy Italian counts and British lords for their daughters.

Daily, you could see how it went to the town's head. California Street, where the big banks were—Billy Ralston's Bank of California, the London and San Francisco Bank, the Merchants' Exchange Bank, the Anglo-California Bank—and where the Big Board of the San Francisco Stock Exchange was, was jammed for two blocks with curbstone brokers and their yelling customers. Police attempted vainly to make way through the crowds for wagons and carriages. "All day long," wrote Lloyd, "their yells and screams are heard for half a block away. They jibber and cavil and quarrel—now howling like enraged beasts, now giving vent to maniacal screams that would almost shock the nerves of the superintendent of an insane asylum."

Pompous, stiff-shirted patrons of the Big Board, when Comstock Lode stocks hit the market, were no better behaved: "They spring from their chairs and rush furiously into the 'cockpit,' or open space in front of the caller's stand. There is no order. All cry out at once. They shout their offers to buy or sell. They jostle and push each other about like frightened animals before a stampede. They rush from one place to another, wildly gesticulating, stamping and chafing as if infuriate. They froth at the mouth from excessive screaming. They yell and scream until their voices grow husky. . . . Bedlam let loose would scarce rival the scene."

It was a world where anything could happen, where Aladdin and his lamp would have been a tawdry side show, and the men who were making it go around began to believe themselves giants of infallibility. They believed this so thoroughly not one of them blinked an eye when a couple of prospectors proposed to dump a new kind of fortune in their laps—a fortune in sparkling diamonds, rubies and sapphires plucked by the bushel basket from the desolate badlands of Wyoming. Up and down California Street, the giants greedily rubbed their hands. At last, they told themselves, this was the game fate had been saving them for. The Comstock had been a mere practice scrimmage, a warm-up rehearsal. Croesus, they said, move over; you're going to have company.

As far as Asbury Harpending was concerned, he said the whole thing began late in 1871, when he was over in London publishing a financial newspaper called *The Stock Exchange Review*. Billy Ralston sent him from San Francisco a cable so long it had cost Ralston $1100.

On reading the cable, Harpending said he thought Ralston had gone out of his mind. It said a great diamond field, worth at the very least $50,000,000, had been discovered in a remote area of the West. The find was so fabulously rich, you could pick priceless gems out of anthills. Ralston and Mining Engineer George D. Roberts had established control over the discovery. "Drop everything. Take the next steamer. We need you for our general manager," the cable concluded.

Ralston and Harpending were two of a kind: they were both plungers. Ralston had arrived in San Francisco in 1854. A few years later, his strange and undisciplined genius had lifted him to a position where, as founder and manager of the powerful Bank of California, he was carving his own personal empire out of the West. He and his associates controlled the richest mines on the Comstock Lode, the Pacific shipping lanes, the inland waterways. He smiled on a man, and that man became a millionaire. Alone, he forged a new trinity in the West, and horny-fisted miners from Virginia City to Hangtown tossed off bottoms-up toasts of forty-rod to "Whisky, God and the Bank of California!"

Harpending, tall, dark, twenty years old, Kentucky-born and a passionate supporter of the Confederacy, had reached San Francisco six years after Ralston with $250,000 in cash and a million more where that came from—in a Mexican gold mine. With sure judgment and without the slightest hesitation, he entered upon a series of spectacular and successful real estate deals that made the wizards of California Street look like a troop of Rip Van Winkles. When they woke up to what was going on, they realized they had a boy wonder on their hands.

They didn't have to worry about him very long. One night in 1863, armed sailors of the United States man-of-war *Cyane* boarded the clipper schooner *Chapman* a few hours before she was due to leave San Francisco for southern waters. On board they found an arsenal of cannon, rifles and ammunition, about thirty armed men, and—Asbury Harpending.

Examination of the ship's secret papers disclosed a fantastic piracy plot. Harpending and his fellow conspirators had planned to seize the steamship *Oregon* at sea, transfer their arms to her and use her to capture two vessels outward bound from San Francisco with cargoes of Comstock gold and silver. Then they were going to sail to Vancouver and there divide the spoils. With this money, they intended to organize and arm a state-wide secret society that would start an insurrection at Sacramento, cut all telegraph lines to the East, board and capture a Sacramento River steamer, run down the river to Benicia, seize the government arsenal there and then capture Fort Point and Alcatraz in San Francisco Bay. When this was accomplished, they would declare California out of the Union and run up the Confederate flag over every city and hamlet from the Oregon line to the Gulf of California.

The ringleaders of this plot, Harpending, Ridgely Greathouse and Alfred Rubery, an Englishman, were convicted of treason and sentenced to ten years in prison and $10,000 fines. Authorities apparently did not consider the young secessionists a serious threat to the Union cause, however, for they were released within a few months.

A year after the Civil War ended, Harpending again bobbed up in San Francisco, his pockets this time bulging with gold he had picked up in a mining venture in California's Tulare County. Now he and Ralston became fast friends and engaged together in various large-scale promotion projects, one of which resulted directly in the construction of Market Street's luxurious, four-hundred-room Grand Hotel, and later in the building of the world-famous Palace Hotel.

This sort of thing had been good, honest speculation and all right as far as Harpending was concerned, but when he received the cable he said he believed his friend had fallen for a myth; the old master had cracked up at last. He wired back that he was too busy to become general manager of the Ralston diamond company. Back came cable after frantic cable filled with expensively worded assurances, pleas and promises. At length, Harpending weakened. He arrived in San Francisco in May, 1872, and before twenty-four hours had passed, he was head over heels in the fantastic affair that has gone down in California Street history as The Great Diamond Hoax.

According to Harpending, the situation when he reached San Francisco was this:

Philip Arnold and John Slack, two prospectors, had walked into the Bank of California one day with a bag of uncut diamonds and several large rubies. Questioned by Ralston, Roberts and William Lent, a financier, the pair said they had found the diamonds in a desert. They refused to locate the diamond field, except to admit that it was about one thousand miles from San Francisco.

Ralston, Roberts and Lent got down to brass tacks: would the prospectors sell any or all of their interest in the diamond mine? Arnold and Slack hemmed and hawed, and at length cautiously said they would, for a certain large sum.

The financiers demanded more concrete evidence of the existence of the diamond field. That was fine with Arnold and Slack, under these conditions: they would conduct any two men selected by the trio to the field and allow them to look it over, but they must be blindfolded while approaching the area and leaving it. Agreeing with these terms, the financiers sent two men (Harpending believed one of them to be David D. Colton, associate of the Central Pacific's "Big Four") to the place in the desert. They returned to San Francisco and reported that it was the truth: there was a diamond field, and it was rich beyond a man's wildest dream.

Now Slack and Arnold further agreed to go into the desert and bring back several million dollars' worth of stones and deposit them with Ralston as proof of their good faith. They were on this expedition when Harpending arrived from London. A few days later, Harpending met the prospectors at Lathrop, California. Weary and travel-stained, they handed him one buckskin package of stones. They had had another, they said, but lost it while fording a river. But what the hell, they added, there was probably a million dollars' worth in the package they had saved, so what difference did it make?

Leaving them at Oakland, Harpending hastened to San Francisco on a ferry and drove swiftly to his Rincon Hill home, where Ralston and the others awaited him impatiently. "We did not waste time on ceremonies," wrote Harpending in his memoirs, *The Great Diamond Hoax.* "A sheet was spread on my billiard table, I cut the elaborate fastenings of the sack and, taking hold of the lower corners, dumped the contents.

"It seemed like a dazzling, many-colored cataract of light."

The play picked up speed. The financiers formed the San Francisco and New York Mining and Commercial Company, with a capital stock of $10,000,000. Twenty-five of California Street's most reputable and respected businessmen were permitted to buy $80,000 worth of stock each; they included one A. Gansl, Pacific Coast representative of Europe's House of Rothschild, which became the company's agent on the other side of the Atlantic. Colton resigned his lucrative position with the Central Pacific to become general manager. Ralston was named treasurer, and Harpending stayed on in the capacity of a sort of general agent. New York offices were opened with Samuel Barlow, a leader of the New York bar, and General George B. McClellan as resident directors. Plans were made to import Antwerp's ancient lapidary establishments, lock, stock and emery wheel, to San Francisco, which would thus become the new center of the world's diamond-cutting industry.

Tiffany's of New York examined a mere handful of the Arnold and Slack diamonds, and valued them conservatively at $150,000. Henry Janin, a nationally known mining engineer, inspected the diamond field and came away so awed by what he had seen that he promptly bought one thousand shares of stock. There were diamonds, sapphires and rubies all over the place, in anthills, in the crevices of rocks and scattered upon the ground. Some members of Janin's party even insisted they had picked diamonds from the forks of trees. After his two-day examination of the field, Janin estimated that twenty-five ordinary day laborers could take $1,000,000 in gems from it in one month.

When his report was made public, letters poured into the company's San Francisco headquarters from all parts of the country pleading for opportunities to buy into the operation, at any price. The *New York Sun* printed a story signed "Old Miner" which located the field in Arizona and stated authoritatively that one of the diamonds found there was larger than a pigeon's egg and worth $500,000. Several expeditions of diamond hunters immediately set out for Arizona.

"The public," recalled Harpending, "was keyed up to the point of a speculative craze such as even the Comstock never saw, not alone in San Francisco but in nearly every financial center of the earth. . . . Not only that, but three other diamond and ruby companies were organized, each with fairly representative men behind them. One of these companies exposed to public view a gem that looked like the headlight of a locomotive, seen through a fog after dark. It was known as the Staunton Ruby. . . . No one seemed able to give more than a guess at its value, but the opinion was unanimous that only some rich and powerful nation could purchase it, to adorn a scepter or a crown. All of these companies were merely marking time, waiting till the great, proved, unquestioned company should say 'play ball' and start a speculative market for everyone."

Meanwhile, the lucky ones on the ground floor cagily held on to their shares, bought out Arnold and Slack for a paltry $660,000 and proceeded with arrangements to legalize their claim to three thousand acres of diamonds that sparkled across the Wyoming badlands.

The blow fell abruptly and without warning November 10, 1872. From a whistle stop in Wyoming, Clarence King, a government geologist, wired the company that he had investigated the diamond field and found it to be salted from one end to the other and a complete fraud. The gems which the company's inspectors had gleefully dug from the ground with jackknives had been skillfully planted in holes made with sharp sticks and then covered with earth, and the earth tamped down. Even the ant-hills that had glittered so prettily with diamond and ruby dust were fakes; they were man-made, and no ant had ever so much as spent the night in one of them. And if the directors didn't believe all this, he could show them a gem which bore the most damning evidence of all—the marks of a stonecutter's tool.

When they got through investigating this appalling news, Ralston, Roberts, Colton and the rest stood revealed as the dupes of the greatest swindle San Francisco had seen since Honest Harry Meiggs sailed away to the South Seas. The stones, they discovered, had been inferior gems bought in wholesale lots in Europe for about $35,000; Tiffany's experts had made a horrible mistake; Janin, the eminent mining engineer, had been too dazzled by the possibilities of the diamond field to be thorough in his examination. There was nothing else for them to do but pay off the twenty-five stockholders, pocket their losses, dissolve the company and stay away from California Street until the town stopped laughing.

Slack, meanwhile, vanished completely, and was never traced. Arnold went back home to Kentucky and opened a bank. When pursued by Lent and accused of perpetrating the fraud, the prospector denied everything. It had all been on the level, he said; if any planting had been done, it had been done by "California scamps" after the diamond company bought out Slack and him. To exempt himself from any annoying litigation over the matter, he quieted Lent with a cash payment of $150,000. The next year he was wounded in a Hardin County shooting scrape, and not long after that pneumonia removed for all time one of the two men who perhaps knew the true story of The Great Diamond Hoax.

Some said there was a third, a master mind behind the plot, for whom Arnold and Slack were but efficient and convincing tools. This master mind, they said, was Asbury Harpending.

Many years after the scandal, and only a few years before his death in New York in 1923, Harpending returned to California to confront these accusations and clear his name and reputation by telling in *The Great Diamond Hoax* "the whole story of that strange incident so far as my knowledge of it extends."

He was only a dupe like the others, he said. He observed that he had had as much money as he wanted, a family of which he was proud and a respected standing in financial circles both in San Francisco and abroad.

"Honor bright," he asked, "does it not seem incredible that a man situated like myself, full of ambition and with everything to live for, would have engaged in an ignoble plot to fleece his friends and the public, a plot absolutely certain to drag him and all belonging to him through the dust?"

San Francisco long since conceded him the benefit of the doubt, but California Street has never answered Harpending's question. It hasn't said yes, and it hasn't said no.

It was, in a way, like an immense and frantic ballet whose participants are not sure whether they have been cast as clowns or heroes. The Diamond Hoax was a dance within a dance, a farce within the farce, amusing and distracting momentarily the mass of dancers, and when it was over the original and larger movement swept them all up once more into their grotesque round of jigs and caperings.

The screaming and bellowing around the curbstone brokers and the stock exchange boards filled the air again, more strident than before. Big buildings rose, towering over the street through whose rotting planks the horse-drawn carts had crashed less than twenty years before. During the noon hour, a place like Wainwright's Pantheon bar swarmed with millionaire capitalists who went there for their midday refreshers and a Lucullan free lunch which might have included anything from terrapin soup and roast pig to imported cheese and crackers. The brokers you would have found at Eppinger's, half a block off California on Leidesdorff, or up above Montgomery at Moraghan's Oyster Parlors, where, it is said, a drunken sailor once poured all the condiments on the counter over a plate of oysters and thus invented the oyster cocktail; or perhaps at Clem Dixon's Ale Vaults on Summer Street, next door to the California Market.

Whatever they did and wherever they went, they danced to music with a mechanical heart, the roar and banging of the stamp mills on the side of the Washoe mountain where those men had swung their pygmy picks, and the clatter of the overland train over those twin rails that now spanned the continent. Gradually, out of the carnival emerged its humpty-dumpty aristocracy, chosen on the principle that might was right and money was might, and where the money came from was that silver peak of the Washoe and those gleaming, bending rails of steel.

Flood, Fair, Mackay and O'Brien, beginning with picks and shovels and a barroom and Mrs. Flood's corned beef and cabbage and getting their start in Hale and Norcross, cannily extending their control to the Gould and Curry, the Best and Belcher and the Con. Virginia, the biggest bonanza of them all, with a jack pot that paid off $50,000 a day, every day; Billy Sharon, going to Virginia City as the agent of the Bank of California, advancing money here, foreclosing there, getting control, consolidating gains, buying low and selling high, getting out from under when the getting was good, cleverly, shrewdly, ruthlessly manipulating the markets and making himself many times a millionaire; Lucky Baldwin, the horse trader, buying in on the Crown Point mine at three dollars a share and selling out at a thousand and banking a cool $2,500,000; Huntington, Hopkins, Stanford and Crocker, plunging with $50,000 that represented the last penny of every one of them and listening to an engineer named Judah who had a dream about a trans-mountain railroad, and then by cold and crafty conquest building a thirty-million-acre empire of the rails which they ruled with a savagery that reaped them hundreds of millions in profits and a billing in Western history as The Four-Armed Cuttlefish.

They and their satellites took their Central Pacific and Comstock millions and went to the top of the California Street hill and there, where all the city could look upon them, and they could look over the roofs of the Chinatown slums upon the shining waters of the Bay, they built their mansions. With crude arrogance they erected their jigsaw and gingerbread palaces and crammed their stiff, gloomy rooms with gilt-framed paintings from France, acres of Persian carpets, marble statues from Italy, bronzes from Germany and nightmarish assortments of Victorian bric-a-brac from everywhere which both distracted and reassured them in their brief moments of doubt and uneasy discontent. They financed the construction of the California Street cable car line, whose dummies and trailers began running up and down the hill in April, 1878, and the masses in the valleys below found a name for their hill: Nob Hill. Today, San Franciscans explain it as a corruption of "nabob," "snob" or "knob," according to their personal philosophies and the history books they read.

So there they sat, on their hilltop high above the city, self-made men every one of them and successes in every sense of the great American tradition. With their millions, they bought everything money could buy, until there were two things left: the respect and devotion of the city they called home. These were things the city would not sell, to them or anyone else; but it gave them away, with morbid and desperate extravagance, to an old man who had nothing to give in return but a fairy tale.

Late on a certain day in January, 1880, a bearded, elderly gentleman strolled slowly along Dupont Street on his way to a meeting of the California Academy of Sciences in the old First Congregational Church building on the southwest corner of Dupont and California Streets. In contrast to his sedate bearing, he was outlandishly dressed in an ancient, brass-buttoned army uniform. Tarnished epaulettes rested upon his square shoulders, and upon his head was a hat with a dusty plume.

When he was almost there, when he had reached the corner opposite Old St. Mary's, this old man suddenly sank to the sidewalk. A passer-by named William Proll hastened to his assistance, dragged him to the building on the corner and lifted him to a sitting position against the wall. But the old man never regained consciousness; the apoplectic blow had been swift and mortal. Thus, without dignity and on a street corner at a quarter past eight in the evening, died Norton I, Emperor of the United States and Protector of Mexico.

At the city morgue they searched his pockets. They found $2.50 in gold, $3 in silver, a five-franc piece dated 1828, a number of the printed notes he was accustomed to give as security for twenty-five- and fifty-cent loans, and a sheaf of telegrams and cables. These were signed by such notables as Governor Perkins of California, John Parnell of Ireland, Beaconsfield, Prime Minister of England, and President Diaz of Mexico. One, from the Czar of Russia, congratulated Norton I on his approaching marriage to Queen Victoria.

The messages were palpable forgeries, sent to the Emperor by practical jokers with the connivance of friends in local telegraph offices. But that didn't matter particularly, because for twenty-three years the old man had lived in a world of make-believe, a world he had fashioned for himself and one in which forgeries were truths and dreams a reality.

Even to his death, some thought Norton I had cunningly contrived this make-believe world to disarm the city and conceal from it a mysteriously acquired wealth. But a curious reporter, visiting his tiny, lodginghouse room in Sacramento Street the night of his death, found only the pathetic furniture of his long illusion.

"There were many hats," the reporter wrote. "There was first an old stovepipe hat resting side by side with a little plaster cast of himself on the table. Directly above, hanging in a row on the wall, were three more—the first a derby hat. Next to this hung an old army cap bound with red lace, and next in line a regulation army hat, also trimmed with red, and which had apparently once adorned the cranium of a martial bandmaster, as was attested by the lyre which graced its front. On the wall opposite, over the bed, hung the well-known sword of the Emperor, and in the corner, against the bed, stood four canes, the gift of devoted 'subjects.'"

This room had for seventeen years been his palace. A chair at the table had been his throne, and on the table he had written his imperial proclamations. If he had any secrets, this room knew them, but it was as mute as he.

The facts were that Joshua A. Norton had been born about 1815 in the British Isles. Early in life he had sailed to South Africa and served for a time as a colonial rifleman. Leaving South Africa, he crossed the Atlantic to Brazil, where he prospered as a trader. In the fall of 1849, he boarded the Hamburg vessel *Franzika* at Rio de Janeiro, and arrived in San Francisco on November 5 of that year with $40,000 in his trunk.

In the booming real estate market, he increased his fortune to $250,000, and in 1854 he thought he saw a way to double it, maybe triple it, almost overnight. Quietly, he began to corner all the rice in the city. He bought every boatload in the harbor, and every one known to be at sea and en route to San Francisco. Slowly but steadily he forced the price of rice higher and higher, from fifteen to thirty-five cents a pound, from thirty-five cents to sixty. Soon he would push it even higher, to a dollar, two dollars. Then he would start to sell.

Three ships he had somehow overlooked came sailing through the Gate. They bore cargoes of rice, and Norton's ticket to ruin. Flooding the market, they destroyed his artificial price structure; Norton was wiped out. He paid off what debts he could and left the city.

When autopsy surgeons examined the brain of Norton I, they found no indications of insanity. On the contrary, they learned that it was in remarkably healthy condition and that it was in fact an ounce-and-a-half heavier than the average brain. But with the collapse of his rice corner, or sometime during his subsequent, three-year absence from the San Francisco scene, something must have snapped inside that brain, for he came back in 1857 convinced that he was a monarch.

He began the play by proclaiming himself Emperor of California. Soon, however, he decided it was unconstitutional for California to be an empire when it was one of the United States, so he legalized his claim by summarily broadening his dominion to embrace the entire nation. Later on, he assumed responsibility for the protection of Mexico.

All these moves were made publicly and by means of personal releases to the press. Joining in the game, the newspapers printed his fantastic documents with a straight face, and the Emperor became an accepted figure in the life of the city. Although he seldom drank, he was hailed and toasted when he wandered into bars in search of the free-lunch counters. When his old uniform grew shabby and he issued a decree ordering his subjects to provide a new one, the San Francisco Board of Supervisors solemnly appropriated the funds for it. In royal recognition, he bestowed a title of nobility upon each Supervisor.

The hours which were not occupied with affairs of state were spent sauntering about the streets, graciously bowing to his subjects, checking to see if the policemen were on their beats, inspecting the sidewalks and making certain the city ordinances were being faithfully observed. Until they died in 1865, his two most devoted attendants were a pair of curs known throughout the city as Bummer and Lazarus. In fact, they were the indirect cause of the only display of regal anger during the Emperor's entire reign. A San Francisco cartoonist drew a caricature showing the Emperor at a free-lunch counter with his two dogs beside him, waiting to devour the crumbs he left behind. The drawing was exhibited in a downtown shop window. When he saw it, Norton I squared his epaulettes. "An insult to the dignity of the Emperor," he flared. He raised his heavy cane, sent it crashing through the window and indignantly strode away.

Financially, the Emperor moved on astronomical levels, frequently seeking loans of hundreds of millions from California Street financiers. But invariably he settled, quite satisfied, for a quarter or a half dollar, in return for which he would hand over a bond of the Empire for several million dollars, payable at four per cent in 1880. When that year approached, he issued a new series payable in 1890.

Diplomatic correspondence occupied a lot of the Emperor's time and attention. During the Civil War, he sent off imperial dispatches to President Lincoln and Jefferson Davis and to Generals Grant and Lee. Later, he stepped boldly into the field of foreign affairs and considered himself responsible for successfully negotiating the end of the Franco-Prussian

War. But he never neglected the domestic front, and in 1869 he issued two decrees which at the time were regarded as characteristically zany. One of them ordered the filling in of the shoals off Yerba Buena Island in San Francisco Bay. Now, Treasure Island, man-made site of the 1939-1940 Golden Gate International Exposition, roughly represents what the Emperor had in mind. The other decree demanded the construction of a suspension bridge from Oakland to Yerba Buena Island to Sausalito (across the Golden Gate from San Francisco and in Marin County) and from there to the Farallon Islands some thirty-two miles at sea. When this command was not immediately carried out, the Emperor amended his decree and called for another bridge, this one to reach from Oakland to Yerba Buena Island to San Francisco, the exact points now touched by the world's longest bridge, the San Francisco-Oakland Bay span.

And so he ruled to the end, issuing his proclamations, strolling regally through the streets, distributing his bizarre notes, dropping into the theater of an evening (entire audiences would rise to their feet as he made his entry), visiting the markets and the wharves, the California Street banks and exchanges, passing out candy to children, ignoring always the banging tumult of the Comstock stamp mills and the chuffing of the overland train, and stepped gravely and deliberately in time to a strange music audible to him and to him alone.

Two days after he died, ten thousand San Franciscans filed past the royal rosewood casket as he lay in state at Lockhart and Porter's funeral parlors in O'Farrell Street. Thousands more were turned away at the doors. In 1936, when it became necessary to transfer his remains from the old Masonic Cemetery to Woodlawn Cemetery south of the county line, San Francisco civic leaders placed wreaths on his new stone, the San Francisco Municipal Band played dirges and an infantry battalion fired a three-volley salute above his grave.

The empire ruled by the bonanza kings and the railroad kings of Nob Hill was broad and powerful and rich, while the kingdom of the penniless old man was a dream and a phantom. But San Franciscans cherish dreams above riches, and they will say that the gentle madman found the better and more enduring realm, after all—a realm no bigger and no smaller than the city's heart.

Even a big bonanza does not last forever; the great veins pinch out, the stamp mills fall silent and the men they enriched grow old and die, and railroads that span a continent outgrow their wonder and are absorbed in the progression of living.

These things happened. The strident music stopped. The milling throng ceased its capering, and the dance was over. Life in California Street— and the street itself—became almost humdrum.

The valleys north and east and south of the city were stirring now, rippling with wheat and grain, green with leaves of the grapes that mellowed in the sun, trembling beneath the driving hoofs of many cattle. So it was wheat and wine and beef now that California Street money bought. Later on, there would be other excitements—gold in Alaska, gold on the Klondike, silver at Tonopah, oil in the South below the Tehachapi —but old-timers of the street would vow they were drops in the bucket compared to the Comstock.

There came the Champagne Days of the Nineties, and life in the mansions of the Nob Hill rich was a Greenway cotillion, a Mardi gras, a Sunday ride in Golden Gate Park on a bicycle built for two, a bon mot by Addison Mizner, a Hunt Ball at the Palace, a plate of oysters at Gobey's, summer in San Rafael or Del Monte or San Mateo, White Hat McCarty tooling Lord Talbot Clifton's tallyho down Market Street, a performance of *Trilby* at the Baldwin Theater, high tea at Mrs. Abby Parrott's, diamond dog collars and thousand-dollar gowns from the Rue de la Paix.

There came a day, too, when an earthquake and a fire, as swiftly as they destroyed the cribs of Morton Street and the wretched hovels of Chinatown, brought to earth the gross and pretentious mansions that crowned the hill at the top of California Street. The brownstone pile that Comstock silver had built for Jim Flood, the Washington Street saloonkeeper, was still standing when it was all over, but the others lay in ashes, and the stone steps that had marched to their massive doors were now steps to nowhere and nothing.

But halfway down Nob Hill, the brick tower and scorched walls of Old St. Mary's still were there, still were lifting their strong, true lines to the blue April sky.

It was at a midnight mass on Christmas Eve, 1854, that Old St. Mary's had been blessed and solemnly dedicated as the cathedral seat of the Catholic archdiocese of the Pacific Coast, whose spiritual leader was the Dominican pioneer, Most Reverend Joseph Sadoc Alemany.

San Francisco was proud of it. The largest religious edifice in California, it had been built not only with the wood and granite from China, but with brick and iron that had come around the Horn. Its tall, Gothic, stained-glass windows had come from the art centers of Europe. People in all parts of the city could tell the time of day by the four-faced clock in its square tower, and the city's youth was swayed from temptation by the wise words from the Book of Ecclesiasticus that were inscribed over the church door: "Son, observe the time and fly from evil." In its loft was a fine organ, brought from New York by clipper ship—"a secondhand instrument, but will compare with any in town for tone and power," the papers said.

For nearly forty years—until the construction of a larger, more impressive one in Van Ness Avenue—Old St. Mary's remained the city's Catholic cathedral. Then, after a few years of direction by diocesan priests, the church passed into the hands of the Paulist Fathers, who still conduct the affairs of the parish. Zealously, they tackled the parish's two major problems: Chinatown, whose disease-ridden tenements stretched from the back door of the parish house six blocks north to Broadway, and the small but lively red-light district that lay across California Street where the grass of little St. Mary's Park now grows green in the springtime. Their work on the first problem resulted in the establishment of a Chinese parochial school, a Catholic social center and a mission, the first Roman Catholic mission to the Chinese in America. Where the second problem was concerned, the fathers received most material aid from the same fire which leveled the mansions higher up the hill. Burnt out, the dives never returned, and the nice appropriateness of the warning above the church door lost some of its edge.

If San Franciscans are sentimental about the Ferry Building, they are sentimental about Old St. Mary's, too, whether they are Catholic or not. For there is a wonderful sweetness and dignity about the old church. In the most turbulent years, it seemed to watch over the city and was a symbol of a certain peace and a way of steadiness. Day after day for almost a century, the sound of its mellow bell has been carried down across the lower city by the wind that blows from the west and the sea. San Franciscans know its tone, and love it.

Down California Street and to the east, there is little left of the city of those years. If you know what it was like from books and old maps and old-timers, you can try to see it. There, just above Montgomery, you can say, was the California Market, whose stalls were so festive and cheerful at Christmas time. There, on that corner, stood Leidesdorff's cottage, and across the street was the Parrott block, four stories of Chinese granite, in whose courtyard one year a porter unwittingly opened a case of Dr. Nobel's Patent Blasting Oil with a hammer and chisel, and blew himself and sixteen others to bits. There yet, in the shadow of the tall office buildings, is the cast-iron hitching post to whose four rings Milton S. Latham, president of the London and San Francisco Bank, used to hitch his horse and buggy in the Comstock days. Across the street was the Marine Exchange, where the shipping men gathered and where they tolled a ship's bell whenever a San Francisco vessel was lost at sea. There, on the corner of Sansome Street, was Billy Ralston's Bank of California, which closed its doors on that Black Friday in '75, at the height of the Comstock madness; and there, around the corner, must have been the door by which Ralston left the bank the next day to go swimming in the Bay and die of drowning in the whitecaps between Black Point and Alcatraz.

And almost at the end of the street, just a few doors from Market, is the old chronometer shop that was founded so many years ago by Louis Weule, the German watchmaker. He's dead now, too, but his son and grandson keep the shop going, just as it always was. On its shelves are old, square, ticking boxes bearing on mother-of-pearl plates the names of their makers: Thomas Mercer, St. Albans; Alex Cairns, Maker to the Admiralty, 12 Waterloo Road, Liverpool; M. F. Dent, 33 Cockspur Street, London; Ulysse Nardin, Suisse. There are more than a hundred chronometers from more than a hundred ships, and on the walls are many ships' clocks of brass. When the hour passes, they fill the narrow shop with the sound of their melodious bells and chimes. But the founder's son and his grandson keep on working, oblivious to the muted, manifold ticking, to the dying hours and the rumble of the streetcars that slide past the end of California Street to the Bay.

Up California Street and west of Old St. Mary's is another Nob Hill, a hill of tall apartment buildings with many-windowed walls, of luxurious hotels, of a barroom in the sky and a bar that's like a merry-go-round and places called the Zebra Room, the Tonga Room, the Popagayo Room, Peacock Court and the Birch Room. Carmen Cavallaro plays there, and Hildegarde sings there, and it's the closest San Francisco gets to glamor.

The traces of those other years linger in a few names and a bleak, brownstone mansion with a $30,000 (or is it $60,000?) brass fence around it. That is Jim Flood's old place, and now the Pacific Union Club, whose only sign of life is a millionaire member sometimes standing at a window staring into the street. The Stanford Court apartments cover the site of Leland Stanford's mansion, and the Hotel Mark Hopkins has replaced the $2,500,000 Victorian Gothic monstrosity that Mark Hopkins built with his Central Pacific profits, dying before it was finished. Huntington Park, a little square beside the Pacific Union Club, is where D. D. Colton's imitation marble palace stood, and Grace Cathedral towers above the site of Charlie Crocker's four-story, redwood château.

Beyond Nob Hill and farther west, California Street is block after block of bay-windowed houses and flats, stopping at Lincoln Park, which is near Land's End and the ocean. But there on the hill, the street reaches for the stars, aspiring through the night sounds: dance music, laughter, the grinding of taxicabs, the whine of cables beneath the street and the sighing of the wind that drives evening fog in from the sea.

10. UNION STREET

FROM WATERFRONT TO PRESIDIO · THE LAKE. DREAMS OF THE "CONQUIS-
TADORES." ANZA'S CARAVAN. THE WILDERNESS FORT. THE BOX OF DATES.
EL POLIN · OUTPOST FOR AMERICA · WASHERWOMAN'S LAGOON. MEMORIES
OF THE KING OF COW HOLLOW. HARBOR VIEW PARK. ONE-ARMED HARRY ·
THE ECCENTRIC DOCTOR COGSWELL. THE SIGN OF THE GOLDEN TOOTH.
A NIGHT AT BONANZA INN · LILLIE HITCHCOCK COIT, HONORARY FIREMAN ·
TELEGRAPH HILL, AND HOW IT WAS NAMED. "SIDE-WHEEL STEAMER!" THE
IRISH AND ITALIAN IDYLL. "LAYMAN'S FOLLY," AND THE KNIGHTS OF THE
BROADSWORD. FIRE AND DYNAMITE. WHISTLE-STOP MONTPARNASSE. THE
ISLAND IN THE SKY

PARALLEL TO Bush, California and Washington Streets and Broadway, but
farther north than these, Union Street starts west at the Embarcadero, and,
three blocks from the piers and the Bay, meets the steep, burnt-sienna
cliffs of Telegraph Hill. At the top of the hill, where it crosses Montgomery, the street takes another start, slides down the other side of Tele-

graph Hill, past Grant Avenue, past Washington Square, then climbs
once more, across the shoulder of Russian Hill, and falls to the west again
to Cow Hollow, crossing the dry fill that replaced Washerwoman's Lagoon, and then runs flat, skirting the bright stuccos of the Marina, to the
eucalyptus trees, the rolling mesas, the barracks and the shady winding
roads of the Presidio.

Union Street is an old street, not so old as Broadway or Montgomery
Street, but nevertheless a street of the old town, of old North Beach. From
the top of Telegraph Hill to Washington Square with its weeping willows
and two statues and Cathedral of SS. Peter and Paul (whose biggest,
brightest day was the day Joe DiMaggio got married there), the street is
Little Italy. From the square to the Presidio, it is anything, but mostly the
two- and three-story flats with bay windows bellying out over the sidewalks, seeking some of the light and warmth distributed over the city by
the sun.

It is not an important street in the life of the city. But it is a significant
one, and its significance lies in what it links and binds together: three
things, and if you do not know them, if you know, say, only the Ferry
Building and Nob Hill, a hotel and Fisherman's Wharf, a few restaurants
and the view from Twin Peaks, then San Francisco is a half-read book,
an image without depth and distorted as if by a fun-house mirror.

The first begins with a lake, the second with a lagoon, and the third
with the island in the sky.

The little lake beside which they were camped is still there, beside a
boulevard, and it's called Mountain Lake. The trucks and automobiles
on their way to the Marina or the Golden Gate Bridge roar past it now,
but on that evening Fray Pedro Font could hear the westward surf as he
carefully wrote, perhaps by firelight, the following words in his diary:

"March 28, 1776. The commander decided to erect the holy cross on
the extremity of the white cliff at the inner point of the entrance to the
port, and we went there at eight o'clock in the morning. We ascended a
small low hill, and then entered a tableland, entirely clear, of considerable
extent, and flat, with a slight slope toward the port; it must be about half
a league in width and a little more in length, and keeps narrowing until

it ends in the white cliff. This tableland commands a most wonderful view, as from it a great part of the port is visible, with its islands, the entrance, and the ocean, as far as the eye can reach—even farther than the Farallon Islands. The commander marked this tableland as the site of the new settlement, and the fort which is to be established at this port can be defended by musket fire, and at the distance of a musket shot there is water for the people. . . ."

The commander was Lieutenant Colonel Juan Bautista de Anza. The white cliff today is called Fort Point, and it now lies beneath the high arching span of the Golden Gate Bridge. The fort to be established was the long-delayed Presidio of San Francisco.

One by one, as the explorers and the empire seekers had crossed its deserts and mountains, Spanish dreams of the fabulous land in the north had faded away and perished. The dream of the Fountain of Youth. The dream of Cufitachiqui, land of pearls. The dream of Gran Quivara, where golden bells sang the king to sleep. The dream of the Seven Cities of Cibola, with their streets of turquoise and flashing towers of diamonds. The dream of the desert Lake of Gold, west of the Rio Grande. The dream of the Passage to the Indies.

So the pathfinders had lost the quest; but in losing it—in finding out that their dreams were nothing but dreams, after all—they had added half a continent to a vast Spanish empire that for two centuries had reached from the heights of Chapultepec to Buenos Aires.

For many years, the Spanish paid little attention to this half a continent. Then the English colonists pushed out from the east, beyond the Adirondacks, the Appalachians, the Great Smokies. Russian seal hunters dropped farther and farther south from their Alaskan outposts. The golden Manila treasure galleons began to vanish from the Pacific, seized, ravished and scuttled by marauding buccaneers. When the Seven Years' War ended in 1769, Carlos III, King of Spain, decided to act.

He fortified the Spanish border of the Mississippi. He ordered a chain of forts built from the Gulf of Mexico to the Vermilion Sea (Gulf of California). And he commanded Don Antonio Maria Bucareli, Viceroy of Mexico, to undertake the colonization and fortification of the Pacific Coast.

It was late in 1774 when Bucareli wrote to the Spanish Minister of the

Indies, "It now appears necessary . . . to establish a presidio at the port of San Francisco, which by all means ought to be occupied to support our conquests in that region. . . ."

The man he picked to lead his expedition was Anza, who had been the first white man to cross the mountains to California and the sea. Bound for San Francisco Bay, some seventeen hundred miles to the northwest, Anza's caravan left Sonora in northern Mexico in October, 1775. It comprised two hundred thirty-five soldiers, colonists and their wives and children, and eight hundred twenty-five head of livestock. They arrived in Monterey the next March with the loss of only one life, an achievement that has gone down brilliantly in the history of the West.

Leaving the colonists there, Anza pushed on a hundred more miles to the great harbor of San Francisco with Father Font, Lieutenant José Joaquín Moraga, eight soldiers and several guides and servants. Other pathfinders had been there before him—Portolá, Palóu, Ortega, Fages, Rivera, Ayala—but it was Anza who, at this journey's end, selected the presidio site so glowingly described in the journal of Father Font. Then, his mission accomplished, Anza returned to Monterey, left Moraga in charge of the colony and turned south and homeward.

It was in August, 1776, two months after the celebration of the first mass on the site of Mission San Francisco de Asis, which Anza had also marked out a few miles inland from the Bay, that Moraga with the soldiers, the colonists and the crew of his supply ship, the *San Cárlos,* began construction of the rude wilderness fort. Within a month, most of the buildings—the log barracks with the flat roofs, the chapel, the warehouse, the guardhouse—were completed, and they chose September 17, the Feast of the Stigmata of St. Francis, as the day of dedication. There were about one hundred fifty present at the simple ceremonies.

"A solemn mass was sung by the ministers," Father Palóu wrote in his diary, "and when it was concluded the gentlemen performed the ceremony of taking formal possession. This finished, all entered the chapel and sang *Te Deum Laudamus,* accompanied by peals of bells and repeated salvos of cannon, muskets and guns, the bark (the *San Cárlos*) responding with its swivel guns. . . ."

That was the beginning of the Presidio of San Francisco.

Lieutenant Moraga and his band of soldiers and colonists were brave and filled with hope for the new settlement in the wilderness, but the days of Spanish conquest were over; the far-flung empire was tottering. And in a few years, the outpost on the shores of the great Bay was a burlesque bastion.

They had an adobe house for the commandant built within two years, and a church and a few more warehouses, but struck once by lashing winter rains and they almost dissolved. "During a rainfall in the month of January, 1779," reported Acting Commandant Hermenegildo Sal, "the stores, the slaughterhouse, the church, the house of the commandant and of the troops and the greatest part of the four pieces of wall fell in such a way that at the end of the year 1780, none of the houses built in the year 1778 were standing."

The reconstruction was less than impressive. For one thing, timber for palisades was thirty miles away, tule rushes for the roofs nine miles away. For another, appeals for financial and material aid were quite disregarded by the government officials in distant Mexico.

When, in 1792, Captain George Vancouver sailed into the Bay, his ship was saluted by a brass three-pounder tied to a log at Fort Point. At the Presidio, he found one other cannon, mounted on a rotting carriage. There had been a third, Commandant Sal explained apologetically, but it had burst into ten pieces while firing a salute on a saint's day. The Presidio, Vancouver said, was garrisoned with thirty-five soldiers and looked to him like "a pound for cattle."

Suddenly, however, the Spaniards decided to strengthen their coastal defenses; part of the program was the construction of the Castillo de San Joaquín on Fort Point. This horseshoe-shaped fort, with eight mounted cannon commanding the mouth of the harbor, was completed and dedicated December 8, 1794. But it had been hastily planned, and in the interest of economy its builders had cut too many corners. Within two years, the fort's brick-faced adobe walls were shaking to pieces every time its guns went off.

It was all very discouraging, and the earthquakes didn't help any. In 1808, Lieutenant Luis Arguëllo, the commandant, plaintively complained to California's Governor José Arrillaga, "I notify you that since the 21st day of June there have been felt at this Presidio some earthquakes, eighteen shocks to date, and among them some so violent that as a result of them the walls of my house have been cracked, being badly built, so that one of its rooms was ruined."

Arrillaga, an old hand at earthquakes, was unsympathetic. It is said he wrote the commandant and told him to repair the damage himself and pay no attention to such trifling occurrences as earthquakes. Along with his reply, to console the commandant, he sent a box of dates.

The end of Spanish rule in 1821 brought little change. Commandants came and went, their pleas for aid still ignored by higher officials in Mexico, most of whom were too busy with their own affairs to care about the outpost in the north, or the dreams of dead *Conquistadores*. Colonel Mariano G. Vallejo, the new commandant of the Mexican northern frontier, with headquarters at Sonoma above the Bay, begged for both men and money, but his pleas, like the others, went unanswered. By 1845, he had given up asking and had withdrawn the officer and twelve men he had stationed at the Presidio three years before. By 1846, the rains did as they pleased with the walls and roofs of the Presidio buildings, and nobody cared. In the little hollow now called Tennessee, amid the willows, the waters of the spring El Polin made a lonely sound over the pebbles of the creek bed; once, hoping the Indian legend was true, garrison maidens drank there in the light of the full moon so they would be blessed with many babies and eternal bliss, but now the grass grew tangled and high on the banks above the spring. Where, across the old parade ground, there had been the tinkling of guitars, there was the moaning wind. Where the Russian Rezánof and Doña Concepcion Arguëllo danced the fandango and fell in love, there was a crumbling ruin.

And when the Bear Flag rebels, tatterdemalion troops of the short-lived and comic-opera California Republic, sailed across the Gate from Sausalito and spiked the impotent guns of San Joaquín, the only defenders they routed were the gulls that rose screaming, and flapped away.

For a time after the Presidio of San Francisco became United States soil, the Americans had their troubles, too.

Colonel Jonathan Drake Stevenson's regiment of New York Volunteers arrived early in 1847, too late to take any action in the conquest of California. Three companies were sent to Santa Barbara; two remained at the Presidio. They were the first American troops to occupy the post so hopefully dedicated to the greater glory of Spain and Carlos III seventy years before.

Mustered out the next year, Stevenson's men lost no time, once the gold strike was made, in heading for the diggings. Their replacements, Second Infantry troops from the East Coast, deserted left and right, and took off after them. Sometimes, soldiers sent to catch the deserters went A.W.O.L. themselves.

But as the Gold Rush tapered off, instability in the army routine gave way to Yankee drive and purpose. By the middle Fifties, a visitor to the Presidio wrote, "The old adobe buildings, and a portion of the walls are there; but the hand of modern refinement has swept away the dust and dilapidation which, in the mind of the traveller, throw around these ancient structures their highest charm. The castle of the Mexican commandant and the fort are now occupied by American troops; and neat, white-washed picket fences supply the place of old walls."

By this time, too, the army had torn down the Castillo de San Joaquín and hacked away the bluff on which it stood, cutting it down to the water's edge. At the cost of nearly $3,000,000, army engineers put there a grim brick bastion with water cisterns cut in the solid rock beneath its floor and one hundred forty-nine guns to rake the approaches to the Gate. Called Fort Point at first, it was renamed in 1882 for Brevet Lieutenant General Winfield Scott. It was occupied during the Spanish-American War by two artillery batteries and three companies of the Eighth California Volunteers; but by 1905, when construction began on a new post to be called Fort Winfield Scott, the old fort was obsolete. Its battery was abandoned in 1914. Thousands who cross the Golden Gate Bridge pass over it every day and never know it is there, hard by the bridge's south anchorage.

Between the Civil War and the next one in 1898, under such commanders of the Division of the Pacific as Major General Halleck and Major General Irvin McDowell, the Presidio developed into a major installation. Telegraph lines were installed. Water pipes were laid. Trim frame barracks replaced the adobe ruins. Gardens and trees were planted, roads and streets excavated and graded. By 1884, when the Presidio burial ground was officially designated as the National Military Cemetery, two hundred seventeen known and thirteen unknown soldiers lay sleeping beneath the green grass and the trees.

More than ever, the Presidio became a warm and vital part of San Francisco in 1898, when it organized and equipped thirty thousand men to fight the Spanish-American War. It was in May of that year, the *Overland Monthly* reported, that twelve companies of California Volunteers "marched through the city from the Presidio to the Mail docks to the accompaniment of the cheers and sobs of 200,000 people. It was the going of the first home regiment from the mainland of the United States to fight a foreign foe, and the concentrated fever was something not to be forgotten by those who witnessed it."

That was a half century ago. Now, two more wars have come and gone, and between then and now the white headstones in the Presidio have increased to eighteen thousand five hundred, and there is no more room there for the soldier dead.

Within the Presidio walls, there are markers to tell where Anza paced off his varas for the wilderness fort in the month the patriots wrote the Declaration of Independence, and they are lost on the fifteen hundred acres and amid the hundred buildings of the mighty reservation of today.

The sites of the old cantonments, the old encampments, are there—the tenting grounds of the First Tennessee, the Thirteenth Minnesota, the First South Dakota, the Seventh California, the First Idaho, the Twentieth Kansas and the Second Oregon—and there are markers of redwood to tell you where.

Read the names on them and think of those men and where they came from and why they were there, and it is clear that those rolling Presidio hills, those trees, those rocks washed by the sea, that earth, are America. But they belong to San Francisco, too. From beyond the beginning, they have been part of her, and they always will be.

The picture windows of the mansions of the rich on Pacific and Presidio Heights look north to the Bay; they look down on the roof tops of the district known to San Franciscans as the Western Addition, on the tile roofs of the Marina residential district, then on the masts of the yachts and sailboats that ride at their moorings in Yacht Harbor, then on the Bay and the northern shores of the Bay and then, if the day is clear, to the low, blue outlines of the Mayacmas Mountains, up St. Helena way.

The lagoon was below the heights, where the Marina is now, and in the Fifties and later when the boys in Union blue were tenting those nights on the camp grounds of the Presidio, it was called Washerwoman's Lagoon.

From the first days of the Gold Rush, there was a laundry situation in San Francisco. You couldn't get anybody to do your washing, and even if you could have, the charge would undoubtedly have been four or five times the worth of the garments. Consequently, you sent them to Hawaii to be washed, sometimes even to China.

Although it was beyond Russian Hill and out by the Presidio and almost three miles from the plaza, several enterprising Chinese finally decided to establish a laundry beside the lagoon. Then a man named Pratt started another one, a big one that eventually became the Occidental Laundry. And thrifty San Francisco housewives began to go to the lagoon to wash their clothes by hand. They would make a Sunday outing of it, taking their families and their picnic lunches and, in wheelbarrows and dump carts, their washing. After scrubbing and rinsing it down by the shore, they would hang it on the chaparral to dry, and then that night would take it home and iron it. And so the lake became known as Washerwoman's Lagoon.

About the time the Chinese began their laundry, George William Hatman and his wife came around the Horn to San Francisco. Hatman got a job driving a white mule in a brickyard, and for a week's wages he received an octagonal gold piece worth $50. One day Mrs. Hatman asked him to bring home some potatoes. They were so expensive, he easily carried home all he could buy for $2.50 in his coat pocket. Not long after that, a few hundred yards south of the lagoon, Hatman went into the truck-farming business. In 1861, he bought a couple of acres along the present line of Union Street for $500. On this land he built a house and started a dairy ranch. His boy Bill was born in that house in 1868. A few years ago, Bill was still living in Union Street and was greeted by friends all over the city as "the King of Cow Hollow."

Hatman's dairy was one of the first on the grazing lands near the lagoon, and by the early Seventies there were at least thirty of them between the western slope of Russian Hill and the Presidio. His ranch, with about sixty cows, was the average size, although there were some that had as many as two hundred. San Franciscans called that district Cow Hollow, a name that persisted long after the lagoon had been filled in and long after the Eighties, when the San Francisco Board of Health ordered the dairies to other, less populated sections of the city. Once in a while you still hear the name, and when you do, you're listening to a San Franciscan who's an old-timer, and damned proud of it.

"The King of Cow Hollow" said that one of the best things about it in those days used to be Harbor View. The Union Street cable cars, he said, started at Montgomery Street and Montgomery Avenue (now Columbus Avenue) and ran out Montgomery Avenue to Union Street, and out Union to Steiner. From there, a steam paddy took you to where Yacht Harbor is now, and you were at Harbor View.

There were two places at Harbor View: the Seaside Gardens and Herman's Harbor View Park. And on Sundays, brass bands would board special cable cars at the beginning of the line and play all the way out to the View. Later in the day, at the pavilions, they would play for dancing, the music drifting out over the water. It was like Meiggs' Wharf had been earlier; you went there with the wife and kids for a Sunday picnic, and while the young folks were dancing in the pavilion, you took a hot salt-water bath at Herman's, or spent your money in the shooting galleries, or ate cracked crab and drank steam beer. It was a place like that until they took over most of that waterfront for the 1915 Panama-Pacific Exposition.

Cow Hollow had its share of celebrities. Emperor Norton, it is said, lived there at one time. Lotta Crabtree went to primary school in Cow Hollow, and it was the destination of Frank Pixley, the *Argonaut* editor, when he guided his mule team homeward nights over the Pacific Street planks on Russian Hill. Abe Ruef, the politician, who was later to be indicted on one hundred twenty-nine counts of civic graft and sent to San Quentin, lived there. The late Pete McDonough, the celebrated bail-bond broker, was a Cow Hollow boy, and it was the home district of the late Mayor Angelo J. Rossi.

Also, there were the ballplayers. It was in the late Seventies that a

Mr. Long organized the Young Presidios, who used to play on the sand lots where the Army's Letterman General Hospital stands now, proudly sporting the first uniforms ever worn by a San Francisco amateur baseball team. Old Cow Hollow residents still remember and revere their names: Bob Romer, Joe McCarthy, Jack Welch, Charlie Long, Jimmy Costello, Ed Long, Tom Taylor and Buck Lange, who as "Little Eva" Lange went on to the big leagues to play for the Chicago Cubs. Another to learn the game on these sand lots was the colorful Ping Bodie, the "Cow Hollow Kid," who went on to the San Francisco Seals, and later to the New York Yankees.

The life of the district had a rough vitality, and it was a world away from the crystal-chandeliered Palace Bar, the stock exchanges, and the carriage-and-champagne society that lived on the other side of Russian Hill. There were slaughterhouses down by the Bay shore, near Harbor View. There were two gashouses, and one of them, Cow Hollow boasted, was the finest gashouse of its kind in the world.

The gashouse terriers had a saloon they were fond of, at the foot of Fillmore Street, a few blocks from Union. It was Andy McLane's Crab House, and they'd go there after work for their tall steams. McLane was a whisky man, himself. That's where his profits went, and it was a Cow Hollow saying that Andy was drunk half the time and the other half he wasn't sober. When he wanted to go any place he couldn't reach by a short stagger, he'd clamber aboard his trained pony, Billy, and Billy would see that he got there. "Left, Billy," McLane would say, and Billy would dutifully turn left. "Right, Billy," he would say, and Billy would turn right. When he reached his destination, he said, "Stop, Billy," and Billy stopped, and he fell off, and there he was.

One-armed Harry Conamar was another Cow Hollow character. Near Harbor View were the Fulton Iron Works, and Harry was working there on the ship *Progresso* when she blew up. That was when he lost his arm. But he still had a wife and kids to support, so he practiced rolling dice. For months he practiced, and subsequently he was regarded as the greatest crapshooter on the Coast. Name your point, and nine times out of ten, they say, Harry could roll it—with your dice. He didn't starve, and neither did his family.

Lucky Baldwin had a house in the western end of the Hollow, not far from the Presidio, and there was a high board fence enclosing its land-scaped grounds, which the neighbors used to call Baldwin's Park. Henry Casebolt's carriage factory was on the line of Union Street; that was where they built the cars for the Union Street cable road. Mutton-Toe Flanagan was another Cow Hollow boy, and so was the mild-mannered Felix Mendelssohn, the little barber called "Punch," who used to travel to the County Jail every day to shave Ruef during the time of his graft trials.

They didn't have much money or much glamor, but the first one who told them they weren't San Franciscans would have been knocked flat on his back and tossed into the street. And even though it has been seventy years since a cow set foot in Cow Hollow and the pastures have dwindled to a vacant lot or two, there are plenty of Native Sons who will say that Cow Hollow, San Francisco, is heaven on earth, and that's where they want to go when they die.

From Union Street, by the side of Washington Square, you can see three monuments, two on the square and the third rising above you and to the east, high and white atop Telegraph Hill. One of them is the figure of Benjamin Franklin upon a pedestal which contains a casket to be opened in 1979; this was a gift to the city from the eccentric Dr. Henry Daniel Cogswell. The second is a group of three firemen, one of whom bears in his arms a woman he has rescued from a burning building. The third is the white shaft on the hilltop. These two were paid for with funds left San Francisco by Lillie Hitchcock Coit.

It is quite curious that Doctor Cogswell and Mrs. Coit should be thrown into each other's company—even thus remotely—in death, for in life they would have had less than nothing to say to each other. Doctor Cogswell was perhaps the dullest San Franciscan who ever walked down Market Street. Lillie Coit was, in more ways than one, the most picturesque.

Any claim to romance in the doctor's life begins and ends with the statement that he was a Forty-niner. Born in Tolland, Connecticut, in 1819, Cogswell survived a poverty-ridden childhood, moved to Providence, Rhode Island, and became a dentist's apprentice. Later, he opened his own dental offices in Providence and Pawtucket. He is generally credited with having, at some time during this period, devised the vacuum method of securing dental plates in the mouth.

Two years later, he went around the Horn to California. Being a shrewd and practical fellow, he took with him a stock of miners' goods which he peddled on horseback through the mining country. With the $3000 profit, he set up a dentist's chair in a tent in lower Washington Street. He did so well there that he opened an office on Portsmouth Square, hanging out a sidewalk shingle that bore the words, "The Sign of the Golden Tooth." It was there, in 1853, that one Mrs. S. Martin submitted to chloroform before Cogswell extracted three of her teeth. Thus he became the first California dentist on record to use chloroform as an inhalation anesthetic in a dental operation.

As fast as he made money, and he made it hand over fist, he invested in real estate, city scrip and mining stocks. In 1856, estimating himself to be worth a conservative million, he retired from the tooth-pulling business to devote his entire time to the management of his business affairs. About 1870, he and Mrs. Cogswell toured Europe, the Holy Land and Egypt, and it was undoubtedly during this trip that he got the idea of perpetuating his memory by scattering statues all over America. At one time, sixteen cities owned Cogswell monuments, most of them artistic catastrophes. In San Francisco, there remain two: a twenty-four-foot obelisk near the Palace of the Legion of Honor and the Benjamin Franklin statue in Washington Square.

In 1887, the doctor founded Cogswell College, the first technical school west of the Mississippi. This project cost him about $1,500,000 in cash and real estate, and is his worthiest memorial. Among its ten thousand alumni have been, and are, some of the city's most important men. Probably the most notorious was Theodore Durrant, the Belfry Killer of Bartlett Street and San Francisco's candidate for the "criminal of the (nineteenth) century."

Personally, the doctor seems to have impressed everyone he met as a handsome but vastly boring bellow, lacking in imagination and making up for this in infamous thrift, unflagging perseverance and a generous amount of self-esteem. Until his death in 1900, he frequently descended upon his college classrooms to see how much chalk was being used, and to check on other details of petty economy. One time, he concluded he had wondered long enough what life in the Palace Hotel was like; he would spend some of his millions and find out for himself. He packed a bag, walked to the hotel, registered, went to bed and returned home the next day after a good night's sleep, satisfied and proud that he had at last sampled life at its headiest, in the world-famous Bonanza Inn.

Whether his millions and his college and his statues brought him any happiness, no one can say. You get the impression he may well have considered happiness a waste of time, something frivolous and fancy whose returns are intangible, and therefore worthless. Perhaps, when the box in the base of the monument on Washington Square is opened, the doctor, in the message to posterity it undoubtedly contains, will settle the question himself.

Lillie was another matter.

The story goes that one day, just about a hundred years ago, the members of three volunteer fire companies labored up Telegraph Hill, pulling on the long ropes that drew their engines. They were on their way to fight a fire already licking the roof of a flimsy wooden shack near the top of the hill.

Short of hands that day, the proud Knickerbocker Engine Company No. 5 fell behind. All at once, a slender schoolgirl standing beside the road threw her books to the ground and ran into the street. She grasped the Knickerbocker rope in her small strong hands. Over her shoulder to gaping bystanders she shouted, "Come on, you men! Everybody pull, and we'll beat 'em!" Spurred by the challenge, half a dozen men followed her to the rope, and the first water on the fire that day streamed from the nozzles of the triumphant Knickerbocker 5.

The schoolgirl was ten-year-old Lillie Hitchcock, daughter of Dr. Charles McPhail Hitchcock, a West Point army surgeon who in that year, 1851, had arrived in San Francisco as medical director of the Pacific Coast. From the moment she set her hands to the Knickerbockers' rope, she was their mascot. She raced with them to fires. In street parades, she rode atop the Knickerbocker engine, surrounded by flags and flowers. So strong and loyal was her affection for the company, the Knickerbockers made her an honorary member, a tribute paid no other woman in San Francisco history.

Lillie responded to this honor with a lifelong devotion. For the rest of her days, she wore the company pin with the numeral "5" on it. She had a "5" embroidered on all her clothing, and always wrote her signature "Lillie Hitchcock 5." Whenever she could, she appeared at the company's annual banquet, wearing a fireman's red shirt and carrying her fireman's helmet. If she was abroad, she remembered the event with a cablegram.

The tomboy that had run to the aid of the Knickerbockers that afternoon on Telegraph Hill developed into one of San Francisco's most spectacular women. In the Sixties, her soft, dark hair and eyes, her independence, her spirited wit, all combined to make her the toast of society. From California Street's Pantheon and Montgomery Street's Bank Exchange to the parlors of Rincon Hill and South Park, Lillie was the talk of the town. "Silverheels," men called her, because she always wore heels of silver on her dancing slippers.

Obviously, Lillie was not the spinster type, and in 1868, in a brilliant wedding at the Church of the Advent, she was married to B. Howard Coit, a young financier. From an around-the-world honeymoon, during which she was presented at several European courts, she returned unchanged. In a manner that must have baffled her social rivals, she managed to break nearly every rule of society's code without loss of prestige and, more importantly, without offense. Lillie smoked, and remained uncensored. She was an excellent rifle shot in a day when the heaviest thing most women handled was a lace fan, and won many medals for her marksmanship. She rode like a cavalry officer, and played poker like one.

For a number of years after her husband's death in 1885, Lillie lived in what had been a childhood summer home, near St. Helena; but eventually she returned to a permanent residence in the Palace Hotel. There, in her rooms, in 1903, Major J. W. McClung, an old friend, was fatally wounded by Alexander Garnett. Garnett, a distant relative hired by Mrs. Coit as a rent collector, shot McClung in a fit of insane rage when he became convinced the officer was influencing her to discharge him from his job.

An anecdote lives to indicate that Lillie's spirit was unshaken even by this unfortunate event. The story says that when she was reading an account of the shooting in a newspaper the next day, she suddenly tossed the paper scornfully to the floor. "It says the shooting occurred in the apartment of 'a Mrs. Coit,'" she snapped. "*A* Mrs. Coit, indeed!"

But a few years later, when Garnett was paroled from San Quentin, she grew fearful for her own life and moved to Paris. She returned to San Francisco in 1924, a sick and aging woman of eighty-three. She died five years later, leaving among her bequests $100,000 for the beautification of the city and $50,000 for a monument to the valiant volunteer firemen she had always loved. Both bequests have been fulfilled, and you see her memorials now from Union Street, by the side of Washington Square.

To her old volunteer fire company, which went out of existence with the others in 1866, Lillie was loyal to the end. At her cremation, the flames that consumed her consumed the badge that bore the number "5." She had been wearing it when she died.

Telegraph Hill has been many things to San Francisco.

It has been her sentinel peak, her watchtower, and its rugged shoulders sheltered the square-rigged ships that rode at anchor in the little cove whose waters lapped Montgomery Street nearly a hundred years ago.

It has been where the wild mustard bloomed yellow in the springtime, and where the people have gathered to see ships come beating through the Gate, and where people have gone to laugh and to cry. The city has burned its triumphal fires upon its crest, and it has been an island in the sky, high above the streets, far from the world, with lights that were reflections on the water, with music that was the sound of the wind in the trees, a gull's cry, and foghorns blowing somewhere.

It has been a sanctuary for murderers and saints, for the brave and the weak, and many dreamers. It has been a place of strange songs— a Neapolitan boat song and a Killarney lament, a drinking song and a lilting serenade, ballads of all kinds of love and blues as deep as any Beale Street ever heard.

And so the hill stands there, lifting its fluted white shaft to the sun and the stars, apart and yet not apart, serene and unattainable, yet reached and touched and in a way possessed by all who have ever known this fabulous city, and loved her.

In the beginning, the Spanish saw it, round and brown against their azure Alta California sky, rising from the water's edge north and west of Yerba Buena cove. They called it Loma Alta—High Hill—and it was Loma Alta for many quiet years.

When the Americans came, when the American flag first flew over Portsmouth Square, the hill was still the home of quail and the mustard and the wild blue lupine, and for a while they left it that way. Jealous of their new land, they installed a battery of guns (the guns that gave Battery Street its name) beneath the brow of the hill and called the battery Fort Montgomery; but soon the fort was abandoned, and the guns rested there rusty and silent, their muzzles pointing harmlessly to the Bay.

As the city grew, as it developed, almost overnight, from a sleepy settlement to a hectic, frantic boom town, as the immigrant population swelled and bargaining and trading swept to a feverish tempo, the arrival of a ship with mail and merchandise from back home became the most important thing in the life of San Francisco. And to signal that a ship was standing through the heads, to give the city the good news, a Scotch dealer in nautical instruments named Joseph MacGregor leased the very summit of the hill from M. L. Callender and E. V. Joice, and there erected a two-story lookout with an observation platform on its roof. The tiny building, eighteen by twenty-five feet, was pinned to earth by a pole which passed from the roof down through the center of the house and fourteen feet into the ground. For a few months, MacGregor operated his signal station, flashing word of the arrival of a vessel, it is said, by heliograph code.

It was in 1850 that George Sweeny and Theodore E. Baugh, founders and proprietors of the Merchants' Exchange, bought the lot and the house for $6000 and installed, on the lookout platform, the semaphore tower with the wide, black arms that became so intimately identified with the city in those Gold Rush days.

But impatient San Franciscans wanted the news of coming ships even before they reached the Gate, so Sweeny and Baugh put up another lookout station on Point Lobos on the southern heads, linking it to the one on the hill with the first telegraph line ever operated in California. Now, even though a ship was still miles at sea, the city could be told that it was on its way. And now the city had a name for that slope that stood out against the northern sky. The name was Telegraph Hill.

Soon the improved signal station was as important to the city's life as Portsmouth Square. Wrote Bancroft, ". . . when the signal flag was unfurled, and the windmill-looking indicator on Telegraph Hill stretched forth its long ungainly wooden arms and told the town of a steamer outside, a thrill went through the heart like that which Gabriel's trumpet sends into the fleshless bones of the dead."

One of the signal station's first and happiest tasks in 1850 came when the semaphore heralded the approach of the mail steamer *Oregon,* flags flying from every inch of her and bearing the news that California had been admitted to the Union. That night, the bonfire beacons of manifest destiny blazed high on Telegraph Hill.

It would seem that even babes in arms knew the longed-for and looked-for signal for the Pacific Mail Steamship Company's side-wheel steamers—the two outstretched, and slightly uplifted, black arms of the semaphore—and when they appeared that way against the sky over Telegraph Hill, everything stopped. Like school children unexpectedly released from classes, shopkeepers, croupiers, bartenders, merchants, carpenters, lawyers—everyone, in fact, who could walk—rushed into the streets and headed pell-mell for the waterfront to watch the steamer round Clark's Point and come in for her landing.

There is a classic story about this particular signal. One night, during the run of *The Hunchback* at the American Theater, the action had reached a point where, after a bitter argument between two of the characters, a third character, wearing a somber black suit, rushed upon the stage from the wings, flung up his arms and cried, "What does this mean?" Roaring out of the balcony came the reply, "Side-wheel steamer!" An appreciative and tickled audience gave the quipster a hand that all but brought down the roof.

With the passage of a few years, however, and as the town shed some of the crudeness of its early, almost wilderness existence, the arrival of a steamer no longer inspired the town to kick up its heels, shut up shop and dash to the wharf, and the semaphore signals, in 1855, were abandoned.

Nevertheless, the bare crest of the hill, with its scrub oak and wild flowers, was where San Franciscans went for their Sunday picnics, toiling up the hillsides, eating their lunches on the summit, looking down at the ships at anchor beneath them or across the Bay to the hills of Marin and Oakland, the men adjourning, perhaps, after lunch, to the signal station bar for a long and cool milk punch, or maybe climbing still higher to the station's observation tower to look through its strong telescope.

That was the year Charles Warren Stoddard, later the noted author but then a lad of twelve, arrived on Telegraph Hill with his family. The house they took, on Union between Montgomery and Kearny, stood, he remembered, on the "snow-line" of the hill. "Beyond it, the hill was not inhabited save by flocks of goats that browsed there all the year round, and the herds of boys that gave them chase, especially of a holiday." There were high cliffs on the northern and eastern slopes, where the blasters and the earth movers had been at work getting fill for the tidelands and the water lots, and digging ballast for the freight ships bound back around the Horn to the ports of the Atlantic.

Above the cliffs, there were the cottages (Junius Brutus Booth, Jr., and his brother Edwin lived in one of them, No. 5 Calhoun Street). "Nestlike," Stoddard called them, ". . . so small, so compact, so cozy, so overrun with vines and flowering foliage . . . as delicate and dainty as toys."

You reached them by Jacob's ladders which clung to the faces of the cliffs, or by long, never-ending flights of steps up from Broadway, by precarious bridges flung across gullies, by sidewalks made of planks that came from the hulls of old ships. The carts of the vegetable man, the grocer, the baker and the water vender zigzagged up the steep, unpaved streets to ease the pull and the climb for their plodding horses. Caged parrots and bright canaries sunned themselves in the small gardens, and, even as they do today, geraniums bloomed vividly red and soft pink in the window boxes.

Life on Telegraph Hill in those days, then, was a simple and happy thing. Hell broke loose with metronomic regularity in the Devil's Acre of the Barbary Coast, but that was down at the foot of the hill and across Broadway. Sailors were duped, doped, bludgeoned and shanghaied, but that, too, was down at the foot of the hill, in the rat warrens and honky-tonks of the waterfront. On the steep sides of the hill, above all this and looking down, or away to the blue San Bruno hills in the south or out over the moving tides, were the sea captains' cottages, the shacks and shanties of the Irish longshoremen and the dock workers and the Italian fishermen.

Out in Twentieth Street, a few blocks from Mission Dolores, lives Jim Garbarino, a retired employee of the San Francisco City Engineer's office. He can remember being a boy of nine, and being led by the hand by his father to the top of the hill to watch the blowing up of Blossom Rock almost eighty years ago. He and his family lived on the southern slope of the hill, two blocks from Union Street, and for six years before that and a dozen years after, the hill was where he and the other boys of the neighborhood played and fought.

He and the others that are still alive remember the lateen-sailed fishing boats moored at the Fisherman's Wharf that was where Vallejo Street met the Bay, and the songs of the fishermen and accordion music drifting over the hill at night. Playing hooky from the school over on the other side of the hill and spending those days of freedom climbing Nob Hill and playing in the cisterns up there, or hiking out to Lone Mountain and carving their initials in the wooden cross that stood on the mountain-top. Buying half a dozen shoulder chops for a dime in the corner store, where the Italian patriarchs sat drinking Chianti and quarreling over their games of pedro. Gathering wood on the India Docks at the foot of the hill, tying it in bundles and carrying it up the goat trails and home for the kitchen stove. Crushing the wine grapes with bare feet in the autumn and watching the drilling Garibaldi Guards swagger down Broadway. Watching the China steamers make their landings below the hill and swimming off Cowell's dock, flying kites from the hilltop and capturing the nanny goats of the Irish families and milking them. Picking Tahitian oranges out of the water with crab nets as they dropped overboard while Kanakas were unloading them from the white fruit schooners from the South Seas.

"It was a wonderful place," these old-timers say. "All the people were friendly, happy people."

Sheriff Dan Murphy, who grew up on the hill, can remember the way the Italian fishermen used to drape their nets from the back porches of their houses and mend them and sing arias as they worked, the bass voices blending with the baritones, the baritones with the tenors. . . .

When, in 1871, the wind blew down the old Sweeny and Baugh signal station, it destroyed a symbol of the life and times of the Forty-niners, and a venerable San Francisco institution. It was estimated that the board sides of the tiny structure bore forty thousand sets of initials, painstakingly carved there by men, women and children from all over the world who had scaled the hill to visit the lookout and see the view.

For eleven years after that, the summit was bare, a place for the goats to graze, but in 1882, teams of horses dragged load after load of lumber up Filbert Street, a block north of Union, and workmen hammered together the "German" castle that was to be a picturesque Telegraph Hill landmark for another two decades. It was a strange and gloomy structure of notched parapets and turrets, and beneath its flat roof were installed a concert hall, a bar, a restaurant and private dining rooms. On top of the building, they put an observatory, a fifty thousand-candle-power lamp (the strongest on the Coast at the time) and a time ball, which dropped from its tall shaft on the dot of noon so masters of ships anchored in the Bay could check their chronometers.

The Castle was primarily the idea of Frederick O. Layman, who hoped it would become a fashionable resort, rivaling, perhaps, even the Cliff House in popularity. When people complained it was too remote, Layman organized the Telegraph Hill Cable Railroad Company and laid down a set of tracks that ran from Powell Street up Greenwich to the Castle's front door. This cable car line, climbing what was then the world's steepest right of way, began service in 1884 and was known amiably, but prophetically, as "Layman's Folly."

Even this added attraction did not fill the empty dining rooms and the bar of the Castle. Adolph Sutro took it over, and failed to make the resort pay its way. As for the cable road, the legend is that one day a loaded car got out of control, tore down the hill and crashed, killing several passengers. The cars never ran after that.

For a time, the Castle enjoyed a limited prosperity under the proprietorship of Duncan Ross, a noted swordsman, who supplemented the Castle's medieval qualities with appropriate exhibitions of jousting and broadsword battles. Every Sunday, before throngs of goggling picnickers, he and a Captain Jensen garbed themselves in suits of armor, mounted a couple of stalwart plow horses and had at each other with a hacking and clashing of steel that sent the goats scrambling down the hillside braying with terror.

Attracted, perhaps, by these bizarre spectacles, sporting characters of the town frequented the Castle. John L. Sullivan tossed off many a drink in its paneled bar, and so did Charlie Mitchell and Paddy Ryan and other celebrities of the prize ring. But Ross couldn't make a go of it, either. It became, in swift succession, the headquarters of the Telegraph Hill Observatory Athletic Club, a vaudeville theater, an art studio, a cheap boardinghouse. About the turn of the century, it was bought by the Gray brothers, who had started their blasting of the hill, and they used it as a dormitory for their laborers.

In July, 1903, five months after it reopened as a tourist resort under the managership of Mrs. A. Vincent, the now dilapidated and weather-beaten structure caught fire. Flames raced up its walls, broke through the roof and crackled across the quaint battlements. Only one fire engine, pulled by six horses, reached the top of the hill. Scores of neighborhood gamins helped the firemen drag the hoses up the steep inclines, but they were too late. "Suddenly," said one account, "the whole burning mass fell with a terrific crash, sending up thousands of blazing cinders, which gave the appearance of the bursting of a mammoth skyrocket."

One section of the burning building broke loose from its foundations, roared over a cliff and crashed in a fiery mass two hundred feet below.

Three firemen were injured, and all they could save from the building was Mrs. Vincent's Italian greyhound. A week later, the charred shell that remained standing on the hilltop was unable to withstand the ocean winds, and it toppled to the ground, and the destruction of the ill-fated Castle was complete.

Once again the summit of the hill was bare. Many of the Irish had already moved from the hill, drawn by real estate developments and by Catholic parishes more solidly Irish, to Bernal Heights and The Mission, and the boys that played there now were still Italian, but Spanish, too, and Mexican and sometimes Chinese. The hill was still far away from the city, and the sky still was touched with Mediterranean blue, and the men still sang to their accordions in the warm evenings. It was still a peaceful, happy world, somehow more of Europe than America, but a world that wouldn't last.

The first thing that happened was the earthquake.

There is a picture which was taken during that disaster of 1906, and its caption reads: "Refugees on Telegraph Hill—These people sought a safe place and are watching their houses and the city burning." It shows men, women and children, dressed as if for an outing—men in overcoats and bowler hats, women in long dresses with lace collars, sweeping cloaks and straw sailor hats with wide bands. They are sitting around on the rocks of the hill's crest, surrounded by the odds and ends and the curious scraps of possessions that people always risk their lives saving in times of emergency: quilts, bedding, chairs, pictures, books, toys, a canary, a frying pan.

The reason why Telegraph Hill was a relatively safe place is also part of the city's legend, and everyone knows how the Italians and the Spanish kept it from burning by quenching, with buckets of red wine and wine-soaked blankets, the flames that threatened their tindery frame houses and board shanties.

But the calamity interrupted the smooth and happy tempo, the tone, of life on the hill, and the cliff dwellers there had hardly recovered and settled down again when the Gray brothers, Harry N. and George F., resumed the dynamiting of the hill to obtain rock for their stone-crushing plants.

One August evening, four months after the earthquake and fire, a violent blast shook the eastern side of the hill, lifting the small houses from their foundations, showering debris and bringing down into Sansome Street at the hill's base a great slide of rock. Although the Gray brothers had planted the dynamite on their own property, the explosion carried away fifteen feet of one Vallejo Street lot, and a quarter of another homeowner's lot on Montgomery Street. That night, hysterical women and their angry husbands, armed with loaded pistols and brickbats, stood on the cliffs above the Gray brothers' quarry and shook their fists at the workers below.

Two weeks later, fifty property owners gathered for a protest meeting at Union and Montgomery Streets and listened to a shocked and stirring speech by Father Terence Caraher, militant pastor of St. Francis' Church, at the foot of the hill. "I know the Gray brothers have political protection and I know who protects them," he cried, "but political pull can be overcome and we shall overcome it."

But the blasting continued. Wide fissures opened in the hill, and houses that had been many yards from danger now teetered on the rim of man-made cliffs. The explosions shook plaster from the walls and ceilings, jarred doors out of line and cracked foundations. Some of the residents fled in fright to other parts of the city. One Italian said, "The blasting has terrified every person on the hill. Those who can are hurrying away. Our wives are sick from the shock, our children cry all night long."

The next year, a twelve-room house whose tenants had moved out the week before slid down the hill, toppled over the brink and crashed to splinters in Sansome Street. Broken water pipes played streams of water over the face of the cliff, and the air was filled with escaping gas. The year after that, two entire lots fell down the hillside in an avalanche of earth and stone. In 1909, while Presidio guns boomed a Fourth of July salute, a terrific explosion shook every house on the hill, in spite of an injunction forbidding the Gray brothers to continue their destruction. Denying his men had touched off the blast, Harry Gray explained, "It must have been the cannons that they heard."

By this time, however, the Gray brothers were over their heads in trouble and spending most of their time in court defending themselves against a swarm of attachment suits, contempt of court proceedings and suits to collect unpaid wages. One disgruntled employee, maddened by his inability to collect his pay, shot and killed Caroline Brasch, the Gray brothers' cashier. At length, after some six years of blasting, Judge F. J. Murasky issued a permanent injunction against the brothers, and the now scarred and defaced hill was saved. Violence and a bullet brought an end to the firm in 1914, when a discharged employee, in a fit of rage, murdered George Gray.

For years before this, history-conscious San Franciscans had urged the preservation of the hill, and the creation of some sort of park or memorial upon its summit, so that in years to come the people would know how important and how close it had been to the city's life in the Gold Rush days. But it wasn't until the 1920's that the city got around to paving a road to the top of the hill. Then the Park Commission brought down a storm of indignant protest upon its head by erecting upon the hilltop a balustrade ornamented with huge urns which effectively blocked the view on all sides. "We have a new game up here now," one hill dweller wryly observed at the time. "We call it 'Find the Bay.'"

Defeated and chastened, the Commissioners had the whole thing taken away, and with the $100,000 left by Lillie Hitchcock Coit they erected the white tower that points to the stars and the sky above the hill the Spaniards called Loma Alta.

In the Twenties and in the Thirties, this hill won a reputation as the Montparnasse of the West, the Left Bank of every whistle stop from the Coast to Kansas City, the destination of kids from the country who came seeking congenial companionship with art in their hearts, easels under their arms and copies of Freud and Joyce in their battered suitcases.

In a way, that was true of a certain section of the hill, a quarter of it, perhaps, whose geographical center would be close to the intersection of Filbert and Montgomery Streets. The rest of it was, and still is, inhabited by Spanish and Italian elements leading simple, normal lives, bearing many children, going to mass on Sunday, growing grapes in the tiny backyards and string beans on the roof, gossiping over the back fences and going quietly to bed at nine or ten o'clock every evening.

But from the early Fifties, when the Booths lived in Calhoun Street, the hill attracted the poets and the painters because it seemed a world apart where they could indulge in personal irregularities without fear of bourgeois reproach, because the view was inspiring and the rents were ridiculously cheap.

But somehow, not much work got done. Over the red wine and salami sandwiches, and by the romantic light of candles stuck in bottlenecks, the bohemians assured each other they were geniuses and believed it, but the next morning, the mood to write or to paint was not upon them. In the late 1920's, there were some serious artists on the hill—Otis Oldfield, Ralph Stackpole, Tony Sotomayor and a few others—and they sensed the

richness around them in the lives of the Spanish peasants and the Italian fishermen, and learned from it. But this richness and this vitality went right past the bohemians. They were too busy acting the way they believed geniuses should act, making love, racing turtles at Mickey's speakeasy on the Filbert Street steps, sun bathing in the nude, playing drinking games in the wine cellars, swooning over scratchy records of Stravinsky and Hindemith, and talking. Above all, talking. A few years later they found their heroine in Lady Honoré Cecelia Bowlby-Gledhill, who stepped outside her Dead Fish Café one night, said, "Boys, I don't like that silo," and emptied a small revolver at Coit Tower. When the bohemians forced themselves to create, they created bad imitations of Picasso and austere and incomprehensible verse that reminded their friends of e.e. cummings.

They were a merry and sterile crew, capering at their own wakes, and the laughter on their hill rang with a strong and unsuspected note of irony, because it was they, the laughers, who were pathetic and absurd. Only the most honest and brave of them came to see this, that art is hard work and is born in the streets and alleys of the living city and not on a magic mountain, on an island in the sky. So if you were one of them and you saw this and had the courage to work, you packed up and got off the hill; if you didn't, you stayed there in the sun, languidly devouring lotus, setting off its flavor with sharp gin or raw, red wine and telling yourself that some day, when the party was over, you'd settle down and write your masterpiece.

So the lotus-eaters made their few blocks of the hill a vagabond's house, an animated exhibition of failure in action, a showcase containing a representative collection of individuals who were endlessly fascinated by themselves and whose favorite picture was the one they saw in the mirror. Some of them grew up; some of them didn't, and never will.

It was in the middle Thirties that the cold white apartment houses went up on the hill, cutting off the views, cutting off the north light from the studios and convincing landlords that they were robbing themselves when they let their shacks go for $15 a month. Telegraph Hill entered a new era, a fashionable, expensive era, and the geniuses of the red-wine-and-salami set got their portable typewriters down off the closet shelves, collected their unused tubes of paint, took the Van Gogh and Matisse prints from the walls and moved to yet-unexploited areas in Montgomery Street or on Potrero Hill or the slopes of Twin Peaks.

Not all of them are gone, but in the shacks and studio apartments you're likely now to find a bank clerk, a bartender, a department-store model, a radio announcer, a bond salesman. In the glass-brick and view-window apartments live executives and socialites who pay their staggering rents out of five-figure incomes. Tourists with cameras and field glasses dangling from their necks tramp the alleys George Sterling once roamed. On one corner, children's swings and a slide and a sandbox stand in the sun; on another, a well-tended vegetable garden defies the hill's rocky soil.

The wind sings a mournful song in the electric wires overhead, and through the yellow broom and the eucalyptus trees up by the tower; the bells on the Belt Line engines down on the waterfront toll in the night, and from the Bay bridge drifts the rumble of the trains. And Loma Alta, the sentinel peak and signal tower of the pioneers, the fabled hill of dreams, sleeps on, confronting the sounds and its people with silence, breaking promises it never made.

Main Stem

11. MARKET STREET

THE PATH OF GOLD · JASPER O'FARRELL AND HIS PLAN · STEAM-PADDY
HEWES · MONTGOMERY STREET SOUTH: A PLAN THAT FAILED · HUBERT
HOWE BANCROFT. HIS ARRIVAL IN "DANTE'S INFERNO." FROM TRAFFICKER
IN BOOKS TO HISTORIAN. THE HISTORY FACTORY · SOUTH OF MARKET DAN-
DIES. DRAGOONS AND HUSSARS. THE MIRACLE OF MARKET STREET · THE DEDI-
CATION OF LOTTA CRABTREE'S FOUNTAIN · BONANZA INN · THE FAST RIDE
OF THE LIGHTNING TRAIN · LUCKY BALDWIN'S HOUSE OF GOLD · THE
LINE · PHILOSOPHER PICKETT · TOM BLYTHE'S MIRAGE · SOCIETY IN THE
EIGHTIES · THE GREAT BLIZZARD · THE STREET IN THE GAY NINETIES. WAX-
WORKS AND QUACKS. THE TAMALE MAN, AND OTHER CHARACTERS. WHITE
HAT MCCARTY AND THE DOUGHNUT. TOD SLOAN'S MILK BATH. STEVE
BRODIE, AND THE GOAT THAT DRANK BEER. THE BATTLE OF THE CEN-
TURY · THE BALDWIN HOTEL FIRE · THE GREAT DISASTER OF 1906 · CHRIST-
MAS EVE, 1910

SAN FRANCISCO'S Fifth Avenue, its Champs Elysées, its Main Street or
Great White Way or Path of Gold, cuts down through the town that lies

213

east of Twin Peaks for three miles, straight and broad and true to the waterfront. Of all the streets, it represents the lowest common denominator of all the city and all its people.

As you will see, Market Street got off to a late start in the development of the city, but for the last three-quarters of a century it has been what the plaza was in an earlier time—a place to promenade, a mart, a meeting ground, a stage, a king's highway and a beggar's wasteland, a forum of fraud, a garden of truth, a pathway of hopes and a boulevard of broken dreams, in the vulgarest, teariest, most hill-billy-ballad sense of the phrase.

You can say that the last best time came to Market Street on that Christmas Eve in 1910. Then, for a few moments, a multitude was united there as one never was before or has been since, united by a song, a sweet and melancholy sadness, and caught, for a starlit instant, in a soft web of peace.

Things happened after that—Didier Masson, the French birdman, flew down the line of the street the next year; Ishi, the last of the Yahis, the last Stone Age man on the North American continent (they had trapped him, half-starved and cowering in a tattered skin garment, in an Oroville corral), stood there and marveled at the man-made cliffs; Market Street parades captured in shimmering fanfares of trumpets the excitement of the opening of the Panama-Pacific International Exposition, and the jubilant people, their shouts muffled by the influenza masks they wore, danced there the night of the first Armistice Day; the year after that, Laura Fair died in an outer Market Street shanty and lay lonely on the board floor until the neighbors wondered why her cats were mewing; White Hat McCarty, the swaggering playboy of the Nineties, died in the poorhouse dreaming of Market Street; strikers rioted in Market Street, and Golden Gate International Exposition bands played there; fires blazed in the Market Street car tracks, store windows splintered and crashed and a mad and devilish carnival held sway there the day the Japs surrendered; and Eden and Molotov, Stettinius and Bidault, in the days of the United Nations Conference, sped up Market Street, waving to the crowd from the windows of their lean limousines—these things happened, but more than any one of them, or all of them, that Christmas Eve was San Francisco, the best of San Francisco, the beating of the heart of San Francisco, its life breath and essence.

Physically, the street hasn't changed much since then. There are fewer sand lots, more automobiles, more theaters, and there are solar windows now, but its standards are about the same. Coney Island hot dogs, Alice-in-Wonderland hamburgers and penny arcades, five rooms of Monterey furniture for $189.50 and ready-to-wear dresses, passport photographs and cut-rate drugs, luggage stores and tattooing parlors, corned-beef-and-cabbage restaurants and pinball arenas and honky-tonks, assembly-line dentists and easy-credit, no-down-payment, as-long-as-you-like-to-pay opticians—you'll find them all in Market Street, then and now the Side Show Row and Installment Plan Avenue of the West.

It's got lots of lights and neon signs, a great deal of glitter and always lots of noise and people; and if you like the sensation, the sound and smell and look of any kind of life, crowds, movement and clamor and the shuffle of a million footsteps, Market Street is the street for you. Cheap, gaudy, noisy, dirty it always is and always will be, and no special place to look for loveliness; but it's there if you want to see it and if you can't see it you don't love San Francisco the way a San Franciscan does. It's in the people's faces, in the way they walk. It's in the sunshine slanting down across the office-building roofs and into the late afternoon street. It's in the heat haziness and the sometimes electric smell of the air. It's in the crooning of the old man who sells lavender powder there at Christmas time, in the everlasting pounding and clatter of the street-cars charging and swaying along the street, and in the red and powerful fire engines that lunge into Market from the side-street engine houses, careening for that turn with wide-open sirens. It's in the white fog that rolls over and smothers Twin Peaks at the far, western end of the street, and the blue sky above the Ferry Building tower. It's in the clear salt smell of the ocean wind that's bringing the fog with it, and in the December rains, borne also on the wind and moving swiftly down the street and above it between the buildings in long slowly descending gusts, making the short afternoons shorter and making the stores and the motorists turn their lights on early in the early dusk, jamming the traffic so the street fills with the sound of car horns and streetcar bells, and sending all the people, the Christmas shoppers, running for store entrances and awnings and side-street shelters.

Those are just some of the things about Market Street, and they include

some of the things some people hate most about San Francisco. But it's got them, and if you love a town you take everything that goes with it, its people and its rain, its noise and its dirt and its cheapness, and you don't apologize for them, because they're San Francisco, and if another man doesn't like them you tell him to go some place else and leave you alone. That's the way you get to feel about San Francisco, and even about Market Street.

The man who put Market Street where it is, who struck it off on a tangent, on a bias, from the rest of the streets, was a Dublin Irishman named Jasper O'Farrell, a civil engineer who reached Yerba Buena in 1843, at the age of about twenty-six. A picture shows him as a rugged fellow with a long, thin nose, dark, bushy hair and a dark, bushy beard. He is holding a rifle and has a revolver and a knife stuck in his belt, and a dog has its head on his lap.

For a couple of years after his arrival, he worked for the Mexican government, surveying Spanish and Mexican land grants in the San Francisco Bay region. After the American occupation, he was given the job of mapping out the streets of Yerba Buena on the basis of an original survey made in 1839 by Jean Vioget. He squared Vioget's angles (they were two and one-half degrees off right angles), swinging the east-west streets into line, and went on to lay out the streets of North Beach and extend the official survey to new streets west of Dupont and south of California. Market Street, the biggest, broadest street of all, cutting diagonally across the checkerboard pattern of the older streets from the cove shore straight as an arrow to Los Pechos de la Choca—The Breasts of the Indian Maiden, as Twin Peaks were called in that less-inhibited era—was his idea, and it so enraged the hotheads of the time that he nearly swung for it.

Wrote Thomas F. Prendergast in *Forgotten Pioneers,* "When the engineer had completed his map of Market Street and the southern part of the city, what was regarded as the abnormal width of the proposed street excited part of the populace, and an indignation meeting was held to protest against the plan as wanton disregard for rights of landowners; and the mob, for such it was, decided for lynch law. A friend warned

O'Farrell, before the crowd had dispersed. He rode with all haste to North Beach, took a boat for Sausalito, and thence put distance behind him on fast horses in relays until he reached his retreat in Sonoma. He found it discreet to remain some time in the country before venturing to return to the city."

There were undoubtedly some San Franciscans (O'Farrell included) who wondered what all the fuss was about; the right of way of Market Street, as it appeared on O'Farrell's map, was blocked by sand dunes, one rising not far from the waterfront (about where the Palace is now) to the height of more than sixty feet, and a hundred yards west of that was another one nearly ninety feet high. Furthermore, in relation to Portsmouth Square, Market Street was far out in the sticks and obviously had less than no future. The only reason anyone ever went near it was to hunt bear on Rincon Hill, a mile or so to the south, or to go to Happy Valley, a tent settlement near the cove shore south of Market Street, or to reach the main trail that meandered west to the Mission, which stood beside a willowed lagoon at the base of Twin Peaks.

But most of those very pioneers who were so intent on lynching the Irishman lived to praise him for his foresight, and probably, while living off the real estate profits it earned for them, told their grandchildren they knew Jasper was right, all along.

Charles Warren Stoddard, in his *In the Footprints of the Padres,* also remembered how, in the Fifties, he stood in Market Street and watched a white top come down the street in the dusk. It had crossed the plains, the deserts and the mountains, and now, dusty and dried out and creaking, it had reached the end of the long trail. Its driver turned the four weary horses into Montgomery Street, and it came to a sand lot where the Crocker First National Bank is now. On this lot, the emigrants unhitched the horses and turned them loose, and built their campfire and sat there in its flickering light, cooking their supper.

Perhaps that was the last covered wagon to roll on its high wheels through the San Francisco streets, ending that pioneer era for the city; even so, it was still a muddy, rutty straightaway, and it looked like a Hollywood-horse-opera set for the main drag of Tombstone with its hitch racks and corrugated-iron sidewalk awnings. But Dave Hewes' steam shovels were cutting through the hills and leveling some of them, and there were plank sidewalks running out past the end of St. Ann's Valley, where Powell met Market.

By that time, it was getting a built-up look about it, even two or three blocks west of Montgomery, for beyond St. Ignatius' College at Fifth Street stood Henry Casebolt's carriage factory until he moved it out to Cow Hollow. It had originally been in Market Street closer to the waterfront, but one day he had finished a couple of carriages and discovered they were too large to fit through the front door. When the owner of the property in the rear of his shop promised to charge him $1500 for the privilege of moving them out the back door and across his land, Casebolt tore out the front wall of the factory, pushed the carriages into Market Street and promptly set about transferring his plant to a new and less complicated location farther out the street. Just to the west of Casebolt's factory was the residence of Hewes, the Welsh contractor.

There was, at the time, an Irish orator whose inspired verbal blunders were uproariously appealing to San Franciscans. One of his most quoted remarks was, "Not being a bird, I cannot be in two places at once." Another was his prediction that a certain piece of legislation "would transform every barren hill into a fertile valley." (The same type of thinker as San Francisco's late Supervisor McSheehy, noted throughout the state for his quaint rejoinders. One McSheehy classic: "This has all the earmarks of an eyesore.")

Nevertheless, San Franciscans on second thought declared that was exactly what Hewes and his steam paddies were doing—transforming the city's barren sand hills into fertile valleys—and pointed to Market Street as proof. That was a little premature, however, for in 1860, when the tiny steam trains of the Market Street Railroad Company began running on Market Street (offering the city's first mechanical, public transportation), it ran through sand-hill cuts all the way out to the Italian truck gardens of Hayes Valley. Service was constantly interrupted by sand slides on the right of way; and conditions were no better at the eastern end, for there, near the waterfront, reclaimed land frequently sank below grade and became so flooded during the rainy season it was called "McCoppin's Canal," in honor of Frank H. McCoppin, general manager and superintendent of the company.

That was about the time that Asbury Harpending blew into town, a twenty-year-old, self-made millionaire. In his boy-wonder way, he had the imagination to see a future in Market Street, and, after the unpleasantness surrounding his Civil War privateering venture had died down, he set about cashing in on that future. His Harpending Block, between First and Second Streets, was the street's first big building. Constructed in 1869, it was a three-story, brick structure with a two-hundred-fifty-foot frontage. But even before that, he had launched a scheme which, though unsuccessful in itself, contributed directly to the development of Market Street as the town's No. 1 boulevard.

One day, the Bank of California's Ralston had sent for Harpending. The financier, himself an all-out believer in San Francisco's potentialities, told Harpending he was interested in young men with ideas; did he, Harpending, have any particular plans in mind?

Yes, replied Harpending, he had. He had a plan that would make Montgomery Street the biggest and busiest thoroughfare in the West. It now ran to Market Street, and stopped. He wanted to extend it across Market Street, past Mission Street, past Howard Street, right through Rincon Hill to the Bay. With earth dug from Rincon Hill to make way for the avenue, some one hundred fifty acres of tideland, he estimated, could be filled in along the waterfront and sold to the city for $5,000,000 profit. And along the new thoroughfare, which would in effect join Telegraph Hill on the north with the great piers on the southern waterfront, tall buildings would rise. There would be parks and trees beside it, and it would be a great metropolitan artery. This, he said, was his plan.

When the interview was over, Harpending and Ralston were partners. Their organization: the Montgomery Street Land Company, to which Ralston pledged the unlimited backing of the Bank of California; their goal: to drive Montgomery Street across the city, from Market Street to the Bay.

By 1868, they had acquired one essential piece of Market Street property from the Catholic Church, and from Selim Woodworth the adjoining lot east. (This transaction was good for a chuckle in Harpending's memoirs. Woodworth, a pioneer who is rarely identified now except as "the son of the man who wrote *The Old Oaken Bucket*," had bought the lot for pin-money terms, but, when approached by Harpending and Ralston, demanded $300,000 for it. At this, the financiers balked. Not long after that, San Francisco was jolted by the stiff earthquake of 1868. The next day, Harpending spied Woodworth with a carpetbag in each hand, heading for the Sacramento Street pier. "I don't like earthquakes. I'm getting out of here," explained Woodworth. "I'm not leaving, and I'll give you $150,000 for your Market Street lot," replied Harpending. "Sold!" cried Woodworth, and so the Montgomery Street Land Company acquired one of its key properties.)

Immediately, Harpending and Ralston started cutting New Montgomery Street through their property at their own expense, and began construction of the luxurious, three-story, four-hundred-room Grand Hotel on the southeast corner of its intersection with Market. To them, the advantages of their project were so obvious they took it for granted they would receive universal support and cooperation. But when the street reached Howard, two blocks south of Market, they ran head-on into a situation which defeated the whole magnificent scheme: Milton S. Latham and John Parrott, who owned the sections of land next on the line of the extension, refused to sell. Latham, according to Harpending, "asked such a fabulous price . . . that even Ralston and myself, who were accustomed to brush any minor obstacles out of our way without counting costs, stood aghast." The only response they got from Parrott was a tart and testy promise to fight them "every inch of the way."

Into the project had gone more than $2,000,000 of Ralston's Comstock Lode riches, and hundreds of thousands of Harpending's personal fortune. As a last resort, they tried to persuade the Legislature to condemn the land that blocked their way, but this failed, and they and their Montgomery Street Land Company were through. What started out to be the biggest and busiest boulevard in the West is still the two-block street connecting Market and Howard, between Second and Third.

But the Grand Hotel was there, standing on the corner of Market and New Montgomery, the best hotel in the West, and the vacant lot on the other corner was where Ralston would outbuild and outclass and surpass the Grand in every way with his Palace. Market Street, in spite of itself and shortsighted San Franciscans, was, in the late Sixties, on the verge of being great.

There was a young man in his thirties who did not exactly see this, but he thought it might be true and took a chance on it. He was a pioneer bookseller named Hubert Howe Bancroft, who, when he thought of his childhood, remembered the low round hills, the waving cornfields and a stone house of Ohio's Granville, the sturdy Puritanism of a Massachusetts father and a Vermont mother, raking hay in a blazing summer sun, and camping in the snow beneath the bare maples in sugaring time.

He had wanted to go to college and then become a Congressman. "But we were not rich," he wrote later in *Retrospection;* "there were no rich men in those days, all being honest. And long years of study would impose a burden upon my parents for my maintenance to which I could not subject them." So he got a job as a clerk in his brother-in-law's bookstore in Buffalo. Four years later, in 1852, his brother-in-law sent him to San Francisco to see if he couldn't peddle a few books on the Coast. Landing there, he said, was "a dump into Dante's *Inferno.* The streets were slush knee-deep in winter, and in summer the strong unobstructed ocean wind laden with fine particles of sand brought regularly every day at ten o'clock stinging to the face and bad words to the tongue."

The frontier town was a little rugged for the young book agent, and he went back home. A few years later, however, he returned to stay. He spent several weeks in the mines near Sacramento, made a living briefly as a merchant in Crescent City and then went back to the city where, as he put it, God sometimes ruled the day, and Satan ruled the night, every night. He opened a bookstore in Montgomery Street and became "a West Coast trafficker in books, handling them as one handles bricks, not for the knowledge, but for the profit in them." It was in 1858 that he began to change his ideas. In that year, he started collecting books on California.

Like most collectors, the more he got, the more he wanted. His interest expanded, crossed the boundaries of California, spread south to Mexico and Central America, north to Alaska. He bought every book, manuscript and map he could find that had been written or printed about the western half of the continent. He sent copyists to Mexico City, to the California Missions, to Alaska and St. Petersburg in Russia to reproduce archive reports. He raided eastern bookstores to fill out his reference shelves, and he himself traveled thousands of miles in a feverish quest for the history and legend of the West.

"I studied the Mormons at Salt Lake," he wrote, "the Mexicans at the lakes of Tenochtitlan, the Hudson Bay people in British Columbia, and the early Oregon pioneers by their jubilee campfires. Crossing the Atlantic, I visited many times the capitals and universities of Europe, my agents attending the public and private sales."

This went on for more than ten years. Then he began to wonder what he was going to do with all these books, all this material. He thought of writing an encyclopedia, or using them as the foundation for a great newspaper, like the London *Times*. But instead of these, he found himself one day sitting at a table, writing history.

Before this happened, however, the Montgomery Street quarters became too cramped for his thriving book-and-stationery business. He decided to build a larger establishment. But where? There were no sites available on Montgomery Street or Kearny Street. Market Street from the waterfront to Third was solid with hotels, bars, stores, lumberyards, stoneyards. Finally, Bancroft made up his mind to risk Market Street west of Third; and on the south side, between Third and Fourth, in 1869, workmen started construction of an elegant, five-story, brick building with an ornamental iron front.

"There was a good deal of surprise and even merriment at the choice of such a location," wrote Lloyd. " 'Bancrofts are going to move their store to the country,' was a common joke in the city, and dealers in the southern counties rejoiced that the house was getting so much nearer as to materially diminish freight charges."

In April of the next year, Bancroft moved into the new building that towered over the street's shabby and weather-beaten frame shacks, and from whose fifth-floor windows one could look down at the wide plank sidewalks, the horse-car tracks in the dust or the dark mud of the street, and across the house tops to the new and bulbous twin towers of Temple

Emanu-El north on Sutter Street, and the yet bare crest of the California Street hill beyond.

As far as Bancroft was concerned, the move marked a turning point in his life. He saw that at last conditions were shaping themselves so he could get to work on what he wanted to do. His business was growing and prospering, and the time when he could devote himself to writing had arrived. He knew, too, that if he didn't take advantage of it, the loss to students and scholars of the future would be irreparable.

"I appreciated the situation only so far as to see that howsoever crude might be my effort, there was here an opportunity to do for this Western America more extensive and complete work than had ever been accomplished for any other country in the way of gathering and preserving its early history. I was here upon the scene at the psychological moment, able and willing to do an important work which no one else would undertake and which could not be done later."

And pulling on Bancroft was a force more fundamental: he was tired of working only for money; he wanted to contribute something. So there he was, with some sixty thousand maps, books and manuscripts, and thousands of newspapers in many languages, and committed to sorting their information, sifting it, evaluating it and arranging it in intelligent and readable order. It was, he knew, enough work to occupy twenty men for twenty years. How was he to do it alone?

The answer was simple: he wasn't. In radical departure from the standard method of writing history, where the historian gathers, checks, analyzes and writes alone, Bancroft cast about for a staff of men who could do most of it for him.

He established his history factory on the top floor of the new building in a great room one hundred seventy feet long and forty feet wide. He hired twenty workers, all of them well educated and competent, and some with a facile grasp of half a dozen languages. He put them to work nine hours a day, six days a week, indexing and digesting his millions of words of material. The hub of all this industry was an immense revolving table in the center of the room. Beside the table was a desk, and at the desk, standing up, Bancroft took from the table the summaries and references supplied by his assistants, studied them, organized and arranged them, and wrote.

In the next twenty years, across that desk passed, page by page, the manuscripts of Bancroft's monumental history—five volumes on the Native Races of the Pacific States of North America, three on Central America, six on Mexico, eleven on California, and others on eleven other Western states and Alaska, all covering historically an area comprising one-twelfth of the earth's surface. In his thirty-ninth and final volume, *Literary Industries,* he told the story of his history factory. It was, said Franklin Walker in his *San Francisco's Literary Frontier,* "the greatest feat of historiography since Thucydides."

Frequently criticized because he accepted credit for sole authorship when probably nine-tenths of the work was actually composed by his hard-driven assistants, Bancroft replied: 1) if it hadn't been done that way, it never would have been done; 2) the material they used was gathered and owned by him; 3) although they did do much of the spadework and first-draft composition, it was he who was the central and organizing force, and 4) he fulfilled all obligations to them by frankly acknowledging their aid in *Literary Industries.*

Anyway, the job was finished; he had accomplished what he had set out to accomplish. And when that time came, it was nearly a quarter of a century from the day when, as a thirty-seven-year-old bookseller with ambition and an idea, he bought that land on Market Street, and changed his life, and gave the town wags something to crack jokes about.

The movement, the fantastic ballet, the carnival, the ten-ring circus, the loud rout of the Seventies had something desperate about it over on California Street; there was a macabre touch to it, the suggestion of evil and even tragedy about all the gold groveling; and there were logic and consistency to it when it ended for someone in a lonely, single and final shot and the final wound in the temple or the mouth or the chest, or when it ended with the dark, lank hair and beard of Ralston, wet with the salt sea water, clinging damply to his pale face and throat as they drew him dead from the Bay into their small boat. That made sense on California Street, because what they were doing over there had souls mixed up in it, sick souls.

Market Street was healthier. The jokes about Bancroft's moving to the country were losing their point, because the street was beginning to boom. It was shedding its cow-town, frontier look. It would be another few years before the Palace Hotel was completed and the Baldwin was up and the Central Pacific moved its ferry terminal from Pacific Street to Market and Market was in for good as the Big Drag and the Main Stem, but, even so, it was accumulating drive and bustle and vitality.

It was getting them from the immigrants, the Scotch, the Irish, the Jews, the gashouse terriers, the iron-foundry bully boys who swaggered uptown from Tar Flat and Happy Valley and Irish Hill, south of Market, to show off their double-breasted, beaver coats, their peg-top pants, their flowered vests and their shining, high-heeled boots. They probably never heard of H. H. Bancroft, and to them Ralston was a failure compared to Professor Dave FitzGibbon, the dapper, goateed dancing master who ran the academy in Charter Oak Hall over McFarland's Livery Stables on Market Street, next door to the Bancroft Building.

There they would go to learn the mazurka and the schottische and another dance called "the racket," rigid as ramrods but stepping lightly to the Professor's calling, and holding their South of Market doxies at arm's length and gracefully wheeling and gliding. When the dancing class was over, they might all descend on the public dance hall at the City Gardens and dance a few hours more and have some steam beers, and then on the way home sing and get into fights and break up a horse car, but what the hell, that was all in a good night's fun.

A lot of these boys, too, belonged to the military companies that were the pride of San Francisco in those postwar years. In the parades of those days, you could count thirty-five or forty of them swinging smartly up Market Street in their bright and dazzling costumes while the bands played and the girls cheered and threw flowers from the curbing. They had their headquarters and drill halls in second- and third-story lofts on Market Street, and the rolling of their drums and the stamping of their feet on their practice nights were as much a part of Market Street life as the tinkle of horse-car bells and the clatter of carriage wheels over cobblestones. There, in the blocks between Third and Fifth, were the First Light Dragoons, the Jackson Dragoons, the San Francisco Hussars, the California Tigers, the Union Guards, the Franklin Light Infantry, the Ellsworth Rifles, the Ellsworth Zouave Cadets, the Germania Guards.

Closer to the waterfront, between First and Second, were the headquarters of the colorful Irish companies: the MacMahon Grenadier Guards (named in honor of the famous French marshal), the Hibernia Greens, the Mission, the Montgomery, the Meagher, the O'Neil, the Shields, the Emmett Life and the Wolf Tone Guards.

Their uniforms reflected a variety of influences, ranging from the Oriental to the French and British. The San Francisco Cadets, one of the most spectacular of the companies, wore baggy, Turkish pantaloons of red, tunics of bright blue, and red fezzes. The MacMahon Guards wore uniforms presented to them by Napoleon III and patterned after those of Emperor Napoleon's Old Guard: skintight white trousers, high boots, blue cutaway coats with tails reaching below the knee, belts that crossed on the chest and huge bearskin shakos. Other Irish companies adopted modifications of this costume, the Montgomery Guards, for example, wearing scarlet cutaways, and the Meagher Guards, green cutaways, with white shakos.

They added a dash, a glitter, a brassy fanfare to Market Street that California Street never had, and on St. Patrick's Day, say, when they stepped up Market Street, a San Franciscan could look at them and get a wonderful feeling; God was in His heaven, and he was in his, with the sound of a parade band and the tramp of marching feet in his ears, with flags flying and uniforms dazzling in the sunlight. It stirred his soul, made his heart beat faster and made him know that surely this was the best town in the world.

Train whistles were hooting down the overland tracks, the stamp mills were pounding on the Comstock, the ships were leaning through the Gate from China and the seven seas, and here she was, only twenty-five years old and already the Queen City of the Pacific. Comstock silver was building the biggest and the best hotel in the universe right there on the corner of Market and New Montgomery, where General Vallejo had shot a bear forty years ago, and Comstock silver, a few blocks up the street at St. Ann's Valley, was building the theater that was going to make New York's finest look like a Barbary Coast minstrel house. It was a miracle, that's what it was, and here he was standing right in the middle of that miracle; he was part of that miracle himself, and this parade and all this color and those brave lads in their bright uniforms were part of it, too.

Even that Black Friday of 1875 and the closed doors of the Bank of California and the death of Ralston, the Comstock prince, couldn't get Market Street down, and while the Stock Exchange boys over in California and Montgomery Streets schemed and trembled, a jovial crowd collected there where Market and Geary and Kearny came together (Cape Horn, they called the corners, because they were always so windy) to witness the unveiling and dedication of Lotta's Fountain.

Lotta Crabtree—the little girl who had come West with her mother in 1853, who had learned her first songs and dances from Lola Montez while her mother ran a boardinghouse in Grass Valley on the northern Mother Lode and who had gone to school in Cow Hollow when her mother brought her to San Francisco, the vivacious, red-haired, black-eyed kid who had jigged on barrelheads in waterfront saloons, toured the mining camps in a theatrical troupe's buckboard and then had become the toast of the nation—Lotta, the California Diamond, was giving San Francisco this pillar with the drinking fountain in its base because she loved the town and the warm applause of its audiences, and a goodly but unruly crowd gathered at Cape Horn that September day. Most of them were burly larrikins who ambled down from the Barbary Coast to jeer because there was no beer or whisky in the fountain pipes. One reporter described the audience as a mixture of "idle hoodlums to whom it was apparent water would be a precious boon," and "a few women, maidens and children who loved water for its own sweet sake."

By three o'clock, when the ceremony was to have begun, those near the fountain, said the reporter, were being crushed "almost to a jelly" by shoving roughnecks. "Women and children in danger of death from suffocation escaped with great difficulty, assisted by the strong arms of sympathetic gentlemen." The day was saved fifteen minutes later by the arrival of two companies of soldiers who pushed back the crowd, "stood very straight, looked very handsome, and when the canaille crowded upon them too fiercely, trying to break up their serried ranks, pushed them back and brandished their shining muskets in their terrified faces with a heroism unparalleled since Waterloo." Meanwhile, both sides were cheered by onlookers who hung out of Market Street windows, stood on roof tops or looked down on the scene from the white-and-gold Palace Hotel, which was nearing completion across the street.

When order had been restored, Harry Edwards, the popular actor, made a flowery presentation speech in behalf of Lotta, who was on tour in the East. Mayor Otis made a brief and equally flowery speech of acceptance and ceremoniously turned the fountain's brass spigot. The first drink went to a Mrs. Vernon, Lotta's aunt. The Mayor and several other dignitaries took a drink, and then the soldiers were withdrawn and the spectators were permitted to help themselves. It was undoubtedly the first time in months that some of them had swallowed water.

By the time the *hoi polloi* got to the fountain, however, Mayor Otis and his official party and the soldiers had repaired down the street to the Grand Hotel and were hastily clearing the taste of water from their mouths with bumpers of champagne. "After all," observed the Mayor, with a jerk of his thumb in the direction of the fountain, "water and wine are both good—in their places." Everybody agreed the Mayor had hit the nail on the head, and had another bumper.

San Francisco had plenty of hotels, but Ralston had decided to build another one on that corner of Market and New Montgomery, the street he and Harpending had dreamed of pushing through to the south and to the piers down by China Basin. Like most everything else Ralston did or thought of doing, the concept was the answer to a megalomaniac's prayer, and as it went up (at the rate of three hundred thousand bricks a day) newspapers kept San Franciscans fully informed of its world-shaking features: walls two feet thick, a quarter of a mile in circumference and enclosing an area of two and one-half acres; seven stories and eight hundred rooms (all with sun-catching bay windows), and accommodations for twelve hundred guests; more than twenty miles of gas pipe, six miles of sewer pipe and twenty-eight miles of water pipe; four hundred thirty-seven bathtubs, and a water closet in every room; private artesian wells capable of supplying twenty-eight thousand gallons an hour; thermostatic fire detectors in every room; pneumatic tubes for mail, and sixteen electric clocks; five hydraulic elevators; a dining room one hundred fifty feet long, and a central court, into which carriages could be driven from New Montgomery Street, rising the full seven stories past balustraded galleries to an opaque glass roof. Cost: $5,000,000.

As far as fittings were concerned, they were no less staggering. To supply the furniture, Ralston bought an entire furniture factory and kept two hundred fifty men working fifteen hours a day for four months. He ordered nearly thirty thousand specially made dishes, cups and saucers from Haviland in France. He imported tons of Irish linens and bought so much carpeting from W. & J. Sloane that to handle the contract the concern opened a branch store in San Francisco, one that has been in business ever since.

The Palace was officially opened to the universe on October 2, 1875. As awed guests strode through its incredible halls, the memory of the five-weeks-dead Ralston lingered wistfully in the shadows of the long, gaslit corridors, and in a short opening address Senator Sharon, who had taken over Ralston's interest in the hotel, paid tribute to him who had conceived "this glorious temple of hospitality"—this cosmic hostelry.

"I miss, as you do," he said, "the proud and manly spirit of him who devised this magnificent structure. . . . I mourn, as you do, that he is not with us to enjoy this scene of beauty. . . ."

Twelve days later, in the great dining room, San Francisco gave a banquet for Lieutenant General Phil Sheridan. It was the Palace's first social affair of importance. There were many speeches, a lot of rich food, Château d'Yquem, champagne and cognac, and as the distinguished guests rode out of the cobblestoned court that night, their rattling carriages were to them so many magic carpets, wafting them home to bed from a dream whose richness and splendor they would never match in all the dreams of their sleep.

It was a "wonders-will-never-cease" time for Market Street and San Francisco, those Seventies; things happened so fast it made a man's head swim. It wasn't just the Comstock and the stock exchanges and the Palace. A few blocks up the street at Powell, where flowers had bloomed not so long ago in Lansezeur and Harbert's St. Ann Gardens, and where boys had floated packing-case rafts in a stagnant pond, workmen were rushing to completion another Bonanza Inn, Lucky Baldwin's hotel, and the crimson-plush-and-gold theater that was to be called Baldwin's Academy of Music.

The year after the Palace opened was the year of the great Philadelphia Centennial, and that March was when Baldwin threw wide the crimson portals of the Academy of Music, next door to his hotel, and gave Market Street its first luxury theater. Splendid as Ralston's California Theater had been, first-nighters gasped at the broad double staircase that swept from the lobby to the balcony circle, at the immense and gleaming mirrors, at the two huge and imported crystal chandeliers that hung from the ceiling of the high, faraway auditorium dome, at the frescoes (done by a New York Italian) that had set Lucky Baldwin back $30,000, at the satin drop that had cost $6000, at the elegantly fitted proscenium boxes and the magnificent mezzanine boxes.

The play they saw was Cibber's version of Shakespeare's *Richard III*, starring the stormy and temperamental Barry Sullivan. If any of them looked hard on their program that night, they might have found, listed as assistant stage manager and prompter, a stage-struck, twenty-two-year-old South of Market boy named David Belasco.

But the event that dazzled the town that year and sent it to the nearest bar for a toast to Progress was the fast ride of the Lightning Train. In fact, the Lightning Train delighted and thrilled the entire nation, and it was a daring and imaginative present to America on her hundredth birthday.

It started out as a promotion stunt in the inventive brain of Henry C. Jarrett, a New York theatrical producer known as "the Barnum of the Footlights." At a time when normal coast-to-coast train travel consumed seven days, he wanted to close an engagement of Shakespeare's *Henry V* in New York's Booth Theater on Wednesday night, May 31, and open it with the same principal cast in San Francisco on Monday night, June 5. Intrigued not only by the challenge of the idea but by the huge national publicity it would mean, railroad officials planned a phenomenal, transcontinental race against time.

The midnight chimes of New York's Trinity Church had scarcely died away in the first few minutes of June 1, when the sixteen through passengers, including Jarrett, leading members of the *Henry V* cast and five newspapermen, piled into carriages outside the Astor House and raced for the Cortlandt Street ferry. Across the Hudson in Jersey City, a mighty Pennsylvania Railroad engine, steam up, chuffed impatiently beneath the train shed at the Pennsylvania Central Station. At her throttle was one of the Pennsy's crack engineers. Behind the engine was a baggage car, and behind that a hotel coach, the *Thomas A. Scott,* and behind the *Scott* a sleeping car, the *Yosemite.*

It was minutes before one o'clock in the morning when the passengers scrambled aboard, and baggagemen began loading fifteen thousand copies of the *New York Herald* and five hundred pounds of mail into the baggage car. It was three minutes after one on the dot when, to the cheers of spectators and the blazing of fireworks, the Lightning Train pulled out for the Golden Gate.

Until then, the fastest time to Chicago had been twenty-six hours. The Lightning Train made it in twenty hours, fifty-five minutes. Twelve hours later, she rolled into Omaha, averaging fifty miles an hour on the long run from Chicago. Three minutes for refueling, and once more she was pounding down the rails that spanned a continent.

She reached Ogden, Utah, at nine-forty-four Saturday morning. There the Central Pacific took over with its mighty McQueen Engine No. 149 and Hank Small, the line's most daring engineer. Ahead of them, across the perilous Sierra divide, engines were spaced at fifty-mile intervals, ready to speed to the Lightning Train's assistance if she got into trouble. A mile behind, another engine trailed her like a shadow; in case of accident, it would back to the nearest station for help.

On level stretches, she was rocking down the flimsy roadbeds at a break-neck sixty-six miles an hour. At whistle stops men, women and children lined the right of way to cheer on the speeding iron horse. At Terrace, near the end of the Salt Lake division, fifty men shoveled six tons of coal into her tender in less than two minutes.

"So fast are we whirling," wrote *Chronicle* correspondent J. F. Latham, "that the lights of the station seem as near to each other as street lamps. . . . We dash along at an awful pace. . . . Great bonfires are burning at intervals, illuminating the landscape, and we return the compliment with fireworks."

Up the great Sierra divide she panted, from Truckee to Summit, and then plummeted down the steep, eighty-five-mile descent to Rocklin. Through Sacramento she flew, through Stockton, through Niles. Then, at nine-twenty-two Sunday morning, with a long, hoarse blast of triumph from her whistle, the Lightning Train pulled into Oakland.

Seven minutes after that, the elated but travel-weary passengers were on board the Bay ferry. At nine-forty-four o'clock, as the first one stepped to the ferry pier at the foot of Market Street, a twelve-pound mountain how-itzer on the Palace Hotel roof boomed the signal to the whole city that the Lightning Train had finished the most spectacular run in the nation's railroad history. A few minutes more, and the carriages carrying her pas-sengers rounded the corner from Market Street on two wheels, dashed down New Montgomery and rumbled into the galleried courtyard of the Palace. It was eighty-four hours, less six seconds, from the time they left New York.

San Franciscans, reading Reporter Latham's stirring account of the trip in the next day's *Chronicle,* could look back and remember when it took them that long, or longer, to go to Sacramento, across the Bay and ninety miles away.

The next year was the year Market Street got its first Ferry Building (three sheds roofing the Central Pacific and South Pacific Coast ferry slips), and the year Lucky Baldwin, the one-time brickmaker, opened, at Powell and Market, his $2,000,000 House of Gold, with its six floors, mansard roof and dome, its four hundred richly furnished rooms, its roof garden and ladies' billiard room, its paintings on glass hanging in the lobby and illustrating memorable events in the life of Baldwin ("Crossing the Plains," "An Attack by Indians"), its Tiffany clock that Baldwin bought for $25,000 at the Centennial Exposition and that told the time, the day, month and year, the phases of the moon and the condition of the tides, its imported $30-a-yard carpets, its twin mechanical birds (made in Paris) that twittered over the long mahogany bar in the hotel taproom.

The hotel and its Academy of Music did something for that part of Market Street, gave it distinction and glamor. Fashionable shops opened in nearby locations, and it became a San Francisco custom of an afternoon to stroll window-shopping, preening and flirting along The Line, a six-block promenade from the hotel down Market to Kearny and Lotta's Fountain, and down Kearny to Bush. The other side of the street, the south side, was derided as Market Street's "two-bit side" because of its shabby façades, its beer cellars, its medicine shows and cheap restaurants.

To step along The Line, to see the girls in their finery, to catch the mischievous glances they tossed from under the brims of their cart-wheel hats, to watch a tipsy broker swagger from the Baldwin bar scattering $5 gold pieces to the newsboys at Powell and Market, you'd never know there was a depression, but there was. With the collapse of the Comstock market, a tenth of the town was on relief and taxes were rising steadily.

The fabulous Baldwin himself, who had staggered into the Bank of California under the weight of $40,000 in gold coin to demonstrate his confidence in the institution in its unsteadier days, was down to his last string of trotters. Within a year or two after the opening of the hotel, a wholesale liquor dealer attached the hotel safe and its contents for an unpaid bill of $9000. Jim Marvin, chief clerk of the hotel, quoted in C. B. Glasscock's *Lucky Baldwin,* recalled: "Another time he was so badly pressed for cash that he literally pleaded with the Bank of California for a loan of one hundred thousand dollars. The hotel was mortgaged and I guess everything he owned was in the same fix. The bank wouldn't give him the money. He came back scratching his head.

" 'By gad, I'm not licked yet,' he said to me after sitting quietly behind the desk for a while. 'Jim, you come with me.'

"We went to the bank together, and he made a proposition that all the receipts of the hotel should be impounded in the safe under my absolute control until they amounted to enough to pay off his note for one hundred thousand dollars. On that arrangement the bank gave him the money. . . .

"But he was mighty hard up, though he owned thousands of acres of the finest land in the city. The hotel was losing a lot of money. . . . Two or three times while I was there, between 1877 and 1882, I remember the help struck because they weren't paid their wages. Sometimes the management had to get out and rustle up the pay roll before we could serve a meal or get the beds made."

The Palace wasn't doing very well either (less than a year after it opened, Sharon appealed to the city for a lower tax assessment, succeeded in getting it reduced from $2,000,000 to $1,500,000), but Market Street was down on the city map once and for all as The Big Street, and it set itself to ride out the depression. With the establishment of the ferry terminal at its waterfront end, streetcar lines fought for franchises to operate on Market Street, and in the first years of the Eighties it got cable cars and its four sets of tracks. With the laying of the cable-car tracks and the cable slots, Tar Flat, Happy Valley, South Park, Rincon Hill, the lower Mission district and all the rest of the sprawling southern city got a new name, one by which old-timers still call it: "South of the Slot."

But while the street was developing, some of the old faces and the old figures were dropping from The Line. Emperor Norton, for one, had gone in 1880, and two years later, in a Mother Lode hotel room with a stranger at his bedside, Charles Edward Pickett, known from Oregon City to San Diego as "the Philosopher," raised a trembling finger toward the ceiling, whispered, "The gate is open," and then turned his face to the wall and died.

An iconoclast and a one-man revolution wherever he went, "the Philosopher" had added a sort of Donald Duck touch to the frontier side show. Born in Virginia in 1820, Pickett started west to Oregon when a young man with a change of clothing, $200 in cash and a dog-eared copy of Byron's poems. On his arrival in the Willamette Valley a year later, he refused to build cabins or hunt and fish along with the other male members of the community, and contributed what he considered his share by scrawling philosophical gems on shingles, and nailing the shingles to trees.

In 1845, he started the first English-language newspaper on the Coast, a bi-weekly sheet of twelve copies written in longhand and called *The Flumgudgeon Gazette and Bumble Bee Budget.* Under the *nom de guerre,* "The Curltail Coon," Pickett industriously attacked various territorial officials with whose policies he disagreed, calling them liars and rascals. They retaliated by calling him a thief and a debaucher of squaws. After a while, however, Pickett grew bored with picking on officials and Methodist missionaries, and drifted south to California. Picturing himself as a country squire, he ordered from Hawaii five Merino sheep, the first wool-bearing sheep imported to the state, and settled down in Sonoma to become wealthy.

When the Gold Rush put an end to schemes like this, Pickett opened a trading post at Sutter's Fort, ultimately killed a man in self-defense and became the defendant in the first trial conducted at the fort. One feature of this trial was the amount of brandy consumed by judge, jury, defendant and spectators. Another was Sam Brannan, who at one point stepped down from the bench he had been occupying as judge and proceeded to make an impassioned plea for the prosecution.

"Wait a minute," protested Pickett. "You can't do this. You're the judge."

"I know it," replied Brannan, "and I'm the prosecuting attorney, too."

After he had argued the case before himself, Brannan resumed the bench to consider the points he had raised as prosecutor. In the end, the jury disagreed. Pickett was tried again, and acquitted.

For the next twenty years, "the Philosopher" peppered San Francisco editors with lampooning pamphlets and letters on subjects ranging from *The Corruption of Politics in California* to *American Education Analyzed, or a Synoptical Disquisition on the Quality, Culture, Development, Rank and Government of Man.* It was in 1871, however, that he hit the peak of his rebellious career. As a result of a contemporary technical dispute over Supreme Court tenures of office, Pickett became convinced that Justice J. B. Crockett was holding his seat on the bench illegally. When no one in authority would do anything about it, "the Philosopher" decided to act. One morning, as the dignified Justices filed into the courtroom and prepared to take their seats, Pickett charged from the lawyer's enclosure, ran across the platform and sat down in Crockett's chair.

While shocked spectators gasped, Chief Justice Wallace cried, "Where is the bailiff? Who is this man that intrudes himself?"

When the bailiff failed to appear, the Chief Justice collared Pickett, who clung fast to the chair and yelled, "Crockett is a bogus Justice! I have as much right to this seat as he does!"

He began to wrestle with Wallace, and, a moment later, he and the Chief Justice were wildly scuffling on the Supreme Court floor. After a brisk free-for-all, Pickett was overpowered by court attendants who rushed belatedly to the defense of the tribunal and its dignity. He was summarily fined $1000 for contempt and tossed out of the courtroom. Unable to pay, he spent fourteen months in the Broadway Jail, and then, when on the verge of becoming a martyr and a public hero, was released. He promptly turned around and sued the Supreme Court for $100,000 for false imprisonment. But at the end of six years' litigation, a new Supreme Court ruled against "the Philosopher," and his most spectacular revolt came to an end.

For the next year or two, he was a Market Street character, distributing pamphlets that still carried a sting, and amusing his friends with a slapstick review of his battle against the Supreme Court. While on a trip to Yosemite, he was stricken with an intestinal ailment, and died at a Mariposa hotel operated by a Mrs. Jane Gallison, who befriended the eccentric in his last days. At his dying request, she attended his funeral and, as the gravediggers covered his pine coffin, read aloud Pickett's favorite poem, Byron's gloomy and misanthropic *Inscription on the Monument of a Newfoundland Dog.*

Another to go was the aloof, reserved and sardonic Tom Blythe. Strollers along The Line used to see him standing outside his office at 724 Market, dressed always in a black suit and top hat, and standing or sitting beside him would always be his four huge dogs, of which he prized most highly a St. Bernard he called General Grant. The promenaders all recognized him, and nodded to him, and with a cold dignity he would nod back. His presence there on the street was a tiny cloud, a sudden chilly, sobering draught, and it would be a moment or two before the strollers, passing him and nodding to him, would smile again and turn their eyes once more to the bright shop windows. If Tom Blythe realized this, it did not disturb him; he had been there on Market Street before some of them were born. And besides that, and all his money, he had a dream and a passion that must have been a flame in his heart.

Actually, his name was not Thomas Blythe. He had been born Thomas Williams in Mold, Wales, in 1822. As a youth, he worked in Welsh drapers' shops and grocery stores. He was a clerk in a Liverpool clothing establishment. At length, weary of drifting, he started a contracting firm in Birkenhead. It failed. And when it did, Thomas Williams changed his name to Thomas Blythe. More important than that, he changed the entire pattern of his life; breaking all ties, he sailed for California, and arrived in San Francisco on the heels of the first Forty-niners.

Within a few years he had shrewdly laid the foundation for a fortune. By a mortgage foreclosure, he took over the block bounded by Market, Dupont and Geary for an original investment of a little more than $1000. For another song, he bought the adjoining block, bounded by Dupont, Geary, Stockton and O'Farrell. Then all he had to do was sit back, wait for the expansion of the city to catch up with him, and he was rich.

In 1873, during a visit to England, Blythe had a love affair with a girl named Julia Perry. After his return to America, she bore him a daughter. This daughter, who was christened Florence, whom he had never seen and never was to see, became the one, dominating passion of his life. He wrote long letters to the child, dwelling happily on the day when she would be old enough to join him in San Francisco. In anticipation of that time, he even built a house for her; it is 1000 Chestnut Street, standing now on the northern slope of Russian Hill.

Meanwhile, he became fascinated with the idea of establishing a great agricultural empire on the desert wastelands of southeastern California by irrigating them with water diverted from the Colorado River. He filed claim to forty thousand acres along the river under the terms of the Swamp and Overflow Act, and, looking out over those acres, he saw, not the desolation they were, but fields of waving corn, mile after mile of alfalfa, sugar cane and cotton, and melons ripening in the hot sun. At Black Point, on the banks of the river, Blythe's engineers worked night and day, blasting a canal bed through the solid granite to make the mirage a reality.

Blythe visited the project in November, 1882. Dressed in black as he always was, with a black shawl pulled around his shoulders, he stood on the riverbank looking down into the narrow cut of the canal. It was almost finished. "You've done a fine piece of work," he said to the engineer at his side. "Go on with it. Finish the ditch."

Less than six months later, Blythe suffered a paralytic stroke in his rooms at 26 Geary Street, above Radovich's saloon. He fell at the feet of a friend and said, "Oh, I'm cold. Cover me up warm and don't move me." A few minutes after that he was dead.

Work on his Palo Verde irrigation project stopped abruptly, and in Blythe's name was never completed. Most of his four-million-dollar fortune went to the daughter he had never known. As Florence Blythe Hinckley, as Florence Blythe Hinckley Moore and as Florence Blythe Hinckley Moore Musgrave, she became a sparkling member of the champagne set, not only in San Francisco, but in Chicago and in New York and on the Continent. Following the death, in 1927, of her third husband, Dr. William Everett Musgrave, nationally known San Francisco physician, she retired to comparative seclusion and died in Oakland in 1941.

Now there is Hoover Dam, and the All-American canal, harnessing and directing the waters of the Colorado. Cotton blooms and date trees grow and melons ripen in green, fertile valleys that her father dreamed of long ago.

Men like Pickett and Blythe died, and like Senator Sharon. The Fortyniners were dwindling, and the tent city, the boom city, the sand-hill city of the bawdy, lusty, quick-on-the-trigger days was gone, too. Also, the Comstock was dead, and the men who had been pioneers no longer tossed off their forty-rod and bawled *Oh, Susanna* and *Say, What Was Your Name in the States?,* and shot out the lights of the Bella Union bar sheerly because they were alive and their muscles strong and they felt good in their guts. That city and that time were past and lost.

Now, instead of yelling its head off at Lotta Crabtree's buck and wing, the town was jamming Platt's Hall in Montgomery Street to hear and admire the delicate aphorisms of the tall, pale and long-haired Oscar Wilde. Emma Nevada, the California Linnet, sweetly singing *Listen to the Mocking Bird* enthralled the town, and it fell at the feet of Adelina Patti when she arrived on her national tour in her thirty-thousand-dollar private railroad car with its gold plush upholstery, its hand-carved piano, its satin rosebuds and pink bedchamber. Theatergoers were impressed, delighted and charmed by Sarah Bernhardt in *Frou-Frou* and *Camille*. Society, taking itself pretty seriously now, engaged in a polite scuffle for membership in Ned Greenway's Friday Night Cotillion Club, and emerged only slightly flushed and with its Eugénie curls only slightly disheveled. On Mt. Olympus, which rose over the western end of Market Street, Adolph Sutro, another Comstock millionaire, unveiled his gift to the city, the statue *Triumph of Light* (a concrete copy of a Belgian work of art showing Liberty victorious over Despotism), and school children listened with grave interest as the donor concluded his speech with the solemn plea, "May the light shine from the torch of the Goddess of Liberty to inspire our citizens to good and noble deeds for the benefit of mankind." On a different level, Dr. C. C. O'Donnell, the city coroner, blamed thirteen of the city's eighty-six suicides in one year (1885-1886) of this decade on cheap Chinese labor. "Inability to obtain work actuated thirteen of our noble citizens to sacrifice their lives rather than lead a life of crime. . . . (They) were crowded out of every avenue of employment by the base Coolie slaves of Asia," he said in his annual report. He recommended that the Board of Supervisors avert additional suicides from this cause by abating Chinatown and all resident Chinese as a public nuisance.

But in spite of the yearning after elegance, in spite of its trying to act grownup and civilized and cultured and above its crude beginnings, there was still a good brawl or two left in the town, still a time when it could kick up its heels and get out in the middle of Market Street and raise hell.

A day like this came on February 5, 1887, when San Franciscans woke up, looked out their windows and saw such a strange sight they could hardly believe their eyes; the streets, the hills, the house tops, the trees— everything, as far as the eye could see, was covered with snow. Swept into the city on a northwest wind, it had started falling at three o'clock in the morning. When the storm was over, it had mantled the city in depths ranging from three inches downtown to one foot in Golden Gate Park.

A child living in California Street had never seen snow, and thought it was feathers, or bits of white paper, or sugar, or salt. Hastily pulling on his clothes, he ran into the street and scooped up a handful. "I'm going to put it away in my closet and show it to people," he explained to a passer-by. As it turned to water in his hands, he looked bewildered and began to cry.

Young blades made sleighs out of packing boxes and boards, hitched horses to them and drove down Market Street, laughing and waving to pedestrians. Children improvised toboggans out of their mothers' ironing boards and slid down the Powell Street hill.

As the morning wore on, however, and as everyone started throwing snowballs, the situation got a little out of hand. Mayor Pond had his hat knocked off as he stepped outside of City Hall. Dignified judges on their way to court sessions were sent scrambling for the shelters of doorways. Roughnecks pelted streetcar passengers and cable-car gripmen with snowballs containing rocks. What began as genial snow fights ended in free-for-alls and flurries of policemen's clubs. One irate citizen, who took a snowball on the chin, pulled a gun on several small boys and fired four shots at them before he was disarmed by police.

"It would not have been so bad," wrote one commentator, "if the throwers of the snowy spheres had acted halfway fairly and endeavored to send a chill down the backs on only their own kind. But no one was spared. The snow of the clouds was bestowed on rich and poor, dignified and undignified, man and maid, learned and ignorant, washed and unwashed alike. Nor were the balls thrown in a sportive way, but after being pressed as hard as stones were sent with all the force of powerful arms. The result to the recipient was, as may be supposed, far from pleasant, and bruised faces, black eyes, bloody noses and damaged hats were as common as lampposts."

Chinese rash enough to venture beyond the borders of Chinatown drew a merciless volley of snowballs wherever they went. In retaliation, they seized whites they found in Chinatown and thrashed them soundly with sticks and bamboo poles. At City Hall, the tax collector and the assessor rallied their office crews, declared war on each other, and soon snowballs were smacking against the august walls of City Hall corridors. The tax collector's men quickly routed the assessor's forces, and chased the assessor himself into the license collector's office.

Throughout the day, however, attacks on streetcars remained the most hilarious good time. At one Market Street intersection, a gang of hoodlums, becoming bored with snowballs, seized shovels and heaved shovelfuls of snow on streetcar platforms as they went by. A conductor on a Hayes Street line leaped from his car and caught the youth who had hit him in the eye with a snowball. The youth's companions promptly fell upon the conductor, knocked out two of his teeth and were drubbing him unconscious when the gripman sprang to his aid with an iron switch hook and rescued him. Hundreds of car windows were shattered, and, finally, most cable and horse cars stopped running altogether. One street railroad company voted its men half a day's extra pay to compensate them for the indignities they suffered.

The next day, most of the snow was gone, and sunny California was itself again, and it was with an air of relief that the *Chronicle* reported, "The day after the visitation of the snowstorm was one of thaw."

The Nineties came to Market Street, and, if you like the phrase, you can call them "the Champagne Days," remembering that, as at any other time, only a few had the price of champagne and only a few drank it. Thousands of others—in Cow Hollow, say—couldn't afford it, and preferred steam beer, anyway. They also preferred corned beef and cabbage to terrapin *à la* Maryland, and they never saw the inside of the Poodle Dog or Marchand's. If you asked them about the Nineties, they would say that that time was overrated.

In retrospect, though, you can see that it was a time before disaster, and you can see how a memory could look back and call them the good old days—before the Fire. Because, after the Fire, nothing was the same, or ever has been. Market Street and the rest of the town aged a hundred years in four days.

There were events that made some of those years stand out. 'Ninety-one, for example, was the year Kalakaua, King of the Sandwich Islands, died at the Palace and the guns boomed from the harbor forts as the cruiser *Charleston* moved down the stream and out through the Gate, taking him home. And that was the year the California Academy of Sciences moved into the big, five-story building on Market, just east of Fifth (James Lick's money had built it, and it was the finest museum building in America, they said). And the next year was the year Gentleman Jim Corbett, the Hayes Valley boy, knocked John L. Sullivan silly at New Orleans and brought home to San Francisco the heavyweight championship of the world.

If you were a blood in those years, and had money, you drove your team of bays through Golden Gate Park on Sunday afternoons, and had champagne cocktails and pressed duck at the Cliff House that evening; and if you were poor you took the ferry to Marin County across the Bay and hiked up Tamalpais and came back to town in time for dinner at Sanguinetti's. Either way, though, there were certain things you did on Market Street.

You had a game of billiards at the Café Royal, and saw Little Egypt dance at the Midway Plaisance and applauded, until your hands stung, MacIntyre and Heath in *The Ham Tree,* that played at the old Bijou, there between Third and Fourth. You took in the waxworks at the Eden Musée, and the freak shows and the medicine men in the lot near the Café Royal, and everything that went with them: Joaquin Murietta's head, "preserved in purest alcohol"; and the three-legged lady, who got mad one night and picked up her third leg (it was wooden), tucked it under her arm and flounced off the stage; and Oofty-Goofty, the Wild Man of Borneo; and the King of Pain, in flaming red underwear, a robe and an ostrich-plumed hat, screaming his pitch for his aconite liniment—these, and the beating of drums, the cries of the shills and the barkers, the oily smoke from the flaring torches and the sounds of the Market Street traffic going by.

You sat in the bleachers of the sand lots at Market and Tenth (across the way from the canvas panorama of Yosemite Falls) and watched the kids play ball in the summer evenings, and you treated your girl to a strawberry soda at Slaven's Drug Store in the Baldwin Hotel, hearing, maybe, as you stood outside afterward and wondered where to go and what to do next, the sound of the Trinity Church bells drifting down Powell Street from Union Square, and the humming of the west wind in all the electric wires, and the rattling of hack wheels on the cobblestones.

You sauntered down The Line and stared at the characters: the Tamale Man crooning his call and peddling his hot tamales there at Market and O'Farrell; the Astronomer, who for a nickel would let you look at the moon through the long telescope he had set upon its tripod near the curbing, and Floating Annie (Annie Edgar, her real name was), who, on her way to work at Mrs. Mish's millinery store, moved so gracefully the boys on The Line swore she didn't walk, she floated. These, and Anna Held, maybe, and Tessie Wall, the Tinsel Queen of the Tenderloin, and Mayor Jimmie Phelan, and certainly White Hat McCarty. . . .

White Hat was a card for you. Dan was his first name and he'd come from Boston in the Seventies and made his living as a racehorse trainer. In 1887, after he'd won $100,000 backing a fifty-to-one shot in the American Derby at Chicago, he bought himself a white beaver hat, which he wore tilted to one side of his crop of brown, curly hair, a checked suit, a flashy vest, a heavy gold watch chain and a golden horseshoe for the watch chain.

He bought himself a stable—Sorrento, Mollie McCarty and Bridal Veil were his horses—and plunged at the Bay District track, at Emeryville and Tanforan. When he had money, he spent it like a Comstock king, buying champagne for the house at the Baldwin bar or the Palace, and flinging regal tips to every waiter and bartender in sight.

He became the inseparable companion of a young British nobleman who lived for a while down the Peninsula in Burlingame, Lord Talbot Clifton, and he used to tool the Clifton tallyho and its four spanking grays down Market Street and into New Montgomery and then through the Palace's carriage entrance and into the Palm Court, sending a ripple of excitement to every one of its seven balconies and bringing oldsters from their rocking chairs to the gallery railing to look down and watch White Hat toss the ribbons to a waiting lackey, majestically descend from the box and head for the carpeted floor, the sparkling chandeliers—and the bourbon whisky—of the Palace bar.

One day in 1896, he and Lord Clifton drew up in front of the Lick House in Montgomery Street. They looked in vain for a hitching post to which to tie the horses. "I'll take care of that," said White Hat, and disappeared into the Lick House bar. A moment later, he reappeared with a free-lunch-counter doughnut, which he fastened to the bit of one of the horses with a piece of string. The two then repaired to the taproom for a few brandy smashes. They were on their fifth when the cop on the beat tapped McCarty on the shoulder. "White Hat," he said, "you're under arrest for violating the runaway horse ordinance. The law says your horses must be tied to a hitching post, or tethered to a heavy weight."

"We'll fight the case," said White Hat.

In court the next day, Judge Campbell, a whiskery and jovial gentleman, listened gravely to the testimony. Then he slanted a wink at White Hat, and declared solemnly, "In all my career on the bench, I have never presided over so weighty a case. And may I say it is beyond the realm of my imagination that the defendant's horses could possibly have run away when they were tied to a free-lunch-counter doughnut. None that I have ever sampled has weighed less than a ton. Case dismissed."

White Hat was a card, all right, and you saw him often, strutting down The Line like a flock of ducks on the wing, with his white plug hat cocked to one side and the golden horseshoe on his watch chain flashing in the sun. You saw Lucky Baldwin, too, whose red Maltese cross, the emblem of his famous Santa Anita stables, had come home the winner in three Derbys, and who liked his horses high and clean-limbed and his women young and melting. And Tod Sloan, the little jockey who swaggered in and out of the Baldwin bar, and up and down The Line with you and the rest. You heard about the time when a horse-drawn milk truck stopped in front of the Powell Street entrance of the Baldwin every morning with fifty ten-gallon cans of milk for Anna Held's milk baths, and how Tod, joking with friends at the bar, said maybe he ought to start taking milk baths to improve his riding. The friends went to the hotel kitchen, got some of the cans and took them up to a bathroom on the second floor and dumped the milk into the tub for Tod's bath. He splashed around in it for half an hour, and that day rode a winner at Ingleside. Every day after that, while Anna Held was at the Baldwin, Tod took a milk bath, and as long as he took them he never lost a race.

Another character you saw along The Line was Steve Brodie, who had jumped off the Brooklyn Bridge in '86, and you heard the story of why he left the Baldwin Hotel and would never stay there again. Brodie had been passing the time of day in St. Ann's Louvre, the bar across Powell

Street from the Baldwin, when in walked his friend Yankee Sullivan leading a beer-drinking goat. Brodie decided to take the goat up to his room in the Baldwin to show his wife how it drank beer. He and the goat got as far as the hotel lobby, where they were stopped by the clerk. It was against the house rules of the Baldwin, he said, to take a goat up-stairs. One word led to another, and soon he and Brodie were trading punches. When the fight was over, the only thing standing upright in the wreckage of the lobby was the goat. Brodie picked himself off the floor, went upstairs, washed the blood from his face, packed his bags, took his wife by the arm and marched out of the hotel forever.

A year or so after that, you were one of those thousands that milled in Market Street that St. Patrick's Day in '97 to read the bulletins on the screen there on the *Chronicle* Building at Market and Kearny, across from the Palace—the bulletins about the fight in Reno, the battle of the century between Gentleman Jim and Ruby Rob Fitzsimmons. You read the danc-ing words on the screen that said Jim drew blood in the fifth, splitting Fitzsimmons' lip, and heard the yells that rose over the street when the bulletin for the sixth said Fitz had gone down for the count of nine. And you were incredulous and silent with all the others when the words on the screen said Corbett, the Champ, was down and out in the four-teenth, and the fight was all over and Ruby Rob was king of the heavy-weights. (Eastward in Reno, as you read them, Gentleman Jim was rock-ing to and fro on his dressing-room cot and crying over and over, "James J., James J., where are you now?")

That was the Market Street scene in those days, and that's what you saw and heard and did there; that's what you would remember in days to come.

There was another crowd around Lotta's Fountain, outside the *Chronicle* Building, more than a year later, November 22 of '98 it was, and this time the bulletins were telling them of Gentleman Jim's fight against Sailor Tom Sharkey back in New York. When it was finished, they broke up and wandered off to the late bars muttering and shaking their heads and wondering at the strange way the fight had ended (Cor-bett lost the decision when his second leaped into the ring in the middle of the ninth round). Then they went home to bed and didn't wake up until they heard the fire engines racing through the streets. They got up and peered out their windows and saw a glow in the sky, low above the tops of the buildings and looking as though it was coming from Market Street. They pulled on their clothes and ran down the hills and along the dark streets to Market, following the sound of the engines and, as they got closer, the cries, and the crackling of the flames. When they reached Market, they stopped and stared in terror and in wonder. It was the Baldwin Hotel.

It started in the second-floor kitchen, on the Ellis Street side, a little after three in the morning. Thirty minutes later, the flames were licking along every floor, every corridor. Fire Chief Dennis T. Sullivan ordered a fourth alarm, and the horse-drawn engines began arriving from fire stations all over the city. Someone had pulled the hotel light switch, and two hundred fifty guests and some fifty employees, aroused from sleep by the smell of smoke, by the wild cry of "Fire!", by frenzied kicking and pounding on their doors, milled blindly around inside the dark, six-story structure, frantically seeking a way out. Many were lucky, and found it themselves; others were saved only by the heroism of firemen and fellow victims, and four never found it, dying inside the building. The fifth fatality was a traveling salesman who for years had carried a rope in his suitcase for just such an emergency. He secured it fast inside his fifth-floor room, and lowered two women down it to safety. Then he climbed to the window ledge and started down. Between the fifth and fourth floors, the life line snapped. He struck the Market Street pavement on his back and was dead when they picked him up.

At four-twenty o'clock, the great dome and cupola crashed one hundred sixty-two feet to the street. At four-thirty-four, the dome of the Baldwin Theater collapsed to the stage on which, a few hours before, William Gillette had starred in *Secret Service*. By five o'clock, all three fronts of the building were ablaze and flames were soaring two hundred feet into the dark, pre-dawn sky. Behind the fire lines stood thousands of spectators, all silent, all pale, all struck with awe by the sight, all looking up. . . .

Late the next afternoon, reporters saw a frail, white-haired man of seventy, clad in a shabby Prince Albert, hovering about the water-soaked rubble and the charred ruins. It was Lucky Baldwin. He had made $20,000,000 on the Comstock and had lived on Nob Hill with the best of them, but his luck had turned. The rich, wide acres of Santa Anita, his timberlands at Lake Tahoe, his ranchos of La Merced and La Cienega, his Los Angeles real estate holdings—all were mortgaged to the hilt, and he was far in debt; and now, all but beggared by the destruction of his House of Gold, he wrung his hands in despair as he climbed to the ruins of the second floor, where the new hotel café had been. As the reporters watched, he grubbed around in the blackened wreckage. After a while, he found several things he seemed to think worth saving. He wiped them clean on his coat, then bound them in a tablecloth and carefully lowered them on a rope to the street. Curious, the reporters walked over to see what the old man had so tenderly salvaged. They unwrapped the tablecloth. It contained $10 worth of knives and forks.

So that was the end of the brief landmark known as the Baldwin Hotel, and that was the end of the Baldwin Theater, which for twenty-two years had been the town's best, and that was the end of The Line.

A little more than a year after that, the crowds once more thronged into Market Street, this time to dance and blow their horns, throw confetti and cry and kiss the century good-by. The midnight chimes of that New Year's Eve pealed sadly across the hills, and down on the Bay at the end of the street, the whistles of the ships made a brave and lonely sound across the water and the dark, restless tides.

Less than six years later, the street they danced upon was a boulevard of despair and desolation. Not buildings bustling with work and commerce, but the black skeletons of buildings, stretching as far as the eye could see. Not music, or the sound of footsteps, or street cries, or the clip-clop of horses' hoofs, or the clatter of streetcars, but silence broken only by the keening wind that picked up the city's dust and ashes and scattered them to the sky. Not life, but death.

That was the way the earthquake and fire of 1906 left Market Street.

"It is a clear bright day in early September," wrote Thomas Robins for *Scribner's Magazine*. "The hot sun of a long rainless summer is tempered by distant fog upon the Southern ocean. A broad modern boulevard crowded with vehicles resounds with the clear, crisp stamp of horses' hoofs upon the asphalt, mingled with the wail of hurrying automobiles. A leisurely crowd throngs the footways. . . . It is a gay throng, moving to and fro in leisurely fashion, or darting in and out of shops whose windows display in brilliant profusion the costliest fabrics of all countries. . . . Everyone appears to be regardless of any skeleton at the feast; yet in easy sight, to the eastward, above the low sky line of the shops, as far as the eye can reach and farther, following the contour of the hills from the Golden Gate to the Potrero, are four square miles of dust, ashes and desolation, ruins of what were but a few short weeks before the homes of three hundred thousand people.

". . . Can it be possible," he wondered, "that these people, so intent on the diversions of a Saturday afternoon, were but yesterday the inhabitants of those homes? . . . Is it they who escaped with little more than the clothes on their backs, to lie for many nights under the stars on the sand hills? How can they carry the disaster in their memories and yet, to all seeming, put it so completely out of their minds?"

Many articles like this appeared about that time in eastern magazines and newspapers, and they told an admiring world of San Francisco's attitude and comeback. But that San Franciscans recovered from the disaster is not astonishing. Natural calamities have driven no people in the world from the place they called home. In Guatemala, in Tokyo, in Naples, in London, in Chicago, in the Mississippi and the Connecticut valleys—in a hundred other cities and places, fires have burned, earthquakes have struck, floods have surged, and always, patiently, the people have rebuilt their homes and have gone on living their lives on the familiar streets, under the familiar sky, within sight of the familiar trees.

What was exceptional about the San Franciscans was the swift strength of their resiliency, the optimistic power of their bounce that brought them to say, not a month later or a year later, but within a week, "Let's not stand around feeling sorry for ourselves. We've had good times. Now this is a bad time, and there's work to do. Let's get going."

And so there was no brooding, nor even a question of timidity or fear or lost faith; the way their fathers had after the fires fifty years before, they began rebuilding their homes and the city they loved. Feverishly they tore down the shells of buildings until Market Street was a desert of rubble. Then they laid down temporary railroad tracks to dumps at First and Market, at New Montgomery and Market, and other points along the street. Then, with carts and wagons brought from ranches and towns in all parts of the state, they hauled the debris to the dumps, where it was loaded upon freight cars and drawn away. Experts from the East shook their heads and said it would take five years to clear Market Street at that rate. But the street was clear in a matter of months, and twelve-, fifteen- and twenty-story buildings were going up where four- and five-story buildings had stood before.

All the days of her life, San Francisco's approach to personal value has been, "Tell me not what a man has, but what he is." That is engraved upon the city's heart; the words are the embodiment of her spirit. And that is why her people could smile and leisurely promenade on that clear bright day in early September. The important things had not burned to death in the Fire. San Franciscans still had courage and good will and faith in themselves.

What more, they asked, do we need?

Market Street, from the Ferry Building to Civic Center, where they were preparing to build a new City Hall, was the thoroughfare whose permanent buildings were first finished and occupied. Regraded along the stretch the pioneers had called "McCoppin's Canal," relighted, with the old wholesale district down by the waterfront gone and a new retail district in its place, with buildings that had withstood the disaster restored, with towering brick-and-steel structures in place of wooden ones and a new Palace Hotel two months from completion, it looked bigger, better and more impressive than ever to San Franciscans, and they decided to celebrate.

"It was," said the late City Controller Harold J. Boyd, "as if everyone in San Francisco suddenly turned to the next fellow and said, 'Let's get drunk.'"

The party was a gay, five-day affair in October, 1909, and it was called the Portolá Festival in honor of Don Gaspar de Portolá, whose men had discovered San Francisco Bay one hundred forty years before.

Those festival nights, more than a million lights blazed along Market Street. A great Mission bell, made of twenty-five thousand lights and visible for fifty miles at sea, hung over the city. On Battleship Row on the Bay, cruisers from the German, Italian, Japanese, Dutch, British and American navies fired salutes and raked the night sky with searchlight beams. Batteries of fanfaronade and Roman candles, flights of spider bombs, rockets and aerial wrigglers burst in a dazzling fireworks display over Union Square. A daredevil walked across Market Street high overhead on a tightrope, and Nick Covarrubias, portraying Don Gaspar, fell off his horse in the middle of the great Portolá parade.

Once more, the phoenix had risen from the ashes. That was worth a party, and so they had one.

The city was changed, the street was different, the halcyon days were over, and now they had a great good deed behind them to live up to in the eyes of the rest of the nation and the world, but there came a night when time stood still for San Franciscans, and that night, that Christmas Eve in 1910, they gathered slowly in the streets.

Half believing, half skeptical, they came to learn if what they had heard was true, if it was true that Luisa Tetrazzini was going to sing for them beside the fountain Lotta Crabtree had given them half a lifetime before.

They streamed into the great intersection at Market, Third, Kearny and Geary Streets until they were massed in Market Street from store front to store front. They faced Lotta's Fountain and a large platform that had been erected at the curbing before the entrance to the *Chronicle* Building. Some say they numbered one hundred thousand, some say two hundred fifty thousand. They stood quietly, waiting.

A few weeks before, in New York, Luisa Tetrazzini had had contract difficulties. Oscar Hammerstein said she was under contract to him and wanted her to sing in New York. She said her manager was William H. Leahy, who had booked her for an engagement in San Francisco. She issued a defiant statement to the New York press: "I will sing in San

Francisco if I have to sing there in the streets, for I know the streets of San Francisco are free."

She and Leahy won the case, and she was going to keep her promise to the city in which, five years before, she had made her American debut.

Now the crowd stretched as far as she could see, and now she, too, was waiting for the moment when she would step upon the platform, upon the dais at the edge of the platform, and lift her silver voice to the stars.

She and the members of her party were chatting gaily in the *Chronicle's* executive offices on the second floor of the building. From the platform below drifted the voices of a massed choir and the accompaniment of Paul Steindorff's symphony orchestra. The choir was singing Christmas carols.

"I never thought I would be a street singer," Tetrazzini had said, "but I want to do this for San Francisco, because this is the first place in the United States where I sang, and because I like San Francisco better than any other city in the world. San Francisco is my country."

So there she was, her eyes sparkling with excitement, her face radiant with happiness. She had dressed carefully, covering her plump, stocky figure with a trailing white gown that was heavy and stiff with hundreds of flashing brilliants. She wore a broad-brimmed hat and white gloves, and carried a white ostrich boa. Over her gown was thrown a cloak of old rose.

She went to the window once and looked down at the great crowd, and her handkerchief fluttered a greeting. From the street came an answering roar of applause.

A few moments later, the time had come. Atop the Monadnock Building across the street a green light flashed the signal for her appearance. Clinging to Mayor McCarthy's arm, she descended to the street floor, left the building, swept through the door cut into the sound shell at the back of the platform, and stood like a queen before the cheering throng.

They say that no man who was there will ever forget the way it happened—the vast crowd in Market Street, every man with head bared, the people clustered in the office building windows and on the balconies of the Palace Hotel down the street, and Luisa, then thirty-six, at the peak of her career and the greatest coloratura of her time, standing there in the spotlight singing *I Would Linger in This Dream* and *The Last Rose of Summer.*

The song poured from her throat full, clear and flawless, and filled with a stabbing beauty. So resonant and rich was her voice, they say, it seemed to fill the air, and come from invisible sounding boards everywhere. It came back from the walls of the Monadnock Building as from the wall of a cathedral. It soared up to heaven and reached a last high note and held it so long and perfectly there seemed no limit to the breath behind it.

The singing, the wistful words, the spell of Christmas Eve and the knowing it would never come like this again in their lives—a feeling made of all these things, an ache, like saying good-by to someone you love, reached the hearts of the people when it was all over, and they sang *Auld Lang Syne* together with tears streaming down their cheeks.

As the last notes died away, cheer after cheer welled from their throats and echoed across the square, and Luisa bowed and smiled and waved her handkerchief. Then she turned away and shook hands with Conductor Steindorff. Someone gave her a basket of scarlet poinsettias. She threw one last kiss to the crowd, gathered her cloak about her shoulders and left the stage.

The spotlights flicked off. The musicians folded their stands and put their instruments away. The people lingered for a while, and then, as gradually as they had come, drifted from the square. Soon the streetcars were running again past Lotta's Fountain, where the platform lay deserted in the shadows.

People say that peace and good will seemed to lay like a blessing upon the city's hills that night, and she seemed to belong to the stars that burned high in the soft December sky.

South of the Slot

12. MISSION STREET

"TRUE TO THE DOT" · FATHER SERRA'S ROSARY. FROM MONTEREY TO ANZA'S LAGOON. THE FOUNDING OF MISSION DOLORES · CALIFORNIA PASTORALE · THE PLANK ROAD · TAR FLAT AND HAPPY VALLEY · TAKING THE AIR · MEMORIES OF WOODWARD'S GARDENS · FRANCIS L. A. PIOCHE, PIONEER CAPITALIST: HIS LIFE AND DEATH · THE U. S. MINT. OLD WIVES' TALES. "THE SHADOW" · THE BONANZA OF BERNAL HEIGHTS, AND THE GREAT GOLD RUSH OF THE SEVENTIES · SOUTH OF MARKET BOYS. THE PASSING SHOW

TELEGRAPH HILL and Portsmouth Square, Nob Hill and North Beach, California Street, Chinatown and those places are all what San Franciscans call, in a general way, North of Market. Roughly half the city is south of Market, or would be if Market Street were extended from Twin Peaks (where its diagonal thrust down and across the San Francisco peninsula ends) to the coast.

Just as the northern city has divided itself into districts, so has this area. The largest is The Mission, named after Mission Dolores and Mis-

257

sion Street, which, in turn, comprises smaller districts like Eureka Valley and Glen Park, Fairmont and Bernal Heights and Noé Valley. Other comprehensive districts include the specific South of Market—South of the Slot, as it was known in the old days—downtown and hugging the waterfront and also having its component neighborhoods like Tar Flat, Happy Valley, Pleasant Valley, South Park and Rincon Hill; and then, farther south and on the southern hills, districts like Bay View, Potrero Hill, Butchertown and Hunter's Point.

You would never know it to read the books on San Francisco, but there are persons who have lived all their lives in these twenty-two square miles of San Francisco and have never set foot on Nob Hill, have never looked down on Alcatraz from Telegraph Hill, have never got drunk at the Happy Valley Bar in the Palace, have never eaten a Virginia-ham breakfast at the Cliff House or cracked crab at Fisherman's Wharf, and wouldn't know the Hotel Fairmont lobby from the concourse of the Grand Central Station. But that's all right with them; they like it in South of Market. There's a poem they remember, written by a South of Market boy named Miles Overholt, and its first stanza tells how they feel about their side of the city:

> *Whether you know your locations or not,*
> *The heart of the city is South o' the Slot!*
>   *That is the spot,*
>   *True to the dot—*
> *The heart of the city is South o' the Slot.*

So you can read all you want to about how glamorous San Francisco used to be, or is, but never forget that these people are part of it and have been since the Gold Rush; and if Nob Hill and Russian Hill and Montgomery Street and Fisherman's Wharf have given the city charm and romance, these districts and these people have given it punch and toughness, a sense of humor and a crude strength. Their men run the streetcars and are the cops on the beats; they slaughter the steers and stoke the foundry furnaces, and their sons are priests; they build the ships, and load and sail the ships; they drive the trucks and run the trains; they lay the bricks and build the tall buildings, and through their veins runs the red blood of many nations.

Before there was any San Francisco, there was the Mission San Francisco de Asis, almost at the northern and farthest end of the dusty Pathway of the Padres that began at San Diego and wound north along the coast and the coastal mountains to Sonoma. To the Franciscan Father Junípero Serra fell, in 1768, the holy but arduous duty of establishing the Alta California Missions. Leaving Mexico, he and a hardy and zealous band of fathers pushed to the Pacific Coast, founding first the Mission San Diego de Alcalá, and sending exploring parties to the north to choose the sites of other missions. Four were selected, the names for them drawn from the calendar of saints and angels: San Gabriel Arcángel, San Luis Obispo de Tolosa, San Antonio de Pádua, and, the farthest north, on the shores of the Bay of Monterey, San Cárlos Borromeo.

Disturbed because none was dedicated to the patron of his order, Father Serra took the matter up with the military commander of the territory. The general curtly replied, "If our seraphic father, Saint Francis of Assisi, would have his name to signalize some station on these shores, let him show us a good haven."

Not long after that, the explorers found the great Bay, the good haven, and, half believing St. Francis had led them there, named it the Bay of San Francisco. In June, 1776, three months after Lieutenant Colonel Juan Bautista de Anza had selected the site for the Presidio on the rolling mesa by the Bay, and the site for the Mission by a willow-shaded lagoon he called La Laguna de Nuestra Señora de los Dolores, a small expedition set out from the dunes of Monterey, bound for that mesa and that lagoon. The translation of Fray Francisco Palóu's *Historical Memoirs of New California,* edited by Dr. Herbert E. Bolton, describes the little band as follows:

"It was composed of its commander, Lieutenant Don José Joaquín Moraga, a sergeant, two corporals and ten soldiers, all with their wives and families except the commander. . . . In addition there were seven families of settlers . . . other persons attached to the soldiers and their families; five servant boys, muleteers and *vaqueros,* who conducted about two hundred head of the King's cattle and some belonging to individuals, and the mule train which carried the provisions and utensils necessary for the road. All of the foregoing belonged to the new Presidio. And for whatever concerned the first Mission that was to be founded, we two ministers, Father Pedro Benito Cambón and I, went with two servants who conducted the loads, and three unmarried neophytes . . . who drove the cattle for the Mission, numbering eighty-six head. . . ."

Traveling by easy stages, for several of the women were pregnant, the expedition reached the lagoon on the twenty-seventh and there pitched its tents. Indians, bearded and naked, timidly approached the camp, bringing shy gifts of shellfish and wild seeds.

On the next day, Lieutenant Moraga ordered the construction of a small arbor of branches, and in this arbor, on June 29, Father Palóu celebrated the first mass on the site of the Mission San Francisco de Asis.

With happy hearts, the colonists began construction of the Presidio and the Mission that were to be the outpost homes of Spanish might and Spanish faith. A mule train came by land and the *San Cárlos* by sea with supplies and willing help. By the middle of September, the Presidio had been completed and dedicated, over by the white cliffs of the headlands that Father Font had written about in the light of the Mountain Lake campfires, and a few weeks later the Mission chapel, with its crudely hewn timbers of redwood and its roof of tule reeds, was finished. Its interior was brightly decked with the banners and pennants of the *San Cárlos*.

The chapel was dedicated on October 8, the ceremony taking place, Father Palóu wrote, "in the presence of the gentlemen of the bark (the *San Cárlos*) and of the commander of the Presidio with all the troops and citizens, only those that were absolutely required remaining in the fort. I sang the mass with the ministers, and at its conclusion a procession was formed, in which an image of Our Seraphic Father San Francisco, patron of the port, Presidio and Mission, was carried on a frame. The function was celebrated with repeated salvos of muskets, rifles, and the swivel guns that were brought from the bark for this purpose, and also with rockets."

(The ceremonies marking the beginnings of the Presidio and Mission have led to a teapot controversy, which still persists, over the birthday of San Francisco. There are authorities, including the noted Mission historian Father Zephyrin Engelhardt, who support June 29, the date of the first mass. Others say it is October 8, the date of the dedication of the Mission. A third opinion, backed by the Native Sons of the Golden West, contends the city's birthday is September 17, official date of the founding of the Presidio.)

There was a skirmish with the heathen Indian, in which the savages launched a rain of arrows at the Mission buildings and were sent fleeing in helter-skelter panic by a volley of musket fire, and in the end they sued for peace and submitted to sound floggings, and that was all there was to native resistance. On to the blank pages of the Mission books went, with naïve pride and triumph, the names of the first convert, the principals of the first marriage, the report of the first burial. Seeds for the first crop were planted, and the Mission cattle grazed across the peaceful hills and beside the banks of the creeks that fed the Laguna de los Dolores, which, in the days that came to pass, gave the Mission its name, so that this sixth bead of Father Serra's Rosary of Missions was known, not as Mission San Francisco de Asis, but as Mission Dolores.

The next year, the kind Serra paid his first visit to the Mission by the lagoon and celebrated mass in its chapel on the Day of St. Francis in that year of 1777. Afterward, he went to the Presidio, and from its little parade ground looked for the first time upon the moving tides of the Golden Gate. "Thanks be to God," he exclaimed happily, "that now our father St. Francis with the holy cross of the procession of Missions has reached the last limit of the California continent. To go farther he must have boats."

There followed the long, drowsy years of the California pastorale, when a birth, a death, the tilling of the fields, the tending of the herds, the conversion of the heathen and the coming of the Spanish packet—when these things were the Mission life, these and the hot sun that ripened and mellowed the grapes in the Mission vineyards and scorched sere the Mission hills; the rain that made the hills green once more in the springtime, and the fogs that sometimes drifted from the sea, smothering the hills and the valleys in their rolling, gray mist.

A small settlement came to cluster about the chapel and the dwelling of the Mission fathers: small buildings where the Indian neophytes wove their coarse fabrics all day long; rows of huts for the Indians to live in;

shacks for melting tallow and making soap; shops for the smiths and the carpenters; storehouses for tallow and hides, butter and salt and grain. Nearby were the adobe homes of the Spanish ranchers—the Guerreros, the Valencias, the Bernals, the De Haros—whose cattle roamed over acres that lay west to the sea and south to the valley of Santa Clara and east to the Bay.

On certain days—a wedding day, perhaps, a birthday, a Sunday—there would be a fiesta, the dark-haired men and women in their bright clothes dancing all night long, to the music of violins and guitars, the graceful *jota*, the playful *jarabe*, the measured *contradanza*. Sometimes, after the mass on Sunday, there would be a horse race, a bull fight, or a *carrera del gallo*, with the horsemen thundering one by one down the Mission street, leaning far over and reaching down to pluck by the head the live cock buried in the sand at the street's end, or a bull and bear fight, the animals tied together with a *reata*, the bull trying to gore the bear and the bear raking the face of the bull with its claws, the bull lowering its head and bellowing with pain and the bear thrusting its paw far into the bull's mouth, digging its hooks of claws into the bull's tongue and lacerating the tender flesh so that suddenly blood was pouring from the bull's mouth, and it was choking on its own blood, its angry bellow suddenly a bubbling, ghastly and helpless bleating.

In the early 1830's the Missions were secularized, their administration taken from the Franciscans, their vast herds sold or slaughtered, their many miles of hills and vineyards and grainlands auctioned or distributed to parishioners. The languorous lilting music of the pastorale was dying away. The Russian ships had come, and the British ships, and now the Yankee traders were beating past the headland cliffs and the crumbling Presidio walls, dropping their anchors in the Bay and sending their boats to the Mission landings for the hides and the tallow, for casks of fiery *aguardiente* and for wool from Mission sheep for the spinning mills of New England. A few more years in which to die were all that were left, and when they were over, the pastorale would be utterly ended, its last fading strains drowned in the quick bright notes of a bugle, the lusty refrain of a song called *Yankee Doodle*.

On what was left on the lands of Mission Dolores, and with the few Indians that remained at the settlement, the priests raised cattle and hay, but it was a long and arduous way from the town by the shores of the cove, and San Francisco merchants began complaining about the $15 or $20 it cost them to have a load of hay carted across the sand hills, over the Mission trail.

This trail, starting at the Mission, was a little more than two miles long. It extended along fairly level but sandy ground, across a bog and a creek or two, south of the sand hills that were on the line of Market Street, and then turned and went down Kearny Street to Portsmouth Square.

In 1850, to solve the problem of the high cost of transportation and to exploit the increasing flow of traffic to and from the Mission, certain citizens organized the Mission Planks Road Company, named Charles B. Polhemus its president, and built a plank toll road forty feet wide over the Mission trail from Third Street to what is now Sixteenth Street, which would mark the limit of the Mission settlement. For the privilege of traveling on its plank road, the company charged a horseman twenty-five cents, a wagon and two horses seventy-five cents and a four-horse team $1.

The plank road, which was the beginning of Mission Street and which actually opened up all the South of Market region as a suburban living area for the pioneer city, was an instant success. Commented the authors of *The Annals of San Francisco* a year or two later, "This plank road has proved of the greatest service to San Francisco, and the property through which it passes has increased immensely in value for building purposes. Formerly that property was at times nearly inaccessible, and on all occasions was very difficult and troublesome to reach."

Since that beginning, it has been South of Market's big street.

In those Fifties, when horses were floundering in the California Street mud, when there was no Cliff House and Golden Gate Park was a wasteland of sand, Mission Street was the town's boulevard, a frontier promenade that was like Montgomery Street's Ambrosial Path, only with carriages.

Not from Third to "the Bulkhead," as the Mission Street waterfront was called. Down there were rickety wharves, where old men fished for sharks and boys for porgies from the rotting, teredo-ridden hulls of store-ships, and iron foundries and the San Francisco Gas Works, flooding the waterfront with the refuse coal tar so that the residents of the neighbor-hood, with bleak humor, could find no better name for it than Tar Flat. To the south of them and a few blocks away, ranged in cold dignity the well-kept lawns and gardens and mansions of the Rincon Hill and South Park rich, but in their pride and poverty the Tar Flatters found a solidar-ity and a certain warm humanity that would some day distinguish all South of Market from the rest of the city, compensating for and counteracting the snobbery and artificiality that would settle upon the hills and heights. Between Tar Flat and Third Street lay Happy Valley, where in 1850 two thousand emigrants had pitched their tents in the lee of the Market Street sand hills and where, two years later, José Forni plunged his Spanish dagger into José Rodríguez's breast and swung for it from the gallows of Russian Hill.

So not to the left would the carriages turn when they reached Third and Mission Streets, but to the right and westward, toward the open country out by and beyond Mission Dolores. On sunny days, teams and vehicles by the score rocked and rumbled over the plank road, the carriages with their tops down and springs sagging beneath the weight of a curious assortment of passengers—dandies and women of fashion, gamblers, men of consequence (straight-backed, spade-bearded and genteelly holding on to their plug hats), squawling babies in their nursemaids' arms—all tak-ing the air, getting away for a while from the dusty and windy streets of the north side of town, seeing and being seen, smelling the smells of the grass and the country and the sea that was never very far away, no matter where they went or what they did.

Half a mile from Third Street and already well in the open, they would pass over a bog and beyond that would be the trail leading off over the sand hills to the Yerba Buena Cemetery, and then, on the left (across the street from where the main post office is now), the tiny cottage, "not much larger than a full-sized Saratoga trunk," where Stephen C. Massett lived, and a few hundred feet beyond that the two-room cabin Edwin Booth had lived in for the winter of 1853, sharing it with his friend, David C.

Anderson, who had been the first person in California to play the ghost in *Hamlet*. ("We had a horse and wagon," Booth later recalled, "and we drove into town to get provisions. Kidneys were cheap and we bought them whenever we could.")

Beyond that and still beside the plank road were the roadhouses, where you could sit in the shade and sip a milk punch while your horses rested: The Grizzly Bear, owned by Colonel William Greene, father of Playwright Clay Greene, with its mascot—a small cinnamon bear—chained to an oak tree in its front yard; The Nightingale (where Judge Ned McGowan hid from the Vigilantes in '56), The Mansion House and Witzeleben's brewery, hard by Mission Dolores. Farther than the Mission and the end of the plank road were two race tracks, the Union, and the Pioneer, which was operated by George Treat, owner of the great California-bred sorrel Thad Stevens. Across the road from the Union was The Willows, over the field on which the Californians had staged their Sunday bear-and-bull fights and where now was this resort, with its theater where Lotta danced and Irish Joe Murphy put on his blackface minstrel act, with its open-air restaurant and its open-air pavilion for moonlight dancing.

Still farther in the country were The Red House, which proudly advertised "Bird, Chicken and Wine Breakfasts served at all hours of the Day and Night," and Chris Lilley's, a rendezvous for politicians and duelists. That was William Walker's favorite dueling ground, and where George Hunt killed Numa Hubert in '54, and where, in some months, "Pistols for two and coffee for one" was a standing order every morning of the week.

As for the Mission itself, most of the promenaders who got that far kept on going, for it had nothing to offer but the gloomy picturesqueness of its dim clerestory, its hand-hewn redwood timbers, its hand-carved alters, its ceilings decorated with vegetable dyes by the Indians, its tiny graveyard. Sometimes, attracted by the sad glamor Lola Montez had given it when she married Patrick Purdy Hull there (bringing artificial white roses as a gift for the priest) in the July of 1853, a fashionably gowned lady, gathering her rich velvet cloak around her, would descend from her carriage and with her escort peer curiously into the dark chamber and see, perhaps, an ancient Mexican crone muttering her prayers.

The somber shadows, the solemnity, this portrait of humility tacitly reproaching, would be more than she and her escort cared to see, and they would get back into their carriage and drive on toward The Red House for their milk punches or champagne, regretting silently that they had stopped at all.

The Mission was a crumbling relic of another day, another California, and the places where the life was were the plank road and the roadhouses, the race tracks and the parks. Another resort, something like The Willows but without its sophistication, was Russ Gardens.

Christian Russ, the former New York jeweler, had grown tired of his ship's cabin on the sand hills by Bush and California Streets, and in the early Fifties, already a man of wealth and position, he built for himself and his family a mansion "far out in the wilderness," as Bancroft put it, on Sixth Street, two or three blocks south of Mission Street. He planted the grounds with elaborate care, constructing many pleasant arbors, and then threw them open as a public resort. In those early years, to the blare of horns and the pounding of drums, to the rousing phrases of patriotic orators and the rapping of bung starters, the city's various racial groups frolicked in Russ Gardens to celebrate their appropriate holidays, the Americans on the Fourth of July, the Irish on St. Patrick's Day, the French on Bastille Day, the Germans on May Day.

(Of the celebrants, the Germans put on the liveliest show. On May Day in 1853, *The Annals* reported, some eighteen hundred of them, including members of the Turner Gesang Verein in loose brown-linen coats and pantaloons, descended upon Russ Gardens "with banners flying, and musical instruments sounding." Once the party got under way, they "leaped, balanced and twirled, danced, sang, drank, smoked and made merry, as only such an enthusiastic race of mortals could.")

The most popular of these playgrounds, however, and the one that persisted as a local institution almost into the twentieth century, was Woodward's Gardens, now covered by the two city blocks bounded by Mission and Valencia, Thirteenth and Fifteenth Streets. In the end, the arbors of Russ Gardens were destroyed by fire, flood waters from a Mission district creek inundated the romantic pavilions of The Willows and Woodward's was the only one of the old South of Market resorts that you might say died a natural death, although its end was hastened by the development of Golden Gate Park.

Its owner was Robert Woodward, proprietor of the What Cheer House at Sacramento and Leidesdorff Streets. Like Russ, he had made a comfortable fortune during the Gold Rush, and, like Russ, he decided to have an estate over by the Mission plank road, buying this tract of land (on which was a cabin once occupied by John C. Frémont) and turning it into a private park of great charm and beauty. To amuse himself and his friends, he moved there various exhibits that had been features of the What Cheer House: his collection of mineral specimens, the great assortment of souvenirs and knickknacks sailors picked up for him in foreign ports. In the late 1860's, Civil War veterans asked permission to use his grounds for a reunion. Woodward gladly granted it. Other organizations sought the same privilege, and, finally, Woodward opened his garden gates to all the people.

To Native Sons now in their seventies, Woodward's Gardens is still their idea of a wonderland, and that ride out there on one of Henry Casebolt's horse-drawn balloon cars a cherished memory of a trip to paradise. Their eyes light at the mention of the Gardens, at the thought of what they were like:

The main gate, with the carved wooden bears on top, holding the flagpoles. The museum before you as you entered, and, to the right, the large bust of George Washington. A vista of flowered terraces, and a grand stairway leading up the terraces to a conservatory, a lake. The deer park and the bears you fed peanuts to, and the carriage you could ride in, pulled by two white goats. The band platform with its hanging baskets of roses and blue streamers and bright banners. Roller skating, and the Japanese acrobats and the tribal dances of the painted Warm Springs Indians that came down from the Modoc country to put on their shows. Jaguarine, the swordswoman, and Christal, the Frenchman who wrestled the bear. The arena, where you watched the Roman chariot races, and the pavilion where you (and five thousand others) saw the Three Arnold Brothers in their Silver Statue Clog; Major Burke in his rifle drill; Ida Siddons, the rope-skipping dancer; Orndorf and Kidd, the Dutch comedians; the Big 4 Minstrels and the stars of Emerson's Minstrels. The balloon ascensions on Sundays, and Tom Baldwin's parachute falls, and Herman the Great, the man who was shot from the mouth of a cannon. The barking of the seals, the hot, rich smell of popcorn, bands playing and the water lilies you held in your hand, plucked from the surface of the lake for your mother or your girl as you sat in the circular boat on the lake. These, and the sound of laughter across sunlit lawns, the feeling of gay and carefree times.

In their minds, the Native Sons can hear and see it all yet, and in their hearts, though the place has been gone for half a century and more, the gardens of Woodward are as green and lovely as they ever were in those far-off days when life and the city were new.

West of Happy Valley, one of Mission Street's earliest and most distinguished residents was the suave, cultured Francis L. A. Pioche, for whom the Nevada mining town was named. It is odd that in a city that likes to remember its pioneers there is no monument dedicated to him, for he was unquestionably one of the builders of San Francisco. He was a financial operator of stature in the financial district when $50,000 on Montgomery Street was cigar money. He was a noted *bon vivant* in a city that prided itself on *bons vivants,* and in an era when the term meant someone besides a man who likes a New York cut smothered in onions, with sparkling Burgundy. Out in front with the rest of the early empire makers, his short, stocky figure sauntered along the Cocktail Route beside those of Ralston and Peter Donahue, Coleman, Sharon and Mackay and all the others. As a matter of fact, Pioche is credited with getting San Francisco off to its start as a happy hunting ground for epicures by importing, bodily, forty Parisian chefs and a boatload of French wines so San Franciscans unable to afford the Grand Tour could find out for themselves what frogs' legs *à la poulette* tasted like, so they would know what vintage champagne was, and how the bouquet of Sazerac brandy smelled.

Born in France in 1818, Pioche left home at the age of thirty to become chancellor to the French consul in Chile. The next year, the year after the gold discovery, he came to California hunting a fortune. With J. B.

Bayerque, who accompanied him from Chile, he started the merchandising firm of Pioche and Bayerque on the north side of Clay Street, just off Portsmouth Square. In 1851, he went back to Paris, boosted San Francisco and its future to the skies, and returned home with about six million francs to invest, borrowed from French capitalists at 6 and 7 per cent interest. He then proceeded, with shrewd judgment and great faith in California, to channel this money into enterprises which eventually earned millions of dollars, not only for him but for his associates.

His capital constructed one of the first railroads in the state, the Placerville and Sacramento Valley road, from Placerville to Folsom. He bought thousands of acres of land: the San Miguel and Bernal ranches, and great tracts in San Francisco's Visitacion Valley, Hayes Valley and the Western Addition. To open these latter two districts to the city's increasing population, he helped finance the Market Street Railroad, and the sand dunes he bought by the acre he sold by the lot. Along with Peter Donahue and George Newhall, he backed construction of the San José railroad, whose northern terminal stood at Market and Valencia Streets.

As Pioche and Bayerque flourished into a banking house and became the funnel through which much French capital poured into the rapidly developing West, the financier broadened his investment base. He supplied heavy backing to the cattle ranchers of Monterey and Santa Barbara Counties. He sank money in the Temescal tin mines. He financed new processes for treating mineral ores. He discovered the benign virtues of New Almaden mineral water, and had it bottled and placed on the market. It would have been difficult indeed in the Fifties and Sixties to find a financial pie in San Francisco that did not have in it the pudgy but delicately manicured finger of Monsieur Pioche.

There were three dwellings associated with him in San Francisco: the Hermitage; the house in Mission Street just west of Sixth (the Sullivan Block stands on its site today); and an immense, square, mansard-roofed mansion in Stockton Street.

The Hermitage was a sort of country home out by Mission Dolores. There, as wherever Pioche lived, distinguished travelers visited the affable and distinguished banker and enjoyed his abundant hospitality. Once, in a sentimental mood, he wrote a poem about the place. One stanza went,

Away from the din of the city
The busy mart and the street,
Stands the old church of the Mission,
With my Hermitage at its feet.

Pioche was an active man; he tackled his business deals with great energy and imagination, and was a lover of hunting and fishing. But there was a softer side to him, one that made room in his nature for art, creative art as well as the art of living.

Many were the banquets of infinite courses and infinite wine that Pioche served at the house in Mission Street. But there came to be a touch of tragedy about it, for in the rainy winter of 1862 the waters of Sans Souci lake drained from their bed a mile or two to the north and rushed down into the Mission district. The next morning, Pioche's lovely gardens (like The Willows) were deep under water, and his house was all but submerged. This new body of water became known as Pioche's Pond, and at least a dozen Mission lads, swimming in its murky waters, sank from sight and drowned.

Flushed from their stone-fronted mansions by the sounds and smells of the shops and factories that were pushing south of Market Street along the waterfront, and the sounds and smells of the immigrant workers the factories brought with them, the elite were deserting South Park and Rincon Hill. South of Market addresses were not quite so fashionable as they once were, and so Pioche followed society to the other side of the city and moved to 806 Stockton Street, a three-story, brick house that was to be his home for the next ten years.

With its grounds, it covered half a block. Its large bay windows fronted on Stockton Street, and across the rear of the house extended a long balcony where Pioche liked to sit after dinner, sipping his cognac, smoking his rich Havana cigars and admiring the view over the city and Bay. Inside the house, costly paintings imported from the world's art centers hung on the walls. Thick Brussels carpets muffled the footsteps of discreet, well-trained servants.

His banking firm flourishing and his widely scattered investments prospering, Pioche entertained here as lavishly as a millionaire bachelor can. His dinner parties, which he gave almost weekly, glittered with men and women of importance in social, financial and artistic circles. (In *The Fantastic City,* Amelia Ransome Neville tells of the party Mrs. Hall McAllister gave for Madame Parepa Rosa, prima donna of the Carl Rosa Opera Company, which brought grand opera to Maguire's Opera House in 1868. One of the guests had heard her sing a few evenings before at a party at Pioche's house and asked her if she was going to sing for Mrs. McAllister. "Only when it is an engagement for money I sing," replied Madame Rosa artlessly. "But," persisted the guest, "you sang at Mr. Pioche's the other night." She extended a plump arm. "Ah, but Mr. Pioche gave me a bracelet," she said. Above her wrist was a circlet of gold quartz medallions, the largest bearing the letter *R* in diamonds.)

But in back of Pioche's rugged, jovial face, in the mind behind it, there were troubled thoughts, and some kind of fear. Later, friends recalled a horseback-riding accident that left him the victim of severe headaches. They remembered he was said to take opiates. They knew he was gnawed by worry over the war that had come between his native land and Germany. On the other hand, they knew also that his financial position was sound, and they had heard him express himself on the act of suicide. "It is cowardly and unchristian," he had said. "A man should fight the battle of life. He has no right to kill himself."

If Pioche really believed this once, then he fought the last skirmish on the morning of May 2, 1872—and lost.

At seven-five, Louis Reiff, his valet, entered his bedroom, in accordance with the morning custom of the house. The banker was lying in bed reading the morning papers. His back was to the bedroom door, and his gaily colored nightgown was buttoned up under his dark, virile beard.

"Do you care for some water to drink, sir?" Reiff asked.

"I do not wish to talk to you," Pioche replied gruffly. Reiff turned on his heel and left the room, and was the last man to see Pioche alive.

A few minutes later, Pioche got out of bed and took one of a pair of heavy Navy revolvers from a mahogany case which was on a large center table. Then he returned to the bed, lay back against the pillows, placed the cold ring of the muzzle against his forehead, and pulled the trigger. He fell sideways and lay still, in so natural a position that, for a moment, when he re-entered the room a little after eight o'clock, Reiff thought his master was still sleeping.

Basalt blocks replaced the old plank road; those, or, in some places, Nicholson pavement, which was tar-dipped wooden blocks set on edge, hailed as the city's first noiseless pavement and after one winter's rains flung as street-fight missiles or gathered in baskets for firewood when, swollen by water and sun, the blocks buckled and popped out of place and strewed themselves over the street.

Rows of frame cottages set close to the sidewalks appeared along the narrow alleys that paralleled Market and Mission—Natoma, Jessie, Stevenson, Clara, Clementina, Minna and Tehama. The smells were the smells of stew meat cooking and potatoes boiling, of the gashouse and factory smoke, of washing on the line; and the sounds were made by drinkers singing snatches of songs over their tall steams, by babies crying in packing-case cradles, by women gossiping over backyard fences in the brogue of the Irish, in Dutch, in Yiddish, in Polish.

The districts were beginning to shift or consolidate themselves, South of the Slot or South of Market starting at the waterfront and taking in Tar Flat, Happy Valley, South Park and Rincon Hill and all that district west to Twelfth Street. From there, south and west to Bernal Heights and the Mission hills it was called The Mission, still, in the Seventies and even as late as the Nineties, mostly grazing land for cows and sheep.

South of Market wasn't much affected by the rise or fall in the price of Kentuck or Con. Virginia or Hale and Norcross, but, even so, the Comstock, in a way, left there a monument steadier than Ralston's Bank of California and more enduring than his Palace Hotel or the Nob Hill palaces of the bonanza kings. This was the United States Mint at Mission and Fifth Streets. Now it is a shabby building on the busy corner, but when it was new it was South of Market's pride and delight. Tourists from the world over came to gape at its Doric columns and to gaze greedily upon its heaps of gold and silver.

Over in Commercial Street, just off Montgomery and nearer the financial district, there had been a mint, which, in 1855, its first year of operation, had turned out nearly $21,000,000 in gold coinage. When the silver flood poured down from the Comstock, the Commercial Street plant was unable to cope with it, and federal architects planned a new mint. They designed it to be fireproof and earthquake-proof. They specified a copper roof, wrought iron girders from Philadelphia, a base of Folsom granite, sandstone blocks from British Columbia. The columns were to be thirty-foot, thirty-ton pieces of stone, the finest examples of single-stone columns on the Pacific Coast.

Finally, on May 26, 1870, after a year of digging and building of foundations, the city turned out for the impressive ceremony of laying the cornerstone. It was a brilliant, all-Masonic celebration. At two o'clock that afternoon, waiting crowds heard band music in the distance, and out Mission Street from the Masonic Temple at Montgomery and Post Streets came a dazzling procession of uniformed Masons of the Grand Lodge and Grand Chapter of California, and Knights Templar of Commandery No. 1 dashingly garbed in their swinging black mantles, their plumed hats, their aprons and gauntlets. The throng cheered. A woman fainted. Out of Tom Sawyer's saloon across the street (where the *Chronicle* Building stands now) stumbled a score of amiable drunks, who, once they had recovered from the impact of the fresh air, supported the marchers with unruly applause. After the preliminary speeches, the cornerstone (containing a copper casket of coins, newspapers, photographs and other mementos of the occasion) was lowered into place, and over it was poured the corn, oil and wine of the Masonic ritual.

"The genius of republican institutions," thundered Grand Orator Judge James H. Hardy, "has mastered the impediments of space, and the Atlantic and Pacific, bound together by iron bands, speak to each other in the quickness of an electric spark. . . . The work now so auspiciously begun is for all ages . . . a monument to the achievements of the present time."

A choir chanted the *Old Hundredth,* and the ceremonies came to an end.

It wasn't long before the Mint became, in the public mind, a foreboding temple of mystery. South of Market children, passing it on their way to Lincoln school across Fifth Street, stopped to press their faces against its iron fence and listen to the clinking machinery inside, manufacturing more money in a day than they would see in all their lifetimes. Sometimes, behind the barred and grimy windows, they caught a swift glimpse of a flaring blast furnace and the stooped, gnomelike figure of a man silhouetted against it.

South of the Slot housewives repeated legends about the Mint, spicing their gossip with them; some of these tales still persist. For example, it is said that a man tried to tunnel under Mission Street to the Mint's basement vaults. For months, he burrowed there like a mole. Halfway to his goal, the heavy Mission Street traffic jarred loose the ceiling of his tunnel. It caved in, and he crawled from his hole more dead than alive.

There are stories about unscrupulous janitors. One of them killed Mint rats, sewed $20 gold pieces inside of them and threw them on the building's rubbish heap, where, in the nighttime, he would recover them and rip them open for the treasure hidden in their entrails. Another slipped a silver blank into a coining machine each day, coined himself a silver dollar and took it home with him. When officials caught him at last, they found themselves in a quandary; they couldn't charge him with counterfeiting, because he had been making bona fide American currency. He got off with three months in jail—for theft of the silver.

The Mint came to be regarded as a building that was literally worth its weight in gold. It is said that an employee wiped the dust off a transom. Assayed, it was found to be worth $100. A superintendent got a new rug for his office. Gold dust extracted from the old one was worth $200 more than the new rug cost. The building, people thought, was saturated with gold dust. A reporter wrote, "If the Mint was melted in a kettle big enough to hold it, it is believed a fortune would be recovered. But," he concluded regretfully, "this may never be done."

Solid, ponderous, indestructible, the old Mint was one of the few public buildings to survive the 1906 disaster. "For seven hours," recalled Harold French, a Mint employee, "a sea of fire surged around this grand old Federal edifice, attacking it on all sides with waves of fierce heat. Its little garrison was cut off from retreat for hours at a time. . . . When the fire leaped Mint Avenue in solid masses of flames, the refinery men stuck to their windows as long as glass remained in the frames. Seventy-five feet of one-inch hose played a slender stream upon the blazing window sills, while the floor was awash with diluted sulphuric acid. . . . At length, the Mint was pronounced out of danger, and a handful of exhausted but exultant employees stumbled out on the hot cobblestones."

During the conflagration, a dozen looters trying to reach the $200,000,000 in coin and bullion in the Mint vaults were shot down in the street.

From then until the opening of the new Mint in outer Market Street

in 1937, the building's dark dignity has remained unruffled except for a few moments in 1928 when an imaginative crackpot calling himself "The Shadow" warned Superintendent Michael J. Kelly that he was going to blow the place up. "Beware of The Shadow," he wrote Kelly. "The Mint will be blown up on Friday, March 16, 1928. If any false moves are made while this is going on, everyone will be blown to hell by The Shadow." Although the building swarmed that day with Secret Servicemen waiting for him, "The Shadow" failed to carry out his threat, and the Mint calmly went about business as usual.

It is still a United States Treasury Department building and now houses a miscellany of government offices, such as the Bureau of Standards, the Geodetic Survey, the Bureau of Mines and the Civil Service Commission. And in spite of all its janitors try to do to brighten it up, it is still drab, to the point of stubbornness; even the flowers they plant beneath its walls carry their pale blooms with an air of futility and depression. At night, when it is dim and sad and no lights are burning in its grimy lamps, it reminds you of an old man who has outlived his time and usefulness, and wants only to be let alone and to sleep.

Some gold the old Mint never handled—gold, in fact, that no one ever saw—once touched off a hectic, four-day gold rush to the outer Mission district in search of the bonanza of Bernal Heights.

Bernal Heights is now a picturesque and cosmopolitan district of San Francisco characterized by steep, winding streets, hillside cottages, geraniums in window boxes, vegetable gardens in the backyard, and one of the best views in the city. Eighty years ago, it was an isolated settlement, predominantly Irish in tone, a place of milk ranches and goats and truck gardens. Nothing much happened there from week to week, and it was a big day when the boys of Bernal Heights ganged up on the poundmen and beat the daylights out of them for seizing one of Widow O'Brien's cows. Another big day was when Jack Lally fell in Egan's ditch and died just after inheriting $15,000. The wake his widow Rose threw for poor old Jack lasted for a month, and Bernal Heights natives say no man before or since has inspired such a shivaree in his passing. When the keening guests fell asleep, Rose tied them in their chairs to keep them from falling on the floor and to make sure they would stay until the wake was over. A week after the wake, Rose married a German waiter and with what was left of poor Jack's inheritance launched another Celtic bacchanalia that also went down in Bernal Heights history, a bacchanalia which continued for several days after she and her bridegroom set out on their honeymoon to Ocean View in Mike Welch's dumpcart.

The good citizens of the Heights were still talking about how Rose's old man tried to ride the billy goat into the front parlor during the wedding party when, suddenly, their lots and backyards were invaded by a swarm of gold seekers. A Frenchman named Victor Ressayre had announced the discovery of a rich quartz ledge on the summit of the Heights, and estimating it would assay at $1,000,000 a ton, he named it the Eureka Lode and staked out a fifteen-hundred-foot claim.

Hot on the trail of the sensational story, a *Chronicle* reporter sped out Mission Street on a horsecar and toiled up to the top of the barren and windy hill. There he found "not the herds of cattle and goats which scour that elevated locality in search of a precarious subsistence, but about one hundred and fifty men, women, boys, girls and babies, breaking the rock and gyrating to and fro. Dozens of respectable, intelligent-looking men were engaged on the boulders, chipping off small pieces and examining them critically."

Nearby, a post had been driven into the ground. It bore a sign reading, "City of San Francisco Lode." On another sign post eight hundred feet from Ressayre's claim was this proclamation: "Notis:—The Centennial Mine. We the undersine thereof have this day located 1500 feet running S. Easterly Direction with all the Dips, spirs and angles and Claiming in all the Best protections of Gold an mining Laws of Cal. Albert Johnson, Thomas G. Maguire, G. W. Harper, J. F. Cahill, Hugh Curry."

Shortly after the reporter's arrival, a cloud of dust was seen on the winding road leading up the Heights, and out of it, a few moments later, materialized Maguire, riding a sorrel colt and carrying a pick and spade. A large crowd gathered as he dismounted and proceeded to attack the ground with his pick. When he had dug a hole three feet deep without striking a bonanza, he announced that his eyesight was bad and that he would give a twenty-five-cent reward to the first man who discovered a piece of gold quartz on the claim of the Centennial Mine. A score of prospectors promptly abandoned their search for nuggets to compete for the reward. After an hour of fruitless digging, Maguire threw down his pick. "If I was a young man," he snorted, "I'd work for fifty cents a day before I'd mine in such a confounded place as this." Then he remounted his horse and rode back down the hill.

"A hundred men and twice as many women still lingered, however," noted the *Chronicle* man, "and during the day no less than four hundred persons visited M. Ressayre's ledge, all with the anxious query of 'Where's the stuff?'"

But as the day waned, so did the gold fever. And when experienced quartz miners skeptically examined the ground and told the reporter there was no more gold on Bernal Heights than there was in the ordinary backyard, he returned to the office and wrote his story.

A few days later, he trudged back up the Heights to see if the gold rush was still on. All he found at the diggings were a few geese, a couple of scrawny goats. Furthermore, he discovered that the less said on Bernal Heights about the gold rush the better; it was far from funny.

"The joke which the facetious Frenchman had perpetrated—for he could not have contemplated anything more serious—has not been appreciated at all," he wrote. "It is dangerous to broach the subject of gold to anyone living in that locality."

And so the great San Francisco gold rush of the Seventies was over, and the goats and cows and sheep roamed again in peace over the Heights, and its citizens went back to wagging their heads nostalgically over the great wedding party that followed the marriage of Rose Lally and her German waiter.

In the 1920's, a small group of San Franciscans organized a club they called the South of Market Boys, which they dedicated to the perpetuation of the spirit of the South of Market district as it was before the earthquake and fire of 1906. Membership privileges were extended to all who had lived in that area, from the waterfront to Twelfth Street, before the disaster scattered them to all the other parts of the city. Within a year or two, the South of Market Boys boasted a membership roll of more than three thousand, including many men who had risen to high prominence in the city's life. Mayor Jim Rolph was a South of Market Boy, and so was Police Chief Dan O'Brien. David Belasco and David Warfield were South of Market Boys, and Congressman Sol Bloom of New York, and many judges, businessmen and civic leaders.

Many of the members, old when the club was started, have died; the sons did not support the organization or its ideals the way their fathers hoped they would, and now the South of Market Boys, as a social unit of the city, is beginning to flag. But it's to South of Market Boys that are still alive that you go when you want to know what it was like in South of the Slot. They saw it come, and they saw it pass. The alleys that are now lined with machine shops, print shops, garages and the back entrances of the big Market and Mission Street stores were the streets they called home, the streets they played in and grew up in. Today, their sons, and they themselves, live in The Mission or in the row houses of the Richmond or the Sunset district out by the beach, and in South of the Slot, a place of factories and flophouses and secondhand stores and the closest things to slums outside of Chinatown, is no longer the heart of the city.

But the true South of Market Boy thinks back, and in place of the poverty remembers the friendliness, the tolerance—his mother passing a plate of warm jelly tarts across the backyard fence to her neighbor or sitting up with the neighbor's sick child, his father pitching in and helping the people next door move to another house up the street, Father Yorke and Congressman Julius Kahn walking arm in arm along Mission Street, and the six families sharing a three-story house—the Rubens and the Friedmans, the Wobbers and the Friedenbergs, the Healys and the Griffins— living peacefully together and sharing the Wobbers' frankfurters and sauerkraut, the Friedmans' gefüllte fish, the Griffins' corned beef and cabbage.

He remembers the pageant of street scenes: the line of hacks in Fifth Street outside the Mint; the water venders trundling their two-wheeled barrels; the one-horse dumpcarts with no seats and the drivers standing up; the Chinese vegetable peddlers in blue cotton trousers and woven bamboo hats with baskets swinging from their shoulder poles; the Chinese fishmongers haggling with the housewives on Friday mornings and weighing out their silver fish in the portable scales; the wandering minstrels, roaming the streets at dusk with their accordions and triangles and sweetly playing *The Banks of the Wabash* and *Two Little Girls in Blue,* kites with broken spines and streaming tails in the electric wires in the month of February; leather-aproned brewery-wagon drivers rolling the kegs of steam beer through the swinging green doors of the corner groceries; the varicolored sidewalk displays of the dry goods stores; the street-corner bonfires around election time, and the kids roasting potatoes in the coals; the balloon cars going by crowded with children bound for Woodward's Gardens; the pushcart peddlers hawking mallards and wild geese in Sixth Street; the Tar Flat hoodlums hanging around the street corners Sunday afternoons in their pale-blue, spring-bottom trousers and black coats with padded shoulders and buff-colored felt hats, worn always with four dents in their crowns; the liquid-filled jars glowing red and green in the light of the gas jets in drugstore windows; roving bands of boys on their way to steal pretzels from Gus Dunderbecker's saloon, or to throw red pepper on the stove in the Chinese laundry, or to fight it out behind the Mint or in Hobb's lumberyard, or to fish for porgies from the wharves at the foot of Third Street.

He remembers the people: Police Captain Jack Spillane, who always, it seemed, broke up the street fights; Old Doc Thompson, the druggist, who never wore a collar or necktie, and invariably parted his long white whiskers to display to a customer the big diamond in the bosom of his shirt front; Barney Farley, the trainer of prize fighters, who lost his heart the night Peter Jackson knocked out his boy Joe McAuliffe at the Palace Amphitheater at Mission and New Montgomery Streets; Joseph Michael Collins, the world's champion handball player, whose home court was Phil Ryan's Handball Courts there in Howard, just east of Fifth Street; Mrs. Emily Edwards, the Folsom Street tavern keeper who saved three firemen trapped in a burning building and was known from one end of the district to the other as The Fireman's Queen; Captain Thomas Francis O'Malley Baines, the Irish patriot and former soldier of the Irish Papal Brigade, who wore the green ostrich plume in his military hat and never shaved or cut his hair because he had vowed to let them grow until Ireland won her freedom; Professor Norman Beaton, the Nova Scotia Scotsman who ran the popular dancing academy in Concordia Hall at Mission and Mary Streets; Georgia McDermott, the Natoma Street belle, who became Little Egypt; Sid Grauman, who ran the Lyceum Theater in Market

Street; Father Matthew of St. Joseph's parish, who founded the Young Men's Total Abstinence Society of Tenth Street; Bernhard Marks, the principal of the old Lincoln School; and Kate D. Smith, the director of Rincon Hill's Silver Street Kindergarten, whom they later knew as Kate Douglas Wiggin.

They remember Sunday afternoons with their fathers at Canivan's Greyhound Coursing Park out by the county line, or with their best girls on picnics at Shellmound Park across the Bay. They remember old songs, and old faces seen from the galleries of Morosco's Union Hall Theater and the Grand Opera House in Mission Street just west of Third, which Morosco took over after he left Union Hall: *Paddy Duffy's Cart, There Never Was a Coward Where the Shamrock Grows, When This Old Coat Was New, Never Take the Horseshoe from the Door, The Mick That Threw the Brick, Murphy's Little Side Door, Sally in Our Alley, Poverty's Tears Ebb and Flow,* and *I Never Liked O'Regan or His Father;* Theodore Roberts in *The Octoroon,* Melbourne McDowell and Florence Stone in *Antony and Cleopatra,* Darrell Vinton in *Michael Strogoff,* May Nannery in *East Lynne,* George Webster in *At the Bottom of the Sea,* Tom Taylor in *The Ticket of Leave Man,* James T. Brady, the father of Alice Brady in *After Dark,* Idalene and Ben Cotton in *Uncle Tom's Cabin,* Jane Hading and Coquelin the Elder in *Tartufe,* Irving and Terry in *The Bells;* Schumann-Heink singing *Die Walküre,* Nordica singing *Tannhauser,* Calve singing *Carmen,* Melba singing *Faust,* Caruso singing *I Pagliacci.*

They remember these, and a thousand other things no one has ever put down on paper about that San Francisco, and, above all, they remember the forty-eight seconds the earth shook that April morning, and the devastation that came after, shattering the old ways into as many fragments as it shattered the great crystal chandelier of the Grand Opera House. That was the end of South of the Slot; that was the beginning of the San Francisco they see today.

The lineaments of Tar Flat have substance in their minds alone; Happy Valley lives only in their memories, in the name of a hotel bar, in the name of a Market Street newsboy's corner; and Mission Street is six miles and more of stores and bars and streetcar tracks and parking lots and motion picture theaters, with the Bay and Yerba Buena Island at one end and the other end now far beyond the little Mission Dolores chapel and the Twin Peaks that rise behind it. Factories and freight yards sprawl across the reclaimed water lots of Mission Bay, and cars and trolley busses roll over Dolores Street and Eighteenth Street, where the willowed lagoon waited for Anza.

But in their hearts, until the day they die, burns a love for San Francisco—love, and a fierce pride in the knowledge that never in all their lives were they unfaithful to her. They always knew she was the most beautiful and most wonderful city in all the world; never did they waver, never did they desire any other. Their only regret is that they can't have her back, the way she used to be.

13. SOUTH PARK

THE HAPPY ISLAND · THE GORDON TRAGEDY · EADWEARD MUYBRIDGE AND
"THE FATAL AMOUR" · THE AMATEUR EMIGRANT ON RINCON HILL · IN
THE SHADOW OF THE BAY BRIDGE

IN THOSE old days, when the shore of Yerba Buena cove was that inward-curving crescent, Clark's Point and Telegraph Hill formed its northern tip; the southern was made by Rincon Point and Rincon Hill. South from Rincon Point, the harbor waters swept around what was later known as Steamboat Point, and back into Mission Bay. The shacks of the early settlement clustered around Clark's Point, but it could be clear and warm on Rincon Hill when the fog fumed over Russian Hill and down over the plaza a couple of miles away; and some of the Forty-niners, liking that about Rincon Hill, pitched their tents there while they prepared to leave for the gold country. The hill's first resident was Dr. John H. Gihon, who, on November 26, 1849, erected a tent upon its summit amid the

283

scrub oak, the boxwood and the plants that in the next spring would bear lupine and golden poppies. The doctor, who later collaborated with Frank Soulé and James Nisbet in writing *The Annals of San Francisco,* called it his "country home."

Ten years after that, Rincon Hill was one of the two most fashionable and expensive residential neighborhoods in San Francisco. The other was South Park.

The way it started was that in 1852 a smiling, affable and homesick Englishman named George Gordon got an idea for a real estate development. South of Market Street, south of Mission Street and beyond the shacks and the sand hills, he found a few level acres between Third Street and the sharp slope of Rincon Hill. Upon this land he plotted an oval garden about five hundred feet long and seventy-five across at its widest point. Around the oval he extended a broad avenue linked at one end to Second Street and at the other to Third. This avenue he called South Park.

He divided the land on the avenue's perimeter into sixty-four lots, and then offered them for sale to San Francisco's wealthiest citizens. Unhappy with the rough and crude way the town was developing around Portsmouth Square and Dupont Street and Broadway, they were attracted by Gordon's idea, and soon stone-fronted mansions were going up in South Park.

There, and to Rincon Hill above the Park, went the leaders of the city's commercial, professional and social worlds. There was, perhaps, a fine distinction between the two districts. Rincon Hill, with its large, rambling homes and lawns and gardens, its view of the Donahue foundry down on the flats, the waterfront and the shipping on the Bay, was closer to the city's life, and there lived the men who were building the city: Henry Miller, the cattleman, and Isaac Friedlander, the wheat king, the Ralstons and the Selbys, the Donahues, the Tallants, the Donohoes, the Garnetts, John Wieland, the brewer, and the Sathers.

South Park, a little more elegant, a little more frivolous, resisted the frontier instead of exploiting it, and its residents, looking out their lace-curtained French windows upon the green grass, the elm trees and English roses of the little park, could easily imagine themselves in London or in Philadelphia, or Washington or Richmond—almost anywhere, in fact,

but the desolate, dangerous, brawling wilderness city where a year or two
before men had been hanged in the streets. It is said that to help them
forget things like this, Gordon imported English sparrows from London
and listened proudly to them as they quarreled noisily in the garden and
on the park pavement.

"Doesn't that take you back to Berkeley Square?" he would ask, his
eyes alight with amusement and pleasure.

So, as the Sixties came, the people of South Park were moving and living
in a world of their own, a world that touched and met reality only in the
low rumble of the Third Street omnibus that passed the end of the Park
every once in a while, and in the hot, quick sympathy that welled in most
of them whenever the Confederacy was mentioned. For them, it was a
time of water frolics on the Bay and oyster suppers and eggnog parties
at the Senator Gwins'; of champagne picnics in Sausalito, and a garden
party at Fort Mason for the Duc de Penthièvre; of "Follow-Me-Lad"
curls, and flounces and dust ruffles on long, flaring skirts, and brocaded
fans and tiny parasols; of marble statuary and crystal chandeliers and gilt-
framed mirrors in the reception hall; of gold-mounted barouches waiting
at the front door, and summers spent at White Sulphur Springs in the
Mayacmas, high above the sea-coast fogs; of calling on friends on New
Year's Day and drinking champagne-punch toasts to this life and this
world, and hoping with laughter and assurance that they would never
change.

But they did. The drive, the character of the growing city, could not
be denied; its rising tide lapped the shores of the charming island, and,
as the years passed, flowed over it, engulfing it and scattering its inhabitants to ponderous, Victorian sanctuaries far out Mission Street and
Howard Street, or back across the city to Russian Hill and Nob Hill, now
the newest aerie of power and wealth, and to the heights above the Presidio. Fleeing, they held their noses delicately against the gashouse fumes,
the smell of immigrant cooking, the malt odor of stale beer that streamed
down from Third Street on the breeze that shook the leaves of the elm
trees and set nodding the bursting blooms of the English roses. They abandoned the island none too soon, for shipyards and docks, boiler factories
and iron foundries went up on the beach of Mission Bay to the south, and
to bring them closer to the city the earth movers began cutting through

Second Street, where it crossed Rincon Hill, to reduce its grade. The shovels and the engines sent tremors through the foundations of the fine mansions, and raised the red dust and sent it slowly drifting to settle on their sharp roof tops, their long windows, their walks and green lawns.

Two tales of South Park are still alive, and are the most real and most tangible things it left behind. Oddly enough, it was its founder, the Englishman Gordon, who produced the tragedy of the Park. By the time Muybridge came along, the best it could do was the cheapest kind of melodrama. But the Park wasn't altogether to blame for this; it was mostly Muybridge's fault.

If it weren't for Gertrude Atherton, who was born on Rincon Hill, the fantastic story of George Gordon, his wife and their daughter, Nellie, might well be lying forgotten in the newspaper files. On it she based her first novel, *A Daughter of the Vine,* which was published in 1899. The book both scandalized and shocked the members of the carriage-and-champagne set that liked to look back upon the South Park days as their gayest and most invulnerable time.

In the beginning, say the early 1840's, George Gordon was the son of a well-to-do Yorkshire family. He had little of the inclination to wildness about him, reaching the limits of any riotous living in occasional drinking bouts with his friend and neighbor Bramwell Brontë, brother of the noted Brontë sisters. One day, however, Gordon woke from one of these youthful sprees and found himself married to the attractive barmaid of a Yorkshire pub.

Appalled by what he had done, Gordon nevertheless refused to dissolve the marriage; he believed she loved him; it had been his mistake, and as a gentleman he should make the best of it. But he was unable to face a future in England with her—to introduce her to his friends and relatives as his wife was more than he could ask of himself, or of them—and so he took her to San Francisco, and there began his life all over again.

Mrs. Gordon soon learned that this Gold Rush camp and its muddy streets and plank sidewalks and gambling halls, its sand and bone-chilling fogs, were not exactly what she had married her husband for; she had had in mind the comfortable, respectable and easy life of the wife of an

English country squire. She tried cajoling him into a return to England. When this failed, she pleaded with him. And when that didn't work either, she laid her cards on the table. They made an impressive hand, one that had been stacked against Gordon from the moment she first set eyes on him.

She coldly informed Gordon she had arranged the drinking bout that preceded their wedding night; when he was so drunk he did not know what he was doing, she had seen that they were married. There was another thing he might be interested in knowing, now that they were getting better acquainted: she was an incurable alcoholic. She had concealed it from him until now; now she didn't care who in this God-forsaken hole knew it. And one more item: ever since he had demonstrated the shame he felt over their marriage by leaving England, she had hated him, and for it she would hate him as long as she lived. It ought to be clear to him now, she concluded, that if he did not take her back to England at once, he would regret it.

Gordon refused.

Instead of yielding to her demand, he sought relief from his domestic trouble in the business and social life of the community, assigning to a trusted butler the task of taking care of his wife, who, after their scene and his decision, had openly surrendered to her thirst. Gordon entered the sugar business and was soon on his way to a substantial fortune. He grew genuinely to love the city, and identified himself with numerous civic improvement projects, and the development of South Park became his personal hobby. Down the Peninsula, in what is now Palo Alto, he built a large summer home he called Mayfield Grange, and planted a vineyard and grass and eucalyptus trees and flowers across its flat warm acres.

Meanwhile, Mrs. Gordon gave birth to a child, a dark-eyed, dark-haired girl. They named her Nellie, and from the day she was born Gordon idolized her. When Mrs. Gordon realized this, she determined upon her most exquisite revenge. Secretly, cleverly, drops at a time so it would not upset the baby's system, she put whisky in the child's food, to the point where Nellie would not eat or drink anything that was not flavored with it. Whenever the baby was ill, Mrs. Gordon gave her liquor with her medicine. This went on year after year, and Nellie was almost seventeen before Gordon found out that his daughter bore an insatiable craving for alcohol.

She and her mother had hidden it well. Some of the most celebrated belles of the city lived in South Park as their neighbors—the lovely and blonde Pussy de Ro, Helen Ritchie, Patsy Ritchie, Lottie Hall, Rosa Gore. But none of these was more admired or more vivacious and spirited and lovely than Nellie Gordon. A newspaper account described her as "petite, daintily formed and exquisitely neat and attractive. She had inherited her mother's beauty and her father's brains. She was intelligent, well-read and a sparkling conversationalist."

When he discovered the secret, the distraught father sent Nellie to a boarding school to free her from her mother's influence. Mrs. Gordon's answer to this move was to smuggle bottles of whisky to Nellie in her' laundry.

Eventually, Gordon found this out, too. He ordered his wife out of the house and out of South Park. Jeering, she asked him how he would like reading in the San Francisco papers every morning that Mrs. George Gordon had spent the night in jail as a common drunkard. He thought of sending Nellie to England, but in the end decided against it because he was afraid she would disgrace his name and his family.

Nellie tried to help him. Once, he went down on his knees to her and implored her to stop drinking. She promised she would, and, resisting the temptations with which her mother cunningly confronted her at every opportunity, kept the promise for six months. Then she gave in. Gordon pleaded with her again, and once more she tried—and failed. As her lonely struggle grew more and more hopeless, she came to hate herself, to loathe the person she had become.

It is in Mrs. Atherton's book (her husband's family were intimate friends of Gordon, and one of them was at Nellie's bedside when she died) that Nina Randolph, the character based on Nellie, fell in love with an Englishman, decided to marry him and sent him away for a year while she went to a mountain lodge in Lake County, California, to conquer her illness alone. While there, and out of wedlock, she bore his child, a daughter, who died ten days after birth. Letters to him went astray in the confusion of Civil War communications. Letters he wrote from New Orleans and New York never reached her. At last, convinced he had gone back to England and forgotten her, she abandoned the conflict, married a ne'er-do-well cousin, and died a drunkard ten years later at Mayfield Grange. Mrs. Atherton says that that actually is the story of what happened to Nellie Gordon.

The unhappy love affair, the Englishman and the illegitimate child, however, are missing from factual newspaper reviews of the Gordon tragedy. Undoubtedly, reporters were either denied access to information available to Mrs. Atherton, or else were constrained to omit those features of Nellie's career.

In any event, their endings vary only in detail from Mrs. Atherton's. They say that Nellie, much against her father's wishes, married a ship's surgeon whose name was also Gordon, Dr. C. C. Gordon. They say her father (who had retired with a $500,000 fortune, realized in part through the sale of the state's first sugar refinery to Claus Spreckels) died a few years later, brokenhearted and exhausted by shame and worry. Nellie's husband, also an alcoholic, drank himself to death, and then, in the early Seventies, still in her twenties, Nellie herself died. Mrs. Gordon, who had outlived them all, sent back to England for her brother, and he came to Mayfield Grange to keep her company. Both died of alcoholism. Before his death, the brother married the Mayfield Grange cook, and so all that was left of the Gordon estate fell into her hands. When she died several years later, she left it to her peasant relatives who lived on a farm in West Ireland.

In 1876, Leland Stanford bought Mayfield Grange and remodeled it into his country home. It was all but wrecked by the earthquake of 1906, but one wing of it still stands in Palo Alto, on the Stanford University campus. It is part of the Stanford Home for Convalescent Children.

Youngsters who never heard of Nellie Gordon, and perhaps never will, play upon its lawns. In tall straight ranks beside the road now called Governor's Lane rise the eucalyptus trees that Gordon planted and that now stand as a monument to his despair. And South Park, which he created and which was where Nellie's tragedy began, bears no resemblance to the place that knew her step, her infrequent laughter and the shadow of her mother's curse.

Muybridge, the Othello of the horsecars and hero of the South Park period piece that newspapers of 1874 headlined as *The Fatal Amour,* was born Edward James Muggeridge in England in 1830 and arrived in San Francisco in 1854. He changed his name to the more poetic Eadweard Muybridge and opened a bookstore in Clay Street. Somehow, he drifted into professional photography, and by the Seventies had made a name for himself through his photographs of Yosemite, his news pictures of the Modoc Indian War, and his work in Alaska for the United States Coast Survey.

In 1872, Leland Stanford's passionate interest in horses prompted the railroad baron to considerable research into equine locomotion. One day, he announced his conviction that a trotter, at a certain point in its stride, lifted all four hoofs off the ground at once. Frederick MacCrellish, a publisher of the *Daily Alta California,* said it was ridiculous; how could a horse do that? There followed an argument which, legend says, ended in a $50,000 bet, Stanford saying a trotter did, and MacCrellish saying it didn't. (Biographers of Stanford primly scorn the story; they insist the Governor was not a betting man.)

Anyway, Stanford determined to prove his point. Thinking that perhaps photography was the way, he hired Muybridge to take action shots of Occident, one of the first trotters in what later became Stanford's famous racing stable, the Palo Alto Stock Farm. Muybridge, working with the wet plate process and an ordinary stand camera whose fastest exposure was one-twelfth of a second, failed dismally. All he could see of Occident on his plates was a blur.

(Five years later, with greatly improved equipment, he managed to get, out of hundreds of tries, four shots, one of which proved Stanford right. Then he went on, here, in France and in England, to other experiments and activities which earned for him the title "Father of the Motion Picture," as he is even now referred to on a commemorative plaque at Stanford University. In his *A Million and One Nights, A History of the Motion Picture,* Terry Ramsaye expertly and conclusively exposes Muybridge as a fake who contributed exactly nothing to the development of the motion picture. Muybridge, nevertheless, in full knowledge of the facts which Ramsaye later uncovered, benignly accepted the plaudits of his admirers, and after a few years of modest retirement died in 1904 at his birthplace, Kingston-on-Thames.)

It was a couple of years after the failure with Occident that Muybridge achieved the brilliant and dramatic high point of his San Francisco career. In California, where men were men, he reasoned, there was only one thing to do if another man seduced your wife: preserve your honor by shooting the son of a bitch. So he got a gun and shot Major Harry Larkyns.

As personalities went, they were at opposite poles. Muybridge was a ponderous and moody man, with a carefully cultivated air of picturesqueness about him—a shaggy, untrimmed mane of white hair, a long, white and tobacco-stained beard and tattered, unkempt clothes.

Larkyns, on the other hand, was a dashing nineteenth-century Don Juan with a romantic and incredible past that included a wealthy Scotch ancestry, membership in various underground revolutionary societies in Europe, a wound while fighting with the French against the Prussians at Metz, and several fabulous years in India, where an admiring potentate made him a raja and gave him a trunkful of diamonds. How he happened to come to America no one seems to know, but he arrived in Virginia City in the early Seventies and took the town by storm.

A writer of the time, recalling the stir Larkyns made on the Comstock, described him as tall, handsome, witty, debonair, master of seventeen languages, a poet and a musician. Additionally, "he could box like Jem Mace, and fence like Agramonte. . . . He could hit more bottlenecks with pistols at twenty paces than anyone else, and he never sent his right or left into a bully's face but that the bully was carried away on a stretcher."

He drifted off the Lode and down to San Francisco, where for a time he was drama critic for the *San Francisco Post*. It is related that he lost this job through the deceit of a man named Coppinger, whom he had once befriended. After that, whenever Larkyns met Coppinger on the street, he would seize Coppinger's nose with one hand, his lower jaw with the other, force his mouth open and spit in it. Coppinger became known all over San Francisco as "Cuspidor" Coppinger.

In 1871, Muybridge married a divorcee and Mills Seminary graduate named Flora Stone. He was forty-one; she was twenty, invitingly plump and endowed with tender, blue eyes and wavy, brown hair. Full of love for his innocent child bride, as he regarded her, Muybridge installed her in a home in South Park, whose roses now grew unpruned and whose mansions now stood dusty and sullen in the sun. During the photographer's long business trips, the lonely Flora and the dashing Major Larkyns became very friendly. In fact, they got just about as friendly as you can get.

A nurse later testified to this exchange in Flora's bedroom a few days after she had a baby, in April, 1874: "Mrs. Muybridge," she said, "ordered me to bring the baby in for Mr. Larkyns to see. Mrs. Muybridge said, 'Major, who is the baby like?' He smiled and said, "You ought to know, Flo.' She laughed and made no answer. . . . On one of his visits, Larkyns was standing at her bedside, and she said, 'Harry, we will remember the thirteenth of July—we have something to show for it.' She and Larkyns looked at the baby, and smiled tenderly. . . ."

Not long after the baby was born, Muybridge, still with the wool over his eyes, sent Flora and the baby off to relatives in Portland, while he prepared for a photographing expedition to South America. Larkyns, who, with the nurse as go-between, wrote frequent and amorous letters to Flora, joined a mapping party in Napa County.

One day in October, while calling on the nurse about a bill, Muybridge noticed a picture of his baby on the wall. He took it down and examined it. On the back, in his wife's handwriting, were the words, "Little Harry."

His dim suspicions snapping into sharp focus, Muybridge smote his brow with his fist and reeled. Then, trembling, pale and glassy of eye, he turned on the nurse and cried, "Great God! Tell me all!"

Terrified and believing him on the verge of a stroke, the nurse told him all. He tottered from the room sobbing, "Flora, Flora, my heart is broken. I would have given my heart's best blood for you. How could you treat me so cruelly?"

A few nights after that, Major Larkyns was playing cribbage at the home of William Stewart, superintendent of the Yellow Jacket quicksilver mine near Calistoga. There was a knock on the door, and the caller asked for Larkyns. Larkyns excused himself—there were ladies present—and went to the veranda and asked who was there.

"My name is Muybridge," came the reply from the darkness beyond the porch. "Here is the answer to that letter you wrote my wife."

There was a shot, and Larkyns fell back mortally wounded.

One account of what happened next said Larkyns ran through the house and out another door and fell dead at the base of an oak tree. But another and vastly more appealing version showed the Major at his cavalier best: ". . . Larkyns staggered back into the room, and with his hand covering his heart, which had been pierced by a bullet, bowed low to the ladies. 'I am very—sorry—this little trouble—has occurred—in your presence,' he said, with the hesitation of death in his tones, but with a soft, wistful smile playing about his lips. Then, straightening, he started for the door, saying, 'Kindly—excuse me—for—a moment.' With this, he passed through the door, and, reeling, fell dead."

Muybridge, palpably terrified by what he had done, was tried for murder in Napa in February, 1875. His defense of justifiable homicide was presented by State Senator W. W. Pendegast and Cameron H. King, whose son, until his retirement a few years ago, was San Francisco's Registrar of Voters. In a passionate speech to the jury, King nut-shelled the case for the defendant, crying, "I assert that he who would not shoot the seducer of his wife, aye, even if he were to suffer ten thousand deaths, is a coward and a cur! Better, far better death, than that the seducer should boast his conquest and a wife's dishonor with drunken companions over the flowing bowl, and point out the wretched man who walks the streets—a cuckold!"

A jury of horny-fisted, tobacco-chewing ranchers and farmers, all married but one, agreed with King, and returned a verdict of not guilty. "Hell," they snorted after it was all over, "we'd of done the same thing ourselves."

For a few days, Muybridge remained pale and haggard and on the brink of nervous collapse from the strain of the trial, and if it ever occurred to him that he had ambushed his man like the most arrant of cowards, he never admitted it. He moved away from South Park, and in a little while was quite himself again.

A few years later, Robert Louis Stevenson, the Amateur Emigrant, toiled up Rincon Hill and there found Charles Warren Stoddard who, with Ina Coolbrith and Bret Harte, comprised the *Overland Monthly's* illustrious Golden Gate Trinity. The encounter, related as it happened, supplied a brief incident for the San Francisco passage in the career of Loudon Dodd, hero of the novel *The Wrecker,* which Stevenson wrote in collaboration with Lloyd Osbourne.

"I had discovered," says Dodd, "a new slum, a place of precarious, sandy cliffs, deep, sandy cutting, solitary, ancient houses, and the butt ends of streets. . . . The city, upon all sides of it, was tightly packed, and growled with traffic. . . . On a steep sand hill, in this neighborhood, toppled, on the most insecure foundation, a certain row of houses. . . . Thither I used to mount by a crumbling footpath, and in front of the last of the houses, would sit down to sketch. The very first day I saw I was observed, out of the ground-floor window, by a youngish, good-looking fellow, prematurely bald, and with an expression both lively and engaging."

This was Stoddard, whom Stevenson had known by reputation as the author of *South Sea Idylls,* a whimsical and pleasant collection of travel pieces based on Stoddard's experiences as a Tahitian beachcomber. It was a curiously fateful encounter for Stevenson, who was to die fourteen years later beneath a bright Samoan sky; for it was Stoddard, in this and subsequent conversations, who first kindled Stevenson's curiosity about the South Pacific, who urged him to go there and see for himself the charm and loveliness of its islands.

Afterward, looking back on that time, Stoddard recalled how, a few short years after Mrs. Donahue's glass coach rolled sedately along Harrison Street and the little rich boys were fretting over their books at Doctor Huddart's Union College at Bryant and Second Streets and the little rich girls were prettily lisping their French conjugations at Madame Zeitska's fashionable female academy—how, even then, South Park and Rincon Hill had already been destroyed by the earth movers and the Second Street cut.

"The ruin I lived in [he wrote] had been a banker's Gothic home. When Rincon Hill was spoiled by the bloodless speculators, he abandoned it and took up his abode in another city. A tenant was left to mourn there. Every summer the wild winds shook that forlorn ruin to its foundations. Every winter the rains beat upon it and drove through and through it, and undermined it, and made a mush of the rock and soil about it; and later portions of that real estate deposited themselves, pudding fashion, in the yawning abyss below. . . ."

It was a not-long-ago noon, and a warm sun was breaking through the mist; but the man on the bench wore a hat well pulled down and an overcoat with the collar turned up. From the waxed paper package on his knees he selected a jelly sandwich and began to eat his lunch.

To the east rose the incline of Rincon Hill, now a place of factories and warehouses, freight cars and trucks, and dominated by the great overhead ramps of the Bay Bridge. To the west was Third Street, and the mutter of traffic.

"Yes," the man said, "this neighborhood was once the Nob Hill of San Francisco. It reached its zenith before the Fire—long before the Fire."

The bench on which we sat was on Gordon's oval park, roseless and crisscrossed by many footpaths. Clipped sycamore trees were beginning to thrust out thin green branches. There was a weeping willow tree, and, at its base, a drinking fountain. Ranged around the park were shabby two- and three-story dwellings that after the Fire had replaced Gordon's stone-fronted mansions; those, and a machine shop or two and several small warehouses and hotels. They were all gray, and the effect, even in the warm sunshine, was that of a slattern with a hang-over, who wished you would go away and leave her alone.

A big truck left the gas station down at the corner of Third and eased into the traffic stream. The spatter of its exhaust filled the little square and then died away. The man on the bench unwrapped his dessert, a lady finger.

"Who lives here now?" I asked.

"Negroes, mostly. Before the war, there were some Japs. They say they planted the weeping willow tree." He nodded over his shoulder, indicating the dilapidated hotel on the north side of the park. Its sign said, "Hotel Bo Chow." "When the steamers came in from the Orient, a lot of Japs used to get off the boat and come here to the Bo Chow. The war finished that. Now it's Negroes, and some Mexicans."

I thanked him and left him finishing his lunch and went over and sat down on a bench in front of the Hotel South Park, up the street a bit from the Bo Chow. Cars were parked all around the oval, and here and there, on their running boards, sat workmen eating from their lunch boxes. When they finished, one of them produced a softball and they walked into the oval and started tossing it back and forth, near the weeping willow.

A man appeared on the steps of No. 78 South Park. He was tieless, coatless, needing a shave and wearing bedroom slippers. He looked up and down the street, and then, weaving a little, walked a few doors to the Home Grocery, and came back a few minutes later carrying a bottle of beer.

A truck rumbled past on Second Street.

A door up the street opened and a Negro girl came out. Her hair was in a net, and she wore a lavender chenille robe, wrapped tightly to her shapely figure. The men stopped their softball to watch the arrogant swinging of her hips as she, too, entered the Home Grocery. When she appeared again, she had two eggs and a loaf of bread. She went back into her place and shut the door. The men resumed their play.

In a second-floor room across the park, someone pulled down the shades.

Something wakened two young cats sleeping on the hood of a car parked in the sun. They looked around them with staring green eyes. One of them saw a gray and withered leaf drifting along the street. Craftily, fluidly, the cat moved from the hood to the fender, to the running board, to the pavement. There it crouched, and, with its tail slowly flicking, began to stalk the leaf.

14. THIRD STREET

SAN FRANCISCO'S BACK DOOR · NOTES FOR AN UNWRITTEN BOOK. A FOURTH
OF JULY PARADE. LAMPLIGHTERS. THE MILKMEN'S EXCHANGE. CHASING
THE CABLE. THE LITTLE USHER OF THE BUSH STREET THEATER · DAVID
BELASCO. TRUDGING THE WATERFRONT. BARNSTORMING THE WEST. ADE-
LAIDE NEILSON AND THE BLACK PEARL. SUCCESS IN MANHATTAN. "I WAS
TRYING TO IMITATE GOD." REUNION IN SAN FRANCISCO. HIS DEATH · OLD
BUTCHERTOWN. DRINKING BLOOD · IRISH HILL, AND THE BLUE MUDS OF
POTRERO · THE LITTLE MAN OF THE SIERRA

THIRD STREET was one of the big streets in South of the Slot, five miles long
and leading off Market just above the Palace and cutting past South Park
to the waterfront, and then following the Bay beach south all the way to
the road to San José. In its first blocks off Market, it lay across that family
neighborhood of cottages, flats, corner grocery stores, social halls, club-
rooms, shops and bars. Architecturally, the neighborhood was dominated
by the two hundred-foot shot tower of the Selby Smelting and Lead Company. It was dominated aesthetically by the Grand Opera House, politi-

297

cally by the Democrats and racially by the Irish. As for its soul, dominion over that was pretty evenly shared by the beery bartenders of the Third Street taprooms, and the patient, industrious and forgiving fathers of St. Patrick's parish.

That's the way it was in 1906.

Then the shot tower came tumbling down, and the Grand Opera House (where Caruso had sung the night before) fell flaming into Mission Street. The many back-room rendezvous of the Democrats went up in smoke, and the street corners where their political bonfires blazed disappeared beneath debris. All the cottages and flats and stores collapsed in charred ruins. The taprooms vanished, and St. Patrick's was still burning a couple of days later.

Even the canaries that had rolled and twittered their songs in the four great cages above the courtyard of A. Schilling's new spice-and-coffee factory in Folsom Street were silenced, for how could they sing when they lay scorched to death on the floors of their cages?

Brick by brick, St. Patrick's went up again, and, by the time it was finished, most of the people who had lived within the sound of its bells had moved away from that neighborhood to the Mission hills, to Bay View or Eureka Valley or Bernal Heights or Glen Park or some place else. And Third Street, near Market, became a Bowery, a barrel-house haven, a flophouse heaven for itinerant laborers, vagabonds and wrecks from all points north, east and south. Then, as it passed South Park and approached the Southern Pacific station and yards, and the piers of China Basin, they built warehouses and factories upon it, making it the main artery of a compact and crowded industrial district. Beyond that, it led to the slaughterhouses and tanneries whose pungent and richly rotten odors rose over Butchertown hard by Hunter's Point, and from these it struck farther south, though bending slightly west, through the new, monotonous rows of Bay View homes—all one-and-a-half stories, all white or cream or brown, all alike—to the city-and-county line that extended from Candlestick Point on the Bay across the Peninsula to Lake Merced and the ocean.

And that—except that there are more factories and warehouses, more cottages and neighborhood shopping districts and government housing projects out near Bay View, more barrel houses and pawnshops, more

Mexicans and Negroes near Market Street, the Bay Bridge ramp slanting overhead between Harrison and Bryant Streets and a lot more traffic everywhere—that is pretty much the way Third Street is now.

If the Embarcadero is the city's front door, then Third Street at Townsend, where the Southern Pacific station is, is its back door. When The Lark brings you in from Los Angeles some morning, and you get off there at that absurd little station, and get into a cab and drive a mile or so along a bus- and truck-clogged street, past Greek and Mexican lunch counters, past a hundred dreary saloons and a hundred shabby hock shops, and past droves of Skid Road scarecrows out to panhandle early morning pedestrians for the price of a muscatel pick-me-up—when you see this from your taxicab window on your way to the Palace or the St. Francis or the Mark Hopkins, you're in San Francisco, on Third Street.

In the past of Third Street, in the faraway years back beyond all this, you find the background notes for another book about San Francisco that has never been written. Frank Norris could have done it, if he had felt like it. It's too bad someone didn't write it, for it would have had strength and humor and plenty of color, and a hundred times more humanity and life than all the volumes that have ever been written about the four-story iceboxes that pass for homes on Nob Hill.

How David Belasco was born in a basement room at Third and Howard Streets, and how his gypsy mother, smiling, scattered violets upon him when the neighborhood midwife first brought him to her bedside. . . . The thousands of Irish, bareheaded and on their knees in the vacant lot at Third and Brannan during the masses celebrated there on St. Patrick's Day morning, before the big parades. . . . The early days of Third and Townsend, with the revenue cutters and the lighthouse tenders at anchorage off the beach there, and the docks where the sailors landed for their shore leaves, and the hay wharves and lumberyards and brickyards where now the long engines pull in with the streamliners from Los Angeles every day; John G. North's shipyards, where, in 1860, they launched the *Chrysopolis,* a Sacramento River boat and in her day the largest steamer ever built in California; the Pope and Talbot lumberyard, where the kids who went swimming down there off the Long Bridge over the tide flats to Butchertown stole kindling wood by the bagful for their mothers' kitchen stoves; Caesar Brun's grocery and the restaurants of Sarcin and three-fingered Johnny Killa-da-Fly; Huckmeister's fruit stand and Dan Twigg's stationery store and Duff's crockery shop; the rowing clubs, the Pioneer, the South End, the Neptune and the California; red-shirted Tom McNamara, the ferryman, who rowed men out to ships in the stream in his Whitehall boat, and Tom McKelvey, the bumboatman, peddling candy, cigarets and fruit to the ships along the anchorage; Rocky Mountain Jack and three-hundred-pound Slim Jim, who told hair-raising and improbable tales to the kids of the neighborhood, sipping from oyster cans (as they talked) the stale beer they salvaged from used kegs outside the Third and Townsend saloons.

The big Fourth of July parades, turning from Market into Second, from Second into Folsom and from Folsom into Third and moving along Third back to Market, past Doctor Rottanzi's Statuary Drug Store on the Folsom corner, with its marble sidewalk and its Greek and Roman statues, and the secondhand store of Mrs. Attell, mother of Abe the prize fighter; past Uncle Benjamin's pawnshop and Pincus Funkenstein's variety store; past the old bars—the Whale, the New York Casino, The Chief, The Eagle's Nest and Happy Jack Harrington's; past the Third Street clothing stores—I. Magnin's, Mrs. Mark's, J. Bull's, Deasy's Shoe Store, Healy's and Quinn the Hatter's; past the Americus Democratic Club (at Third and Mission), and Ginty and Blanchard's saloon (Dave Blanchard, it was, who took the day's receipts home with him every night, walking the middle of the gaslit streets with a cocked pistol in each hand); past Regan's restaurant ("Two Eggs, Any Style—10 Cents"), and Martin's Oyster House, and Lundy the jeweler's, and Beamish the haberdasher's, and C. C. Keene's music store in the Nucleus Building that was on the corner of Third and Market. The line of march, the loud bands, the bright guards and hussars (the St. Crispins, the St. Patrick Cadets and all the others), the soldiers and the Civil War veterans would move past these old Third Street places and so back to Market, and then across Market, past Lotta's Fountain and into Kearny. And there would be floats on carts, and a long file of milk wagons, patriotically decorated in red, white and blue bunting, and if you were a kid then the thing you used to do for the hell of it was toss lighted firecrackers beneath the milk-wagon horses; maybe once in a while you would be rewarded by seeing the horse bolt and the wagon lurch out of line, off the car tracks they all rode to avoid the cobbles, and up the street away from the parade, strewing its empty milk cans as it went, sending them rolling and banging all over the street and sidewalks.

The long and merry dances—rasping fiddles, and the hall resounding to the quick, rhythmic stamping of the heel-and-toe polka or the measured scraping of the French minuet—at the firehouse of Engine 10 on Bryant Street, just off Third, or at Ixora Hall, or Mother Stoke's place down by the lumberyards on Saturday night. . . . The chants of the ragpickers as they shuffled past the alley cottages, and the droning nasal cry of the razor-grinder, "O-ho, get your razors ground!," backed by the jangling of his hand bell as he pushed his wheeled grindstone up the street.

Bill Dolan, the saloonkeeper, riding grandly along Third Street in his handsome barouche and behind his proud team of black-pointed bays. . . . The cut-glass dishes the housewives carried home as premiums for the tea they'd bought at the Great American Tea Company. . . . The Third Street lamplighters: old Mulcahey on his dolorous and sway-backed nag, reaching up from the saddle with his flame-tipped pole and then withdrawing it, leaving up there in the air the sudden, swift bloom of light, as if the pole were a magic wand turning into light whatever Mulcahey touched with it; and after old Mulcahey, little Charlie Quigley with his stooped shoulders and his red flannel shirt, smiling and cheerfully wishing you the top of the evening as he passed on his rounds, lighting the lamps in the dusk and putting them out in the dawn when you were getting dressed and your daddy was already leaving the house on his way to work at the brickyards or the lumberyards or the waterfront.

The Milkmen's Exchange (the "Bun Racket," they called it) at the corner of Third and Howard, where the deliverymen gathered before setting out on their rounds. They would arrive, the cans on their wagons banging and clashing through the deserted, lamplit streets, just after midnight; they would hitch their horses outside, covering them with blankets of tarpaulins if it was cold or raining, and then go in to the great copper boilers—one for hot milk, the other for steaming coffee—the fresh, warm, sweet-smelling buns stacked on platters, the high stools, the glowing wood stove and the sawdust floor of the Exchange, and there they would eat and drink and gossip, absorbing the bustle and warmth and light and friendliness until it was time to leave for their wagons and their lonely chores. . . . The Italian street singers, with their harps and violins, singing serenades in the backyards of Natoma and Clementina Streets on summer evenings, and, when they were through, smiling and bowing and picking from the ground the pennies and nickels the people threw to them from the back porches and windows. . . . Uncle Sam, the Negro, who wore a swallow-tailed coat and a beaver hat with a red, white and blue band, and hobbled along the street on Sunday afternoons selling molasses candy. . . . Street gamins pegging rocks at the Chinese immigrants as they rode in wagons from the Pacific Mail docks, along Third Street and across the city to Chinatown, or stealing rides on the back ends of horsecars, or playing prisoner's base in the alleys in the evenings, or tying string around a ball of paper and dropping the string through the Howard Street cable slot and then, when the string tangled with the cable, chasing the paper ball as the cable pulled it down the street. . . . Morosco's Union Hall Theater over the carbarns on Howard a half block off Third, and the blood-chilling melodramas that kept you wild to return there Saturday night after Saturday night—*The Wreck of the Night Express; Nellie, the Cloak Model; From Rags to Riches; No Mother to Guide Her; The Bridge-Tender's Daughter; The Hidden Hand*—and then afterward walking your girl to the Greek's candy store out Third Street near Mrs. Attell's and buying ice-cream sodas for a nickel apiece, and, if you were rich that night, splurging with another nickel for a bagful of candy hearts with the love mottoes on them.

The little crowd that used to gather on Clara Street not far from Third, listening to a lad who, like Belasco, had been born in South of the Slot and who, like Belasco, grew up to fall in love with any stage and any footlights and any theater. Belasco himself learned about this one day, and told about it in his reminiscences: "There was an usher at the Bush Street Theater—a bright little fellow with a most luminous smile. He is still small, and his smile is still luminous. I did not then know his name, but I had heard among his family and friends he was quite an entertainer, being able to sing, to mimic and to recite. One day I was at home, in my front room on the top floor, when I heard a voice in the street below. I leaned out, and there on the corner, standing on a box which scarcely raised him above the gaping onlookers, was the little usher from the Bush Street Theater, reciting to a curious crowd. I went down and stood near until he had finished. Then I went up to him and asked him his name. 'Dave Warfield,' said he, giving me the smile that lived long afterwards in Herr von Barwig, during all the rehearsals of *The Music Master,* and that was our first meeting."

That was in the Seventies, and the oldest South of Market Boys tell you those were the best days down there in South of the Slot. Maybe they say that because to most men the days of their childhood are always the best days, no matter where they were lived; but Belasco certainly agreed with them, long after he had left those streets behind him.

None of his classmates at the Lincoln Grammar School in Fifth Street, just off Market, would have thought of giving the slender, dark-eyed boy a vote as the most likely to succeed, but when Belasco died in 1931, people mourned the passing of the greatest producer and showman of the American stage.

Three weeks after his death, misty-eyed San Franciscans honored their South of Market Boy with special memorial services in the vast and lofty City Hall rotunda. Actress Florence Reed told them the theater had worn mourning before. "But tonight," she said, "it wears its rue in a different way, because when David Belasco went away, he took with him the light, the color, the glamor, the very soul of the theater."

Everyone agreed that it was very touching and very fitting, and quite an impressive epilogue to a life that began in that basement room at Third and Howard.

Belasco was the son of Humphrey Abraham and Reina Martin Belasco, who had gone from London to California seeking their fortune. They arrived in San Francisco a few months before David's birth. Failing to prosper, they moved (in 1858) to Victoria, British Columbia. There, curiously (he was born a Jew), David fell under the influence of a Catholic priest named Father Maguire, and William Winter, Belasco's biographer, and Belasco himself, attributed to the priest's training his mental stamina, his respect for scholarship and his rigorous self-discipline. There, too, he had his introduction to the theater, playing several child's parts at the Theater Royal.

At the close of the Civil War, the Belascos moved back to San Francisco, living always South of Market—in Harrison Street, Bryant Street, Louisa Street, Clara Street. It was at 174 Clara Street (now just east of Fifth, about at the site of the Fischer Elevator Company) that David, at the age of thirteen or fourteen, wrote his first play, *Jim Black or The Regulator's Revenge!* Even then, while attending the Lincoln Grammar School, he kept candles and matches and writing materials by his bed in order to jot down ideas that might come to him in the middle of the night.

But the early years were filled with hardship. The gold medal he won at Lincoln as the best reader and performer of Tragedy was pawned for food money. Each Friday, after school, he helped his mother with the family laundry, standing on a box to reach the tubs, and with the household chores. He got a job washing windows and sweeping floors in a cigar factory. He trudged the waterfront, giving recitations in saloons and gratefully picking up coins the maudlin patrons tossed at his feet. As he wandered the city, however, his eyes and ears were open, and he absorbed the richness, the drama and vitality that made the streets of San Francisco more ugly and more beautiful than any other streets in the world. He tried to earn money by haunting gambling halls and hospital emergency rooms and police stations, and writing his observations and peddling them to the city desks of local newspapers.

"As a young fellow," he once told Winter, "I visited the scene of every murder that I heard of—and they were many. I knew every infamous and dangerous place in San Francisco. . . . Only my dear mother seemed to understand me. My adventures and wanderings ('Wandering Feet,' she used to call me) worried her, which I grieve to think of now, but she always took my part. 'Davy is all right,' she used to say; 'leave him alone; he's only curious about life, and wants to see everything with those big, dark eyes of his.' She was right; and, if I didn't see everything, I saw a good deal."

Among his favorite renditions in those times were melodramatic poems like *The Maniac* by Matthew Lewis and *Curfew Must Not Ring Tonight* by Rosa Hartwick Thorpe. He gave such plausible demonstrations of madness along with *The Maniac* that his school mates accused him of chewing soap in order to froth at the mouth with convincing realism.

So, looking back on Belasco's life in those days, you see him as a Lincoln Grammar School boy taking part in public entertainments, declaiming *The Banishment of Catiline* in a costume comprising his father's underwear and a cheap cloth toga. You see him as a newsboy in Augustin Daly's *Under the Gaslight* at Maguire's Opera House, or giving recitations on the stage of Platt's Hall in Montgomery Street, or acting in plays presented at Turnverein Hall in Bush Street by the Fire-Fly Social and Dramatic Club, an organization formed by stage-struck youths and named in honor of Lotta Crabtree after her San Francisco appearance in the play *Fire-Fly*. You see him in the galleries of the California Theater, dark eyes lighted with his worship of McCullough, Lawrence Barrett, William Henry Sedley-Smith and the other matinee idols of the time. And you see him, at last, going on as a super in Frederick G. Marsden's play *Help* at the Metropolitan. That was on July 10, 1871, and that was Belasco's first paid and professional appearance on the stage. He was almost eighteen.

Between then and 1882, when he left San Francisco to go east as stage manager of the Gustave Frohman Dramatic Company, Belasco accumulated an amazing record.

He barnstormed the West from Vancouver to Lower California, sometimes acting, sometimes hawking merchandise from a fairgrounds soapbox, sometimes peddling a gargle and mouthwash manufactured by his mother. "Many a time," he later recalled, "I've marched into town banging a big drum or tooting a cornet. We used to play in any place we could hire or get into—a hall, a big dining room, an empty barn; anywhere. . . ." He acted in the theatrical company playing John Piper's Opera House in Virginia City, and there for a time served as secretary to the playwright Dion Boucicault, who lay in bed, propped up on pillows with a glass of hot whisky beside him, and dictated to Belasco the dialogue of *Led Astray*.

As manager, actor, playwright, director, producer, scene painter and all-round handy man at the Metropolitan, the California, the Baldwin, the Grand Opera House and other San Francisco theaters, he had acted in more than a hundred plays, taking roles ranging from insignificant walk-on parts to Hamlet. And, according to William Winter, he had "altered, adapted, rewritten or written more than one hundred plays, and he had been the responsible director in the production of more than three times that number."

An encounter during one of these productions, as the San Francisco phase of his career was drawing to a close, provided Belasco with one of the strange and inexplicable episodes that marked his life. It is the haunting story of the black pearl.

To begin with, Adelaide Neilson, an English girl, was one of the most celebrated and beautiful actresses of the Seventies. Her dark, tragic eyes, her rich and passionate voice and her magnetic presence were known and acclaimed on every stage of importance from London to San Francisco. She had first attracted attention at London's Adelphi Theater in 1865. A hard worker, a conscientious student, she one day blazed out as the greatest Shakespearian actress of the times.

Her first appearance in San Francisco was in the role of Juliet at the California Theater, March 10, 1874. Belasco, then twenty, was one of the supers in that performance and danced the minuet with her in the ballroom scene of the first act. ("I shall never forget," he said, "how deeply affected I was when, in the dance, for the first time I touched her hand and she turned those wonderful eyes on me.") She played again at the California in 1877, and once more returned to San Francisco in June, 1880, for a five-week appearance at the Baldwin. The last performance she gave there—the last performance she gave anywhere—was on the night of July 17. She acted the Balcony Scene from *Romeo and Juliet* and then appeared in the title role of *Amy Robsart.*

It was the custom for a star, when ending an engagement, to present a memento to each member of the company. Later that evening, she called Belasco to her dressing room. She indicated, on her dressing table, a pile of her personal jewelry—a glittering heap of diamonds, rubies and emeralds—and said, "Perhaps I may never see you again. Look over those things and choose something for yourself . . . to bring you luck."

Belasco, dazzled by the gems, hesitated. . . . "I finally reached forward [he wrote] and picked up a black pearl. I said, 'I'll take this.' Miss Neilson's face turned white and she closed her eyes. 'Oh, David, why do you ask for that?' she cried, and I dropped it as though I had done an evil thing. 'I'm superstitious,' she confessed. 'My truck is full of nails, horseshoes, and the luckiest thing of all is that little black pearl. I dislike to refuse you anything, but I know you will understand. . . .'" Belasco selected a small emerald and left the room.

At the company's farewell supper that night, Miss Neilson talked incessantly of Belasco's curious choice. She said at last, "If I gave up that pearl, I shouldn't live a month. Someone told me that, and I believe it."

The next day, July 18, she left San Francisco bound for Europe.

A few days later, Belasco received a note from Miss Neilson, and it said, "I cannot get your voice out of my mind." The package contained the black pearl.

On August 15, almost four weeks to the day from the time she mailed it to Belasco, Adelaide Neilson died in Paris. Dispatches said she had been stricken while driving in the Bois de Boulogne. By the time they got her to her hotel, she was beyond medical aid.

"Charge it to the long arm of coincidence, if you will," Belasco afterward said, "but in my own career I have met so many occurrences that are stranger than fiction that I cannot doubt the workings of coincidence any longer."

Belasco did not own the black pearl more than a few months. A few days after he told his mother its curious story, she stole the black pearl from his room and destroyed it, lest it bring him bad luck.

When he reached New York in 1882, the young San Franciscan from South of the Slot did not exactly set fire to Manhattan. There followed thirteen years of grueling work, small pay and frequent failure—years he passed as the director of stars like Georgia Cayvan and Richard Mansfield, as a hack dramatist writing or revising or adapting such plays as *May Blossom, Pawn Ticket 210* (in collaboration with the San Franciscan Clay M. Greene), and *The Girl I Left Behind Me* (in collaboration with Franklyn Fyles). All this brought him almost nothing but a reputation. Later, recalling his desperate circumstances in 1894, he wrote: "My private possessions, my library (containing some very valuable historical books)—my few antiques—everything—had been sold. As a last economy, I decided to give up my little office in Carnegie Hall. . . ."

But he had held out, had held on, and his luck was about to change. And less than a year later, at New York's Herald Square Theater, his romantic Civil War play, *The Heart of Maryland,* opened with his first protégée, Mrs. Leslie Carter, in the starring role of Maryland Calvert. The play was a smash hit.

Four years passed during which *The Heart of Maryland* triumphantly toured the United States and won foreign acclaim in London. Then, January 9, 1899, at New York's Garrick Theater, Belasco starred Mrs. Carter in his second great success, *Zaza*. Two nights after a brilliant opening, Belasco had another strange experience, one that impressed him deeply and influenced his thought for the rest of his life.

Lying sleepless and exhausted on his bed, he seemed to see his mother standing beside him. She repeated his name three times, smiled, and kissed him. She told him she was happy, and not to grieve. Then she moved to the door and disappeared. The next day, he received a telegram from San Francisco telling him his mother had died at their old home in Clara Street. He later learned she had died the precise moment that she appeared at his bedside. Her last words had been, "Davy, Davy, Davy."

Unable to reach San Francisco in time for her funeral, Belasco wired relatives and asked them to do something for him. When the funeral services were over, they carried out his wish, and covered his mother's grave with violets, to say good-by for him.

The new century brought with it much fame and success for David Belasco. Before its first five years had passed, he had written and produced *Madame Butterfly*, a play based on a story of the same title by John Luther Long, and the play which inspired Puccini's opera. He had produced *Under Two Flags*, launching the San Francisco actress Blanche Bates (later Mrs. George Creel) in the starring role of Cigarette. He had presented David Warfield in his first major role, Simon Levi in *The Auctioneer*. He had written and produced his sensational *Du Barry*, with Mrs. Carter in the title role. He had given Miss Bates another great part, Princess Yo-San in *The Darling of the Gods*. He had at last opened his own Belasco Theater on Broadway, and had given Warfield his second major role, Anton von Barwig in *The Music Master*. And, as 1905 ended, he had written for Miss Bates and produced *The Girl of the Golden West*. (Six years later, Puccini's *La Fanciulla del West*, based on Belasco's play, had its world *première* at the Metropolitan Opera House.)

And so the South of Market Boy had made good, and for the next quarter of a century he was to dominate the American stage, bringing to it insight, genius and a phenomenal sense of showmanship.

There were many things about Belasco that captured the public imagination. He was a small man, five feet six, and his later pictures show him

with a heavy shock of white hair, and always with the clerical collar and high-necked vest he affected. He spoke slowly, measuring each word, and impressed one with his air of complete simplicity.

In his professional life, he went to bizarre lengths to achieve realism. When stage directions of a play called for letters written by Mozart, Belasco bought originals, in the composer's own hand, although the audience would never see their contents. When, as in *The Easiest Way*, the set called for an Eighth Avenue boardinghouse, he bought one, dismantled it and reconstructed it upon the stage. Yet, in his private life, he often displayed a childlike and wistful sentimentality: after his daughter Augusta died and was buried in Brooklyn, he kept a guard beside her tomb every night, and a light burning there, because she had always been afraid of being alone in the dark.

The seven-room studio he occupied above his theater was a museum of dramatic effects and associations. Light slanted through stained-glass windows. A carved oak desk had come from the sixteenth-century palace of the Italian Collonas. A chair was made from a pew of the Stratford-on-Avon church in which Shakespeare had been buried. His wastebasket was a drum used by the German army in its march on Paris in the Franco-Prussian War. The tile of his fireplace came from the Alhambra in Granada. Around his study stood screens on which were tacked memos to himself, instructions to his staff, manuscript fragments of plays in progress.

When he decided to write a play, he would first of all determine its period. Then he would read all the books he could obtain on that period, absorbing them to the last detail. Next, he would shut himself in a dark room, to insure the utmost concentration. When he emerged hours later, he would have in his mind characters and a plot. He would begin dictating the dialogue, acting out each part as he went along. One stenographer would take down his words, another would record every movement he made. In a day or two, he would have his new play.

He once wrote that "the great thing, the essential thing, for a producer is to create Illusion and Effect," and some of his greatest contributions to the theater were in the field of stagecraft. His use of lighting, for example, was revolutionary for his time (he believed himself the first director to dispense with footlights). Frequently, the expense of his light rehearsals alone would exceed the total of all other production costs. It took him ten months' work before he was satisfied with the lighting of *The Return of Peter Grimm*. And when he staged a storm (as in *Tiger Rose*), or a forest fire, it was a literally terrifying spectacle. To produce the wild Sierra blizzard in the second act of *The Girl of the Golden West,* he employed thirty-two specially trained technicians, all under the control of a centrally placed conductor.

To his friends, when they praised one of these superb storm scenes,

Belasco would reply, "Was it good?—Really?—Then I have achieved the thing I was trying to do. I was trying to imitate God."

In February, 1909, Belasco paid one of his rare visits to San Francisco, to see his aged and ailing father. On February 24, he was the guest of honor at a dinner given at the Bismarck Café by alumni of the Lincoln Grammar School Classes of 1865-1871.

"The night at the Lincoln School dinner was wonderful," he wrote Winter. "There were about seventy of the 'boys' there, and dear old Professor Bernhard Marks, who had been the principal and who was nearly eighty, presided and called the roll, just as he used to do when we were all lads. Sometimes a silence followed a name; many times there came the answer 'Dead,' and now and then somebody responded 'Present.' I cried! Then the principal put us through our paces again, at the old lessons, and dealt out cuts on the hand with very little of the old-time vigor. After that there were speeches, and so many lovely things were said about me that I was too embarrassed to reply properly; I remember that I began by saying it was the happiest night of my life—and then stood there with tears running down my cheeks. . . ."

Twenty years later—twenty years rich in achievement and content— Belasco was interviewed on the occasion of his seventy-fifth birthday. He told reporters he was "confident of the great years ahead. I feel," he said, "as I did at twenty-one. . . . I shall retire when I am carried feet first out of the theater."

Two years after that, after a long struggle against pneumonia, he was struck by coronary embolism. On his deathbed he turned to his physician and said, "I am fighting for my life, doctor."

They were the last words of David Belasco, a South of Market Boy who once said he had made his own world—a world with few people in it, he said, because it was a world of faith and dreams.

In those far-off years (but only yesterday to some who are still alive) when David Belasco was parading into country towns beating a drum or tooting his cornet, Third Street reached to the city's southern hills across the dank tidelands, across bogs and blue mud and through a community whose skies were everlastingly stained with the dark smoke of steel mills

and tainted with gashouse fumes, whose days were filled with the bawling of steers in the slaughtering pens and the incessant chuffing of sand-
laden steam trains reclaiming the land from the sea, and whose life was
a jungle of toil, sweat and poverty.

There went the immigrants—the Irish, the Scotch, the Dutch, and
Russians, the Poles—as they stepped off the trains and the ships with their
belongings in bundles on their backs and leading their grave, somber-eyed
children by the hand. There went the shipbuilders and the mechanics,
the boilermakers and the butchers, steady, sober home builders as well as
all the wandering workers of the world who drifted into Frisco to make
a few dollars, see the sights, get themselves drunk and get themselves a
woman for a while, and drift on again to some other town, some other
place.

You pick up what you can about that San Francisco from the men who
go back that far, like Fred W. Zimmerman, Sr., historian of the South
San Francisco Parlor of the Native Sons of the Golden West, like little
Billy Carr, a retired deputy sheriff who lives in The Mission and whose
round blue eyes still shine with wonder and affection when he remembers
those days, and like Charlie Smith, the lonesome miner of Sierra City.

Most of all, they recall the rough-riding *vaqueros* and the steers that
came in on the cattle trains from the great ranches of the South, and the
Third Street abattoirs where blood gushed in rivers from the severed
throats of the animals.

"Old Butchertown in the Sixties," said Zimmerman, "extended about
from where Seals Stadium is now to Third and Townsend Streets. But
as the Mission Bay flats were filled in, they gradually moved out towards
Hunter's Point, to stay near the water."

Carr, who grew up on Irish Hill (it was leveled by the government
during the First World War and is now the site of the Bethlehem Steel
shipyards), can remember crossing the tide flats on Saturday mornings
to earn a dollar or two.

"A gang of us used to go over the dumps to Butchertown to teach the
consumptives how to drink hot blood. The doctors would send them
down there after it, but they'd be afraid to catch it in their tin cups as it
came out of the throat of the steer that had just been slaughtered. So we
would take their cups and catch the blood for them, while they stood

looking on with their eyes popping out of their head. Then we would take it over and hand it to them. Fifteen cents a cup, they gave us. . . ."

There wasn't much in those days between Butchertown and the county line except grazing land for the dairy farms that moved over there from Cow Hollow in the Seventies, and the dusty road leading over the hills and south to San José, and the roadhouses, like the Four-Mile House and the Five-Mile House, and the Bay View Race Track there on the flats, where the Bay View playground is now.

Those, and a couple of silk factories, a brewery or two and Purcell's South San Francisco Park, where they had church fairs and Sunday picnics and rat-killing matches and dances, and that was about all.

Irish Hill, however, seethed with a raucous and brawny vigor. In the Eighties, when he lived there, Carr said, it was covered with hotels and boardinghouses.

"There was the Green House, run by Mike Farrell. The White House, run by Hans Rasmussen. Cash's Hotel, run by Jimmy Cole. The San Quentin House, run by Jim Gately. Gately took in the parolees from San Quentin prison and got them jobs in the rolling mills at the foot of the hill. There was Paddy Kearn's Hotel, and outside the gashouse was Mike Boyle's steam beer dump. There was also the Shasta House, and McDonald's Hotel.

"In them days," he continued, "we never went to Morosco's, because the shows were better on Irish Hill, where the boys from one hotel would challenge the boys from another hotel and fight all Saturday afternoon in a hay-rope ring outside of Gately's hotel. When the fights were over, we'd all go to Mike Boyle's and knock off tall steams for a nickel apiece.

"You went up on Irish Hill—ninety-eight steps, it was, to the top— when you got off work, and you never left it till next morning. Below it, on one side, stood the blue muds of Potrero, where King McManus and Jack Welch—he was the prize-fight referee, Congressman Welch's brother —where they used to run their hotels and get out in the street and fight for each other's boarders. Below it on another side was Dutchman's Flat, where Dutchmen from the old country lived. The next hill, that's Potrero Hill now, was Scotch Hill, where the Scotchmen lived.

"The Irish'd come from Ireland, with a shillelagh stick and a bag on their shoulder, and a card in their hand telling them to go to work at the Pacific rolling mills. If there was no work there, they'd go to the gas-house. The Dutchmen came over with work cards for the sugar house. The Scotchmen, all mechanical men, would go to work at the Scott Iron Works. . . ."

Charlie Smith, sitting outside his board shanty in Sierra City with the rocky Sierra Buttes looming high against the northern sky and the Yuba's north fork singing down the canyon and through the fir trees a hundred yards away, remembered King McManus and his Union House on the blue muds of Potrero below Irish Hill. (I had stopped at his cabin to ask highway directions, and we'd got to talking, and he told me this. He was a little man, wiry, with a heavy gray beard. He wore overalls and a cloth cap. The questions I asked him I wrote on paper and passed over to him; he couldn't hear without his hearing aid on, and that was no damned good, he said, because the battery'd been worn out for months. His features were clean and delicate. He looked like a little professor on a camping trip. He was seventy-seven.)

He had been born in Downieville on the Mother Lode, and his father had taken him to the mountain mining town of Sierra City in 1881, when he had been twelve years old and when there had been twenty-eight saloons and twenty sporting girls in the place. He had worked in the mines for a while; then he had left Sierra City in about 1890 and had gone to work in the Union Iron Works shipyard in Frisco as a hand riveter on the *Oregon,* the *Monterey* and the *Olympia.*

He had lived in the Nevada House, across the street from McManus's Union House, and one day, he recalled, he was sitting in his room re-writing a letter. When he was through, he tore up the original, tossed the scraps of paper out the window and idly watched them float on the wind to the Union House's front porch. McManus, in a bad humor because one of Welch's boys had shot the hands off his barroom clock, saw the paper littering his front porch, and dashed inside.

"First thing I knew," Charlie said, "he came out with a rifle and put two shots through the window, just over my head. Then another fellow came out of the Nevada House with his rifle—a Virginia City man with a scar on his face where he'd been burned in the Virginia City fire of

'75—and said, 'King, if there's any shootin' goin' on around here, I'm a-fixin' to be in on it.' The King looked sheepish, and put his rifle down, and went back inside. He was sure shut up that time."

Charlie thought about it for a minute or two, and then rambled on.

"I remember the old Barbary Coast. Had a girl there once. When there was the excitement in the Klondike, I got together four hundred dollars— you had to have three hundred before they'd let you off the wharf—and went down to Frisco. Well, I thought I ought to see the girl before I went so far away. She was at Frank and Paul's, the toughest mill on Pacific Street. I went to see her, and there"—he flung his hands out in a gesture of helplessness—"went the four hundred dollars."

He wagged his head over the memory and smiled gently. "Just as well, I guess. I never would have liked that cold climate, anyway."

He talked on about the Tonopah excitement and the Goldfield excitement, and the times he'd had in the State of Sonora, Mexico, working in the copper mines—the times he'd got drunk, the times he'd gone broke, the good times with the mining-camp girls, the way he'd got homesick for California, and the way the fires of the melting furnaces lighted the Sonoran skies at night.

In the First World War, he'd gone back to work in the shipyards on Third Street in Frisco, and had tried again, at the age of seventy-two, to get work at the Richmond yards during the last war. But he had been too old, and they hadn't wanted him.

And now here he was, sitting on his cabin doorstep in a late October afternoon, in the last years of his life, with all the fires out or almost out, looking over his shoulder at the places he'd been, the things he'd done and seen, the life he'd lived. In that moment he seemed the lonely incarnation of all old-timers everywhere—the Percy Montgomerys, the Bill Hatmans, the South of Market Boys, the Billy Carrs and all the others that have ever lived—all the aged men whose hearts have turned to warm vessels of memories, whose words are love songs to bygone cities and bygone streets, whose Grail is the ever-receding day of their youth, who are driven on toward the end, when what they want almost more than life itself is to go back. . . .

High against the northern sky was the looming presence of the craggy Buttes. To the northwest and closer was the drowsy hamlet of Sierra

City, with its deserted, iron-shuttered Wells Fargo office and its old fire bell on a stand beside the pine tree, its three roadside bars for tourists and hunters, its few frame houses. As Charlie sat there, he seemed to be wondering how he got there. Had it all really happened, and that long ago; had he lived all those years? Had he been born so that some day he might sit there on an autumn afternoon and remember those times while the wind whispered in the Sierra pines about his cabin and a buzzard wheeled in the sky near the Buttes and the waters of the Yuba fork, swollen with early snows, said that one more summer (was it the last?) had slipped away and was gone?

Driving away, I waved to him as he stood on the grass before his cabin. Slowly and with dignity, he raised his cap from his white hair, and stood there like that until the car was out of sight. It could have been a salute, a hail and farewell, not to me, but to a life.

The Sea

15. GREAT HIGHWAY

BESIDE THE PACIFIC · LEGENDS OF THE SUNDOWN SEA. TAMALPAIS. THE
GOLDEN GATE. SEAL ROCKS · SAILS WEST · LOS FARALLONES. THE EGG
HUNTERS · THE FIRST CLIFF HOUSE · "GOOD-BY, GRAY OLD GRANDFATHER" ·
THE POINT LOBOS TOLL ROAD · HARD TIMES · THE BICYCLE BANDIT · DYNA-
MITE! · ADOLPH SUTRO AND HIS GARDENS · THE SECOND CLIFF HOUSE, AND
ITS FIERY FATE · THE GATE'S SOUTH SHORE · RALPH STARR, AND THE MYS-
TERY OF THE TIDE MACHINE · SUTRO HEIGHTS. DEATH OF A BALLERINA ·
WINDMILLS, AND A HISTORIC SHIP · CONTINENT'S END

GREAT HIGHWAY is by the ocean. It is the western rim of the city, and for
a few miles the western rim of the continent. Once it has left the short,
gentle downgrade below the Cliff House, it extends straight and very
broad along the beach to the south, curving inland at its southern end to
meet the Skyline Boulevard, which winds down the crest of the blue
Montara mountains toward Santa Cruz.

Inland, it is bordered by the cypressed summit of Sutro Heights, by
Playland-at-the-Beach, the closest most San Franciscans ever get to Coney

321

Island; by the dense, brown and wind-tossed cypresses of the western frontage of Golden Gate Park; by many blocks of the modest, repetitive homes of the outer Sunset district; and then by Fleishhacker Playfield and the San Francisco Zoo. The other side of Great Highway, below the Cliff House, is lined by the long concrete esplanade and, when that ends, by a grassy ledge of sand which drops sharply to the beach.

Beyond the esplanade and the beach lies the Pacific.

Before the coming of the hawk-eyed navigators and the Spanish *Conquistadores,* the red-skinned Costanoans stood on that beach beside the vast and shimmering ocean and called it the Sundown Sea.

Far across the water, on the brink of the world, they saw rocky islands, and there was where dwelled their dead.

On the mainland to the north beside the Sundown Sea rose a blue and sometimes purple mountain they called Tamalpais. Wise men had told them how it came to be: one day, in a past that was moons ago beyond number, the God of the Sun assumed human form and descended to earth, where he fell in love with the beautiful daughter of an Indian chief. When the time came for the departure on his allotted course across the heavens, he seized her in his arms and mounted into the sky. Burdened by her unaccustomed weight, he was unable to reach his celestial path. As he flew westward, he swooped lower and lower. His foot struck Mt. Diablo, and he plunged headlong into the great lake whose waters were divided from the Sundown Sea by a mountain ridge. His huge arm broke a gap through the mountain barrier—the gap which one day John C. Frémont would name the "Golden Gate." Hurled from his arms, the lovely Indian maiden was crushed to death. The God of the Sun tenderly picked her up and laid her to rest beside the Sundown Sea. And now the soft outlines of Mt. Tamalpais were the outlines of her graceful form as she lay there in eternal sleep.

The sea gulls the Costanoans saw wheeling over the headlands were the people of a certain tribe looking for their lost princess, who fell in love with the Lord of Waters and sailed alone in a tiny canoe for his tepee across the sea, and never returned.

They saw the sea lions and heard them barking on the rocks inshore and close to the cliffs at the sea's edge, and remembered another legend of their tribes. Once, while wandering across the hills in back of the sea, the twin daughters of a chief met a maiden who wore a garland of poppies, symbolic flowers of the Spirit of the Land. The maiden warned them of an impending attack by fierce warriors from across the Bay to the north, and gave the sisters a magic iris. Each petal of the iris, she told them, was a charm that would make a wish come true. Urging them to use the iris to ward off the enemy, the maiden vanished into the sky.

All that night, the sisters stood watch on the two peaks whence they could see both the Bay and the sea. At daybreak, they saw the smoke signals which told them the invaders were crossing the Bay. Tearing a petal from the magic iris, they wished for a heavy fog that would blind their enemies. With a second petal they wished for a great storm to wreck the warriors' boats. And, with a third petal, they wished that the invaders be turned into animals.

When the fog lifted and the storm subsided, they looked down from the two peaks and saw their enemies swimming in the water. They had been changed into sea lions and were swimming through the watery gap in the mountain ridge, on their way to the rocks beneath the cliffs, where they were destined to live forever. . . .

Centuries passed, and sails appeared within sight of that Costanoan shore of the Sundown Sea, within sight of the storied Isles of the Dead, the sleeping maiden, and the rocks where the sea lions lived: the sails of a Spanish treasure galleon blown leeward and off its course from Manila to Mexico's Acapulco; the sails of Drake's *Golden Hinde;* the sails of the luckless *San Agustin* of Sebastian Rodríguez de Cermeñon, who named the great outer harbor the Port of San Francisco, never dreaming of the passage through the headlands and the land-locked Bay it joined to the sea; the sails of Sebastian Vizcaino's *San Diego* and *Tres Reyes,* seeking in the inlets and past the California capes the answer to the Northern Mystery—the fabled Strait of Anian that divided this land from Cathay, reaching from the Frozen Sea southward past the country of the Grand Khan to the sunny Isles of Spice.

These sails appeared on the sea west of the sands, and then, at last, on the sands themselves, the prints made by Spanish leather, by the military boots of Captain Fernando Rivera y Moncada, military commander of

California, and four of his soldiers, and by the Franciscan sandals of his expedition's priest, Father Palóu. Up the long beach they trudged, from Lake Merced to the cliffs that beetled above the rocky home of the sea lions. They ascended a nearby hill, and there erected a Catholic cross. Then they retreated south into the wilderness whence they came.

Two years after that, the sails were the white wings of the *San Cárlos* of Lieutenant Juan Manuel de Ayala bringing his ship through the tidal pass made by the mountain-crushing arm of the falling Sun God. When his pilot Juan Bautista Aguirre, exploring the southern arm of the great inland Bay, was rowed ashore in a cove, he saw three Indians sitting on the cove beach, watching his approach. They did not rise to greet him, nor did they flee in fright. Even when he loomed above them and his shadow darkened their downcast heads, even then they did not move, for they were weeping.

For many years after that, the beach beside the sea remained the desolate home of the sea gulls and the plaintive-calling curlew. Only an occasional horseman or wandering soldier from the Presidio disturbed them, or Indians sent over the hills by the Mission fathers to gather mussels.

More attention, in fact, was paid to the foggy, rain-swept cluster of islands that had been the Costanoan heaven. Drake had been the first to set foot upon them—in 1579, on the day after the *Golden Hinde* sailed from under the Point Reyes lee—and had named them the Islands of St. James. Two hundred years later, Vancouver had charted them and called them Los Frayles, or The Friars. But the name that had clung to them was Los Farallones, which was what the Spanish explorers had termed them in their reports—"small pointed islands in the sea."

After these, it was the Russians who, in the declining years of Spain's New World dream, sailed to the Farallon Islands. They left there a small colony of seal hunters, and within three years the colonists killed two hundred thousand seals, a rash and greedy depletion from which the islands were never to recover. When there were no more seals to kill, the hunters sailed away and left the islands to the gulls and petrels, the cormorants and sea pigeons, the murres and sea parrots.

More years passed, and the ships bearing the gold seekers came beating up the coast from the Cape Horn passage, and once more men invaded the Farallon Islands, this time for the speckled eggs of the murres. Clinging to the islands' rocks and cliffs, drenched by spray from the pounding breakers and harried by thousands of screaming sea birds, the Farallon egg pickers went methodically from nest to nest filling their sacks for the mainland markets and restaurants. It was a profitable adventure; in 1853, one boatload of egg pickers sailed out to the islands and returned two days later with twelve thousand eggs which sold along Montgomery Street for a dollar apiece.

But as ranchers became able to supply the demand for eggs, the expeditions to the Farallon Islands, except for infrequent forays, ceased, and once again the island rookery was abandoned to the birds.

Twenty years later, the beach by the Sundown Sea was famous from coast to coast. Tourists from the world over stood there to regard with amused curiosity the antics of the sea lions that barked and clung like monstrous brown slugs to the steep sides of Seal Rocks, a hundred yards offshore; to exclaim with admiration over the loveliness of lofty Tamalpais, and, if the day were clear and fine, to gaze eleven leagues west to the Farallon Islands and marvel at their desolation. But more than these, they journeyed to the beach to sample the food and wine and warm hospitality of Captain Junius G. Foster, host of the Cliff House.

Perched on the headland at the beach's northern end, the Cliff House was a long, low-roofed tavern that had been built for Captain Foster in 1863. (To the erroneous contention that the Cliff House had been constructed for Sam Brannan, J. M. Wilkins, who succeeded Captain Foster as manager, retorted, "Sam's only relation to the Cliff House was that of a good and liberal patron.")

There was little activity at the Cliff House bar that first year. A few enterprising San Franciscans, encouraged by the success of the Mission road, were building a toll highway to the beach, and until it was finished, the trip was still a formidable journey by horseback, undertaken only by parties of picnickers, or quail and rabbit hunters, or men on a day's outing. One day in August of that year, however, two other riders moved across the dunes toward the sea. They were a curious pair, she the lovely.

326

lithe and black-haired Adah Isaacs Menken, and he a thoughtful and oddly poetic young Pony Express rider named Joaquin Miller. It was less than a week before her opening in *Mazeppa* at Maguire's Opera House, and Menken, discouraged by the rehearsals, was embittered and unhappy. In silence, they rode away from the city.

"The road was all sand then—tossing, terrible, moving mountains of sand," Miller recalled later. "At one place a little mountain had thrown itself right in the road before us. Our horses plunged in and wallowed belly deep, and she shouted with delight. . . . Then she talked, talked as I had never heard woman before and never shall again, of the color, the lion color, the old-gold color, the new-gold color, the sun, the light, the life in the moving mountains of sand about us."

But when they reached the beach, there below the Cliff House and beside a sea that was that day a moody gray, the actress leaped from her saddle, flung herself upon the wet sand and sobbed as if her heart were broken. In a few moments, it passed. She rose and went over to Miller and the horses. "I had to do it," she said. "They are killing me at that old playhouse, and I had to come out here and cry or die."

A wave rushed along the beach, and impulsively she ran down to meet it. Into it, she tossed the handkerchief with which she had dried her tears, and as the foaming surf withdrew she cried, "Good-by, gray old grandfather, good-by." Then she remounted, and they turned their backs on the beach and the sea, and rode away.

In the April of the next year, Menken sailed from San Francisco and south past that beach she would never see again, bound for England; and three months after that the detonation of eight hundred kegs of powder in the seaside dunes signalized the opening of the Point Lobos toll road, and the trip from the city, six or seven miles to the east, became something less than an all-day jaunt.

The road was an instant success, taking the carriage trade away almost overnight from the old Mission highway and the San Bruno turnpike. To cater to the city's horse fanciers, the sponsors constructed a mile-and-three-quarter speeding drive beside the toll road. Constantly harrowed, rolled and watered, it was a fast, level, clay straightaway, and before long well-to-do San Franciscans like Financier William M. Lent, Senator George Hearst, Leland Stanford, Charlie Crocker, James Ben Ali Haggin,

Bonanza Billy O'Brien, Captain Abner Barker and dozens of others were whipping their trotters up and down the Point Lobos speedway. Nearby, on the broad, macadam main drive, the slower, family teams tooled smoothly along on their way to or from the beach. Almost daily adding crust and elegance to this procession were the Vandewaters in their rockaway, Mrs. S. J. Hensley and friends in her blue, seashell carriage that was drawn by four horses, Mrs. Milton Latham in her brown, yellow-wheeled barouche with the blue satin lining, and various additional matrons of fashion sitting in their neat broughams or basket phaetons with the inevitable Dalmatians trotting docilely along between the rear wheels.

"Everybody knew everybody, so it was a sort of family gathering," said Captain Foster nostalgically in later years. "There was a continual nodding and buzzing from one carriage to another, while there was a constant succession of spins on the track between the flyers. These matches were almost always impromptu, and were generally just for the fun of the thing, or for champagne all around for the speeders."

Businessmen and stockbrokers went out to the road for drives before breakfast and the daily grind at the offices and the exchanges; mothers took their children there for afternoon airings; lovers spooned along the drive on moonlit nights, and Thursdays and Saturdays everybody in the city, it seemed, was bound for the beach, and sometimes as many as twelve hundred teams would tie up outside the Cliff House during a day and hundreds of others would have to turn around and go back, or drive on down the beach and hope for tethering space when they returned, because there was no room left at the Cliff House hitch racks.

Inside, while waiting for their dinner of Hangtown fries or terrapin or breast of guinea, the patrons relaxed as they pleased, the men at the bar drinking cocktails or (if it was brisk) toddies and Tom and Jerries, the ladies sitting on the glass-enclosed balconies, looking at the sea lions or ships through the binoculars and sipping their port and sherry. On special holidays, men and women alike gathered at the big seaside windows to thrill at the sight of the fearless James Cook or the daring Rose Celeste walking a tightrope stretched high over the booming surf to Seal Rocks.

As the city developed, the Cliff House and the beach grew more and more accessible. Omnibus lines ran out from Portsmouth Square, and streetcar lines pushed out to the Lone Mountain cemeteries, and there connected with stages on regular runs to the ocean. The Golden Gate Park project was forging ahead, and soon four of the streets branching from downtown Market Street led to Park drives that wound past the newly planted lawns and shrubs of its thousand acres and finally converged on the beach to the west. To San Franciscans, it all became the *dernier cri* in style and refinement and good living, and not one of them could disagree with Lloyd when he wrote, "A drive to the 'Cliff' . . . a hearty welcome from Captain Foster, and an hour passed over his hospitable board discussing the choice contents of his larder, and a return to the city through the charming scenery of Golden Gate Park, tends to place man about as near to elysian bliss as he may hope for in this world."

But with the waning of the Comstock in the middle Seventies, things changed. A man could no longer afford a $10,000 team of Kentucky grays, or a rattling brace of trotters, or gold-mounted four-in-hand coaches and the uniformed liverymen to go with them. The family teams dwindled from the Point Lobos road, and the "flyers" from the speedway. Finally, the road and the clay track lay neglected altogether, and, in 1877, the owners sold them both to the city for $25,000.

This, as well as another factor, combined to enlarge the field of Cliff House attractions to something besides Captain Foster's wine list and the choice contents of his larder. The other factor was competition. From the timbers of a derelict cast up by the sea, a man named Morton had constructed a rambling tavern on the dunes a few miles south of the Cliff House. Conveniently located at the beach end of the Ocean road, which started at the Mission, skirted Twin Peaks and meandered west across the sand hills, the resort became known as the Ocean House, and it soon built up a roistering and well-heeled clientele among the gamblers and sportsmen who frequented the popular Ocean View race track. Still others who might have found their way to the Cliff House at the end of a day's racing card wound up instead at Cornelius Stagg's Ingleside Inn, which was on the Ocean road near Barney Farley's training quarters, a mile or two from the beach. (The Ingleside Inn continued to cut into the Cliff House trade until the late Eighties, when a burglar broke into the roadhouse, killed Stagg and escaped with the contents of the safe. The murder was never solved; but it was generally attributed to the notorious "Bicycle Bandit," who briefly terrorized San Francisco during that period, striking boldly into every section of the city and leaving no clue except the tire treads of the bicycle on which he sped from the scene of his crimes.)

So, out at the Cliff House, Captain Foster became a little more broad-minded. And as he saw less and less of the Nob Hill and tallyho set, he welcomed more and more warmly a heavy-spending crowd that liked what it heard about wine, women and song, and had the money to find out if it were true. Society matrons sipping imported sherry vanished from the imposing galleries, and in their place swaggered flashy, generous and good-natured demimondaines who took their whisky straight, and wore golden double eagles for heelpieces on their slippers. And as long as they were buying champagne, Captain Foster let the parties go on a little longer and a little more loudly in the upstairs rooms; if they were miners and their wenches from the Barbary Coast dance halls, what difference did it make as long as they paid their bills, and settled for the breakage?

In fact, the genial captain came to respect his rough-and-ready customers. Once, one hundred seventy Massachusetts tourists and their wives visited the Cliff House, and during the day they spent there all he served them was two hundred glasses of water and three glasses of lemonade. "Hell," he snorted as they filed out the door, "two prospectors and their girls spend more money for one dinner than the whole state of Massachusetts does in an entire day."

So these came to be free-and-easy times at the Cliff House, but let it be said in Foster's favor that even though the boys from the mining camps drank and scuffled with their doxies in the private dining rooms upstairs a man could still take his family there in all propriety without fear of getting pushed around or hit on the head with a bottle.

The days of happy tolerance, however, were short-lived. In 1883, the Cliff House was bought by studious, book-loving Adolph Sutro, the one-time San Francisco cigar dealer who had ridden to the Washoe on mule-back, had solved the problems of ventilation and drainage for the mine operators by driving a five-mile tunnel into the side of Mt. Davidson and the sumps of the Comstock shafts, and had quietly but triumphantly returned to San Francisco a multimillionaire. After a thorough, firsthand observation of the goings on at the Cliff House, the relaxed attitude of Captain Foster raised Sutro's eyebrows. A few months later, he politely handed the captain his hat, and installed Wilkins as his manager. The scuffling ceased. The Cliff House quieted down.

It remained quiet until the night of January 16, 1887, when the schooner *Parallel,* laden with forty tons of dynamite, went on the rocks under the Cliff House's back porch. The resultant blast, which was felt one hundred miles inland, took off the tavern's entire north wing. Patched and put back together again, it catered to tourists and Sunday visitors for another seven years. Then, on Christmas, 1894, fire started by a defective flue raced along its balconies and roof. In a matter of minutes, it was evident that the old building was going. Wilkins managed to save a painting or two, but was driven out by the flames before he could rescue the precious guest register, which bore the signatures of three Presidents and many other world-famous figures. Attracted by the glare in the night sky, hundreds of San Franciscans arrived in hacks and surreys to watch the historic landmark perish. While they watched, and above the crackle of the flames, they could hear the bellowing of the sea lions as, made frantic by the heat and dancing light, the frightened beasts plunged into the waters that swirled around Seal Rocks.

At daybreak, the sea lions returned to their home, for the fire had burned itself out, and the Cliff House was a ruin.

So firm an institution had the Cliff House become that the beach without it was as forlorn as a San Francisco hill without cable cars; but it was not long before another one went up there on the headland, above the surf and inshore from Seal Rocks. Four years before the end of the Nineties, the tinkle of thin-stemmed glasses, laughter and the popping of champagne corks rose once more over the muffled beating of the waves and the barking of the lions; once more its lights cast a glow over the waters and twinkled far out to sea. This Cliff House was more to Adolph Sutro's taste, one he could look down upon from the gardens upon his heights above the headland and be proud of.

Years before, he had been struck by the possibility of the city's expansion to the west and the sea. Not only had he bought the Cliff House, but the desolate crag above it, and there he had planted palms and firs and cypresses, Norfolk pines and the stately eucalyptus, importing it from Australia, and along with it a shipload of Australian soil to foster its growth on the dunes above the beach. Beneath the trees, in tasteful arrangement amid the geranium beds, he had erected white plaster statues of Grecian satyrs and wood nymphs, mythological deities, and the better-known characters of the works of Charles Dickens. He had placed his large mansion with the castellated lookout upon its roof at the western edge of his groves, and, on the very rim of the heights, a granite parapet adorned with additional plaster statues and urns. There, he had divided his days between study in his imposing library, the supervision of the duties of his fifteen gardeners and three caretakers, the development of his stable of thoroughbred horses, the management of his real estate and transportation interests and the distribution of a princely but cultured brand of hospitality among his friends.

On one unforgettable summer evening, several hundred of them, representing the best San Francisco society had to offer, had driven to Sutro Heights to witness Ada Rehan and John Drew interpret the sylvan charm of *As You Like It*. Presented on the beautifully clipped lawns in front of the mansion and before Japanese lantern footlights, it had been conceived and executed (the guests assured each other afterwards) on the grandest scale since the glittering days of Cañada de Diablo, Billy Ralston's spectacular villa down the Peninsula in Belmont.

There was something of the Ralston touch, too, in Sutro's new Cliff House; Foster's roadhouse had been a mere stable compared to the seven-story château that now raised its spires and towers above the edge of the sea. Getting off to a rousing start in 1896 (the same year work began on the famous Sutro Baths—six of the world's largest indoor swimming pools—just north of the Cliff House), the new hostelry brought Nob Hill once more to the beach for mussels Bordelaise, broiled-Virginia-ham breakfasts, a look at the sea lions, a stroll on the sand amid bathers garbed in ankle-length suits, the few moments of amusement that could be afforded their fashionably jaded and *fin de siècle* spirits by Johnnie the Birdman's trained canaries, Professor Baldwin's parachute falls from a hot-air balloon and the spectacle of Millie Lavelle sliding down a wire cable to Seal Rocks as she hung by her teeth.

Most of them, however, were content to eye these attractions from the ornate balconies of the Cliff House, for they were both dismayed and depressed by the throngs that were now streaming to the beach on steam trains, bicycles, carts and wagons for Sunday and holiday excursions. Meiggs' Wharf had closed, and Woodward's Gardens had been surren-

dered by their creator to less able and conscientious hands; now, shabby and neglected, the Mission Street resort was losing its popularity. Furthermore, the great Midwinter Fair of '94 had accelerated the growth and development of Golden Gate Park, and it was there, where some of the exposition pavilions were still standing, that the people now went for their walks and picnics. When these were over, they would continue on out to the beach for a tamale or an enchilada, for a crack at the swinging targets with the .22's, for a look at the ocean and a promenade along the sands.

The earthquake of 1906 didn't do much to change the beach, for it was still there when the shaking stopped, and so were the Cliff House, and Sutro Baths and Sutro's mansion on the heights. Excited reports that the Cliff House had slid into the sea raced through the downtown city, but when Sutro and Wilkins took inventory and totaled the damage, they found cause to shake hands and congratulate each other: it amounted to $300.

Less than two years later, it was clear that fate had been saving the incredible castle (now that some of the glamor had rubbed off, people were openly calling it "the Gingerbread Palace") for a different kind of disaster. On the afternoon of September 7, 1907, Manager Wilkins saw a dark puff of smoke shoot from a hole which electricians had just bored in a balcony floor. He dashed to a telephone and called for help. But even before the firemen arrived to send their inadequate streams into the leaping flames, the building was doomed.

The baying sea lions once more abandoned their rocks. By now they had had enough of these mainland disturbances; they swam out to the Farallon Islands and didn't come back for two years. When they returned, a third Cliff House stood on the headland, and, except for modernization, that's the one that stands there now.

From the white cliff of Fort Point where Anza erected a holy cross in that March of 1776, from that point where the massive cables of the Golden Gate Bridge hold fast to the land, the Gate shore falls back in a rugged shingle south to Baker's Beach and China Beach, then moves west for about a mile, beneath the entrance bluffs, to Land's End. There it curves off to the southwest, for another mile, perhaps, to treacherous Point Lobos.

Together, the shingle and the beaches and the rocks form the shoulder the San Francisco Peninsula opposes to the sea. Out there, on clear days, the air above that piece of the continent's end is a soft and luminous blue, the heaving sea beyond the breakers is green and the spindrift from the waves that fling themselves against the rocks is blown away in rainbows. And when the fogs come twisting through the Gate—the Italian fishermen say it is Santa Niebla, Our Lady of the Fogs, drawing her gray veil in from the sea—that is when the diaphones begin moaning and crying all over the Bay, warning the mariners of the reefs and rocks, the shoals, the ledges and the islands that lie hidden beneath the thick and billowing mists.

Thirty ships and maybe more have been pounded to pieces on this southern shore of the harbor entrance, and their cargoes and broken timbers have been claimed by the sea. But a bleak wreck of another kind rears high upon a pointed rock fifteen fathoms off the Land's End shore. Its weathered scaffolding, its curious wheels and splintered beams are all that is left of one man's promise to harness the tides and revolutionize, with their unlimited power, the industries of the world.

The legend is that his name was Ralph Starr; that many years ago he invented a tide machine, and on the performance of a working model obtained heavy backing from San Francisco capitalists. With this money, he started construction of a full-scale machine upon the pointed rock. Day after day, intrigued San Franciscans went to Land's End to watch the workmen as from their precarious rigging they bolted the beams together, hung the big wheels in position and strung the heavy cables that were to play so important a part in the ponderous mechanism. Some imaginative onlookers, unaware of the machine's purpose, believed it a newfangled aid to navigation; others thought it was a preparation for the erection of a huge monument, and still others vowed it was to be an instrument for extracting gold from the ocean.

Starr soon put an end to this speculation. He publicly announced that it was a tide machine and that on a certain Sunday, at ten in the morning, it would be given its first official test. When the appointed morning arrived, hundreds hiked or drove to the Land's End heights and waited patiently to see what would happen. Down closer to the shore stood the tense group of men who had invested their money in Starr's dream. Ten o'clock came, and passed. Then ten-thirty. The crowd became restive. Nervously, the backers compared watches.

"Where's Starr? What do you suppose is keeping him?" they asked each other. To the rocks below them rushed the sea, and out from shore, on the lofty pinnacle, the machine waited, its shining wheels motionless.

When eleven o'clock came and Starr still had not arrived, his backers got in their carriages and drove to the inventor's house. There was nobody there. The beds were made, furniture and clothes were neatly in place, breakfast dishes lay stacked in the sink, but Starr, his wife and his son had vanished. No one in San Francisco ever heard from them again.

Without the builder, the only man who knew the intricate workings of the tide machine, the backers were helpless. There was nothing they could do but abandon it to the wind and the waves. Its massive wheels never turned. It stands there now, corroded and weather-beaten, and a roost for the wheeling gulls.

Southwest of Starr's rock and a few hundred yards away is Point Lobos. From there the rough shoreline continues south past Seal Rocks and the Cliff House, and then becomes the tawny beach that parallels the four-mile straightaway of Great Highway. The toll road to which the point gave its name is now Geary Boulevard; the white Cliff House and Seal Rocks are as famous as they ever were (it is a rare time when cars from four or five other states are not parked outside the restaurant), and that purple shadow tourists see low on the western horizon on a clear day, the Costanoan paradise, the twelve-mile chain of islets the Spaniards called Los Farallones, is now the home of half a hundred coastguard-men, whose life there is the mournful blast of a fog signal, the monotonous boom of the surf and the screech of sea birds.

The baths of Sutro—"Tropic Beach"—are still there, too, but his look-out manor is gone and his heights, which now belong to the city, lie neglected. Driven sand is choking his trees and reclaiming the dells of his garden, and the few plaster statues that remain look depressed and sad. Several years ago, Beatrice Lewis, a beautiful and talented San Francisco dancer, brought them to life in a ballet, a fantasy inspired by the gloomy desolation of the old estate. Her program note said, "It is midnight at a deserted spot in historical Sutro Gardens. The statues are standing frozen on their pedestals, when suddenly . . . we behold the Pans dancing into view. They awaken Bacchus and beckon him to follow them in their frolic. One by one the Gardens' other gods come to life and make an evening of it; then all return to their pedestals." Four weeks after the dance's triumphant *première,* the blonde ballerina stood upon Sutro's stone parapet and then plunged to her death in Great Highway, two hundred feet below. No one has ever known whether it was accident, or suicide.

There are suggestions of decay and death not only in Sutro Gardens, but also along Great Highway. Guarding the entrances to Golden Gate Park are the Dutch mill and the Murphy mill, said to be the biggest windmills in the world. Their tall, latticed arms stand motionless in the face of the ocean winds, lashed fast and anchored, because the city has allowed their timbers to rot, and they are no longer safe. Also, in a Great Highway shed lies all that is left of the sturdy *Gjöa,* Roald Amundsen's ship and the first ship in history to sail the Northwest Passage from the Atlantic to the Pacific. She has been there since 1909, presented to the city by San Francisco's Scandinavian colonies. Funds to keep her in condition were exhausted long ago, in spite of generous contributions from private citizens, and the termites are turning her ribs and planks to powder. Still farther south is the site of Morton's Ocean House, which became the "Ocean House of Mystery" (it was believed to be the temple of a cult of fire-worshippers) and then later the famous roadhouse Tait's-at-the-Beach. After thirteen years of patronage by celebrities and gourmets, the resort failed in the last years of Prohibition. It burned to the ground in December, 1940.

But from up there on those heights of Sutro, from beneath his rustling eucalyptus trees, you can look down on a lot of San Francisco—the serried homes of the Sunset district that in the last two decades have marched avenue after avenue to the city's western shore; the brown tree-tops of Golden Gate Park, the midways of Playland, the broad boulevard, and the beach up which Rivera and Palóu and the four soldiers plodded so many years ago.

Here is where Great Highway's life is: in the laughter of children on the Playland merry-go-round, in the bustle of its restaurants and sandwich stalls, in the movement of the traffic flowing down its wide lanes, in the singing of the surf lines as the casters swing their rods and send their leads and hooks flying across the breakers, in the pounding hoofs of riding horses cantering along the wet sand, in the tan flesh of youths and girls sun-bathing, in the swift soaring flight of gulls, in the white crests of the combers racing for the beach, in the clouds drifting across the wide sky.

Stevenson stood upon that strand and looked west across the ocean and likened himself to an ancient legionary standing upon the wall of Antoninus and gazing northward toward the mountains of the Picts, "each of us," he mused, "standing on the verge of the Roman Empire (or, as we now call it, Western civilization), each of us gazing onward into zones unromanized." Millions less gifted have stood there looking west, and thought of an ancient Spanish caravel leaning from the wind, or dreamed of Mandalay.

Some time in your life, watch the sun go down from those heights or that boulevard or that beach, and you'll feel the mood of that part of San Francisco—how and why it is a thousand and one places to San Franciscans. A place to go with thirty thousand others for a Sunday ride and a glimpse of the ocean and the smell of salt air. A place to get a Coney Island hot dog, or a hamburger smothered in onions, or a bowl of Sinaloan chili, or the best meat pies west of St. Louis. A place to take a girl for a ride on the giant swing or the roller coaster and hug her tight when she screams and holds her hat. A place to roller skate or ice skate, or swim in the world's largest indoor pool or the world's largest outdoor pool or, for that matter, the world's largest ocean. A place to dance, and posture before the crooked Fun House mirrors. A place to stare at chimpanzees and peacocks. A place to ride a horse or a bicycle or a merry-go-round swan. A place to make love, or a place for someone that's lost to say good-by to the world and turn his back on and leave behind in the lonely walk across the sand to the tides, the undertow and the end of everything. But above all, and for by far the most, a place to sit and watch the low-flying pelicans skimming the offshore sea, and a red sun sinking beyond the edge of the world, and the fishing fleet standing north for the Gate and home, with its riding lights twinkling in the dusk. That is calmness, that is peace, and such serenity and beauty as San Franciscans never look for in any other city, by any other shore.

So no matter where you were born, or what town you call home, stand there for a moment and feel what they feel. At your back will be the Sunset district lights, and Twin Peaks, and all the city proudly poised upon her hills, and beyond her the moving tides of the Bay and then the beginning of the great curve of the continent. Westward, and before you, will surge the vast dark sea. The cries of the barkers, the strains of the merry-go-round calliope, the crack of shooting gallery rifles will come to you faintly, and there, closer, you will hear the night waves as they spend themselves at last and run whispering down the sand.

INDEX

A

Abolitionists, 101-102
Aguila de Oro gambling hall, 141
Aguirre, Juan Bautista, 324
Aitkin, Jim, 73
Albion Hotel, 67
Alcatraz, 4, 11, 13, 85, 167, 181, 258
Alcatraz ferry, 73
Alemany, Most Reverend Joseph Sadoc, 180
Allen, James E., 90-91
Alta California Missions, 259
"Ambrosial Path" (see Montgomery Street)
American Hotel, 67
American River, 9, 28
American Theater, 146
Amundsen, Roald, 337
Anderson, David C., 264-265
Angel Island, 44
Anglo-California Bank, 165
Anza, Lt. Col. Juan Bautista de, 185-186, 190, 259
Apollo Hall cotillions, 116
Arnold, Philip, 168, 170
Arriloga, José, 187-188
Artists, 207, 209-210
Asbury, Herbert, 76, 87, 144
Atherton, Gertrude, 286, 288-289
Auction Lunch saloon, 146, 161
Ayala, Don Juan Manuel de, 6-7, 324

B

Baker, Col. Edward D., 110
Baker's Beach, 334
Baldwin, Lucky, 173, 193, 231, 233-235, 245, 248
Baldwin Hotel, 234, 243-248
Baldwin Theater, 179, 226, 247-248, 306-307
Baldwin's Academy of Music, 231, 233
Baldwin's Park, 194
Ball teams, 192-193
Bancroft, Hubert Howe, 31, 38, 40, 43, 69, 164, 200, 222-226, 266

Bank of America, 33
Bank of California, 102, 165-166, 168, 172, 181, 220, 228, 234
Bank Exchange, 36, 38-39, 43-44, 52-53, 146, 148, 197
Barbary Coast, 9, 14, 53-54, 87, 99, 118, 126, 150, 201, 316, 330
Barker, Capt. Abner, 328
Barlow, Samuel, 169
Bars, 82-83, 86, 93, 116, 143, 182, 301 (See also Drinking; Saloons)
Bates, Blanche, 309
Bathhouse Jack, 72
Battery Street, 199
Battle Row, 87
Battleship Row, 251
Baugh, Theodore E., 199, 203
Bay Bridge, 3, 54, 295, 300
Bay District race track, 78, 244
Bay View, 258, 298
Bay View race track, 314
Bayerque, J. B., 268-269
Beale, E. F., 96
Beckhardt, Phil, 100
Belasco, David, 231, 279, 300, 303-312
Bell, Teresa, 103, 106-107
Bell, Thomas, 101-103, 106
Bella Union saloon, 136, 141, 239
Belt Line, 85
Benicia, 42, 97, 167
Bergez, Jean, 109
Bergez-Frank, 107
Bernal Heights, 204, 258, 276-278, 298
Bernhardt, Sarah, 240
Best and Belcher mine, 172
Bierce, Ambrose, 57, 133
Big Rich Bar, 122
Bigler, Governor, 42
Bird in Hand, The, 30, 33
Biscaccianti, Elisa, 139, 145
Black Friday, 1875, 181, 228
Black Point, 129, 181
Blandings, William, 48
Bloom, Sol, 279
Blossom Rock, 11-12

Blue Blazer cocktail, 143-145
Blue Star line, 80
Bluebird saloon, 40
Blythe, Tom, 237-239
Boarding houses, 14, 16, 29, 62, 102, 160, 314
Bohemian Club, 133
Bolton, Herbert E., 259
Bolton, James R., 129
Booth, Edwin, 57, 139, 201, 207, 264
Booth, Junius Brutus, Jr., 57, 201, 207
Booth, Newton, 71
Bosqui, Edward L., 129
Botts, Billy, 48
Bowlby-Gledhill, Lady Honoré Cecelia, 209
Boyd, Harold J., 250
Brader, Henry, 126
Branch Extension, 146
Brandt, Henri, 51
Brannan, Sam, 28-29, 32, 67, 236, 325
Brasch, Caroline, 206
Brenham Place, 137
Breweries, 72
Brick building, first, 30
Bridges, 5, 20, 28-29, 123
    (See also names of bridges)
Broadway, 14, 28, 36, 83-84, 116-118, 124-125, 128-130, 132, 184
Broadway Hotel, 118
Broadway Jail, 119-122, 125-126
Broderick, David C., 45-46, 105, 111, 136
Brodie, Steve, 245-246
Bronson, Mother, 16
Brothels, 14, 90, 102, 129-130
    (See also Cribs; Harlots)
Brother Jonathan, 9-11
Brown, John, 102
Bryant's Minstrel, 145
Bucareli, Don Antonio Maria, 185
Bucket shops, 62
Bulkhead, the, 264
Burgess, Gelett, 57
Bush, John, 99   [183
Bush Street, 81, 94-102, 107-110, 151-152,
Bush Street Music Hall, 68, 95, 97
Bush Street Theater, 99-100, 303-304
Butchertown, 258, 298, 313-314

C

Cable cars, 54, 63, 80, 111, 116, 136, 148-151, 158, 173, 192, 194, 203, 235

Cadenasso family, 129
Café Royal, 243
Calhoun Street, 201, 207
Calico Jim, 16
California, admission to Union, 200
    Chinese in, 73-74, 76, 79-80, 82-83, 125, 180, 240-241
        (See also Chinatown)
    first telegraph line in, 200-201, 203
    first wool-bearing sheep in, 236
    irrigation in, 238-239
    missions in, 259-263
    Spanish in, 184-188, 199, 202, 204-205, 207, 209
California Academy of Sciences, 153, 156, 173-174, 243
California Diamond (see Crabtree, Lotta)
California Guard, 67, 119
California Market, 172, 181
California Steam Navigation Company, 10
California Street, 31, 54, 150, 160-183, 225, 227, 257
California Theater, 99-100, 148, 231, 306-307
Calle de la Fundacion, 66
Callender, M. L., 199
Calvary Cemetery, 125
Camels, 95-98
Camille's, 109
Cañada de Diablo, 332
Canivan's Greyhound Coursing Park, 281
Cannon, Big Joe, 123
Canyon Creek, 122
Cape Horn, 8, 67, 102, 151, 195, 325
Capitana, 127-128
Caraher, Father Terence, 206
Carr, Billy, 313-314
Carroll, Curly Jack, 137
Carson, Mrs. Mary, 151
Carter, Mrs. Leslie, 309
Casa Grande, 66, 82
Casebolt, Henry, 194, 219, 267
Casey, James P., 36-38, 120
Castillo de San Joaquín, 187-189
Castle, the, 203-204
Cathedral of SS. Peter and Paul, 184
Celeste, Rose, 328
Centennial Mine, 277
Central Pacific railroad, 168, 173, 226, 232-233
Charcoal Flat, 122
Charlemagne Private College, 126

Charter Oak Hall, 226
Chickasaw Indians, 48, 50
Chicken Devine, 54
China Basin, 230
China Beach, 334
Chinatown, 58, 73-83, 94, 99, 116, 125,
    153, 173, 179-180, 240-241, 257, 279,
    303
Choctaw Indians, 49
Chrysopolis, 300
Church of the Advent, 197
Churches, 52, 66-67, 76-77
    (*See also* names of churches)
City Gardens, 226
City Hall, 68, 124, 140, 241-242, 250
City Hotel, 61, 137, 141
Civil War, 97, 99, 167, 176, 189, 220
Clark, William Squire, 111, 117-118
Clark's Point, 28, 117, 200, 283
Clark's Wharf, 118, 132
Claude Lane, 107, 109-110
Clay Street, 31, 66, 136-137, 149-150, 158
Cliff House, 18, 71, 73, 203, 243, 321-322,
    325, 327-334, 336
Clifton, Lord Talbot, 179, 244
Clipper restaurant, 146
Cloonan, William (*see* Donahue, Cut-Face)
Cobweb Palace, 71-73
Cockney White's museum, 71
Cocktail lounge, first, 39
Cogswell, Henry Daniel, 194-196
Cogswell College, 195
Coit, B. Howard, 197
Coit, Lillie Hitchcock, 194, 196-198, 207
Coit Tower, 21, 207, 209
Colby, Zachariah, 72
Coleman, William T., 48
Collins and Wheeland Grill, 54
Colton, David D., 168-170, 182
Columbus Avenue, 192
Committee of Vigilance (*see* Vigilantes)
Compound, the, 130, 132
Comstock, Old Pancake, 163-164
Comstock Lode, 48, 56, 99, 103, 120, 144,
    147, 164-167, 173, 178-179, 181, 221,
    228, 234, 248, 272, 291, 329-330
Con, Virginia mine, 165, 172, 272
Conamar, One-armed Harry, 193
Congregation Emanu-El, 126
Contra Costa County, 35, 42
Cook, James, 328
Coolbrith, Ina, 294

Coppa's restaurant, 57, 133
Coppinger, "Cuspidor," 291
Cora, Charles, 37-38, 120
Corbett, Gentleman Jim, 243, 246
Corruption and graft, 32, 34-36, 76
Costanoans, 322-324, 336
Cousins, Capt. Jack, 68, 70
Coutard, Louis, 109
Couzen's slaughterhouse, 118
Covarrubias, Nick, 251
Cow Hollow, 129, 184, 191-194, 219, 228,
    242, 314
Cowboy Mag, 54
Cowboys' Rest, 53
Cowell's dock, 202
Crabtree, Lotta, 57, 136, 192, 228-229, 240,
    265
Cribs, 30, 87, 91, 179
    (*See also* Brothels; Harlots)
Crimps, 14, 16, 53
Crisis Hopkins, 52
Crittenden, A. P., 30, 89, 120
Crocker, Charlie, 160-161, 173, 182, 327
Crocker First National Bank, 218
Crockett, J. B., 236-237
Crow, Jim, 122
Crown Point mine, 173
Cummings, G. P., 34
Curran, John, 90-91
"Curtail Coon, The" (*see* Pickett, Charles
    Edward)
Cypress Lawn, 110

D

Daffodil Festival, 93
Dairies, 191-192
Davidson, Ellinor, 154-157
Davidson, George, 153-154, 156
Davidson, George, Jr., 154-155
Davidson, Thomas, 154-156
Davis, William Heath, Jr., 135, 137
Davis Street, 16
Dead Fish Café, 209
Deady, Matthew P., 104
Demarest, Pop, 130, 132
Dennison's Exchange, 136, 141
Denver, Gen. James W., 42
Devil's Acre, 126, 201
De Wolf, Capt. S. J., 10
Diamonds, 166-171
Di Maggio, Joe, 184

Dixon, Maynard, 57
Dixon's Ale Vaults, 172
Dobie, Charles Caldwell, 76
Doherty, George, 72
Dolbeer, John, 129
Dolores Street, 38
Donadieu's, 152
Donahue, Cut-Face, 90-91
Donahue, Peter, 269
Donohoe-Kelly Bank, 48
Douglas, Thomas, 61, 139
Downie, Maj. William, 122
Downieville, California, 122, 161
Drinking, 40-41, 53, 57, 72, 123, 132
    (*See also* Bars; Pisco Punch; Saloons;
    Thomas, Jerry)
Driscoll's Salt Water Tub Bathing Empo-
    rium, 72
Duels, 41-46, 265
Duperu, Numa, 129
Dupont Street, 66-67, 74, 85, 90, 102, 125,
    149-150, 160, 173-174
    (*See also* Grant Avenue)
Durgan's Flat, 122-123
Durrant, Theodore (Belfry Killer), 195
Dutch Nick's saloon, 161
Dutchman's Flat, 314
Dwinelle, Samuel, 120

E

E Clampsus Vitus, 38
Earthquake-proof building, first, 35
Earthquakes, 179, 187-188, 205, 221, 248
    (*See also* San Francisco fire of 1906)
Easter cross, 154
Eclipse mine, 165
Eddy's Sandwich Shop, 63
Eden Musée, 243
Edgar, Annie (Floating Annie), 244
Edwards, Harry, 229
Eighties, the, 100, 192, 239, 314
Elaine (a painting), 88-91
El Dorado, 8, 136-137, 141-144, 158, 161
Elleard, Charley, 138
Ellis, A. J., 29
Embarcadero, 3-4, 9, 11, 17, 19, 21, 23,
    85, 183, 300
Emerson, Billy, 100
Emperor of California (*see* Norton, Joshua
    A.)
Engelhardt, Father Zephyrin, 260

Eppinger's, 172
Esche, Otto, 97
Eureka Lode, 277
Eureka Valley, 258, 298
Evans, Al, 129
Everding, John, 72
Excellent Hotel, 67

F

Fair, James G., 56, 147, 172, 182
Fair, Laura D., 89, 120-121, 214
Fairfax, Charley ("The Baron"), 48
Fairmont, 258
Farallon Islands, 6, 178, 185, 324-326, 336
Farley, Barney, 329
Fauntleroy, Ellinor, 154
Fay, Jack, 72
Feather River, 9, 40, 161
Fennimore, Jim ("Old Virginia"), 163
Ferguson, William I. (Yip-see-Doodle), 44
Ferry Building, 3, 19-22, 82, 180, 184, 215,
    233, 250
Ferryboats, 20-21, 30, 42, 120, 152, 233,
    235
Field, Stephen J., 105-106
Fifth Street, 124, 219
Fifties, 153, 207, 263, 266
Filbert Street, 203, 207, 209
Fillmore district, 110
Fires, 31-32, 34, 57, 140, 247, 250
    (*See also* San Francisco fire of 1906)
First Baptist Church, 145
First Congregational Church, 66, 174
Fisherman's Wharf, 3, 21-22, 67, 84, 184,
    202, 258
Fitzgerald, M. J., 17
Fitzgibbon, Dave, 226
Fitzsimmons, Ruby Rob, 246
Flanagan, Mutton-Toe, 194
Fleishhacker Playfield, 322
Floating Annie (*see* Edgar, Annie)
"Floating Fortress" (*see* Montgomery Block)
Flood, James C., 56, 146, 161, 172, 179, 182
Fong Ching, 77
    (*See also* Little Pete)
Font, Fray Pedro, 184, 186, 260
Fook Yam Tong burial ground, 79
Forni, José, 119, 264
Forrest, Edwin, 147
Fort Gunnybags, 37, 120
Fort Montgomery, 199

Fort Point, 7, 19, 167, 185, 187, 189, 334
Forty-niners, 5, 8-9, 41, 67, 122, 126, 138, 160, 194, 203, 238-239, 283
    (*See also* Gold Rush)
Foster, Capt. Junius G., 325, 328-331
Four-Armed Cuttlefish, 173
Fourth of July parades, 301-302
Franciscan Fathers, 259-262
Francisco Street, 72
Franklin, Louis, 126
French, Harold, 274
French restaurants, 107-110
Friday Night Cotillion Club, 240

G

Gabarino, Jim, 202
Gambling, 48, 63, 66, 76, 81, 119, 123, 136, 140-143, 193
Gambling halls, 9, 31, 141-143, 145, 158
Gansl, A., 169
Garnett, Alexander, 197-198
Geary Street, 91
German Coffee Shop, 93
Gi Sin Seer, 73, 77
Giannini, A. P., 33
Gihon, John H., 9, 283
Gilbert, Edward, 42
Gilbert's Melodeon, 136
Gillette, William, 247
Gin mills, 14
Girard's French Restaurant, 93
Gjöa, 337
Glasscock, C. B., 234
Gleason, Paddy, 72
Glen Park, 258, 298
Globe Hotel, 67
Gobey's Steak House, 93, 179
Gold, 28, 140-141, 163, 167, 179, 276-278
Gold Canyon, 161-162
Gold Rush, 5, 9, 29, 34, 36, 62, 107-108, 118, 189, 191, 199, 207, 236, 258, 267, 286
    (*See also* Forty-niners)
Golden Gate, 4-7, 10, 17-19, 21, 34, 69, 79, 116, 134, 178, 188, 198, 249, 322, 334
Golden Gate Bridge, 21, 185, 189, 334
Golden Gate International Exposition, 157, 178, 214
Golden Gate Park, 71, 133, 179, 241, 243, 267, 322, 329, 333, 336

Golden Hinde, 5, 323-324
Golden Spike, 13, 39
Goldenson, Aleck, 124-125
Gordon, C. C., 289
Gordon, George, 284-289
Gordon, Nellie, 286-289
Gould and Curry mine, 165, 172
Grace Cathedral, 182
Graft and corruption, 32, 34-36, 76
Grand Hotel, 103-104, 167, 221-222
Grand Opera House, 281, 297-298
Grant Avenue, 66, 80-85, 94, 184
    (*See also* Dupont Street)
Grass Valley, 228
Gray brothers, 204-206
Great Diamond Hoax, 167-172
Great Highway, 321-322, 336-337
Great White Fleet, 21
Greathouse, Ridgely, 167
Green, Jim, 51
Greene, Clay, 265, 308
Greene, Col. William, 265
Greenway, Ned, 240
Grizzly Bear, The, 265
Grosch, Edgar Allen, 162, 164
Grosch, Hosea B., 162, 164
Guttersnipe, The, 48
Gwin, William M., 43

H

Hager, J. S., 30
Haggin, James Ben Ali, 153, 327
Hale and Norcross mine, 165, 172, 272
Hall of Justice County Jail, 34, 37
Halleck, Henry W., 34-35
"Halleck's Folly" (*see* Montgomery Block)
Hallelujah Cox, 52
Hallidie, Andrew S., 111, 149-150
Hangings, 119-120, 122-125, 264
Hangtown, 162, 166
Happy Valley, 119, 226, 235, 258, 264, 268, 281
Harbor Station, 16
Harbor View, 73, 192-193
Hardy, James H., 273
Harlots, 9, 14, 30, 66, 74, 76, 87-88, 91
    (*See also* Brothels; Cribs)
Harpending, Asbury, 166-171, 220-221, 229
Harpending Block, 220
Hart, Jim, 163
Harte, Bret, 57, 294

Hastings, Lansford W., 62
Hatman, George William, 191
Haunted houses, 101-107, 126-128, 155-157
Havens, F. C., 133
Hayes, Kate (Irish Linnet), 145
Hayes Valley, 219, 243, 269
Hearst, George, 327
Held, Anna, 244-245
Henry, A. G., 10
Hensley, Mrs. S. J., 328
"Hermit of Russian Hill" (see Demarest, Pop)
Hermitage, the, 269-270
Heron, Matilda, 146
Hewes, Dave, 219
Heydenaber's Atlantic Hall, 72
Hill, Sarah Althea, 103-106
Hinckley, Florence Blythe, 239
Hitchcock, Charles McPhail, 196
Hitchcock, Lillie (see Coit, Lillie Hitchcock)
Honky-tonks, 14
Hopkins, Mark, 161, 173, 182
Hopkins, Peter, 125
Horse racing, 62, 78
Hotel Bo Chow, 295-296
Hotel Fairmont, 182
Hotel Mark Hopkins, 182
Hotel St. Francis, 67, 108
Hotel South Park, 296
House, first, 66
"House of Demons," 126-128
House of Gold (see Baldwin Hotel)
Howard Street, 11, 116, 221
Hoyt, Henry, 73
Hoyt and Dockstadter's Minstrels, 100
Hubert, Numa, 43-44, 265
Hull, Patrick Purdy, 265
Hunt, George T., 43, 265
Hunt, T. Dwight, 66
Hunter's Point, 21, 258, 298, 313
Huntington, Collis Potter, 161, 173
Huntington Park, 182

I

Illinois House, 118
Immigrants, 226
    (See also Chinatown; Irish; Italian section)
India docks, 202
Ingleside Inn, 329
Ingleside track, 78

International Hotel, 45
Iodoform Kate, 87-88
Irish, 202, 204, 298
Irish Hill, 226, 313-315
Irrigation in California, 238-239
Irwin, Wallace, 57
Irwin, Will, 57
Island of the Angels, 4
Italian section, 83-85, 184, 202-207

J

Jackson, Helen Hunt, 129
Jackson Street, 9, 67, 149
Janin, Henry, 169, 171
Jarrett, Henry C., 232
Jeffers, Robinson, 133
Jenkins, John (The Miscreant), 32
Jenny Lind Theater, 140, 158
Jersey Flat, 122-123
Job's ice cream parlor, 145
Johnson, Mrs. R. M., 88-89
Johnston, George Pendleton, 43-44
Johntown, 161, 163-164
Joice, E. V., 199
Jones Street, 72, 149
Jordan, Capt. Fred ("Lucky"), 18
José, Dick, 100
Juanita, 122-124
Judah, construction engineer, 173

K

Kalakaua, King of the Sandwich Islands, 242-243
Kane, Joe, 73
Kearny Street, 14, 31, 34, 86, 136-139, 149-150
Kelly, Maggie, 53
Kelly, Mamie, 124-125
Kelly, Michael J., 276
Kennebec House, 62
Kenovan, Jimmy, 72
Kentuck mine, 165, 272
King, Cameron H., 293
King, Clarence, 170
"King of Crimps," 17
"King of the Dumps," 73
King of William, James, 30, 35-38, 127
Kipling, Rudyard, 57, 148, 152
Kloppenburg's Grocery, 31

Knickerbocker Engine Company No. 5, 196-198

Kremlin, the, 62

L

Ladies' Canyon, 122

Lafayette Hotel, 118

Lafayette Square, 153, 155

Laguna Saluda, 117

Lake Merced, 45, 324

Lalanne, Calixte, 109

Lalanne, J. C., 110

Lally, Jack, 276-277

Land's End, 18, 182, 334-335

Langton Street, 90

Larkin Street, 124

Larkyns, Maj. Harry, 291-293

Last Chance mine, 162

Latham, J. F., 233

Latham, Milton S., 181, 221

Latham, Mrs. Milton S., 328

La Tosca café, 84

Laurel Hill Cemetery, 110-111, 117

Laurel Village, 110

"Law and Order" group, 37, 45

Layman, Frederick O., 203

Leahy, Dan, 73

Leahy, William H., 251-252

Leavenworth Street, 149

Lees, Police Capt. I. W., 90-91

Leese, Jacob, 28, 66-67

Leidesdorff, William Alexander, 59-62, 117, 160, 181

Leidesdorff Street, 62-63, 172

Lent, William, 168, 171, 327

Lewis, Beatrice, 336

Lick, James, 153-154, 243

Lick House, 153, 244

Lick Observatory, 154

Lightning Train, 231-233

Lincoln, Abraham, 10, 34, 46, 176

Lincoln Grammar School, 304-306, 312

Lincoln Park, 182

Line, The, 234-235, 237, 244-245, 248

Little Chile, 118

Little Egypt, 243

Little Italy, 184

Little Pete, 73, 77-80

Little Rich Bar, 122

Lloyd, B. E., 74, 108, 165, 223, 329

Lockhart and Porter's funeral parlors, 178

Loma Alta, 199, 207, 210
(See also Telegraph Hill)

Lombard Street, 126

London, Jack, 57, 133

London and San Francisco Bank, 165, 181

Lone Mountain, 110, 202

Lone Mountain Cemetery, 37, 46, 329

Long Bridge, 300

Long Wharf, 30, 32, 48, 62, 147

Longford, Police Sgt. Tom, 16

Looting, 32

Los Angeles, 50-51, 93, 96, 105

Lost Pegleg Mine, 48-52

Loti, Pierre, 57

Lotta's Fountain, 20, 233, 246, 251, 253

Lotteries, 77

Lovejoy's Hotel, 118

Lütgen's Hotel, 31

Lynching, 33, 36-38, 74, 122, 124-125

M

McAllister, Hall, 48

McAllister, Mrs. Hall, 271

McAllister Street, 124

McCarthy, Mayor, 252

McCarty, Dan (White Hat), 179, 214, 244-245

McClellan, Gen. George B., 96, 169

McClung, Maj. J. W., 197

McCoppin, Frank H., 220

McCoppin's Canal, 250

McCorkle, J. W., 43

MacCrellish, Frederick, 290

McDonough, Pete, 192

McGowan, Ned, 265

MacGregor, Joseph, 199

MacIntyre and Heath, 243

MacKay, John W., 56, 147, 161, 172

McLane, Andy, 193

McLane's Crab House, 193

McLaughlin, Pat, 163-164

McLean, Louis, 48

McManus, King, 314-316

McNear, Johnny, 53

Macondray Lane, 129

Magnin, I., 80, 301

Magpie, The, 30, 33

Maguire, Thomas G., 139-140, 145-147, 277-278

Maguire's Opera House, 145-148, 306, 327

Maiden Lane, 86-93

Mailhebeau, Camille, 109
Maison Dorée, 108
Mammie Pleasant (see Pleasant, Mammie)
Manila Avenue (see Maiden Lane)
Manrow, Col. J. P., 127-129
Mansion House, The, 265
Marchand's, 108, 242
Mare Island, 11
Marin County, 178, 243
Marina, the, 84, 134, 184, 190
Marine disasters, 10-11, 17
Marion Rifles, 119
Market Street, 29, 54, 66, 68, 80, 94, 100, 167, 213-253, 257
Market Street Railroad Company, 219, 269
Marshall, James, 162
Martinez, Maria Antonia, 65
Martini cocktail, 143-144
Marvin, Jim, 234-235
Mason Street, 29
Masonic Cemetery, 178
Massett, Stephen C., 139, 264
Mayfield Grange, 287, 289
Mechanics' Institute Fair, 1857, 46
Meiggs, Harry, 67-71, 84-85, 170
Meiggs, John C., 68
Meiggs' Wharf, 12, 17, 71-73, 84-85, 192, 333
Mendelssohn, Felix ("Punch"), 194
Menken, Adah Isaacs, 147-148, 327
Merchants' Exchange Bank, 165, 199
Metropolitan Hall, 124-125
Metropolitan Theater, 43, 146
Mexican fandango parlors, 118
Mickey's speakeasy, 209
Midway Plaisance, 243
Midwinter Fair of '94, 333
Mile Rock, 7, 18
Military companies, 227
Milkmen's Exchange, 302-303
Miller, Joaquin, 133, 327
Miners, 48-52, 81, 123, 136, 144-146, 161-163, 166, 194, 330
   (See also Forty-niners; Gold Rush)
Minstrel shows, 100
Miramontes, Candelario, 136-137
Miscreant, the, 136
Miss Burke's finishing school, 116
Mrs. Moon's Cottage, 62
Mission, The, 89, 204, 218, 257, 272, 298
   (See also Mission Dolores)

Mission Bay, 283, 285
Mission Dolores, 62-63, 65, 97, 257, 263-266, 282
   (See also Mission San Francisco de Asis)
Mission Dolores Cemetery, 38
Mission highway, 327
Mission Planks Road Company, 263
Mission Point, 69
Mission San Francisco de Asis, 186, 259-260
   (See also Mission Dolores)
Mission Street, 100, 258, 263, 266, 268-270, 281, 285
Missions in California, 259-263
Mitchell, Charlie, 204
Mizner, Addison, 179
Monadnock Building, 252-253
Mongolian Bactrians (see Camels)
Montara mountains, 6, 321
Monterey, 6, 8, 32, 138, 151, 186
Montez, Lola, 48, 57, 136, 145, 228, 265
Montgomery, Percy, 54, 56-58
Montgomery Avenue (see Columbus Avenue)
Montgomery Block, 33-37, 57, 133
Montgomery Street, 27-58, 61-62, 66-67, 96, 98, 117, 160, 192, 198, 205-207, 210, 218-220, 258
Montgomery Street Land Company, 220-221
Monumental firehouse, 36-37
Monuments, 194
Moody, Joseph L., 129
Moraga, Lt. José Joaquín, 186-187, 260
Moraghan's Oyster Parlors, 172
Morphy, Edward, 16, 109
Morrell, Capt. Benjamin, 64-65
Morton Street, 87, 89-91, 179
Mother Lode, 62, 81, 139, 161-162, 228, 315
Motion pictures, 290
Mt. Davidson, 154, 162, 330
Mt. Hamilton, 154
Mt. Olympus, 240
Mountain Lake, 184, 260
Muggeridge, Edward James (see Muybridge, Eadweard)
Murasky, F. J., 206
Murphy, Dan, 202
Murphy, Irish Joe, 265
Murray, Ed, 78
Muybridge, Eadweard, 286, 290-293

N

Naglee's building, 32
National Military Cemetery, 190
Native Sons of the Golden West, 45, 260, 313
Neagle, David, 105-106
Negroes, 295, 300
Neilson, Adelaide, 307-308
Nevada, Emma, 240
Neville, Amelia Ransome, 271
New Joe's, 119
New Montgomery Street, 221-222, 228-230, 233
Newhall, George, 269
Newspaper, first, 67
Nicol, Duncan ("Pisco John"), 38-40
Nightingale, The, 265
Nineties, the, 108, 120, 179, 214, 242, 272, 331
Nisbet, James, 9-11, 284
Nob Hill, 54, 83, 102, 116-117, 173, 178-179, 182, 202, 248, 257-258, 285, 294, 330
Noe Valley, 258
Norris, Frank, 57
North, John G., 300
North Beach, 22, 66-68, 71-73, 84, 89, 116, 119, 184, 217, 257
North of Market, 257
North Point, 12
Norton, Joshua Abraham (Emperor), 30, 48, 136, 174-178, 192, 235

O

Oakland, California, 133, 178
O'Brien, Dan, 279
O'Brien, William S., 56, 146, 161, 172, 328
Occidental Hotel, 143
Occidental restaurant, 146
Ocean Beach, 111
Ocean House, 329, 337
Ocean View race track, 329
Octavia Street, 101-102, 107
O'Donnell, C. C., 240
O'Farrell, Jasper, 99, 217-218
O'Farrell Street, 80
Oil, 179
Old Orthodox, 52
Old St. Mary's, 58, 82-83, 160, 174, 179-182

Oldfield, Otis, 207
O'Neill, James, 90
Ophir company, 163-165
Opium, 14, 19, 66, 77
Opium dens, 74
O'Riley, Pete, 163-164
Osborne, J. A., 163-164
Osbourne, Lloyd, 294
Otis, Mayor, 229
Overholt, Miles, 258

P

Pacific Heights, 80, 116, 153, 190
Pacific Mail Steamship Company, 18-19, 62, 200
Pacific oil refinery, 72
Pacific Street, 14, 16, 53, 87, 118, 129, 192
Pacific Union Club, 182
Palace Hotel, 80, 104, 152, 167, 196-197, 222, 226, 229-231, 233, 235, 244, 250-252
Paladini fish market, 63
Palo Alto, California, 289-290
Palo Alto Stock Farm, 290
Palo Verde irrigation project, 239
Palóu, Fray Francisco, 186, 259-260, 324, 337
Panama-Pacific Exposition, 1915, 192, 214
Pantheon, 172, 197
Parker House, 30, 137-138, 140-141
Parks, 133, 153, 180, 182, 194, 207, 209, 294
Parrott, Mrs. Abby, 179
Parrott, John, 221
Parrott, Tiburcio, 88
Parrott block, 181
Patti, Adelina, 240
Paul, Almarin Brooks, 127-128
Pauper Alley, 62-63, 152
Pendegast, W. W., 293
Peninsula, the, 54, 81, 244
Penrod, Manny, 163-164
Perry, Julia, 238
Peters, Charles Rollo, 129
Peters, F. C., Company, 78
Phelan, Jimmy, 244
Pickett, Charles Edward ("the Philosopher"), 235-237, 239
Piggott, Miss, 16
Pine Street, 62-63, 109
Pioche and Bayerque, 269

Pioche, Francis L. A., 268-271
Pioche's Pond, 270
Pioneer race track, 43
Pisco John (see Nicol, Duncan)
Pisco Punch, 38-40
Pixley, Frank, 129-192
Placer County, 162
Placerville and Sacramento Valley railroad, 269
Platt's Hall, 240, 306
Playland-at-the-Beach, 321, 337-338
Pleasant, John J., 102
Pleasant, Mammie, 101-107
Pleasant Valley, 258
Point Bonita, 7, 18
Point Lobos, 18, 199, 327-328, 334, 336
Point Lobos speedway, 327-329
Point Reyes, 6, 324
Poker Flat, 122
Polhemus, Charles B., 263
Policemen, graft among, 32, 76
   weapons of, 16
Polk, Willis, 129
Pon, Jean B., 109-110
Poodle Dog, 73, 95, 99, 107-109, 242
Port Wine, 122
Portolá, Gaspar de, 6, 251
Portolá Festival, 251
Portsmouth House, 28
Portsmouth Square, 30-31, 43, 48, 52, 66, 99, 117, 136, 141, 145, 147-153, 158, 199-200, 218, 257, 329
Post Street, 91, 110
Potato patch, 136-137
Potrero Hill, 210, 249, 258, 314
Powell Street, 150, 203, 219, 231, 241
Prendergast, Thomas F., 217
Presidio, 65, 116, 136, 184-192, 206, 259-260, 285
Presidio Heights, 190
Presidio Trail, 67, 117
Prohibition, 39, 109, 337
Proll, William, 174
Protector of Mexico (see Norton, Joshua Abraham)
Public schoolhouse, first, 139
Purcell's South San Francisco Park, 314

R

Race tracks, 265
   (See also names of tracks)

Racketeers, 77-78
Railroads, 173, 179
   (See also names of railroads)
Ralston, William C. (Billy), 56, 99-100, 160, 165-170, 181, 220-222, 225-226, 228-231, 332
Ramsaye, Terry, 290
Real estate, 34, 38, 64, 68, 99, 117-118, 153, 166, 195, 218, 284
   during Gold Rush, 29-30, 175, 238
Red House, The, 265-266
Reed, Charley, 100
Ressayre, Victor, 277-278
Rhodes, William H. (Caxton), 127-128
Richardson, William Anthony, 65-66, 82
Richardson, William H., 37-38
Riley's shooting gallery, 72
Rincon Hill, 48, 169, 197, 218, 220, 235, 258, 264, 270, 283-286, 294-295
Rincon Point, 283
Ritz restaurant, 110
Rivera y Moncada, Capt. Fernando, 323, 337
Roberts, George D., 166, 168, 170
Roberts, Capt. Martin R., 153
Roberts, Theodore, 153, 281
Robins, Thomas, 249
Rodríguez, José, 119, 264
Rolph, Jim, 279
Rosa, Madame Parepa, 271
Rosenthal, Toby E., 88
Ross, Duncan, 204
Rossi, Angelo J., 192
Rowe's Olympic Circus, 31
Rubery, Alfred, 167
Rubies (see Great Diamond Hoax)
Ruef, Abe, 192, 194
Russ, J. C. Christian, 98, 266
Russ Building, 61, 99
Russ Gardens, 266
Russian Hill, 29, 37, 116-117, 119, 126, 128-130, 132, 134, 191-192, 238, 258, 283, 285
Ryan, Paddy, 204

S

Sacramento, California, 45, 119, 139, 167
Sacramento River, 9, 11, 21, 159, 167
Sacramento Street, 32, 74, 82, 174
St. Ann's Louvre bar, 245
St. Ann's Valley, 219, 228
St. Charles gambling hall, 141

St. Charles Hotel, 123
St. Francis' Church, 206
St. Francis Wood, 80
St. Joseph's Church, 125
St. Mary's Park, 180
St. Patrick's, 298
Saloons, 30-31, 53, 81, 193
    (*See also* Bars; Drinking)
Salvation Army, 52-54
Sam Yup Company, 73, 77
San Bruno turnpike, 327
San Cárlos, 5-7, 186, 260, 324
San Francisco Bay, 6, 12-14, 17-18, 20-22, 29, 62, 64-65, 84-85, 118, 138-139, 152, 167, 178, 186, 190-191, 217, 251, 323-324
San Francisco Civic Center, 124, 250
San Francisco fire of 1906, 57, 62, 66, 91, 109, 180, 242, 248-250, 274, 294, 298, 333
    (*See also* Earthquakes)
San Francisco Hall, 145
San Francisco Marine Exchange, 17, 181
San Francisco Municipal Band, 179
San Francisco and New York Mining and Commercial Company, 169
San Francisco Zoo, 322
San Joaquin River, 11
San José railroad, 269
San Quentin, 78, 91, 120, 124
Sandbagging, 30
Sanguinetti's, 243
Sansome Street, 146, 181, 205-206
Sapphires (*see* Great Diamond Hoax)
Sausalito, California, 117, 178, 198
Sausalito ferry, 73
Scannell, David, 36-37, 111, 120, 146
Schmidt, Col. A. W. von, 11-13
Schwarz, Charlie, 72
Scotch Hill, 314
Seal Rocks, 325, 328, 331, 333, 336
Secessionist plot, 167
Second Street, 116
See Yup Company, 77-79
Selby Smelting and Lead Company, 297
Senator's Hill, 111
Serra, Father Junípero, 259
Seventies, the, 11, 100, 192, 225, 231, 244, 272, 278, 289-291, 304, 307, 313, 329
Shafter family, 129
Shanghai Kelly, 16-17, 54
Shanghaiing, 14, 16, 201

Sharkey, Tom, 246
Sharon, William (Billy), 56, 102-104, 111, 172, 230, 235, 239
Shellmound Park, 281
Sheridan, Lt. Gen. Phil, 230
Sheriff, first, 111
Sherman, Clay and Company, 53
Sherwood, Mrs. L. M., 106
Shipping trade, 13
Sierra City, 122, 315
Silver, 162-164, 167, 179, 228
    (*See also* Comstock Lode)
Sinclair, Catherine, 43
Six Companies, 76
Sixth Street, 152, 266
Sixties, the, 16, 54, 285, 313
Skyline Boulevard, 321
Slack, John, 167, 170-171
Slate Creek, 122
Sloan, Tod, 245
Slums, 82, 279
Small, Hank, 232
Smith, Charlie, 313, 315-317
Smith, James W., 101-102
Smith, Jedediah, 49
Smith, Pegleg, 48-51, 96
Smith, Thomas L. (*see* Smith, Pegleg)
Smith, Viola Bell, 106-107
Smuggling, 65
Snow & May, 89-91
Snow storm of 1887, 240-242
Society, early, 108, 129, 240, 284-285
Solari, Fred, 86, 93
Sotomayor, Tony, 207
Soulé, Frank, 9, 284
South of Market (*see* South of the Slot)
South of Market Boys, 278-282
South Park, 48, 197, 235, 258, 264, 270, 286-289, 292-294
South of the Slot, 235, 263, 270, 272-273, 278, 281, 297, 303-305, 308, 310
Southern Pacific Company, 20
Spanish in California (*see* California, Spanish in)
Spanish-American War, 189-190
Spanish Kitty, 87
Spinelli, Juanita ("The Duchess"), 122
"Spoony the Dumper," 73
Spreckel, Claus, 289
Squiro's, 62
Stackpole, Ralph, 207
Stagg, Cornelius, 329

Standard Theater, 99-100
Stanford, Josiah, 72
Stanford, Leland, 72, 173, 182, 289-290, 327
Stanford University, 289-290
Starr, Ralph, 335
Staunton Ruby, 170
Steamboat Bar, 122
Steamer Day, 9, 118
Steindorff, Paul, 252-253
Steiner Street, 192
Steiner's saloon, 100
Sterling, George, 57, 133-134, 210
Steuart Street, 16
Stevenson, Col. Jonathan Drake, 188-189
Stevenson, Robert Louis, 57, 136, 152, 158, 294, 337
Stidger, Oliver Perry, 57
Stock Exchange, 165
Stockton Street, 79, 86, 88, 151-153, 269-270
Stoddard, Charles Warren, 148, 201, 218, 294
Stone, Flora, 292
Stranglings, 91
Street preaching, 48, 52
Stuart, James, 33
Sullivan, Barry, 231
Sullivan, Dennis T., 247
Sullivan, John L., 204, 243
Sullivan, Yankee, 246
Summer Street, 172
Sun Yat Sen, 57
Sutro, Adolph, 203, 240, 330-333
Sutro Baths, 332-333, 336
Sutro Heights, 332
Sutter Street, 134
Sutter's Fort, 236
Sutter's Mill, 28
Sweeny, George, 199, 203
Sweringen sisters, 48
Sydney Ducks, 30, 32-33, 118
Sydneytown, 33, 118
Synagogue, first, 126

T

Taafe, William P., 129
Taafe and McCahill building, 31
Tait's-at-the-Beach, 337
Tam o' Shanter, The, 33
Tamalpais mountain, 243, 322, 325

Tar Flat, 73, 226, 235, 258, 264, 281
Taylor, Bayard, 137-138, 141
Taylor, William, 52
Taylor Street, 130
Tehama House, 160
Telegraph Hill, 4, 9, 12-13, 21, 27, 31-32, 63, 84, 116-118, 125, 183-184, 194, 196, 198-210, 220, 257-258, 283
Telegraph Hill Observatory Athletic Club, 204
Tenderloin, the, 95, 244
Terry, David S., 45, 102, 105-106
Tetrazzini, Louisa, 251-253
Theaters, 99-100, 139, 145-146
    (See also names of theaters)
Third Street, 90, 264, 295, 297-304, 312
Thomas, Jerry, 143-145
Thornton, Tip, 53-54
"Toddy Time-Table," 40-41
Tom and Jerry, 143
Tontine gambling house, 31
Top o' the Mark, 22
Transportation, public, first mechanical, 219
Treasure Island, 21, 178
Treat, George, 265
Trinity Church, 243
Truman, Maj. Ben C., 45
Turner Gesang Verein, 266
Twain, Mark, 57
Tweed, William M., 143
Twentieth Street, 202
Twin Peaks, 54, 184, 210, 214-215, 217-218, 257, 282, 338

U

Underwriters' Salvage Company, 37
Union Hall Theater, 281, 303
Union Hotel, 46
Union Square, 86, 93, 251
Union Square Avenue (see Maiden Lane)
Union Street, 23, 183-184, 191-194, 198, 201-203, 206
United States Army, 96-98
United States Mint, 124, 272-276
University of California, 156

V

Vallejo, Col. Mariano G., 188, 228
Vallejo Street, 126, 202, 205
Van Ness Avenue, 129, 153, 180

Vancouver, Capt. George, 187, 324
Vandewater family, 328
Vaudeville, 100
V-E Day, 21
Verandah, the, 136, 141
Vigilantes, 30, 32-34, 36-37, 45, 48, 119-120, 127, 265
Vincent, Mrs. A., 204
Virgin, George W., 32-33
Virginia City, 120, 144, 164, 166, 172, 315
Visitation Valley, 269
V-J Day, 21-22
Volunteer fire companies, 31-32, 38, 137, 146-147, 196-198
Voodoo, 101, 103-106

W

Walker, Franklin, 225
Walker, William, 265
Wall, Tessie, 244
Wall Street Shoe Shine Parlor, 63
Wallace, Chief Justice, 237
Wallace, Tommy, 90
Ward, Capt. William, 18-19
Warfield, David, 279, 304, 309
Warner, Abe, 71-73
Washerwoman's Lagoon, 97, 184, 191
"Washington Block" (see Montgomery Block)
Washington Hall, 139
Washington Square, 184, 194, 196, 198
Washington Street, 39, 73, 136-157, 160
Washoe, the, 159, 164, 172, 330
Waterfront, 3-5, 9, 14-17, 20-22, 37, 62, 66, 73, 117-118, 202, 220, 264, 270, 272
Webster Street, 106
Welch, Jack, 314-316
Weller, John B., 123
Wells, Maj. Alfred, 52-53

Western Addition, 190, 269
Weule, Louis, 181
Whale, The, 53
Wharf, first, 118
What Cheer House, 62, 267
Wheeler, George, 91
Whisky Diggings, 122
Wilde, Oscar, 240
Wildman, Rounsevelle, 18-19
Wilkie's lemonade factory, 31
Wilkins, J. M., 325, 331, 333-334
Williams, Albert, 67
Williams, Mary E. (see Pleasant, Mammie)
Williams, Thomas (see Blythe, Tom)
Williamson, Maj. R. S., 11-12
Willows, The, 265-266
Winn, M. L., 146
Winter, William, 304-306
Winters, J. D., 163-164
Wong Sam Ark, 57
Woodlawn Cemetery, 178
Woodward, Robert B., 62, 267
Woodward's Gardens, 71, 266-268, 280, 333
Woodworth, Selim, 221
Wooster, John, 86
World War I, 21
World War II, 21-22
Wright, Selden S., 129

Y

Yacht Harbor, 191-192
Yellow Jacket mine, 165
Yerba Buena, 5, 8, 28, 61, 65, 82, 99, 111, 117, 135, 199, 217, 283
Yerba Buena Cemetery, 264
Yerba Buena Island, 4, 11, 73, 178
Yuba River, 9, 122

Z

Zimmerman, Fred W., Sr., 313